Paragraph Essentials:

A Writing Guide

Paragraph Essentials:
A Writing Guide

Linda Wong

Houghton Mifflin Company Boston New York

Editor-in-Chief: Patricia A. Coryell
Senior Sponsoring Editor: Mary Jo Southern
Senior Developmental Editor: Martha Bustin
Associate Editor: Kellie Cardone
Associate Project Editor: Cecilia Molinari
Editorial Assistant: Kristin Penta
Production Design Coordinator: Lisa Jelly Smith
Senior Manufacturing Coordinator: Marie Barnes
Marketing Manager: Annamarie Rice

Text credits appear on page 485.

Printed in the U.S.A.

Library of Congress Control Number: 2001131565
ISBN: 0-618-000399

1 2 3 4 5 6 7 8 9 – WEB – 05 04 03 02 01

BRIEF CONTENTS

CHAPTER 1 The Writing Process 1

CHAPTER 2 Writing Effective Paragraphs 43

CHAPTER 3 Narrative Paragraphs 93

CHAPTER 4 Descriptive Paragraphs 143

CHAPTER 5 Process Paragraphs 179

CHAPTER 6 Comparison and Contrast Paragraphs 223

CHAPTER 7 Exemplification and Classification Paragraphs 263

CHAPTER 8 Definition Paragraph 311

CHAPTER 9 Cause-Effect Paragraphs 347

CHAPTER 10 Summary Paragraphs 377

CHAPTER 11 Paragraph Answers for Test Questions 409

CHAPTER 12 Essays 429

APPENDIX A Student Answer Key 459

APPENDIX B Helpful Charts 481

TEXT CREDITS 485

INDEX 488

CONTENTS

CHAPTER 1 **THE WRITING PROCESS** 1

Writing Warm-Up 1 1
Becoming a Strong Writer 2
Seven Steps in the Writing Process 2
- Step 1: Generate Ideas 3
- Step 2: Get a Focus 10
- Step 3: Gather and Organize Information 15
- Step 4: Write a Rough Draft 22
- Step 5: Revise, Revise, Revise 25
- Step 6: Proofread and Edit 27
- Step 7: Prepare the Final Version 28

Grammar and Usage Tips 30
Internet Enrichment 40
Parts of Speech Review 41

CHAPTER 2 **WRITING EFFECTIVE PARAGRAPHS** 43

Writing Warm-Up 2 43
Writing Effective Paragraphs 44
The Structure of a Paragraph 44
- Developing the Topic Sentence 45
- Developing the Body of the Paragraph 48
- Developing the Concluding Sentence 49

Three Qualities of an Effective Paragraph 52
- Unity 52
- Coherence 53
- Adequate Development 59

Kinds of Paragraphs 62
Writing a Cover Letter 65
Writing Assignment 70
Grammar and Usage Tips 71
Grammar and Usage Tips Summary 88
Proofreading and Editing Exercises 89
Internet Enrichment 91
Grammar and Usage Review 91

CHAPTER 3 NARRATIVE PARAGRAPHS 93

Writing Warm-Up 3 93
The Narrative Paragraph 94
First-Person Narrative 94
Third-Person Narrative 95
The Structure of a Narrative 97
Developing the Topic Sentence 97
Developing the Body of the Paragraph 99
Developing the Concluding Sentence 103
The Writing Process for Narratives 104
Step 1: Generate ideas. 104
Step 2: Get a focus. 105
Step 3: Gather and organize your information. 106
Clustering 106
Developing the Topic Sentence 107
Step 4: Write the rough draft. 108
Step 5: Revise, revise, revise. 108
Step 6: Proofread and edit. 114
Step 7: Prepare the final version of your narrative. 115
Writing Assignment 116
Narrative Planning Sheet 117
Partner Feedback Form 118
Grammar and Usage Tips 119
Grammar and Usage Tips Summary 138
Proofreading and Editing Exercises 138
Internet Enrichment 141
Grammar and Usage Review 141

CHAPTER 4 DESCRIPTIVE PARAGRAPHS 143

Writing Warm-Up 4 143
The Descriptive Paragraph 144
Subjective and Objective Description 144
The Structure of a Descriptive Paragraph 146
Developing the Topic Sentence 146
Developing the Body of the Paragraph 148
Developing the Concluding Sentence 152
The Writing Process for Descriptive Paragraphs 153
Step 1: Generate ideas. 153
Brainstorming 153
Step 2: Get a focus. 155
Step 3: Gather and organize your information. 155
Clustering 155
Selecting a Central Impression 155
Writing the Topic Sentence 157
Step 4: Write the rough draft. 157
Step 5: Revise, revise, revise. 158

Step 6: Proofread and edit. 159
Step 7: Prepare the final version of your descriptive paragraph. 159
Writing Assignment 160
Descriptive Paragraph Planning Sheet 161
Partner Feedback Form 162
Grammar and Usage Tips 163
Grammar and Usage Tips Summary 175
Proofreading and Editing Exercises 175
Internet Enrichment 177
Grammar and Usage Review 177

CHAPTER 5 PROCESS PARAGRAPHS 179

Writing Warm-Up 5 179
The Process Paragraph 180
Informational Process Paragraphs 180
Directional Process Paragraphs 181
The Structure of a Process Paragraph 183
Developing the Topic Sentence 183
Developing the Body of the Paragraph 185
Developing the Concluding Sentence 188
The Writing Process for Process Paragraphs 189
Step 1: Generate ideas. 189
Step 2: Get a focus. 190
Step 3: Gather and organize information. 190
Listing the Steps 191
Writing the Topic Sentence 191
Step 4: Write the rough draft. 192
Step 5: Revise, revise, revise. 194
Step 6: Proofread and edit. 196
Step 7: Prepare the final version of your process paragraph. 197
Writing Assignment 198
Process Paragraph Planning Sheet 199
Partner Feedback Form 200
Grammar and Usage Tips 201
Grammar and Usage Tips Summary 219
Proofreading and Editing Exercises 220
Internet Enrichment 221
Grammar and Usage Review 221

CHAPTER 6 COMPARISON AND CONTRAST PARAGRAPHS 223

Writing Warm-Up 6 223
The Comparison or Contrast Paragraph 224
The Structure of a Comparison or Contrast Paragraph 225
Developing the Topic Sentence 225

Developing the Body of the Paragraph 228
The Point-by-Point Method 230
The Block Method 231
Developing the Concluding Sentence 234
The Writing Process for Comparison and Contrast Paragraphs 235
Step 1: Generate ideas. 235
Step 2: Get a focus. 236
Identifying the Two Subjects 236
Deciding to Compare or Contrast 237
Step 3: Gather and organize information. 237
Create a Grid of Details 237
Write the Topic Sentence 238
Develop an Outline 238
Step 4: Write the rough draft. 240
Step 5: Revise, revise, revise. 240
Step 6: Proofread and edit. 243
Step 7: Prepare the final version of your comparison or contrast paragraph. 243
Writing Assignment 244
Comparison or Contrast Paragraph Planning Sheet 245
Partner Feedback Form 246
Grammar and Usage Tips 247
Grammar and Usage Tips Summary 257
Proofreading and Editing Exercises 258
Internet Enrichment 260
Grammar and Usage Review 261

CHAPTER 7 EXEMPLIFICATION AND CLASSIFICATION PARAGRAPHS 263

Writing Warm-Up 7 263
Exemplification and Classification Paragraphs 264
The Exemplification Paragraph 264
The Classification Paragraph 265
The Structure of Exemplification and Classification Paragraphs 266
Developing the Topic Sentence 267
Developing the Body of an Exemplification Paragraph 269
Developing the Body of a Classification Paragraph 275
Developing the Concluding Sentence in Exemplification and Classification Paragraphs 280
The Writing Process for Exemplification and Classification Paragraphs 281
Step 1: Generate ideas. 281
Brainstorming 282
Media Searching 282

Step 2: Get a focus. 282
Step 3: Gather and organize your information. 283
Creating a Hierarchy 283
Writing a Topic Sentence 284
Step 4: Write the rough draft. 285
Step 5: Revise, revise, revise. 285
Step 6: Proofread and edit. 287
Step 7: Prepare the final version of your exemplification or classification paragraph. 287
Writing Assignment 288
Exemplification/Classification Paragraph Planning Sheet 289
Partner Feedback Form 290
Grammar and Usage Tips 291
Grammar and Usage Tips Summary 306
Proofreading and Editing Exercises 306
Internet Enrichment 309
Grammar and Usage Review 309

CHAPTER 8 DEFINITION PARAGRAPHS 311

Writing Warm-Up 8 311
The Definition Paragraph 312
The Structure of a Definition Paragraph 313
Developing the Topic Sentence 314
Methods to Use to Develop Your Topic Sentence 315
Developing the Body of the Paragraph 317
Developing the Concluding Sentence 322
The Writing Process for Definition Paragraphs 325
Step 1: Generate ideas. 325
Step 2: Get a focus. 326
Step 3: Gather and organize information. 326
Gathering Different Kinds of Details 326
Creating a Basic Outline or a List of Details 327
Writing a Topic Sentence 328
Step 4: Write the rough draft. 328
Step 5: Revise, revise, revise. 328
Step 6: Proofread and edit. 331
Step 7: Prepare the final version of your definition paragraph. 331
Writing Assignment 332
Definition Paragraph Planning Sheet 333
Partner Feedback Form 334
Grammar and Usage Tips 335
Grammar and Usage Tips Summary 342
Proofreading and Editing Exercises 343
Internet Enrichment 344
Grammar and Usage Review 345

CHAPTER 9 CAUSE-EFFECT PARAGRAPHS 347

Writing Warm-Up 9 347
The Cause-Effect Paragraph 348
The Structure of a Cause-Effect Paragraph 350
  Developing the Topic Sentence 350
  Developing the Body of the Paragraph 352
  Developing the Concluding Sentence 355
The Writing Process for Cause-Effect Paragraphs 357
  Step 1: Generate ideas. 357
  Step 2: Get a focus. 358
  Step 3: Gather and organize information. 358
    Identifying Pertinent Details 358
    Diagramming the Cause-Effect Relationship 359
    Writing the Topic Sentence 359
  Step 4: Write the rough draft. 359
  Step 5: Revise, revise, revise. 359
  Step 6: Proofread and edit. 360
  Step 7: Prepare the final version of your cause-effect paragraph. 360
Writing Assignment 362
Cause-Effect Paragraph Planning Sheet 363
Partner Feedback Form 364
Grammar and Usage Tips 365
Grammar and Usage Tips Summary 373
Proofreading and Editing Exercise 374
Internet Enrichment 374
Grammar and Usage Review 375

CHAPTER 10 SUMMARY PARAGRAPHS 377

Writing Warm-Up 10 377
The Summary Paragraph 381
  Reading for Meaning 382
Writing Informal and Formal Summaries 388
  Writing Informal Summaries 388
  Writing Formal Summaries 389
  Developing the Topic Sentence 390
  Developing the Body of the Paragraph 391
  Developing the Concluding Sentence 392
The Writing Process for Summary Paragraphs 396
  Step 1: Generate ideas. 396
  Step 2: Get a focus. 396
  Step 3: Gather and organize information. 397
  Step 4: Write the rough draft. 397
  Step 5: Revise, revise, revise. 397
  Step 6: Proofread and edit. 398
  Step 7: Prepare the final version of your summary paragraph. 398
Writing Assignment 398

Summary Paragraph Planning Sheet 399
Partner Feedback Form 399
Article 1: *Misuse of Native American Symbols* 401
Article 2: *Technological Wonderland* 402
Article 3: *Yes, America Is Mine . . . and Yours* 403
Article 4: *Why We're Destroying the Earth* 404
Proofreading and Editing Exercise 408
Internet Enrichment 408

CHAPTER 11 PARAGRAPH ANSWERS FOR TEST QUESTIONS 409

Answering Definition and Short-Answer Questions 410
Understanding Direction Words 410
Using Key Words 411
Preparing for Tests 413
Using Prewriting Techniques 415
Writing Your Paragraph Answer 416
Practice Writing Test Answers 417
Excerpt 1: *Europeans in the Americas* 417
Excerpt 2: *Cultural Factors Influencing Leadership Practices* 419
Excerpt 3: *Sexual Harrassment* 422
Excerpt 4: *Responding to Environmental Threats* 423
Paragraph Answers for Test Questions Planning Sheet 425
Partner Feedback Form 426
Learning from Your Tests 427
Internet Enrichment 428

CHAPTER 12 ESSAYS 429

From Paragraphs to Essays 430
The Structure of an Essay 433
Writing the Introductory Paragraph 433
Developing the Body of the Essay 434
Developing the Concluding Paragraph 436
Understanding Your Essay Assignment 437
The Writing Process for Essays 438
Step 1: Generate ideas. 438
Step 2: Get a focus. 439
Step 3: Gather and organize information. 439
Gathering Information 439
Organizing Information 440
Writing a Thesis Statement 442
Step 4: Write the rough draft. 444
Step 5: Revise, revise, revise. 444
Step 6: Proofread and edit. 445
Step 7: Prepare the final version of your essay. 445
Learning from Model Essays 446

Writing Assignment 454
Writing Essay Answers on Tests 454
Preparing for Essay Tests 455
Preparing for Essay Tests When Topics Are Unannounced 455
Preparing for Essay Tests When Topics Are Announced in Advance 456
Preparing for Open-Book Essay Tests 457
Organizing and Developing Answers for Take-Home Essay Tests 457
Additional Test-Taking Strategies for Essays 457
Enjoy the Process of Writing Essays 458
Internet Enrichment 458

APPENDIX A **Student Answer Key** 459

APPENDIX B **Helpful Charts** 481

TEXT CREDITS 485

INDEX 488

PREFACE

Paragraph Essentials: A Writing Guide is a carefully structured, easy-to-use work text designed to teach fundamental paragraph-writing skills to college students. It provides a strong and thorough foundation for the advanced writing skills students need in higher-level writing courses. As students master the paragraph-writing skills in this textbook, they gain confidence and interest in the process of writing.

Instructional Approach

The instructional approach used in *Paragraph Essentials: A Writing Guide* has been carefully developed and class tested with students to focus on *what works*. The key features of this book include the following:

- A step-by-step approach to understanding the basic paragraph structure, which includes a focused topic sentence with a controlling idea, a well-developed body of a paragraph with unity, coherence, and adequate development, and an effective concluding sentence
- A clearly defined seven-step approach for writing effective paragraphs
- The seven-step approach to use for narrative, descriptive, process, comparison, contrast, exemplification, classification, definition, cause-effect, and summary paragraphs
- "What Do You Think?" exercises that promote critical-thinking skills, analysis of paragraphs, and written responses
- Easy-to-understand definitions and explanations of new paragraph elements, supported with model paragraphs written by students

- Interesting writing assignments with comprehensive planning sheets and partner feedback forms
- A wealth of informative and challenging exercises effective for classroom activities, small group or partner collaborative learning, and for independent homework assignments
- Grammar, punctuation, sentence patterns, and sentence-combining instruction incorporated into the study of paragraph essentials
- Grammar and Usage Tips (sentence-level skills) presented in easy-to-understand language without the confusion frequently caused by extensive use of complex terminology. Ample sentence-level exercises with student answer keys promote independent learning
- An ongoing review and application of skills learned in previous chapters
- Emphasis placed on strategies to correct common writing errors:

    fragments
    run-on sentences
    comma splice errors
    subject-verb agreement problems
    pronoun-antecedent agreement problems
    dangling participles
    shifts in verb tense
    informal language and diction

- The textbook's web site (**http://college.hmco.com.** Click on "Students." Type *Paragraph Essentials* in the "Jump to Textbook Sites" box. Click "go," and then bookmark the site.) includes companion activities, indicated with the icon .

Special Features

Chapter Introductions

Chapter introductions provide students with a visual representation of the type of paragraph discussed in the chapter and a list of objectives for the chapter.

Writing Warm-Up

Each chapter begins with a paragraph-writing assignment that students later use for proofreading and revision work.

Introduction of the New Kind of Paragraph

Before writing specific kinds of paragraphs, students learn to recognize and critique the structure and key elements of each type of paragraph. Understanding the different kinds of paragraphs by examining a variety of model paragraphs provides a strong foundation that students can then apply to their own writing.

Paragraph Structure

Techniques for developing the topic sentence, the body of the paragraph, and the concluding sentence provide students with the essential skills to develop effective paragraphs. Checklists for each part of a paragraph are easy to understand and provide students with guidelines to use for writing their own paragraphs.

Student Paragraphs

Paragraph Essentials: A Writing Guide proudly presents student paragraphs throughout the textbook. Students in developmental writing programs nationwide submitted paragraphs for Houghton Mifflin's paragraph-writing contest. The twenty paragraphs chosen as winners enhance this textbook.

Transition Words

Convenient charts of appropriate transition words appear in each chapter. Effective use of transition words enhances the coherence in paragraphs.

What Do You Think?

"What Do You Think?" exercises promote critical thinking, analysis, and written expression. These exercises are ideal for total class instruction, small group or partner work, or for independent homework assignments. Students should use complete sentences and sufficient details to answer each question. Instructors have the option of grading the written responses for sentence-level skills and content accuracy.

Charts

Comprehensive charts appear throughout this textbook. The charts serve as quick references for lists of transition words or parts of speech that students frequently use in their writing.

Seven-Step Writing Process

Each chapter reinforces the seven-step writing process. Prewriting and writing techniques and clear, direct instructions guide students through each of the seven steps. Sample paragraphs and exercises demonstrate the application of the new skills.

Writing Assignments

Writing assignments focus on the skills discussed in each chapter. In addition to topics that students generate in the prewriting step, each writing assignment includes a wide variety of additional high-interest, motivational topics for students to consider.

Planning Sheet

Reviewers of *Paragraph Essentials: A Writing Guide* applauded the Planning Sheets in each chapter. The Planning Sheets provide step-by-step instructions that help students organize their information and produce a well-planned, effective paragraph.

Partner Feedback Form

Each Planning Sheet includes a Partner Feedback Form. Higher-quality writing frequently occurs when students realize that classmates will be reading and analyzing each other's work. The Partner Feedback Forms also provide students with feedback that can be used to guide the revision process and strengthen the final revision.

Grammar and Usage Tips

Each chapter provides instruction and review work for grammar and usage skills. Rules, definitions, and techniques use easy-to-understand wording and explanations and appear with ample examples. Each exercise is self-correcting; the answer keys appear in Appendix A. Students can score their own work and write questions to ask in class about the work and the skills.

Grammar and Usage Summary Chart

The Summary Chart restates the tips discussed in the chapter. A compiled list of Grammar and Usage Tips Summary charts is available in the Instructor's Resource Manual.

Proofreading Exercises

Proofreading exercises appear in Chapters 2–10. Paragraph proofreading exercises promote the application of grammar and usage skills and strengthen students' ability to proofread carefully and thoroughly. Students do not have access to the answer keys for these exercises. Answer keys appear in the Instructor's Resource Manual.

Grammar and Usage Reviews

Chapters 1–9 conclude with a Grammar and Usage Review, which can be used as a review exercise, a quiz, or a test. Students do not have access to answer keys for the Grammar and Usage Reviews.

Internet Icon

The icon that appears throughout the textbook indicates that supplementary activities or Internet links to related sites are available on the web site for this textbook. Instructors may assign web site activities, or students may use them as supplementary practice or drill work.

Content and Organization

Chapter 1: The Writing Process introduces students to the steps in the writing process and emphasizes the recursive nature of writing.

- In Step 1: Generate Ideas, students learn techniques for understanding the assignment, selecting an appropriate topic, brainstorming, clustering, and freewriting.
- In Step 2: Get a Focus, students learn techniques to narrow a topic, know their audience, and identify a purpose.
- In Step 3: Gather and Organize Ideas, students learn techniques to use resources to gather information, take notes, accumulate the right amount of information, develop an effective topic sentence, and develop a prewriting organizational plan, which includes outlining, listing, and clustering.
- In Step 4: Write a Rough Draft, attention focuses on recognizing the goals of the rough draft, using the basic paragraph structure, and citing sources.
- In Step 5: Revise, Revise, Revise, students become aware of the need for multiple revisions; the chapter provides students with convenient checklists for revision work.
- In Step 6: Proofread and Edit, attention focuses on a checklist of sentence-level skills to use for proofreading and editing work.
- In the final step, Step 7: Prepare the Final Version, students learn an appropriate format to use for their final revisions.
- The Grammar and Usage Tips in Chapter 1 discuss the eight parts of speech. Short, self-correcting exercises provide students with practice identifying each of the parts of speech.
- The chapter ends with a Grammar and Usage Review.

Chapter 2: Writing Effective Paragraphs introduces students to the structure of paragraphs.

- Students learn the key elements for developing an effective topic sentence, the body of a paragraph, and a concluding sentence.
- Bulleted checklists state techniques clearly and directly.
- "What Do You Think?" exercises provide practice analyzing paragraphs, identifying effective elements in paragraphs, and responding to questions in writing.
- This chapter defines and demonstrates the effective use of *unity*, *coherence*, and *adequate development* in the body of paragraphs.
- A comprehensive chart of transition words, to show a variety of relationships, is a highlight of this chapter.
- This chapter also introduces students to the different kinds of paragraphs they will learn to write in this textbook.
- To emphasize the value of writing beyond the classroom, students learn to write powerful cover letters to use with job applications.
- Grammar and Usage Tips for Chapter 2 focus on identifying subjects and verbs in sentences, writing complete sentences, and avoiding fragments.
- The chapter ends with paragraph-level proofreading exercises and a Grammar and Usage Review.

Chapter 3: Narrative Paragraphs introduces students to first-person and third-person narratives.

- Students learn the unique characteristics of a topic sentence, the body, and a concluding sentence for narrative paragraphs. Model paragraphs demonstrate the use of these key elements.
- "One Mysterious Night," a student-authored paragraph selected from Houghton Mifflin's national writing contest, provides students with a clear example of the kinds of revision work that occur throughout the writing process.
- "What Do You Think?" exercises provide students with practice analyzing, critiquing, and responding in writing to questions about narrative paragraphs; such analysis equips students with the skills to analyze and critique their own work and their classmates' work.
- This chapter guides students through each of the seven steps for writing a narrative paragraph. An array of model paragraphs, checklists of essential paragraph elements, and specific guidelines for each of the seven steps build student confidence and success.

- A Narrative Planning Sheet with a Student Feedback Form guides and encourages students through each of the seven steps for writing a narrative paragraph.
- Grammar and Usage Tips in Chapter 3 focus on past tense verbs, compound sentences, and identifying and correcting two kinds of fused sentences: run-on sentences and comma splice errors.
- The chapter ends with paragraph-level proofreading exercises and a Grammar and Usage Review.

Chapter 4: Descriptive Paragraphs introduces students to subjective and objective descriptive paragraphs that focus on a central impression.

- Students learn the unique characteristics of a topic sentence, the body, and a concluding sentence for descriptive paragraphs. Model paragraphs demonstrate the use of these key elements.
- Chapter 4 introduces students to five organizational patterns for developing coherence: *spatial*, *emphatic*, *deductive*, *inductive*, and *chronological*.
- "What Do You Think?" exercises provide students with practice analyzing, critiquing, and responding in writing to questions about descriptive paragraphs; such analysis equips students with the skills to analyze and critique their own work and their classmates' work.
- "Clayton," a descriptive paragraph about a cancer survivor, demonstrates the use of clustering to select and focus a central impression and the types of revisions that strengthen the draft of the paragraph.
- This chapter guides students through each of the seven steps for writing a descriptive paragraph. Students work with *brainstorming* and *clustering* to generate and organize details.
- An array of model paragraphs, checklists of essential paragraph elements, and specific guidelines for each of the seven writing steps build student confidence and success.
- A Descriptive Planning Sheet with a Student Feedback Form guides and encourages students through each of the seven steps for writing a descriptive paragraph.
- Grammar and Usage Tips in Chapter 4 focus on working with dependent and independent clauses, creating complex sentences with subordinate conjunctions and relative pronouns, identifying and correcting fragments, and using eight comma rules correctly.
- The chapter ends with paragraph-level proofreading exercises and a Grammar and Usage Review.

Chapter 5: Process Paragraphs introduces students to informational process paragraphs, which explain how an operation, an event, a system, or a procedure works, and directional process paragraphs, which explain the steps to do, make, or repair something.

- Students learn the unique characteristics of a topic sentence, the body, and a concluding sentence for process paragraphs. Model paragraphs demonstrate the use of these key elements.
- In addition to using brainstorming and clustering to generate and organize information, Chapter 5 uses *freewriting* and the *listing of steps* to help students generate and organize writing topics.
- Students continue to practice analyzing, critiquing, and responding in writing to questions about process paragraphs by completing the "What Do You Think?" exercises that appear throughout the chapter.
- This chapter guides students through each of the seven steps for writing a directional process paragraph. After reading this type of process paragraph, the reader should be able to duplicate the steps and achieve the outcome the writer describes.
- An array of model paragraphs, checklists of essential paragraph elements, and specific guidelines for each of the seven writing steps build student confidence and success.
- A Process Planning Sheet with a Student Feedback Form guides and encourages students through each of the seven steps for writing a process paragraph.
- Grammar and Usage Tips in Chapter 5 focus on simple verb tenses, verb phrases, shifting verb tenses, progressive forms of verbs, and participles. Instruction includes ways to avoid common errors with the progressive forms of verbs, perfect tense verbs, and fragments formed by present or past participles.
- The chapter ends with paragraph-level proofreading exercises and a Grammar and Usage Review.

Chapter 6: Comparison and Contrast Paragraphs introduces students to comparison paragraphs, which show similarities between two subjects, and contrast paragraphs, which show differences between two subjects or points of view.

- Students learn the unique characteristics of a topic sentence, the body, and a concluding sentence for narrative paragraphs.

- Model paragraphs, outlines, visual graphics, and grids demonstrate the use of the *point-by-point* and *block methods* for organizing the details in the body of the paragraphs.
- In addition to providing practice analyzing, critiquing, and responding in writing to questions about comparison or contrast paragraphs, "What Do You Think?" exercises provide students with opportunities to apply the sentence-level skills that they learned in previous chapters.
- This chapter guides students through each of the seven steps for writing a comparison or a contrast paragraph. An array of model paragraphs, checklists of essential paragraph elements, and specific guidelines for each of the seven steps build student confidence and success.
- A Comparison or Contrast Planning Sheet with a Student Feedback Form guides and encourages students through each of the seven steps for writing a comparison or a process paragraph.
- Grammar and Usage Tips in Chapter 6 focus on creating and using appositives (nouns, noun phrases, or noun clauses) and participial phrases (adjective phrases). Students learn to identify and correct dangling participles and fragments caused by participial phrases posing as complete sentences.
- The chapter ends with paragraph-level proofreading exercises and a Grammar and Usage Review.

Chapter 7: Exemplification and Classification Paragraphs introduces students to two kinds of paragraphs that share the same paragraph structure: topic sentence, a body that consists of subtopics with secondary details, and a concluding sentence.

- Students learn the unique characteristics of a topic sentence, the body, and a concluding sentence for both exemplification and classification paragraphs. Model exemplification paragraphs demonstrate the use of examples to develop the topic sentence. Model classification paragraphs demonstrate the use of categories or parts of a whole to develop the topic sentence.
- Students learn to use *hierarchies* as a prewriting method to organize subtopics for both exemplification and classification paragraphs.
- Students continue to practice analyzing, critiquing, and responding in writing to questions about exemplification and classification paragraphs by completing the "What Do You Think?" exercises that appear throughout the chapter.

- This chapter guides students through each of the seven steps for writing exemplification and classification paragraphs, including narrowing the topic and organizing details emphatically, spatially, and chronologically to achieve coherence.
- An array of model paragraphs, checklists of essential paragraph elements, and specific guidelines for each of the seven writing steps build student confidence and success.
- An Exemplification and Classification Planning Sheet with a Student Feedback Form guides and encourages students through each of the seven steps for writing either an exemplification or a classification paragraph.
- "Bosses Are Not All Alike" provides students with practice eliminating wordiness and tightening up the language of a classification paragraph.
- Grammar and Usage Tips in Chapter 7 focus on singular and plural nouns, collective nouns, indefinite subject pronouns, subject-verb agreement, and pronoun-antecedent agreement.
- The chapter ends with paragraph-level proofreading exercises and a Grammar and Usage Review.

Chapter 8: Definition Paragraphs introduces students to definition paragraphs that include definitions expanded through the use of formal definitions, informal definitions, synonyms, antonyms, negatives, etymology, quotations, examples, anecdotes, comparisons, and contrasts.

- Students learn to cite sources for direct quotations from dictionaries or textbooks.
- Students learn the unique characteristics of a topic sentence, the body, and a concluding sentence for definition paragraphs. Model definition paragraphs demonstrate a variety of methods to expand a definition.
- Students learn to gather and then select a variety of details to support the topic sentence and to organize these details in an *outline* or a *list*.
- Students continue to practice analyzing, critiquing, and responding in writing to questions about definition paragraphs by completing the "What Do You Think?" exercises that appear throughout the chapter.
- This chapter guides students through each of the seven steps for writing a definition paragraph.
- An array of model paragraphs, checklists of essential paragraph elements, and specific guidelines for each of the seven writing steps build student confidence and success.

- A Definition Planning Sheet with a Student Feedback Form guides and encourages students through each of the seven steps for writing a definition paragraph.
- Grammar and Usage Tips in Chapter 8 focus on using denotation, connotation, and formal language, and avoiding cliches and euphemisms in formal writing.
- The chapter ends with paragraph-level proofreading exercises and a Grammar and Usage Review.

Chapter 9: Cause-Effect Paragraphs introduces students to paragraphs that explain why or how one or more actions cause one or more events to occur. This chapter emphasizes that analytical thought processes and critical-thinking skills are essential to understand and to write cause-effect paragraphs.

- Students learn the unique characteristics of a topic sentence, the body, and a concluding sentence for cause-effect paragraphs.
- Model paragraphs demonstrate the ways in which singular or multiple causes and effects form causal relationships.
- Students learn to create *diagrams* to show the number of causes and effects and their relationship to each other.
- Students continue to practice analyzing, critiquing, and responding in writing to questions about cause-effect paragraphs by completing the "What Do You Think?" exercises that appear throughout the chapter.
- This chapter guides students through each of the seven steps for writing a cause-effect paragraph. A Cause-Effect Planning Sheet with a Student Feedback Form helps students with the writing process.
- An array of model paragraphs, checklists of essential paragraph elements, and specific guidelines for each of the seven writing steps build student confidence and success.
- Grammar and Usage Tips in Chapter 9 focus on effective use of parallelism in words, phrases, and clauses. This section also includes techniques for avoiding wordiness by combining phrases and clauses effectively.
- The chapter ends with a partner proofreading exercise and a Grammar and Usage Review test.

Chapter 10: Summary Paragraphs introduces students to writing summary paragraphs, condensed versions of longer articles or pieces of writing. The chapter includes informal and formal summaries.

- Writing effective summaries must first begin with careful reading for meaning. This chapter promotes reading for meaning. Techniques include using the title and introductory materials for background information, surveying, reading one paragraph at a time, marking the reading text, notetaking, and identifying the thesis statement.

- "From Vietnam to Hell" uses *marginal notes* to show application of the steps for reading for meaning.
- In this chapter, students learn to include the title of the article, the author's full first name, present tense verbs, and thesis statement in the topic sentence of a formal summary. They then learn to include only main ideas and key details in the body of the paragraph.
- Four articles that instructors can use for summary writing assignments appear in this chapter. Instructors may allow students to select one of the articles, or instructors may assign one specific article for all students to use for a summary paragraph.
- A Summary Paragraph Planning Sheet with a Partner Feedback Form guides students through the process of writing an effective formal summary.

Chapter 11: Paragraph Answers for Test Questions provides students with the opportunity to apply their paragraph-level writing skills to test-taking situations. Instruction in this chapter begins with understanding direction words and the type of answer each direction word requires on a test. Students also learn to identify and use key words in questions in order to write effective answers that directly address the questions.

- This chapter provides students with effective techniques to prepare for tests. These techniques include planning time, taking and using notes, ongoing studying, quizzing, reviewing, working with a study buddy or in a study group, developing a five-day study plan, making summary notes, and learning as much as possible about the test before the test date.
- This chapter applies the prewriting techniques and paragraph development techniques that students learned in previous chapters to test-taking situations.
- Chapter 11 includes four textbook excerpts and test-related questions to use for students to practice writing strong paragraph-level answers to test questions.
- A Paragraph Planning Sheet with a Partner Feedback Form guides students through the process of writing answers to test questions.
- The chapter concludes with tips about learning from tests after the instructors grade the tests and provide feedback on students' written answers.

Chapter 12: Essays introduces students to the elements of an essay: an introductory paragraph with a thesis statement, a multi-paragraph body, and a concluding paragraph.

- This chapter includes model essays that use a standard five-paragraph structure as well as essays with fewer or more than five paragraphs.
- Prewriting techniques start students with Step 1 of the writing process. In Step 2, students learn techniques for gathering information, recording information and sources, using *clustering*, *hierarchies*, *grids*, and *outlines* to organize the paragraphs for essays, and developing an effective thesis statement.
- "What Do You Think?" exercises include model essays for students to analyze, critique, and strengthen.
- The chapter concludes with test-taking tips for writing essay answers on tests.

Appendix A: Student Answer Keys provides students with answers to the Grammar and Usage Tips exercises that appear at the end of each chapter. These answer keys provide students with instant feedback on their work and promote independent study. Students can score their own work and compose questions to ask in class about the exercises and the skills.

Appendix B: Helpful Charts provides students with quick-reference charts for the past participles of irregular verbs and the different types of conjunctions used in compound, complex, and compound-complex sentence patterns.

Ancillary Materials

Instructor's Resource Manual

The Instructor's Resource Manual for *Paragraph Essentials: A Writing Guide* includes the following:

- Sample lesson plans and record-keeping suggestions
- Rubrics and assessment forms for Writing Warm-Ups and paragraphs
- Teaching suggestions for each chapter
- Convenient masters for overhead transparencies
- Suggested answers for the "What Do You Think?" exercises
- Answer keys for the proofreading exercises and the Grammar and Usage Reviews

- A compiled list of all the Grammar and Usage Tips
- Information about this textbook's web site

Textbook Web Site

A comprehensive web site accompanies this textbook. Icons throughout the text indicate supplementary activities that are online to reinforce paragraph-writing skills and the skills presented in Grammar and Usage Tips. To access this textbook's web site go to: **http://college.hmco.com**. Click on "Students." Type *Paragraph Essentials* in the "Jump to Textbook Sites" box. Click "go."

Author Contact

The author welcomes feedback, comments, and questions from teachers using *Paragraph Essentials: A Writing Guide.* The author's email address is posted on the textbook's web site.

Acknowledgments

Developing and producing an effective textbook requires the expertise of many individuals. I would like to thank the following reviewers for their insightful and helpful feedback and recommendations:

Patsy Krech, University of Memphis
Linda G. Matthews, South Suburban College
Carol Miter, Riverside Community College—Norco Campus
Dee Pruitt, Florence Darlington Technical College
Cherry Wardrip, Gateway Technical College

I would also like to extend my appreciation to the many individuals in Houghton Mifflin's College Division Developmental Writing Department who were instrumental in the development and production of this textbook. Without their work, dedication, and interest, *Paragraph Essentials: A Writing Guide* would not have been possible. Thank you, Mary Jo Southern, for your leadership and steadfast support of this textbook. Thank you, Martha Bustin, Kellie Cardone, and Cecilia Molinari, for your expert editing skills, attention to detail, and commitment to working as a highly orchestrated team. Finally, thank you, Danielle Richardson, for your fine work coordinating the national student paragraph writing contest. I appreciate you all and feel honored to be a part of your team.

Linda Wong
Author

To the Student

You are about to begin the important study of paragraph-writing skills, which includes generating topics, gathering and organizing details, and presenting your ideas effectively in a standard paragraph structure. A primary goal of this textbook is to provide you with easy-to-understand instructions and a seven-step writing process, a set of practical skills that will help you develop an attitude of appreciation and enjoyment for the process of writing. In addition to learning about writing different kinds of paragraphs, you will also have the opportunity to strengthen your sentence-level skills and your proofreading skills and to analyze and critique model paragraphs, classmates' paragraphs, and your own original paragraphs.

You will find the following key elements in this textbook:

- An easy-to-understand seven-step approach for developing ten different kinds of paragraphs. Step-by-step planning sheets guide you through the writing process.
- Instruction that begins with recognition and analysis of paragraph elements in prepared paragraphs, many of which have been written by college students. With this approach, the learning sequence begins by *seeing* and *understanding* other writers' work, and then *applying* the skills to your own writing.
- Ample examples of paragraphs with a wide variety of topics to help you understand effective paragraph development. You will become comfortable analyzing and critiquing topic sentences, the organization and content of the body of paragraphs, and concluding sentences.
- Sentence-level exercises designed to strengthen your sentence-writing skills. After you complete the Grammar and Usage exercises, you will be able to check the accuracy of your work with answer keys in Appendix A and receive immediate feedback about your work.
- An instructional approach that is flexible and encourages working with classmates to express your opinions and reinforce the skills in the textbook through lively discussions. You will find that many of the activities in this textbook encourage small group and partner work.
- Interesting and informative content and intriguing, thought-provoking, and meaningful writing topics. Careful attention has been given to the selection of material to use for this book.

- An instructional approach that is sequential. Skills are continuously reviewed and applied throughout the textbook. As you progress through the chapters, you will find yourself building a strong foundation for writing that will make higher-level writing classes easier to complete successfully.
- A comprehensive web site for additional exploration and practice. The web site for this textbook includes companion activities that reinforce the skills in the textbook and links to other web sites with related information. Many exercises are interactive and scored online. You may repeat the exercises as frequently as you wish. You will find that the activities and links on the web site for this textbook are valuable tools and resources for supplemental work.

As you work through the chapters in this textbook, you will become more aware of the fact that writing is a *recursive* rather than a linear process. In other words, you will often revisit earlier stages of the process in the course of revision and rethinking. Because of the recursive nature of writing, the writing process is never truly finished. There are always numerous ways to reword your ideas and restructure your paragraphs and your sentences. Your goal as a writer should be to understand the options that are available to express your ideas clearly in language that is free of grammatical or sentence-level errors. Learning the skills in this textbook will empower you with the strong skill foundation that is essential for higher-level writing.

Special Features Designed for You

To gain the greatest benefits from this textbook, use the following features in each chapter:

Chapter Introductions

The short chapter introductions provide you with a "big picture" of the chapter's contents. At a glance, you will be able to see the key elements in the paragraph that the chapter emphasizes.

Writing Warm-Ups

Before learning the skills of the chapter, you have the opportunity to express your ideas in a paragraph that you will later use for additional proofreading and revision work.

Paragraph Structures

A variety of paragraphs demonstrate effective techniques for developing topic sentences, bodies of paragraphs with unity, coherence, and adequate development, and concluding sentences.

What Do You Think?

What Do You Think? exercises encourage you to analyze and critique paragraphs so you can identify effective paragraph elements and provide suggestions for strengthening paragraphs. These exercises provide you with practice expressing ideas clearly in well-developed sentences. Each time you write answers to the questions in these exercises, strive to answer in complete sentences and to provide an adequate number of details to explain your opinions.

Steps in the Writing Process

Each chapter guides you through the seven steps to writing effective paragraphs. You will learn effective techniques for selecting an interesting topic, getting a focus, gathering and organizing details, writing effective topic sentences, developing the paragraph, revising, proofreading, and editing to produce a polished paragraph.

Planning Sheet

The Planning Sheet simplifies the seven-step process for writing paragraphs. As you complete each step, you are closer to producing the final version of your paragraph. The Partner Feedback Form provides you with additional suggestions and feedback for strengthening your paragraph.

Writing Assignments

Unless your instructor provides different instructions, in each chapter you will be able to choose your own topic to write about in your paragraph. Use the techniques in the chapter to identify a meaningful, interesting, and informative topic. Every chapter provides you with possible topics or topics that you can use as "springboards" for your own ideas. Your writing will be more interesting and have more passion if you select topics that interest you.

Grammar and Usage Tips

Each chapter introduces you to Grammar and Usage rules and tips that will strengthen your sentence-level writing skills. The language is straightforward and easy to understand. Examples demonstrate how the rules work in sentences. The exercises in the Grammar and Usage Tips sections are self-correcting. The following suggestions will make the self-correction process effective and easy to use:

1. Remove Appendix A from the back of your book. Punch holes in the pages so you can keep them in your notebook. Separating the pages from the book makes self-correcting easier.
2. After you correct your work, examine any errors that you made. Try to understand why you made the mistakes. Write any questions you have in the margins of your book next to the exercises. Discuss your questions in class with your instructor. Write your score next to each exercise. (The answer key tells you how to record the number of errors you made.)

3. Use a colored pen to write the correct answers. The learning process always involves correcting and refining, so look at errors as simply a part of the learning process.

Grammar and Usage Tips Summary

Carefully read each Grammar and Usage Tips Summary. After you read an item on the summary, pause to think about the information. Can you picture the concept clearly? Can you visualize examples? Can you explain the concept in your own words and with additional details? If you answer *no* to any of these questions, review the section of the chapter that discusses the specific skill or concept.

Proofreading Exercises

Proofreading can be a difficult skill to master. However, through practice, you can acquire the skills necessary to proofread paragraphs for grammar, punctuation, and sentence-level errors. The proofreading exercises emphasize the grammar and usage skills that you have learned. Work carefully and attentively. You do not have answer keys for the proofreading exercises.

Grammar and Usage Review

Each chapter includes a Grammar and Usage Review. Read the directions carefully. Allow yourself sufficient time to complete the work. You do not have answer keys for the Grammar and Usage Reviews. Your work will be corrected by your instructor or in class.

Web Site Activities

Throughout each textbook chapter, this icon indicates topics that can be reinforced through activities on the Internet. Your instructor may assign some of the online activities, or you may wish to explore them on your own. If you own a computer, consider *bookmarking* the web site so you can quickly go to the site for supplementary work. If you do not own a computer, locate a place on campus where you can gain Internet access. Type in the web site address (the URL) in the address box that appears on the top of the screen after you are connected to the Internet.

To access the web site for this textbook, go to: **http://college.hmco.com**. Click on "Students." Type *Paragraph Essentials* in the "Jump to Textbook Sites" box. Click "go."

A Closing Comment

You are now ready to begin the process of building a strong foundation for paragraph-level writing. The value of learning these new skills reaches far beyond the classroom and the completion of this course. You are building a strong writing foundation that will benefit you in higher-level classes, in your personal life, and in the work force. May you enjoy the process and feel an empowering sense of confidence and success as you become an effective, powerful writer!

CHAPTER 1

The Writing Process

Generate Ideas → Get a Focus → Gather & Organize Information → Write a Rough Draft → Revise, Revise, Revise → Proofread & Edit → Prepare the Final Version

In Chapter 1, you will learn about the following:

1. Becoming a strong writer
2. Seven Steps in the Writing Process
3. Eight parts of speech

WRITING WARM-UP 1

Select one of the following topics and write one or more paragraphs about it. The purpose of this writing sample is to introduce yourself to your instructor. This writing assignment will not be graded.

Choose one: My greatest interest, hobby, or talent
My attitude about writing
My goal in college
My greatest achievement
My most prized possession

Becoming a Strong Writer

Many of us, both students and instructors, strive toward the goal of becoming a strong writer. Exactly what does it mean to be a strong writer? There is no one answer, for strong writers vary in their styles, methods, and abilities. However, if you are a strong writer in the college environment, you probably can do the following:

- Put thought into what you are going to write, generating ideas so your writing has interest, substance, depth, creativity, and freshness.
- Focus on your topic, developing it so the topic is neither too broad nor too narrow.
- Gather information on your topic as necessary and become familiar with it through a combination of personal experiences, observations, reading, and research.
- Organize the information about your topic so you can present ideas and facts effectively and in a logical sequence.
- Connect with your readers as you draft your paper, keeping your audience in mind.
- Allow time for careful revision, proofreading, and editing, always asking, "How can I make what I have written even clearer and more effective?"
- Have strong grammar skills that allow you to proofread, edit, and revise to produce error-free work.

After reviewing the wide range of writing skills necessary to be a strong writer, most people do not assume they can become effective writers by working on a few writing exercises, reading a grammar manual, or finishing a handful of writing assignments. Writing is an ongoing process that continues over the course of our lives with diverse writing experiences, formal instruction, discussions and analyses of personal writing and the writing of others, studying, and reading on a regular basis to become more familiar with a wide variety of writing styles. Writing is a process that has no real end.

Seven Steps in the Writing Process

The writing process would be greatly simplified if it were possible to simply say, "This is how you write." However, the writing process, which is a creative process, involves individual steps or stages that vary from one writer to another and from one writing assignment to another. Instead of working through a fixed series of steps for every writing assignment, writers often find themselves weaving back and forth among the various steps of writing until they feel confident and pleased with a final version. The illustrations in this chapter show a common sequence of steps that you can follow for the process of writing, but keep in mind that you are free to alter the sequence of the steps or move back and forth from one step to another as needed throughout the writing process. Following is a logical sequence of steps that serves as a starting point to get your ideas on paper so they can be refined and strengthened to produce a finished piece of writing:

1. Generate ideas.
2. Get a focus.
3. Gather and organize information.
4. Write a rough draft.
5. Revise, revise, revise.
6. Proofread and edit.
7. Prepare the final version.

STEP 1: GENERATE IDEAS

Step 1: Generate Ideas

Sometimes you may find yourself writing for the personal joy of expressing your thoughts on paper. Perhaps you want to write a personal letter, keep a daily journal, or write as a means of seeking answers to perplexing personal questions. The majority of the time, however, you will be writing to fulfill an assignment for one of your college classes. You will be expected to complete the assignment within a specific time period. Getting started right away, not putting off the writing until the last minute, will benefit you in many ways. Giving yourself as much time as possible to work through the writing stages will make the process easier on you, will give you ample time to produce an assignment that shows quality, and will result in a piece of work that is interesting and informative and that shows your writing ability.

Understanding the Assignment

The Writing Warm-Up at the beginning of each chapter in this textbook assigns a specific topic or a choice of topics for a writing assignment. For Writing Warm-Up 1, you had to make a choice. Did you want to write about your greatest interest, hobby, or talent, explain your attitude about writing, discuss your goals in college, tell about your greatest achievement, or discuss your prized possession? Often, as in this instance, your instructor will offer one or more topics for your writing assignment. Your task is to select a topic and develop it as fully as possible. For other writing assignments, your instructor may give you liberty to select your own topic. For example, you may be asked to write a narrative, a process, or a definition paragraph. You are expected to use the key elements of that given style of paragraph, but you are in control of selecting the topic. As a student and a writer, you need to be prepared to write to fulfill this range of writing assignments. Finally, as on tests, you will be asked to explain or discuss a very specific aspect of a very specific topic. In such cases, the instructor has limited the topic and the range of your answer.

Some students find that open-ended writing assignments are easier to write than those with assigned topics. Other students prefer writing assignments that clearly state what topic or topics can be used. Regardless of which approach you prefer, you must be ready to perform for each type of assignment. To get yourself on the right path, begin by clearly understanding the writing assignment. Seek answers to these key questions:

1. Is the topic specific or open-ended? Am I told what to write about or do I have a choice? If I have a choice, are there boundaries or specific requirements for the assignment?
2. What are the key words in the directions? How do those key words affect the direction of my writing?
3. What are the expectations for length and the due date?
4. What else is required? Do I need to turn in my prewriting and my drafts? If I research the topic, do I need to turn in copies of the sources? Do I need to have another student or a tutor give me feedback?

If the assignment is not clear or you are not exactly sure what is expected from you, ask questions in class or schedule a time to meet with your instructor. You do not want to waste your precious time working on a writing assignment only to find out that you did not meet the expectations, understand the assignment, or produce acceptable or quality work.

Selecting a Topic

If a specific topic is not assigned, your next task is to select a topic that is interesting, informative, or entertaining. This initial step is one of the most difficult for some students. Before the writing process begins, some students feel that they are already experiencing a "writer's block"—that no topic seems appealing, they feel no interest or passion, and no ideas flow into their minds or onto their papers. Fortunately, many strategies exist to jump-start the flow of potential ideas. One starting point is to commit yourself to selecting something that interests you. If you try to write about something that does not really interest you, your lack of interest will be passed on to the reader. Answers to the following questions can help you select an appropriate, interesting topic.

1. What topic do I know something about, really care about, or have a passion about that would be interesting to the reader?
2. What topic could I read more about in order to use it for this assignment?
3. What have I recently read about in a newspaper or a magazine or seen on television that would be interesting and meet the expectations of this assignment?
4. What topic could I use that somehow connects to my own family, reflects my cultural background, or exemplifies my personal values?
5. Do any of the topics or example paragraphs in the book trigger associations to other topics that I could use? Could I use them as springboards to my own ideas?

Writing is a form of communication. Your writing should communicate something of meaning to your reader and capture your reader's attention and interest. Your writing should not evoke a "So what? Who cares?" response from your reader. Notice the differences in reader responses to the opening sentences students wrote for a short personal story (a narrative) in which they were asked to tell about a specific event in their lives.

Student 1: I do my grocery shopping every Saturday.
[Possible reader response: So what? Who cares? What's the big deal?]

Student 2: My life flashed before me on the day I got forced off the road by the semitrailer that had a blowout right in front of me. Pieces of tires were flying through the air directly toward me.
[Possible reader response: Wow! That's frightening! What did you do?]

Student 3: My first accident happened when I rear-ended a car; unfortunately, the car I hit was a police cruiser.
[Possible reader response: Oh, this is going to be a good story!]

Three excellent prewriting techniques can help you generate ideas for topics for writing assignments. After you learn to use each technique successfully, you can then select the most effective technique to use each time you need to generate your own ideas. The three techniques are these:

1. Brainstorming
2. Clustering
3. Freewriting

Brainstorming to Generate Ideas

Brainstorming will help you generate writing topics for open-ended writing assignments. Brainstorming involves quickly listing as many ideas as possible without judging the ideas you write down. Your brainstorming list may include single words, short phrases, or whole sentences. Push yourself to brainstorm for five or ten minutes without stopping. After brainstorming, evaluate your ideas and identify those that you want to consider further and those that you can instantly discard.

1.1 What do you think?

Following are writing topics for two different classes. Assume you are in these classes. Under each question, brainstorm possible topics for each writing assignment. Quickly list as many possible ideas as you can for the assignment. Do not judge the ideas at this time; instead, aim for quantity.

1. Literature class: The theme we have explored for the last four weeks focuses on family traditions, cultural values, and family rituals. Write about a tradition, cultural value, or ritual that your family practices.

   Brainstorm possible family traditions, cultural values, or family rituals:

2. Personal health class: Discuss the physical and emotional effects of stress on the human body. Include effects on the nervous, respiratory, muscular, and circulatory systems.

   Brainstorm effects of stress:

Clustering to Generate Ideas

Clustering, also known as mapping, is a form of brainstorming that uses a graphic format. Write the general topic or the writing assignment in the middle of a blank piece of paper. Extend spokes or branches from the middle of the paper outward to show as many ideas as possible. Randomly surround the center of the page with writing ideas or topics. In the following example, students were asked to create a clustering of possible topics for a story about one significant event in their personal lives.

Clustering, like brainstorming, is not limited to generating writing topics. You can also use these techniques to generate details to use in the body of a paragraph. The following example shows a cluster made for Writing Warm-Up 1. This student decided to write about a favorite hobby, quilting. Possible ideas or details to include branch from the topic.

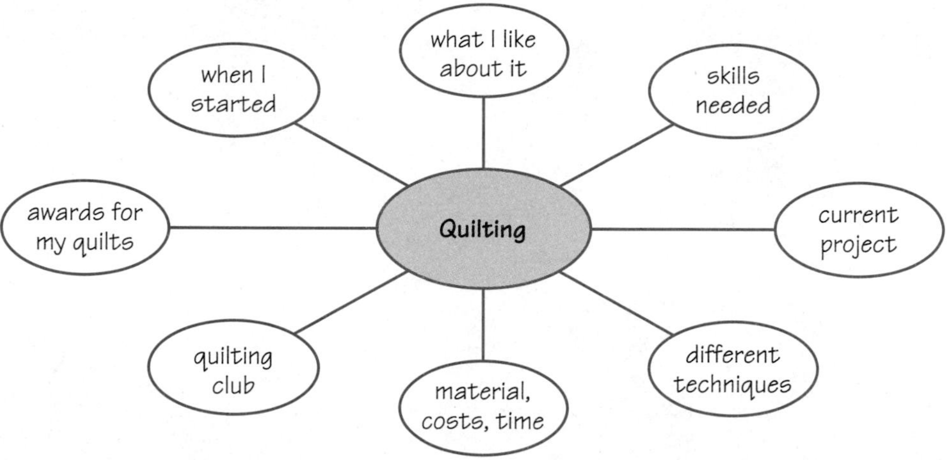

1.2 What do you think?

Create a cluster for possible topics for a writing assignment that asks you to write about one significant event in your life.

Freewriting to Generate Ideas

Freewriting can be used to either identify a topic or narrow a topic to a manageable size. For freewriting, set a period of time to write, usually five or ten minutes. Instead of writing lists as is done with brainstorming, plan to write a continuous stream of sentences. Write down whatever pops into your mind. Do not worry about sentence structure, spelling, or other elements of grammar. The goal is to get the ideas to flow from your head onto your paper. The direction of your ideas will likely shift, which is what you want to happen. If you get stuck, simply continue to write the last word on your paper until new ideas pop to the surface. You can reorganize, expand, or discard ideas later.

In the following example of freewriting, students were asked to write a definition paragraph for the term *apathy*. This freewriting demonstrates how one student jotted down all ideas that came into her mind.

> Apathy—that's where you don't really care. It's when you don't give a rip. A lot of people have a lot of apathy. Look at how some people look away at a homeless or a hungry person. They don't even take the time to consider how other people think or feel. Apathy is everywhere. Teenagers have it. Lots of times toward their parents and their peers. But I think everyone feels it at some time or another. Is it because we don't want to be bothered or upset? I wonder why we have that emotion. Can it ever be good to have? I can't think of situations where I would want apathy. Apathy. Apathy. It seems kinda empty. A denial kinda thing. Men probably have it more than women. Hmmm . . . I wonder if that's true. Reporters—lots of apathy. Look how they stick cameras in the faces of people at accidents or housefires . . . or any kind of tragedy. Do we have it when we watch the reports or do we feel something? Don't they stop to think how much pain a person has? They don't want to be interviewed when they are wailing or in shock. Apathy I bet happens in every culture . . . culture . . . culture . . . Is it the opposite of sympathy? What about empathy? Why do those words kinda sound the same?

While generating ideas may seem challenging at times, you will find that with practice, you can think of an abundance of topics. Your challenge then becomes narrowing down your choices and committing your attention to one specific topic. Save your prewriting work so you have alternative topics available if your original choice does not work out or if you need another topic for a later assignment.

1.3 What do you think?

Select one of the words or phrases below. On separate paper, freewrite about this word for five minutes. Let your ideas flow onto the paper. Do not be concerned with grammar, punctuation, spelling, or sentence structure.

justice freedom of speech diversity human rights patriotism

Step 2: Get a Focus

Once you have selected a topic, you will want to get a strong focus on the topic in order to create a powerful, interesting paragraph instead of a "Ho-hum. Who cares?" kind of paragraph. You can establish a clear focus by

1. Narrowing the topic
2. Knowing your audience
3. Identifying your purpose

Narrowing the Topic

After you select a topic, consider whether you need to narrow the topic. Narrowing the topic involves limiting what you will cover in your paragraph to a manageable size. Limiting the scope of information and the length of the time frame covered in the paragraph sharpens the focus of your paragraph.

Notice in the following examples how one student started with a broad or general topic and then narrowed the topic twice to achieve a manageable topic well-suited for a paragraph. Sometimes you can narrow a topic once to reach a well-suited topic; other times you may need to narrow the topic multiple times before reaching a well-suited topic that has a sharp focus.

Student's initial topic:	Inventors
First narrowing:	1. American inventors
Second narrowing:	2. Alfred Nobel (dynamite)

Student's initial topic:	Personal story about flying
First narrowing:	1. Small, private planes; not commercial jets
Second narrowing:	2. Emergency event over Copper Harbor, Michigan

Student's initial topic:	Problems on American freeways
First narrowing:	1. Road rage
Second narrowing:	2. Efforts that are being taken to stop road rage

1.4 What do you think?

Narrow each of the following broad topics twice to achieve a manageable topic well-suited for a paragraph.

1. Endangered species

   First narrowing: ______________________

   Second narrowing: ______________________

2. American politics

   First narrowing: ______________________

   Second narrowing: ______________________

3. Natural disasters

   First narrowing: ______________________

   Second narrowing: ______________________

Knowing Your Audience

Writing is a form of communication that is designed to share ideas and information. For writing to be effective and for your paragraph to have a sharp focus, you must consider your audience and realize that their backgrounds and experiences may differ greatly from your own. Answers to the following questions will help you know your audience and adjust your writing to your readers:

1. Who is my audience? Who will be reading this writing?
2. How much knowledge can I safely assume the reader has about this topic?
3. Will the reader understand technical terms or will the terms be too unfamiliar?
4. What level of vocabulary or level of formality is best to use with this audience?
5. What kind of language or topics are appropriate so I will not alienate my audience?

Often your classmates and your instructor are your audience. If you are writing about a topic specific to a particular course you are taking, you can assume that your audience is familiar with the technical terminology and concepts used in the course. If you are writing about topics unrelated to the course, you will need to consider carefully the amount of background information and degree of familiarity your audience has with your topic. For example, if you write a paragraph explaining how to change the configuration of a computer, you will write differently depending on whether your audience is your computer science teacher and other computer majors or a general audience with limited computer knowledge and experience. When you believe members of the audience are unfamiliar with your topic, you will need extra details and explanations.

In a work environment, knowing your audience is even more significant. Your writing may on some occasions need to include sophisticated, technical, job-specific language for your superiors or your coworkers. On other occasions, you may be expected to change the language and the tone of your writing to match the knowledge level of the general public or personnel in other departments who may not have the same technical skills. Regardless of your setting or situation, you as a writer need to think about your audience and adjust your writing accordingly. Powerful, effective writing always reflects a compatibility with the audience.

The following example shows how the content of a paragraph varies for different audiences. For example, assume that your topic, which you will need to narrow, is *drugs*. The topic and the content of the paragraph will vary for each of the different audiences.

Audience	**Possible focus and content of the paragraph**
teenagers	Dangers of common street drugs
parents	Indicators of drug use in teenagers
rehabilitation counselors	Success rates of different drug therapy programs
police officers	Efforts to reduce drug use in the community

Identifying a Purpose

Just as your audience of imagined readers affects your writing, so should the specific purpose you intend your writing to serve. Identifying a clear purpose in your writing will help you select the appropriate details to develop your topic effectively. Perhaps you want to teach a process to the reader, entertain with a story, explain the differences between two subjects, or vividly describe a specific person, place, or event. Writing with a clear purpose in mind also helps the reader understand the significance of your writing. You want to create a response in the reader that says, "That was informative. I learned something new. I now understand this concept." or "That was entertaining." or "Your writing stirred some emotions in me." Such responses show that you accomplished the specific purpose you established for your work.

Patterns of discourse is a term used to categorize different kinds of writing based on their purpose. The patterns of discourse are *narrative* to tell a story; *descriptive* to describe a person, place, or event; *persuasive* to convince the reader to accept your point of view; and *expository* to expose, reveal, demonstrate, or disclose information and concepts. Expository writing, which includes process, comparisons, contrasts, exemplification, classification, definition, cause/effect, and summary, is the most frequently used pattern of discourse in college classes. The following chart shows ten different types of paragraphs, each with a specific purpose. Each of these types of paragraphs will be discussed later in this textbook.

TYPES OF PARAGRAPHS	
PARAGRAPH TYPE	THE PURPOSE IS TO:
Narrative	Tell a story about a specific incident or event of significance.
Descriptive	Create a vivid picture of the appearance or nature of a person, place, thing, or idea.
Process	Explain how to do, make, or repair something; explain how something was already done.
Comparison	Show the similarities between two subjects.
Contrast	Show the differences between two subjects.
Exemplification	Explain a statement or a point of view through the use of specific examples.
Classification	Explain a subject by breaking it into categories, groups, or individual parts.
Definition	Define the meaning of a term through an expanded definition.
Cause/Effect	Tell causes (reasons) or effects (outcomes) of a specific event, situation, or series of actions.
Summary	Give the highlights and key points or main ideas of an article or an essay.

In the following example, notice how a single topic, *eyeglasses,* can move in many directions depending on your purpose for writing about eyeglasses. If you were given the assignment to write about eyeglasses, you would first need to narrow the topic, consider your audience's background, and then identify your purpose for writing your paragraph. Clearly identifying your purpose before proceeding to the next step in the writing process is essential.

Purpose	**Focus or direction of your paragraph**
narrate	Tell a significant story about adjusting to your first pair of glasses or an incident that occurred when you could not find your glasses.
describe	Describe a specific pair of eyeglasses worn by a specific person.
show process	Explain the steps for manufacturing prescription lenses.
show similarity	Compare non-prescription magnifying glasses to prescription reading glasses.
show contrast	Contrast contact lenses with eyeglasses.
exemplify	Give examples of different kinds of eyeglasses.
categorize	Categorize different types of eyeglasses.
define	Define the term *bifocals.*
cause/effect	Discuss the causes of vision problems that require the use of glasses.
summarize	Summarize an article in a medical journal that discusses safety factors for sunglasses.

Answering the following questions will help you focus on the purpose of your writing and relate your topic to your specific audience:

1. What do you want your reader to know, feel, believe, or do after reading your writing? What is your intent?
2. Which of the following shows your purpose?
   - Tell a story with a specific emotional appeal, moral, or significance.
   - Create a vivid image of a person, place, thing, or event.
   - Explain how to do, make, or repair something.
   - Explain how something works.

- ☼ Show similarities or differences between two subjects.
- ☼ Explain a concept through the use of appropriate examples.
- ☼ Break a subject down and explain its different categories or parts.
- ☼ Explain causes or effects of a specific event or situation.
- ☼ Define an unfamiliar term.
- ☼ Summarize a literary work, such as an article, a short story, or an essay.

3. Is your purpose to write a narrative, a descriptive, an expository, or a persuasive paragraph for your readers?

Step 3: Gather and Organize Information

At this point in the writing process, you have narrowed your topic to a manageable size for a paragraph, considered your audience, and identified a purpose for writing. Now the work of gathering and organizing information gains importance. Because the writing process is not linear, gathering information for your writing will help you to see your topic from a new perspective or discover information that sways you to revise your focus. Enter into the writing process with a flexible mind. Allow yourself to shift the focus in these early stages and to explore options for your writing as you become involved in the following prewriting tasks:

1. Using resources to gather information
2. Taking notes
3. Accumulating the right amount of information
4. Writing a topic sentence with a controlling idea
5. Developing a prewriting organizational plan

Using Resources to Gather Information

Though your personal knowledge and your personal experiences are valuable foundations for your writing, expository writing frequently demands additional sources of information, such as factual information, quotes, statistics, definitions, and pertinent examples. The paragraphs you write will usually be more effective if you spend time reading and gathering information beyond your level of personal experience.

Many resources exist to locate the information you seek. Answering the following questions will lead you to many valuable resources:

1. Does your course textbook contain the information you need? Check the index.
2. Does your course textbook have a bibliography? Often the books or articles listed in the text's bibliography are available at your library and can provide pertinent information.
3. Is your topic one that would appear in periodicals (magazines)? Check with your reference librarian.
4. Is the topic currently in the news? Check newspapers for articles you can use as sources.
5. Have you conducted Internet searches for the topic? Try several browsers and key words in doing your search.
6. Have you checked the databases and the CD-ROMs in your library? Ask a reference librarian to help you locate the information you seek.
7. Are there experts, other classmates, friends, family members, tutors, or instructors whom you could interview? People make excellent resources.

Taking Notes

As you locate possible information for your writing, you will want to create a notetaking system to keep track of the information and the sources used for your writing. That way you will be able to give proper credit to your sources and create your bibliography, or list of sources that you used in your writing. Creating a **writing file system** is one quick and effective form of notetaking. Photocopy pages of books or clip out newspaper or magazine articles that contain potentially useful material. If the name of the book, newspaper, or magazine is not included on the page, handwrite the information on the page before you place it in your file system. Include the name of the book, magazine, or newspaper; the publisher; the copyright date or the date of issue; and the page numbers.

If the source of your information is the Internet, print a copy of any information for your files and be sure it contains its URL (Web address). Highlight important ideas or details that you might want to use in your writing. Create one or more file folders to house your pages of information.

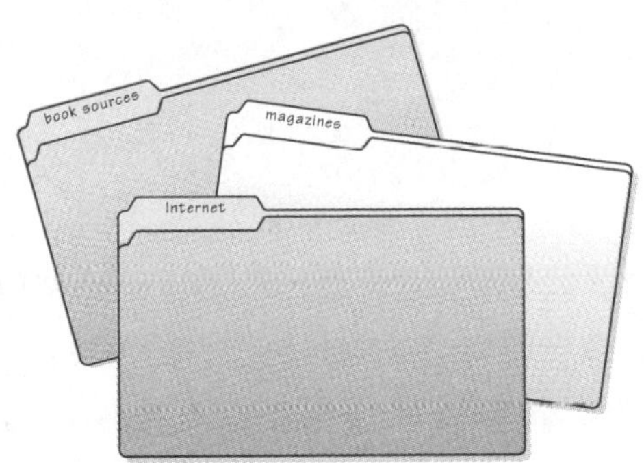

Notetaking on **index cards** is a system that students frequently use to gather information for a writing assignment. Each time you encounter a statistic, definition, quote, example, or fact, jot it down on an index card. Limit one idea per card so the cards can easily be reorganized with similar items grouped together. On the back of each card, write the source of the information or a number code that refers to a master list of sources. This master list needs to contain the kind of information you would need for a bibliography for an essay or a report:

- author's name
- name of the book, magazine, newspaper, or Internet article
- publisher
- copyright date or date of issue
- page numbers

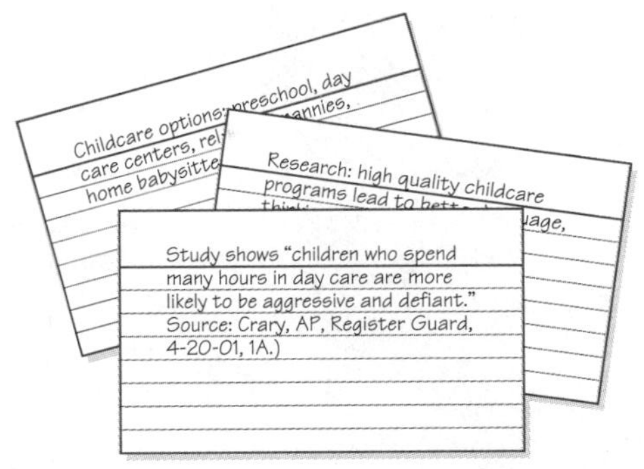

Index cards can serve other functions as well. Frequently, when writers are contemplating a topic, ideas to develop sometimes appear "out of nowhere." An interesting point may come to mind as you wait for a bus or drive to school, mow the lawn, or take a shower. Possible ideas can be quickly jotted down on index cards to be considered more carefully at a later point. You can also use index cards to record comments on the topic that you hear on television, among family and friends, or in the course of an interview with an expert in the field.

Accumulating the Right Amount of Information

The "right amount" of information is extremely difficult to define. How much is too much? How much is too little? The quantity of information required to effectively develop a topic will vary from person to person, topic to topic, and assignment to assignment. You need considerably less for a paragraph than for a research report, but in both cases, your writing needs adequate development. *Adequate development* refers to the quantity and the quality of the details in a paragraph. An effective paragraph needs to have a sufficient number of different details in order to develop the topic sentence effectively. Too little information will result in an underdeveloped paragraph. Too much information is often easier to handle, for you can readily eliminate or discard excessive information when you organize your information and write the first draft. (See Chapter 2, page 59.)

Remember that writers must remain flexible throughout the writing process. Begin by gathering what you feel is sufficient information. Once you begin writing the first draft, or later when you begin to revise your work, you can always march off to the library, the Internet, or other resources if you sense a lack of sufficient details. Ideally, writers have the necessary information gathered and at their fingertips before they begin writing the first draft, but it is not unusual after the first draft has been written for a writer to sense that more content is needed to develop the paragraph effectively.

Developing a Topic Sentence

The topic sentence states the main idea for the entire paragraph; it controls the content of the body of the paragraph. The topic sentence consists of two elements:

1. A meaningful, interesting, narrowed **subject**
2. A **controlling idea,** the main idea that conveys your point of view, opinion, or attitude toward the subject

Some students find a focus for their topics and are immediately able to write an effective topic sentence with a controlling idea. They then proceed to gather and organize information to develop the topic sentence. Others prefer to gather and organize the available information first; the topic sentence often emerges as they work with their prewriting materials. Either approach can work effectively.

Keep in mind the following points about topic sentences:

1. Your topic sentence needs to include a controlling idea. Without a controlling idea, a topic sentence becomes simply a statement of fact without any hint or clue as to your point of view, opinion, or attitude (positive, neutral, or negative) toward the subject.

   Lacks a controlling idea:
   Freeways run through the city.

   Contains a controlling idea:
   Freeways running through the heart of the city is one example of our city's poor infrastructure planning.

2. Your topic sentence is a significant sentence in the paragraph because it controls the information or the details in the remainder of your paragraph. Details that do not support or develop your topic sentence and the controlling idea should not be used in your paragraph.
3. Because topic sentences are controlling sentences and are key elements to the overall development of the paragraph, you need to dedicate ample time to writing a strong topic sentence. (See Chapter 2, page 45.)

4. Writing one sentence, the topic sentence, may sound easy; however, oftentimes you will find yourself searching for the most effective way to state your point of view, opinion, or attitude toward your narrowed subject. Often you may find yourself revising and completely changing the topic sentence several times before an effective topic sentence that clearly states the controlling idea emerges.

The topic sentence is one of three parts of a standard paragraph. Though seasoned writers may vary this pattern, the basic structure provides you with a solid foundation for developing your topic into a paragraph. The following diagram shows the basic paragraph structure.

BASIC PARAGRAPH STRUCTURE

	Title
Beginning: Topic sentence with a controlling idea (a significant main idea)	**Topic sentence with the main idea** ________________
Middle: Body with sentences that provide supporting details	**Body of the paragraph with sentences that contain the supporting details** ________________
End: Concluding sentence	**Concluding sentence** ________________

Developing a Prewriting Organizational Plan

Many writers find that the actual writing process flows more smoothly by starting with a basic prewriting plan on paper to guide the writing process. Be aware, however, that some writers work in the reverse order. They write a rough draft and then create a writing plan as a way to check whether the paragraph flows in a logical sequence. For now, emphasis will be on creating a prewriting plan that will guide the writing of a rough draft. Three common prewriting plans are outlining, listing, and clustering.

Outlining

You may want to create an **outline** to show how you intend to develop the paragraph. For example, an outline for Writing Warm-Up 1 might look like this:

I. My greatest achievement
  A. Student Leadership Award
    1. only one given to graduating senior
    2. high school, senior year
    3. for work with retirement homes
  B. What the work involved
    1. high school kids signing up for visits
    2. recreational activities
    3. special events
  C. How I felt about the award
    1. proud
    2. compassionate
    3. responsible

A well-developed and well-planned outline guides you through the writing of the draft. As with all organizational plans, outlines force you to think about the relationship of the key ideas and details that will be included in your paragraph. You will find that some instructors require you to provide an outline for writing assignments. An outline submitted with a writing assignment provides your instructor with a roadmap of your work and clarifies the various levels of information and details within a paragraph.

In an outline for a paragraph, a Roman numeral I signifies the topic. The capital letters A, B, C, and so on show the main categories or main points you intend to develop in the paragraph. The numerals 1, 2, 3, and so on show the supporting details. Notice that throughout the outline, only key words or phrases are used; full sentences are not usually written in an outline.

The following outline can serve as a guide for writing a paragraph for the topic "My Attitude About Writing":

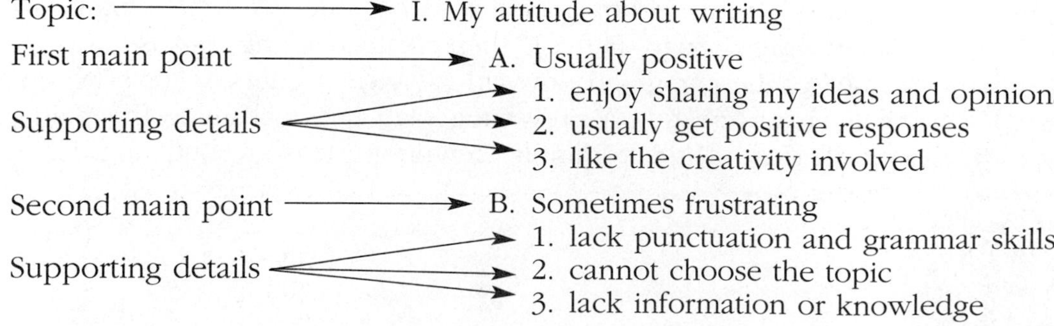

Listing

Details can also be organized in a simple list. The initial list may be in a random order that can later be reorganized in a chronological, spatial, emphatic (degree of importance), or any other order that is logical to you.

My greatest achievement

1. Student Leadership Award
2. working with senior citizens in retirement home
3. getting other students involved
4. organizing volunteers
5. did activities with the seniors
6. special project involving seniors with our school
7. found this really rewarding, exciting, fun to be involved
8. senior year in high school
9. program will continue now every year
10. thirty-five students involved

Clustering

In addition to being used to generate ideas for writing topics, a **cluster** can be used to organize the information and details that will be used in your paragraph. The prewriting stage may include more than one cluster. The first cluster may randomly show ideas or details for the paragraph and then be revised to show the order that you want to present the details. Clusters are usually read from the "11 o'clock position" or from the top of the cluster and then around the cluster in a clockwise direction. In the following clusters, notice the random order of the details in the first diagram and the reordering or sequencing of the details in the second diagram.

Cluster with Ideas in Random Order

Cluster for Organizing Details

Goals in college
- graduate in 2 1/2 years with a dental hygienist degree
- get accepted into dental hygienist program
- get on the honor roll
- pass every class
- study hard

As you work through each of the chapters in this book, you will be guided through activities designed to help you gather information and organize your ideas. By the end of the book, you will know how to use different prewriting plans to organize information. Because writing is an individualized process, you will have the skills and understanding to select and use the techniques that are most effective for you.

STEP 4: WRITE A ROUGH DRAFT

Step 4: Write a Rough Draft

The character in the preceding illustration falsely believes that a paragraph can quickly be "whipped out" since she has completed her prewriting activities by generating ideas, getting a focus, and gathering and organizing information. While the prewriting activities often produce a feeling of being in control and almost finished with the assignment, writing a powerful, effective paragraph (or a longer piece of writing) involves much more than quickly writing a rough draft and hoping that it can work as a finished product. Very few writers are able or willing to present a rough draft as their final, polished piece of work. They know that rough drafts almost always need to be examined carefully and revised in order to be more effective.

Recognizing the Goals of the Rough Draft

A rough draft is exactly that: rough. It is the starting point for later revisions and editing. One goal of a rough draft is to move your ideas from your head onto paper. Another goal is to express your ideas as clearly as possible without worrying about punctuation, sentence structure, grammar, capitalization, or spelling. A final goal is to create a physical form of your paper so you have something to analyze, improve, strengthen, and refine. The basic paragraph structure is the physical form for your rough draft

Using the Basic Paragraph Structure in Your Draft

As shown on page 18, the basic paragraph structure for your draft begins with a strong topic sentence with a controlling idea. The body of the paragraph expresses the supporting details that explain or discuss the topic sentence. For paragraphs that are designed to stand by themselves and are not a part of a larger piece of writing, such as an essay, the last sentence is the concluding sentence. The concluding sentence signals to that reader that you have finished your ideas for the paragraph. (Chapter 2 discusses the key elements of paragraph structure in greater detail.) Understanding and using this basic paragraph structure will help you organize your ideas and information effectively and logically.

Paying Attention to Due Dates

Many students are capable of producing much stronger and more polished writing assignments than the ones they turn in to their instructors. Problems arise when they run out of time to complete the final steps of revising and editing. Writing is a process that requires ample time for both ideas and the writing to be refined.

One effective planning technique is to create a timeline for your writing assignments. On a piece of paper or a calendar, look at the available time between the current day and the due date of the assignment. Estimate the time you will need for each step of the writing process. On your paper or calendar, commit to specific amounts of time on the available days to complete the individual steps in the writing process. For example, assume your assignment is to write a process paragraph that explains how to do, make, or repair something. Jot down the estimated amount of time you feel you would need to complete the assignment by its due date. In the following plan, the assignment is given on Monday and is due on Friday.

		Time Needed
Monday:	Generate ideas; select a topic.	________
	Get a focus; narrow the topic.	________
	Gather information; use resources; take notes.	________
Tuesday:	Organize the information.	________
	Write an effective topic sentence.	________
	Write a rough draft.	________
Wednesday:	Revise the rough draft; use the revision checklist.	________
Thursday:	Revise again if needed; edit.	________
	Write/type the final version.	________
Friday:	Turn in the completed assignment.	

Using Pencil, Pen, or Computer

Whether you write your rough draft with pencil, pen, or computer, plan to double space. Writing on every other line provides you with space to insert words, phrases, and changes in both the rough draft step and the revision step. Some writers prefer to write a rough draft in pencil, some prefer to use pen, and some prefer to use a computer. Each has its pros and cons.

Writing with a pencil:	Pros: Ideas can be changed with the stroke of an eraser. Cons: Pencil is sometimes difficult to read.
Writing with a pen:	Pros: Pen is often easier to read. Cons: Making changes is more difficult.
Writing on a computer:	Pros: Revisions are easier to make. Cons: Slow typing slows down the process of getting ideas on paper.

In some colleges, students are required to type their assignments on a computer. If this is the case for you and you do not type at a reasonable speed, plan to write your rough draft on paper. Later, after you have done your revision work, use a computer for the final revision. Papers that are written on a computer are easier to read, appear more polished, and are more aesthetically appealing to the reader.

Citing Your Sources

In most of your paragraphs, you will be using your own words to express your ideas. However, when you use exact words taken directly from one or more of your sources, you must give credit to the authors of the information. For a paragraph, stating the author's name within the paragraph is the easiest method to use. The author's exact words are placed inside quotation marks.

> In the article "Gunning for a Solution to School Shootings," Paul Chance, Ph.D., claims, "None of these measures is likely to do much good."

Footnotes may also be used. Immediately following another author's words or ideas, write a small number, called a superscript, above the last word of the sentence. Below the paragraph, write the number; then give the author's name, the name of the article, magazine, or book, the publisher, the copyright date, and the page number. Your instructor can provide you with his or her preferred method for citing your sources.

> "The result is a shifting from hostility to tolerance: Outsiders no longer feel so far outside; insiders feel less smug."[1]

1. Paul Chance, Ph.D, "Gunning for a Solution to School Shootings," *Psychology Today,* September/October 2000, p. 74.

STEP 5: REVISE, REVISE, REVISE

Step 5: Revise, Revise, Revise

Revision is the process of carefully reading what you have written, giving it deep thought and attention, and then rewriting as necessary. In revising, you think about your purpose, the ideas, and the information you want to communicate and then make changes to improve and strengthen your work. Many writers revise several times; each revision focuses on one aspect of the paragraph. The first revision may examine the assignment, the purpose, and the audience. The second revision may critique the structure of the paragraph—the topic sentence, the body, and the concluding sentence. Another revision may focus on word choice and style. A final revision may analyze the individual sentences. Perhaps you should combine or reword some sentences, or use better transition words between sentences.

Use the following checklist to revise your work:

First Revision

1. Does the topic fit the writing assignment?
2. Is the topic narrowed and focused?
3. Does the topic sentence clearly state a controlling idea to show your point of view, opinion, or attitude (negative, neutral, or positive) toward the subject?
4. Does the writing show understanding of the audience?
5. Is the purpose clear? Which parts of the writing identify or state the purpose?

Second Revision

6. Are enough details presented to develop the main idea in the topic sentence?
7. Is every sentence related to the topic sentence and the purpose?
8. Are details organized in a logical way?
9. When the paragraph is read out loud, do the ideas flow smoothly?
10. Does the concluding sentence end the paragraph effectively?

Third Revision

11. Is the choice of words effective? Are action verbs and descriptive words used effectively?
12. Are ideas expressed clearly without excessive wordiness?
13. Are unfamiliar terms clearly defined for the reader?

Fourth Revision

14. Does the paragraph have good sentence variety?
15. Could sentences be combined more effectively?
16. Are transitions words used effectively to connect ideas?

With each new revision, you see your writing evolve into a final, polished product. The number of revisions will vary, but the need for revision will not. In almost every case, revision is essential for effective writing.

STEP 6: PROOFREAD AND EDIT

Step 6: Proofread and Edit

Your final stage of revision work is to put the polishing touches on the final draft by proofreading for errors and editing to correct the errors. **Proofreading** requires careful and accurate reading. When you proofread, you must read what is on the paper, not what you intended to put on the paper. Reading word by word and reading out loud increase the accuracy of your proofreading. Proofreading involves giving careful attention to the mechanical skills of writing: grammar and spelling. **Editing** requires a strong knowledge of grammar rules and options to correct sentence errors such as fragments, comma splices, and run-on sentences. It also requires strong spelling skills. The more you can develop your grammar and spelling skills, the more accurate your proofreading and editing skills will be.

Give close attention to the following aspects of your writing. (These sentence elements will be defined in later chapters.)

1. Are simple, compound, and complex sentences formed and punctuated correctly?
2. Are commas and semicolons used correctly?
3. Are fragments, comma splices, and run-on sentences avoided?
4. Do the subjects agree with the verbs in number and gender?
5. Do the pronouns agree with their antecedents in case, number, and gender?
6. Are unnecessary shifts in verb tense avoided?
7. Are dangling participles avoided?
8. Are words spelled correctly?

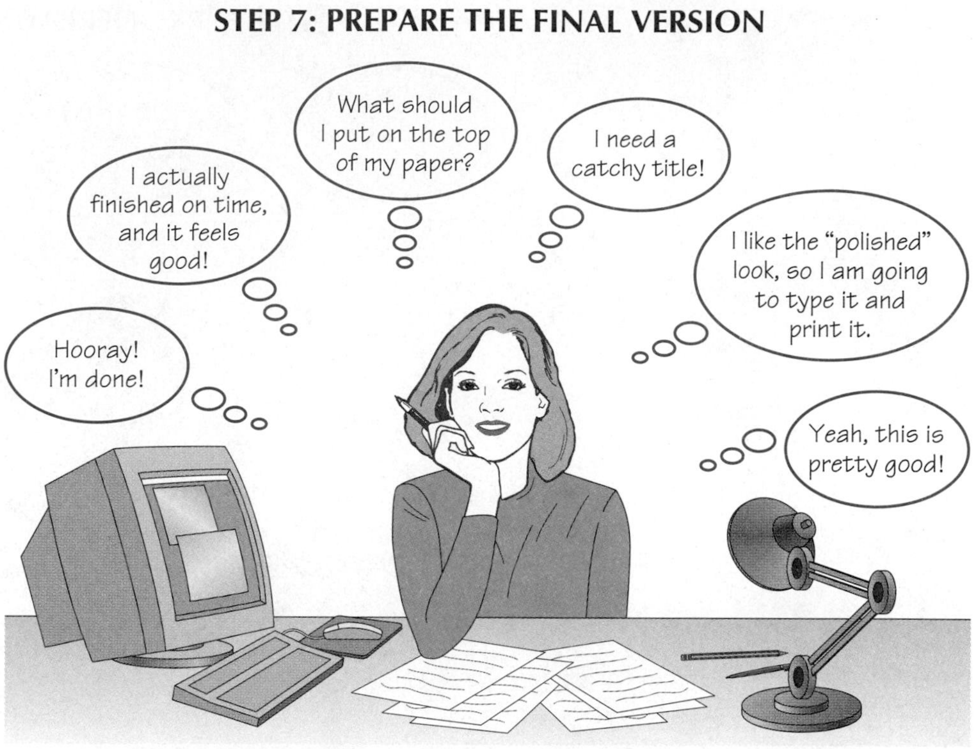

STEP 7: PREPARE THE FINAL VERSION

Step 7: Prepare the Final Version

After you revise, proofread, and edit your writing, you have reached the final stage in the writing process. You are ready to prepare the final version for presentation to your instructor and/or class. You should feel pleased with the final product, for it is a reflection of your time, effort, and commitment to quality work.

Your instructor may suggest a specific format to use for your final version. If a format is not suggested, use the following standard format. The format begins with a **heading** on the top of your paper. After 2–4 blank lines, write the title of your paragraph. On the line after the title, write your paragraph. Use these standards for the paragraph format:

1. Leave a $1\frac{1}{2}$-inch margin on the left and a 1-inch margin on the right of your page.
2. Double space between lines.
3. If submitting handwritten work, use pen and write as neatly as possible.
4. If submitting work done on a computer, use a 12-point font size.

You can use this format for preparing the final version of a paragraph or a longer paper, such as an essay. For longer papers, use the full heading only on the first page. From the second page onward, use a partial heading that consists of your last name followed by the page number: Wong - 2 and Wong - 3. If your instructor prefers an alternative format for the headings, follow your instructor's guidelines.

SUMMARY: STEPS IN THE WRITING PROCESS

Step 1: Generate ideas. Begin by clearly understanding the assignment. Then select a general topic. Brainstorming, clustering, and freewriting are techniques that help you generate ideas.

Step 2: Get a focus. Narrow your topic so it is specific and has a manageable size for a paragraph. Keep your audience in mind and make sure your writing for that audience is appropriate. Identify a clear purpose for your writing so you know what you intend to accomplish.

Step 3: Gather and organize information. Use a variety of resources to gather information for your narrowed topic. Take notes as you read and locate potential information for your assignment. Accumulate a sufficient amount of different details to develop your topic. Write a strong topic sentence that clearly states your controlling idea. Make a prewriting organizational plan by creating an outline, list, or cluster that shows how you intend to organize the details.

Step 4: Write a rough draft. Consider your goals for the rough draft. Make a timeline so you will be able to complete the assignment by the due date, without rushing the process. Use the basic paragraph structure: topic sentence, body with supporting details, and concluding sentence.

Step 5: Revise, revise, revise. Improve and strengthen your work by revising one or more times. Focus on one specific aspect of your writing for each revision until all aspects of your paragraph have been examined and revised. Use the checklist on page 26 to guide your revisions.

Step 6: Proofread and edit. Analyze each sentence carefully. Proofread for mechanical errors such as sentence structure, punctuation, grammar, and spelling. Edit the work by making the corrections. Use the checklist on page 27 to guide your proofreading and editing.

Step 7: Prepare the final version. Keyboard or write a final version. Use a heading on your paper or use the guidelines provided by your instructor.

Grammar and Usage Tips

At the end of each chapter of this textbook, you will have the opportunity to strengthen your grammar and usage skills. Increasing your understanding of grammar and word usage will enable you to proofread and edit to eliminate common writing errors, write more effective sentences, combine sentences for greater sentence variety, and express your ideas clearly and accurately. Chapter 1 lays the foundation for the Grammar and Usage Tips that appear in Chapters 2 through 9. The grammar in this chapter provides you with an overview of the eight parts of speech. The parts of speech indicate the way a word functions in a sentence. To identify the part of speech of a particular word, it is usually necessary to see the word in context—that is, within a sentence.

Each of the eight parts of speech will be discussed in greater detail in later chapters; for now, the point is to gain a general understanding of nouns, pronouns, adjectives, verbs, adverbs, prepositions, conjunctions, and interjections. Short exercises are included. After you have read this section and completed the exercises, check your work with the answer keys in Appendix A in the back of the book. Write the number of errors on the line labeled *Score.*

Nouns

A **noun** names a person, place, thing, or idea. In the following sentences, nouns are in bold print.

> The **evaluators** submitted a lengthy **report.**
>
> Many senior **citizens** use the **bus** as their main **form** of **transportation.**
>
> The **notion** crossed my **mind** before you ever made the **suggestion.**
>
> In **June,** I attended a national **convention** in **Chicago, Illinois.**
>
> Extended **families** consist of **parents, aunts, uncles, cousins,** and **grandparents.**

Nouns can be **singular** (showing one) or **plural** (showing more than one). Nouns can also be classified as common or proper. **Proper nouns** name specific nouns and must always be capitalized. **Common nouns** name nonspecific nouns; they are not capitalized.

Singular	Plural	Common	Proper
movie	movies	movie	*Lethal Weapon*
city	cities	city	Las Vegas

Some nouns are the subjects of sentences—that is, they tell who or what is the "actor" of the sentence. Subjects are key elements of all sentences. Nouns may also be found inside prepositional phrases and as direct objects and indirect objects, which are closely related to the action or the verb part of the sentence. You will learn more about these functions of nouns in later chapters.

EXERCISE 1.1 Identifying Nouns

Score: ______

Circle the nouns in each sentence. Nouns may appear anywhere throughout the sentence. Remember that nouns name a person, place, thing, or idea.

1. The escrow papers arrived in the mail.
2. Homeowners face many expenses.
3. The new development is near a park and a mall.
4. Construction workers toiled under a blazing sun.
5. The house has a shingled roof.

Pronouns

A **pronoun** replaces a noun to avoid repetition of the same word. A pronoun is a noun substitute that is used after the noun has been named or identified. The word *antecedent* refers to the noun that the pronoun replaces. In the following example, the arrow points from the pronoun to its antecedent, or the noun it represents.

antecedent pronoun

My **books** cost eighty dollars this term. **They** cost more than last term's books.

Pronouns can be classified in different ways depending on how they function in sentences. Though we will not be concerned with naming and classifying pronouns, you should be familiar enough with pronouns to be able to identify them in sentences. Some pronouns work as subjects of sentences while others work inside prepositional phrases, as direct or indirect objects, or as adjectives.

KINDS OF PRONOUNS	
Personal Pronouns	I*, me, you*, he*, him, she*, her, it*, we*, us, they*, them
Possessive Pronouns	my, mine, your, yours, his, her, hers, its, our, ours, their, theirs
Indefinite Pronouns**	anyone, anybody, anything, everyone, everybody, everything, someone, somebody, something, one, no one, nobody, nothing, each, another, either, neither, some, both, few, many, several, all, any, none, most, more
Relative Pronouns	who*, whom, whose, which,* that*
Interrogative Pronouns	who,* whom, whose, which,* what*
Demonstrative Pronouns**	this, that, these, those
Reflexive Pronouns	myself, yourself, himself, herself, itself, ourselves, themselves

*These pronouns can work as subjects. (See Chapter 2, pages 72–73.)
**All of the pronouns in this category can work as subjects.

In the following examples, the pronouns are in bold print:

> Mindy plans to sell **her** car. **It** needs extensive repairs.
>
> **Someone** left a strange message on **my** voice mail; **he** did not leave a name.
>
> **Who** borrowed **your** notes yesterday?
>
> **This** is **our** plan for spring break.
>
> **I** drove **myself** across the desert in **their** van.

EXERCISE 1.2 Identifying Pronouns

Score: _______

Circle the pronouns in the following sentences.

1. We invited them to our theme dinner.
2. Many apparently did not see the need to send me an RSVP.
3. Someone delivered your letters to us yesterday.
4. Who placed their shoes by my front door?
5. No one knew who voted for him in the election.

Adjectives

An **adjective** describes or modifies a noun or pronoun. Adjectives provide descriptive details about nouns or pronouns and help create a vivid picture in your readers' minds. The adjectives in the following sentences, which are shown in bold print, appear right before the nouns they modify. Arrows point to the noun each adjective modifies.

> **Angry** protesters marched down the **main** street of the **quiet, little** town.
>
> **Television** crews documented the **momentous** event.
>
> An **extensive** menu at the **new** delicatessen attracts **hungry** customers.

Adjectives can also be placed after a linking verb (*am, is, are, was, were, feel, taste, sound, look, smell, become, appear, grow, seem, remain*). The adjective after a linking verb is called a **predicate adjective.** An adjective in this position describes the noun or pronoun that is the subject of the sentence. In the following examples, the predicate adjectives are in bold print. Arrows point to the noun each adjective modifies.

> The new blanket feels **soft** and **warm.**
>
> Natasha is **athletic** and **intelligent.**
>
> The fumes from the plant are **noxious.**

EXERCISE 1.3 Identifying Adjectives

Score: ______

Circle the adjectives in the following sentences.

1. The marching band performs at sporting events and school concerts.
2. Each of the band members wears red pants and a gold jacket.
3. The band leader stands on a tall ladder to direct the musicians.
4. Loud, energetic music gets the immediate attention of the audience.
5. The special drills and creative formations lead to loud cheers and applause.

Verbs

A **verb** expresses the action or state of being of the subject of the sentence. Verbs and subjects are the key elements of sentences. Learning to use verbs correctly is an essential part of becoming an effective writer.

For now, familiarity with three basic categories of verbs will lay a foundation for future work with verbs.

KINDS OF VERBS	
Action Verbs	**Action verbs** show action or convey something that the subject of the sentence is doing, did, or will do. Words such as *dance, write, carry, run*, and *sing* show action. Some forms of action, however, are "invisible," for example, the verbs *plan, attempt, imagine, organize,* and consider show action that occurs mentally.
Linking Verbs	**Linking verbs** show a state of being, such as an existence or a condition, of the subject. These verbs link the subject to the remainder of the words in the sentence. Linking verbs are used when no action verbs are present. Study these linking verbs so you can quickly recognize them in sentences: *am, is, are, was, were, be, been, feel, taste, sound, look, smell, become, appear, grow, seem,* and *remain*.
Verb Phrases	**Verb phrases** are two or more verbs that work together to show the action that is done by the subject. Verb phrases show a variety of verb tenses or times that the action started and finished. The following combinations are examples of verb phrases: am studying, is running, are planning was skating, were hurrying, do annoy did expect, can pretend, has called have written, could cry, should try may attend, must pay, will cancel might win, had left, would like does work

Verbs can be singular or plural. The correct verb form to use in a sentence is often determined by the subject. Verbs also have tenses. **Verb tenses** indicate when the action occurs, occurred, or will occur. You will learn more about verbs, verb tenses and verb phrases in later chapters. All three kinds of verbs appear in the following sentences in bold print.

> The census takers **knocked** on doors throughout the nation.
>
> The census takers **were trying** to gather the data.
>
> The census **is** a monumental task.

EXERCISE 1.4 Identifying Verbs

Score: ______

Circle the verbs in the following sentences. A sentence may have more than one verb. Remember to circle all the verbs that form a verb phrase.

1. The skies darkened over the valley.
2. The storm front moved quickly.
3. People were running for shelter.
4. Hail the size of golf balls fell from the sky and damaged many automobiles.
5. Lightning and thunder are common in storms of this magnitude.

Adverbs

An **adverb** describes or modifies a verb, adjective, or another adverb and conveys time, frequency, manner, or degree. Adverbs, like adjectives, provide descriptive details in sentences and help your reader form clearer images of the ideas you are expressing. In the following sentences, the words in bold print are adverbs.

My history teacher talks **slowly.**
[*Slowly* modifies the verb *talks* and shows manner.]

Most of the students in the class take notes **very diligently.**
[*Very* modifies the adverb *diligently* and shows degree. *Diligently* modifies the verb *take.*]

Tomorrow, she will give us the questions for our essay exam.
[*Tomorrow* shows *time.*]

I hope that it is not **too** difficult.
[*Too* modifies the adjective *difficult* and shows degree.]

In my major, the instructors **seldom** use objective tests.
[*Seldom* modifies the verb *use* and shows frequency.]

Most adverbs end with an *-ly* suffix, but other words may also work as adverbs. The words *here* and *there,* for example, are adverbs. The adverbs in the following list show time, frequency, or degree. Study these adverbs so you can quickly recognize them in sentences.

ADVERBS					
here	there	anywhere	everywhere	somewhere	nowhere
again	almost	already	also	always	early
enough	even	ever	late	later	least
less	more	most	much	never	not
often	once	quite	rather	really	seldom
sometimes	somewhat	soon	still	then	today
tomorrow	too	very	well	yesterday	yet
Many words that end in -ly: slowly, silently, gently, quickly, assertively					

EXERCISE 1.5 Identifying Adverbs

Score: ______

Circle the adverbs in the following sentences. These adverbs describe or modify verbs, adjectives, or other adverbs. They show time, frequency, manner, or degree.

1. I barely had time to notify my boss about my new job.
2. The news quickly spread around the entire office today.
3. My coworker obviously had not kept the news a secret.
4. I was too embarrassed to confront her directly.
5. I definitely will not tell her confidential information again.

Prepositions

A **preposition** is a connective word that joins a noun or a pronoun to the rest of the sentence. Prepositions may show time, location, direction, or other kinds of relationships between one noun or pronoun and other words in the sentence. Prepositions form **prepositional phrases,** which are groups of words that always begin with a preposition and end with a noun or a pronoun. You can locate the end of a prepositional phrase by saying the preposition and then asking *what* or *whom.*

> People ***with*** migraines should consult a doctor ***for*** treatment.
>
> The prepositions are *with* and *for.* Ask yourself, "*With what?*" and "*For what?*" The correct answer, which must be a noun or a pronoun, marks the end of the prepositional phrase. Thus, the prepositional phrases consist of the words shown in parentheses:
>
> People (**with** migraines) should consult a doctor (**for** treatment).

We walked **between** the pond and the rose garden.

The preposition is the word *between*. To find the end of the prepositional phrase, ask, *"Between what?"* The answer is *between the pond and the rose garden*. Thus the prepositional phrase consists of the following words:

We walked (**between** the pond and the rose garden).

Recognizing prepositions and prepositional phrases will help you correctly identify subjects and verbs. Spend time learning the following prepositions so you will be able to identify prepositional phrases quickly.

PREPOSITIONS				
about	away from	during	next to	subsequent to
above	because of	except	of	through
according to	before	for	off	throughout
across	behind	from	on	till
after	below	in	on account of	to
against	beneath	in addition to	onto	together with
ahead of	beside	in front of	opposite	toward
along	between	in lieu of	out	under
along with	beyond	in order to	out of	underneath
amid	but	in place of	outside	unlike
among	by	in regard to	over	until
around	by means of	in spite of	past	up
as	concerning	inside	per	upon
as to	contrary to	instead of	prior to	via
as well as	despite	into	regarding	with
aside from	down	like	round	within
at	due to	near	since	without

In most sentences, prepositional phrases are "sentence extras" that you can delete from the sentence without altering the general meaning of the sentence. Even though they are considered "sentence extras," they add significant details to sentences and help your reader follow your ideas. In the following examples, the parentheses show the prepositional phrases; the prepositions appear in bold print.

Tiger Woods was (**on** top) (**of** the leader board).

He shot eight (**under** par) and was a strong leader (**in** the tournament).

Other players frequently commented (**on** Tiger's skills and mental abilities).

(**Throughout** the tournament), Tiger made many difficult shots.

He stayed (**out of** the bunkers) and played (**without** any major problems).

EXERCISE 1.6 Identifying Prepositions

Score: ______

Use parentheses to mark the prepositional phrases in the following sentences. Refer to the preceding list of prepositions if necessary.

1. From cradle to ashes, people experience many different events in a lifetime.
2. Elders tell many stories about growing up with different values and beliefs.
3. They often reminisce for hours without ever tiring.
4. During one vacation at our cabin in the woods, Grandpa talked till dawn.
5. We sat by the fire and snoozed under the stars.

Conjunctions

A **conjunction** joins other words, phrases, or sentences. The following three kinds of conjunctions will be discussed in later chapters when compound and complex sentence structures are introduced.

KINDS OF CONJUNCTIONS	
Coordinating Conjunctions	and, but, for, nor, or, so, yet
Conjunctive Adverbs	*Examples:* accordingly, also, consequently, furthermore, however, later, nevertheless, otherwise, then, therefore, thus
Subordinate Conjunctions	*Examples:* after, although, because, before, if, since, than, unless, until, when, while

The three kinds of conjunctions are used in the following sentences. They appear in bold print.

> Lightning can cause forest fires **when** the forests are dry.
>
> The dry undergrowth makes perfect kindling, **and** the trees become the logs for the fire.
>
> Wildfires are difficult to extinguish, **for** many times they are in areas that are inaccessible except by helicopters.
>
> Somefires are left to burn themselves out; **however,** the majority of fires are battled by professional fire fighters **or** trained volunteers.
>
> In some cases, forest fires are beneficial **because** they clean out the dead wood **and** make room for new growth forests **and** plants.

EXERCISE 1.7 **Identifying Coordinating Conjunctions** Score: ______

Circle the coordinating conjunctions in the following sentences. Refer to the preceeding list of the seven coordinating conjunctions if necessary.

1. Uncontrollable fires threaten homes, property, and even entire communities.
2. In my community, we were asked to leave immediately or face the possibility of being trapped.
3. Most left immediately, but some people refused to abandon their homes.
4. Nothing was more important to me than my life, so I left all my belongings in the house.
5. I chose to leave, for I feared getting trapped inside the fire lines.

Interjections

An **interjection** expresses strong or sudden feelings. Interjections stand by themselves; they are not connected to a sentence. Interjections are often punctuated with an exclamation point. The following words are common interjections: **Oh! Ow! Darn Wow! Phew! Aha!**

Summary of Parts of Speech

The part of speech of any given word varies depending on how the word functions in a specific sentence. This overview of the eight parts of speech lays a foundation for grammar work in upcoming chapters. These parts of speech will be examined and applied in more complex ways throughout this book. While emphasis in this textbook is not on analyzing and labeling words according to their parts of speech, understanding the eight parts of speech makes communication about sentence structures and writing options easier to analyze and discuss.

Internet Enrichment

The Internet site for this book includes additional activities and information related to the topics presented in each chapter. For Chapter 1, you will find exercises and links for the following topics:

Generating Ideas

Narrowing the Topic

Clustering

Revising

Proofreading and Editing

The Eight Parts of Speech

Go to: http://college.hmco.com. Click on "Students." Type *Paragraph Essentials* in the "Jump to Textbook Sites" box. Click "go," and then bookmark the site. Click on Chapter 1.

CHAPTER 1 • Parts of Speech Review

Name ____________________

Read each sentence carefully. Identify the part of speech of the word in bold print. Write the letter of the answer on the line.

_______ 1. The **leash** was too loose around the dog's neck.
a. noun b. verb c. conjunction d. adjective

_______ 2. The **fluorescent** lights are highly visible in the fog.
a. adverb b. preposition c. noun d. adjective

_______ 3. I think we should **staple** the worksheets in the right order.
a. adjective b. conjunction c. verb d. adverb

_______ 4. The argument was **between** the secretary and the accountant.
a. preposition b. verb c. noun d. pronoun

_______ 5. **Someone** left the key in the file cabinet overnight.
a. noun b. preposition c. pronoun d. adjective

_______ 6. The message on the answering machine was for **her.**
a. pronoun b. noun c. adjective d. adverb

_______ 7. Gretchen fell on the **slippery** stairs and bruised her ankle.
a. verb b. adverb c. adjective d. noun

_______ 8. Neither my term paper **nor** my midterm exam was difficult.
a. verb b. adverb c. conjunction d. interjection

_______ 9. After I received the notice from the IRS, I **immediately** called my father.
a. adverb b. verb c. adjective d. conjunction

_______ 10. No one **expected** him to confess to the prank, but he did.
a. pronoun b. adjective c. verb d. adverb

_______________ 11. **Prior to** his illness, he prepared a comprehensive will.
a. pronoun b. preposition
c. verb d. conjunction

_______________ 12. I missed my bus **again** this morning.
a. adverb b. adjective c. verb d. noun

_______________ 13. **Procrastination** is often the cause for poor grades.
a. adjective b. verb c. conjunction d. noun

_______________ 14. This **is** my final offer.
a. adverb b. adjective c. verb d. preposition

_______________ 15. **Ouch!** That shot of novocaine hit a nerve.
a. conjunction b. adverb
c. preposition d. interjection

CHAPTER 2

Writing Effective Paragraphs

One topic sentence states the subject and the controlling idea.

Sentences in the body of the paragraph state the supporting details.

A concluding sentence wraps up the writer's final thoughts about the topic.

Topic sentence with a controlling idea ....

Unity + Coherence + Adequate Development ...

Concluding sentence ....

In Chapter 2 you will learn about the following:

1. Writing effective paragraphs
2. The structure of a paragraph
3. Three qualities of a paragraph
4. Different kinds of paragraphs
5. Five grammar and usage tips

WRITING WARM-UP 2

Write about one of the following:

1. The most interesting, challenging, or unusual job you have ever had. Describe the job. Tell why it was interesting, challenging, or unusual.
2. The ideal job you would like to have now or in the near future. Describe the job and the position you would hold. Tell why this would be an ideal job.

Writing Effective Paragraphs

Acquiring strong paragraph-writing skills provides you with an effective way to communicate your ideas, share information, and demonstrate your comprehension of a given topic. A well-written paragraph demonstrates your ability to focus on one specific topic, generate and organize effective supporting details in a logical sequence, and precisely convey your ideas and understanding to your reader.

Writing powerful paragraphs is a skill you will utilize extensively throughout your college years. In college, you will frequently be required to write various types of paragraphs for tests and other course assignments. Some writing assignments will require a one-paragraph answer; other assignments or tests will require a longer piece, such as an essay, which consists of a series of well-written paragraphs that are related by the overall main point (the thesis) of the entire essay. Whether a paragraph stands on its own or is a part of a longer piece, a well-written paragraph is your opportunity to express your ideas, knowledge, and understanding to others.

Your paragraph-writing skills will carry over into your jobs or your career. In the work force, you will use strong paragraph-writing skills every time you write a business letter, report, email, proposal, or memo, as well as in other tasks that involve presenting information in a logical, organized manner.

The Structure of a Paragraph

A **paragraph** is a well-organized series of sentences that develops one main idea about a specific topic you wish to convey to your reader. The main idea of a paragraph is often stated in a **topic sentence,** which can also be called a **main idea sentence** or the **controlling sentence.** With the exception of the concluding sentence, the remaining sentences in a paragraph provide the reader with carefully selected **supporting details** that are closely related to the main idea. The supporting details provide your reader with additional information, understanding, or explanation of the main idea. The paragraph closes with a **concluding sentence** that wraps up your thoughts about the main idea.

You know from Chapter 1 that the structure of a paragraph consists of a beginning (a topic sentence with a controlling idea), a middle (the body of the paragraph with supporting details), and an end (a concluding sentence). In this chapter, you will learn the essential elements of a paragraph. In later chapters, you will learn to use these elements effectively in different kinds of paragraphs.

BASIC PARAGRAPH STRUCTURE

	Title
Beginning: Topic sentence with a controlling idea	**Topic sentence with a main idea** ________________
Middle: Body with sentences that convey supporting details that have unity, coherence, and adequate development	**Body of the paragraph with sentences that contain supporting details** ________________
End: Concluding sentence	**Concluding sentence** ________________

Developing the Topic Sentence

The topic sentence answers the question, "What is the main point or controlling idea the author is saying about the subject?" The topic sentence controls the content of the paragraph. All the sentences that follow the topic sentence must support the controlling idea that is stated in the topic sentence. The **controlling idea** reveals the author's point of view, opinion, or attitude toward the subject. When a topic sentence is well written, the body of the paragraph is easier to develop in a logical manner, and the ideas are more likely to flow smoothly. Spending ample time developing a strong, effective topic sentence is a writing habit you will want to develop. Following are key points about effective topic sentences:

1. The topic sentence should *state a specific, narrowed,* and *well-focused subject* that is a suitable and manageable topic for paragraph-size writing. Subjects that are too general or too broad will require more information than can fit within the structure of one paragraph.
2. The topic sentence should *get right to the point* with the controlling idea so the reader clearly understands your purpose, topic, and point of view, opinion, or attitude that you intend to express about the topic. Your reader should be able to predict some of the content and the direction the paragraph will take. Topic sentences that are vague or ambiguous or that lack a controlling idea do not provide your readers with a sense of the topic you intend to develop, and they make your task of developing the controlling idea with effective supporting details more difficult and frustrating.

3. The topic sentence should *capture your reader's interest.* The choice of words used in the topic sentence has the power to pique your reader's interest or leave your reader feeling neutral or uninterested in reading what you have to say about the topic.
4. The topic sentence should, in most instances, *be the first sentence in the paragraph.* Although the topic sentence does not have to appear in this location, placing the topic sentence at the beginning of the paragraph helps both you, the writer, and your reader stay focused on the main idea of the paragraph.

As an example, assume that you are enrolled in a communications class. Your assignment is to observe and record ways that individuals react to praise and then to write a paragraph describing your observations. You gather information for your paragraph by observing people receiving praise and recording their reactions. With data in hand, you organize it and explore different ways to express the main point in a topic sentence. After writing several possible topic sentences, you can then select the sentence that expresses your ideas most clearly and powerfully:

1. People are born to relate to all kinds of positive stimuli.
2. People seem to have many different reactions.
3. People get embarrassed when they receive praise for their work or appearance.
4. Praise is often given when work is done well.
5. I am going to write about things I observed about people's reaction to praise.
6. One way to respond to praise is to accept it and return the praise with a compliment.
7. People commonly demonstrate one of five reactions when they receive praise.

Sentences 1 and 2 are too broad and do not focus on the assigned topic. Sentence 3 is too limiting; it implies that getting embarrassed is the only response that occurs when people receive praise. Sentence 4 does not get to the point; it implies that the writer is going to discuss when praise is given or when work is done well. Sentence 5 is wordy and does not get right to the point; also, it announces the writer's intentions, which is not effective or acceptable for a topic sentence. Sentence 6 is similar to sentence 3; it more likely is a supporting detail for one of the common reactions. Sentence 7 is an effective topic sentence. The words *five reactions* are specific and appropriate to the assignment. They are interesting, too; the reader becomes curious and wants to know what five reactions are commonly demonstrated.

2.1 What do you think?

1. Read the following sentences carefully. Check the sentences that you find to be specific, well focused, and potentially effective topic sentences.

 ________ a. Instead of becoming fodder or polluting the air when burned, straw can be used to make paper in a process that is environmentally friendly and nontoxic to people.

 ________ b. Straw, a by-product of the harvesting of corn, wheat, and rice, can now be used to make biodegradable, environmentally safe paper products.

 ________ c. The process of making paper products from straw benefits consumers, farmers, and the environment.

 ________ d. The liquid generated in the process can be used for fertilizer.

 ________ e. Traditional papermaking damages the environment, but papermaking with straw generates no pollution or environmental damage.

2. Check only the sentences that get right to the point and could work as effective topic sentences.

 ________ a. Many national monuments falsify the true history of the United States.

 ________ b. King County, Washington, was first named after Alabama Vice President Rufus King, a strong advocate of slavery; in 1986, King County was renamed King County to honor Dr. Martin Luther King, Jr.

 ________ c. Inaccurate history represented on national monuments occurs in the form of omissions, distortions, or euphemisms.

 ________ d. Behind many historical monuments lie two versions of history.

 ________ e. In Tennessee, General Nathan Forest has more state historical markers than any other public figure in any of the fifty states even though history shows Forest was the first Grand Wizard of the Ku Klux Klan.

3. Check the topic sentences that capture your interest and could work as effective topic sentences.

 ________ a. Serena and Venus Williams demonstrate power and grace on and off the tennis courts.

 ________ b. I really like tennis.

_______ c. Sammy Sosa and Mark McGwire have more in common than just their home run records.

_______ d. Many athletes merit the label of role model for young children.

_______ e. Fifteen different guys at Wilson High School in my hometown decided to try out for the water polo team because water polo is a lot of fun and is good exercise, but they had no idea beforehand how difficult it is to play competitive water polo or how much conditioning is involved.

Developing the Body of the Paragraph

The body of the paragraph consists of carefully developed sentences with specific supporting details related to the topic sentence. The sentences in the body of the paragraph develop and strengthen the main idea by explaining, proving, or discussing the statement made in the topic sentence. The type and purpose of a paragraph dictates to some degree the methods used to develop the body of a paragraph. (The different kinds of paragraphs are explained later in the chapter.) For example, the body of a definition paragraph that defines a term or a concept will be different than the body of a narrative paragraph, which tells a story. Following are key points about a well-developed body for a paragraph:

1. Sentences in the body of a paragraph may use *explanations, examples, facts, definitions, reasons, comparisons, contrasts,* or *other kinds of information* as supporting details to develop or explain the topic sentence.
2. The sentences in the body of the paragraph expand the main idea of the paragraph. To have a well-focused paragraph, every sentence and each supporting detail must relate to the topic sentence. This is called *unity.*
3. A well-developed paragraph provides your reader with a sufficient number of details to explain, expand, or discuss the topic sentence. A paragraph with an adequate number of quality details shows *adequate development.*
4. The sentences in a paragraph should flow together smoothly when the paragraph is read. You should present the details in an orderly, logical sequence. Your readers should not have difficulty following your ideas or details. When sentences flow smoothly and in a logical sequence, a paragraph is said to have *coherence.* If there is a lack of coherence, your reader has trouble following your ideas and has trouble understanding the relationships between sentences and between supporting details and the topic sentence.

Developing the Concluding Sentence

The main purpose of the concluding sentence is to briefly pull together or summarize the main idea that you developed by using supporting details in the paragraph. You want to signal to your reader that you have finished your thoughts. You need to leave your reader with a clear impression of the main purpose or intent of the paragraph. If you write a paragraph that lacks an effective concluding sentence, your reader may be left with the impression that you could have added more information, that you simply did not finish the paragraph, that you wandered from the topic sentence, or that you were unable to write a logical conclusion.

A concluding sentence is essential for paragraphs that are written to stand on their own; paragraphs that are a part of a larger piece of writing, such as an essay, do not require a concluding sentence. The concluding sentence of a paragraph that stands on its own usually does one of four things:

1. Restates or echoes the topic sentence.
2. Restates the main idea by including references to the key supporting details.
3. Draws a logical conclusion based on the supporting details used to develop the main idea.
4. Offers a final observation about the main idea and its significance.

The following checklist can be used to evaluate the effectiveness of your concluding sentences.

1. *Does the concluding sentence echo or restate the topic sentence?* If the concluding sentence expresses an idea considerably different from the topic sentence, you wandered from the topic sentence and did not fulfill the intent of the paragraph.
2. *Does the concluding sentence restate the topic sentence by summarizing key points or drawing a conclusion based on the key points?* Though a concluding sentence may do more than "echo" or restate the topic sentence, it should still be closely related to the main idea of the paragraph.
3. *Does the last sentence function as a concluding sentence?* If the last sentence is a continuation of the body and provides a final supporting detail, the paragraph lacks a concluding sentence.
4. *Does the last sentence offer a final observation about the main idea and its significance?* This final statement should reflect the significance stated or implied throughout the paragraph.

2.2 What do you think?

Read the following paragraph. Answer the questions that follow the paragraph. Write your answers on separate paper.

Two Hurricanes

Hurricane Floyd struck North Carolina in October 1999. One month later, the same state got clobbered with Hurricane Irene. Though Hurricane Floyd and Hurricane Irene occurred a month apart, they shared many common characteristics. Hurricane Floyd dumped heavy rains and caused record floodwaters. Hurricane Irene dumped more than a half foot of water in the same region that had been flooded by Hurricane Floyd. When Hurricane Floyd neared the coastal areas, residents were forced to evacuate. Residents were once again evacuated when Hurricane Irene moved steadily in the same direction as Hurricane Floyd once moved. Both hurricanes clocked winds over 80 miles per hour and caused extensive damage and destruction.

[Adapted from: AP, "Irene Inundates North Carolina," *Register Guard*, 10-18-99.]

1. Is the first sentence the topic sentence? Because the topic sentence controls the content of the paragraph, do all the details in the paragraph fit under the content of the first sentence?
2. Identify the topic sentence. Is the topic sentence effective; that is, is it specific, to the point, and interesting? Explain your answer.
3. Is the concluding sentence effective? Explain. (Use the checklist for evaluating concluding sentences.)

2.3 What do you think?

Read the following paragraph. Answer the questions that follow the paragraph. Write your answers on separate paper.

Facilitating Payments

In many cultures, giving bribes—also known as *facilitating payments*—is an acceptable business practice. In Mexico, a bribe is called *la mordida*. South Africans call it *dash*. In the Middle East, India, and Pakistan, *baksheesh,* a tip or gratuity given by a superior, is widely used. The Germans call it *schimengeld,* grease money, and the Italians call it *bustarella,* a little envelope. Companies that do business internationally should be aware that bribes are an ethical issue and that the practice is more prevalent in some countries than in others.

[Ferrell & Fraedrich, *Business Ethics*, Houghton Mifflin, 1997, p. 209.]

1. Is the first sentence the topic sentence? Explain your answer.
2. Is the topic sentence effective; that is, is it specific, to the point, and interesting? Explain your answer.
3. Is the concluding sentence effective? Explain.

2.4 What do you think?

Read the following paragraph. Answer the questions that follow the paragraph. Write your answers on separate paper

Locus of Control

A person's *locus of control* reflects the way a person perceives and responds to the world. A person with an internal locus of control feels in charge of his or her life and has the power within to handle situations. A person with an internal locus of control accepts personal responsibility for his or her circumstances, and after objective analysis of a disappointing or stressful situation, seeks solutions so a similar situation will not reoccur. Problems become lessons to learn. The person who feels in control and empowered sees the world and life as positive, manageable, and rewarding. A person with an external locus of control perceives life quite differently. He or she feels other people, systems, or institutions hold all the power and are responsible for failures, disappointments, and frustrations. This individual feels powerless to control the events and circumstances in his or her world. Instead, a person with an external locus of control blames others for negative predicaments and refuses to accept any personal responsibility. This person feels he or she "got a bum rap" or was treated unfairly. This pessimistic attitude is often accompanied by feelings of helplessness, frustration, and anger.

[Wong, *Essential Study Skills*, Houghton Mifflin, 2000, p. 241.]

1. Which sentence is the topic sentence? Do you think it is an effective controlling idea? Explain your answer.
2. Is the last sentence a concluding sentence? Explain your answer.
3. Write another topic sentence for this paragraph.
4. Write a concluding sentence for this paragraph.

Three Qualities of an Effective Paragraph

An effective paragraph focuses on one specific topic, shows an adequate number of specific supporting details that are directly related to the topic sentence, and organizes details in a logical manner. An effective paragraph clearly conveys your ideas to your reader. After you write a well-developed topic sentence, you then need to focus your attention on the body of the paragraph. To be effective, the body of a paragraph must consistently include three essential qualities:

1. **unity**
2. **coherence**
3. **adequate development**

Unity

A paragraph has **unity** when every sentence supports or is related to the main idea expressed in the topic sentence:

1. Each sentence clearly serves an important purpose to the effectiveness of the overall paragraph.
2. You stay focused on the purpose of the paragraph and the controlling idea expressed in the topic sentence.
3. You do not wander from the topic or the controlling idea in the topic sentence and you do not include supporting details that are unrelated or irrelevant to the topic sentence.
4. Paragraphs that lack unity may confuse, distract, or bore your reader.

2.5 What do you think?

The following paragraph lacks unity. Read the paragraph carefully. Identify the sentences that need to be deleted from this paragraph.

Each sentence in the paragraph is numbered. Write the numbers of the sentences you think should be edited out of the paragraph to strengthen the paragraph and achieve unity.

Hepatitis

[1]Three forms of hepatitis, a contagious liver disease, are common in the United States. [2]Hepatitis A commonly strikes children under the age of fifteen. [3]This form of hepatitis is contracted by eating food or drinking water that has been contaminated by human excrement. [4]Many children, of course, never contract Hepatitis A in school or at home. [5]Two of my friends once contracted this form of the virus and found out about it when they went to the doctor with flulike symptoms. [6]Hepatitis B is more frequently contracted through direct contact with bodily fluids that contain the virus. [7]Hepatitis B is most commonly spread during intimacy and through shared needles that are contaminated with the virus. [8]However, because the Hepatitis B virus can live outside the body on dry surfaces for several days, it can be spread from hand to mouth. [9]I think this is the form of hepatitis that is combated by a vaccine. [10]Some states require children to get vaccinated for hepatitis before beginning school. [11]Hepatitis C is spread by contact with infected blood, contaminated needles, or by sharing drug-snorting instruments. [12]Hepatitis C, for that reason, is similar to HIV, which may lead to AIDS. [13]All three forms of hepatitis attack the liver and cause inflammation, swelling, and tenderness.

[Adapted from: *Register Guard*, "Hepatitis Can Be Highly Contagious," 4-10-2000, p. 5D.]

Delete sentences: ______________________________

Coherence

A paragraph has **coherence** when all the ideas and sentences flow together smoothly. The relationships between ideas and individual sentences are clear and easy to understand. You can achieve coherence by using the following writing methods:

1. Use transition words to connect ideas. Appropriate conjunctions between words, phrases, clauses, and sentences connect ideas logically and continue the flow or continuity of information through the entire paragraph. Many transition words are conjunctions used to join sentences to form compound, complex, or compound-complex sentences. (See Chapters 3 and 4.) The conjunctions accurately reflect the relationship between the clauses or the sentences. Many of the conjunctive adverbs shown in the following chart can also be used at the beginning of a sentence to help the reader understand the connection between ideas.

TRANSITION WORDS			
COMPOUND SENTENCES			COMPLEX SENTENCES
Relationship	**Coordinating Conjunctions**	**; Conjunctive Adverb,**	**Subordinate Conjunction (adverbial clauses)**
addition	and	accordingly again also besides furthermore in addition moreover	
comparison, similarity	and	also in the same way likewise similarly	as as if as though just as
contrast or opposition	but or yet	however in comparison in contrast instead nevertheless on the contrary on the other hand otherwise still unfortunately	although even though though whereas whether while
time	and then	afterward at the same time finally first furthermore in the meantime later meanwhile next second subsequently then third . . .	after as as long as as soon as before once since until when whenever while
illustration		for example for instance in fact	

(Continue on page 55)

TRANSITION WORDS			
COMPOUND SENTENCES			COMPLEX SENTENCES
Relationship	**Coordinating Conjunctions**	**; Conjunctive Adverb,**	**Subordinate Conjunction (adverbial clauses)**
manner			as if as though like
concession	but yet	admittedly however nevertheless	although despite the fact that even though in spite of the fact though whereas
purpose			in order that so that
reason, cause, effect	for so	as a result consequently hence then therefore thus	as as long as because inasmuch as in order that now that since so that such that
condition	so		even if even though if in case only if provided that unless whether or not
summation		finally hence in conclusion in general in short in summary overall therefore	
emphasis		certainly indeed in fact to be sure	

2. Organize supporting details logically. When a paragraph has coherence, details are organized in one of three ways: chronologically, spatially, or emphatically. A **chronological** organization involves presenting the information in a time sequence that moves from the beginning of the event to the end. A **spatial** organization presents details according to their position in space. You may, for example, describe something from top to bottom, left to right, foreground to background, or inside to outside. An **emphatic** organization presents information by order or degree of importance. This involves beginning with the most important or most developed detail and finishing the paragraph with the least developed or least important detail. You can also use the reverse order: least important to most important.
3. Repeat key words or concepts in the paragraph to create a strong impression of the main idea in the mind of the reader.
4. Use pronouns to replace nouns, and make pronoun references clear and accurate.
5. Use parallelism, which involves a consistent form for words, phrases, clauses, or sentences that appear in a sequence. Parallelism moves ideas forward smoothly and with a natural rhythm. (See Chapter 9, page 365.)

Paragraphs that lack coherence often lack clarity. Your reader is not able to follow the development of the topic sentence nor to finish the paragraph with a clear impression of your purpose for the paragraph. The paragraph seems disorganized, disjointed, and unfocused. Your reader may quickly lose interest in reading or understanding the content of the paragraph.

2.6 What do you think?

The following paragraph has problems with coherence. Read the paragraph carefully and answer the questions that follow. Write your answers on separate paper.

Freelance Writing

[1]My first freelance writing job was a fluke. [2]I wanted to be a writer, so I bought *Writers Market* and started contacting magazine publishers for their guidelines. [3]One day I received a request for articles related to the blowing of Mount St. Helens in Washington. [4]An entire issue of a children's magazine was going to be dedicated to the massive eruption of this volcano. [5]I responded immediately to the magazine and claimed I could interview geologists from the U.S. Geological Survey Team, which was monitoring and studying Mount St. Helens. [6]Writers' guidelines for other types of feature articles were also received. [7]I struggled with topics and wondered what I could do that

would be of interest. [8]I had never done a live interview and had never written an article based on geology. [9]I packed up my portable typewriter and set out to find a geologist to interview. [10]The publishing company said it was interested in this article, so I acted as though I knew what I was doing. [11]Fortunately, the geologists at the Mount St. Helens observatory were cordial and cooperative. [12]No one asked for credentials, which was a relief, since I had none. [13]I wrote up a series of questions, got fresh batteries for my tape recorder, and showed up on the doorstep of the U.S. Geological Survey Team's trailer facilities. [14]At the end of the interview, the geologist I interviewed told me I had a very refreshing and different approach from other reporters and that he enjoyed sharing information with me, giving me photographs from inside the crater, and spending time with me. [15]I never told him that was the first time I had ever conducted an interview or attempted writing an article. [16]I raced back to my motel room and pondered how to process all the information on my tapes. [17]Within a few hours, I had written the article and dropped it in the mail. [18]To my delight, the article was accepted without further editing. [19]My first experience with freelance writing was a success and based on a stroke of good luck.

1. Which sentences break the coherence in the paragraph? (Refer to sentences by their numbers.)
2. Does the paragraph have coherence? Should the writer delete some sentences? Should the writer move some sentences to other parts of the paragraph? Explain.
3. Which words are transition words that help connect or link ideas effectively?
4. Does the writer organize the paragraph chronologically, spatially, or emphatically? Explain.

2.7 What do you think?

The following paragraph has problems with coherence. Read the paragraph carefully and answer the questions that follow. Write your answers on separate paper.

Job Application Cover Letters

[1]Writing an effective cover letter for a job application can be done by following six basic steps. [2]First, carefully examine the job description or the classified ad and plan how to compete on paper for the job. [3]Highlight all the desired qualities and skills that are stated in the job posting. [4]On a separate piece of paper, list the qualities and skills under two categories. [5]Title the first category *job-related skills;* title the second category *personal qualities.* [6]Across from each item in your list, jot down specific skills or experiences you have that relate to the items. [7]Try to "read between the lines" to predict what the employer wants from his or her employees. [8]Add these items to your list and your related qualifications. [9]Next, use a standard business letter format. [10]Write a draft with individual paragraphs to present yourself to the employer. [11]In the first paragraph, identify the position and tell where you saw the job posting. [12]In the next paragraph, emphasize the job-related skills you have that qualify you for the position. [13]Include work experience and course work. [14]Be sure to put your address and the date on the top of the paper. [15]Then include the inside address of the business. [16]The salutation, or greeting, should address the person by name if it is known or by position, such as "Personnel Director." [17]In the third paragraph, list the personal qualities that make you a worthy, desirable employee. [18]You can include words such as *responsible, attentive to details, friendly, team player,* and *conscientious.* [19]Finally, close with a short paragraph that tells your availability, interest in an interview, and a contact phone number. [20]Next, revise the draft of your letter. [21]Look for ways to strengthen the content. [22]Finally, sign the letter, make a copy of the letter for your files, and mail the letter without delay. [23]By using these six steps for an effective cover letter, you have greatly increased your chances of being considered for the job. [24]Because the employer will first "meet" you on paper, be sure the letter is neatly typed and free of grammatical and spelling errors.

1. Which sentences break the coherence in the paragraph? (Refer to sentences by their numbers.)
2. How can the writer achieve coherence? Should the writer delete some sentences or move some sentences to other parts of the paragraph? Explain.
3. Which words are transition words that help connect or link ideas effectively?
4. Does the writer organize the details chronologically, spatially, or emphatically? Explain.

Adequate Development

A paragraph has **adequate development** when a sufficient number of specific, relevant supporting details in the body of the paragraph explain or develop your topic sentence thoroughly and clearly. Supporting details that are general rather than specific will not adequately explain or develop the topic sentence. The response you will get from your reader is that your paragraph has nothing of value to say, reveals no new information, or does not fulfill its purpose. If your paragraph lacks adequate development, look at both the *quantity* and the *quality* of details in your paragraph. Return to the third step of the writing process, gathering and organizing information, to seek out and organize more details (or more effective details) to achieve adequate development.

You can achieve adequate development by using the following writing methods:

1. Include an adequate number of different details to develop your topic sentence. Usually two or three sentences for the body of the paragraph will result in an underdeveloped paragraph with too few details; adding additional supporting details to explain or develop the topic sentence will strengthen the paragraph.
2. Avoid overdeveloping a paragraph. Excessive wordiness or too many supporting sentences may reduce the effectiveness of the paragraph and bore your reader. When you overdevelop a paragraph, eliminating weak or unnecessary details and combining relevant details more effectively can reduce the number of sentences and strengthen the paragraph.
3. Decide on an appropriate length and number of sentences to use in the body of your paragraph. A specific number of sentences for an effective paragraph cannot be defined, for the number of sentences necessary to effectively explain or develop the topic sentence will vary from one paragraph to another. However, as a general guideline, you can develop most topic sentences through five to ten well-developed sentences in the body of the paragraph.

In the following example, the paragraph is underdeveloped. It lacks specific details and does not adequately develop or explain the topic sentence.

EXTENDED FAMILIES

In many traditional Asian and African societies, the typical family is often an extended family. Couples live under the same roof as other family members. The family is a clan headed by a mother or a father.

The topic sentence is specific, gets right to the point, and captures the reader's interest. Specific supporting details that strengthen the main idea by explaining, proving, or discussing the statement need to follow the topic sentence. Though the supporting details in the body of the paragraph are accurate, they are insufficient. The result is an underdeveloped paragraph. Expanding the paragraph with additional information will result in a more effective paragraph. Notice in the following revision how the supporting details and the concluding sentence develop this paragraph more effectively.

REVISION: EXTENDED FAMILIES

In many traditional Asian and African societies, the typical family is often an extended family. A newly married couple lives with either the bride's or the groom's family. The couple raises their children under the same roof as their own brothers and sisters, who may also be married. The extended family is a large, three- or four-generation clan, headed by a patriarch or perhaps a matriarch. The extended family encompasses everyone from the youngest infant to the oldest grandparent. Every family member has a place in the extended family, from cradle to grave. This tradition of extended families, however, is diminishing as newly married couples now tend to move to new locations for greater economic opportunities. The traditional extended family is being replaced by nuclear families that establish their own homes and create their individual identities.

[Adapted from McKay, Hill, Buckler. *A History of Western Society*, 4th ed., Houghton Mifflin, 1991, p. 629.]

The following paragraph is overdeveloped. Excessive wordiness and too many supporting sentences reduce the effectiveness of the paragraph and bore you and other readers.

DIVORCE AND A BATTLEFIELD

Divorce has much in common with a battlefield. In a typical divorce, both sides find great difficulty reaching a peaceful accord. Neither wishes to lose ground, compromise, or admit defeat. Both parties want to win at all costs. On a battlefield, both sides see each other as the enemy and have difficulty reaching a peaceful agreement. Neither side in a battle wants to lose its territory. Both sides lack desire to compromise their position or face defeat. Both sides fight, battle, maim, and kill to win. In a divorce, anger, resentment, and hostility increase the more the process is prolonged. On the battlefield, as injuries and mortalities mount, each side loathes the other to a greater degree, and each side becomes more aggressive, hostile, and determined to win the battle. Weapons are used in a divorce as means to achieve a victory. Laws, lawyers, courts, and appeals become the weapons of choice to manipulate and force a final verdict and victory. On the field, light- and heavy-weight artillery manipulate the direction of the battle and attempt to force a verdict and victory. Many emotional and legal strategies are used to get the upper edge in the final divorce decree. Offers and promises are broken. Assets are hidden or protected

> through legal loopholes or business dealings. On the field, emotional and military strategies are used to win the battle. Truthful details of the battle are withheld from the soldiers, and tactics are used to keep the troops fired up and aggressive. Distrust, aggression, and hostility between the sides increase. Peace talks stall or are terminated. In a divorce, people and possessions become pawns that are pushed back and forth across the table as bargaining tools. Children, personal possessions, and bank accounts are moved around, divided, sorted, and shuffled. Their true meaning often gets distorted or lost. On the field, the soldiers are the pawns that are pushed back and forth. Territories, regardless of the people who live on the lands, are pawns. Political policies, principles, and economic and political rights are bargaining tools to splice and shuffle from one side to another. Divorce and battlefields share one final trait: both are damaging, destructive, and painful and leave wounds that are difficult to heal.

The similarities of divorce and a battlefield are interesting, but too many details turn an interesting paragraph into an overly long, drawn-out paragraph. During a revision, the writer eliminated insignificant, weak, and unnecessary details and combined ideas to avoid wordiness. The writer regains readers' interest by retaining the details that create the strongest images.

REVISION: DIVORCE AND A BATTLEFIELD

> Divorce has much in common with a battlefield. In a heated divorce, both sides find great difficulty reaching a peaceful accord, and neither side wishes to lose ground, compromise, or admit defeat. On a battlefield, the same situations exist. The enemies have difficulty reaching peace, and neither side wants to lose its territory, compromise its position, or face defeat. In a contested divorce, cunning strategies, which increase anger, resentment, and hostility, are used to weaken the opponent. Promises are broken, offers are revoked, and assets are hidden or protected through legal loopholes. On the field, cunning strategies, which often breed distrust, aggression, and increased hostility, are also used to win the battle. Peace talks stall; negotiations are postponed or terminated. Promises to find solutions are broken. In a divorce, children, personal possessions, and bank accounts become pawns and bargaining tools. They are pushed back and forth across the bargaining table, divided, sorted, given, taken, and reshuffled. On the field, the soldiers, territories, and trade agreements are the pawns. Political, military, and economic policies are bargaining tools to shuffle and divide from one side to another. Divorce and battlefields share one final trait: both are damaging, destructive, and painful and leave wounds that are difficult to heal.

2.8 What do you think?

Read the following paragraph. Answer the questions that follow the paragraph. Write your answers on separate paper.

Taxes

The federal government collects taxes to pay for government transfer payments. Government transfer payments support welfare and other kinds of social programs. Two kinds of federal taxes are the most significant sources of federal tax revenue. Income tax is one of the most significant sources of federal tax revenue. The revenue from income taxes is transferred to government accounts to pay for welfare and other kinds of benefits for American citizens.

1. Which sentence is the topic sentence? Is it an effective topic sentence? Explain.
2. Does the paragraph have adequate development? Answer each of the following questions, which are related to adequate development in a paragraph.
   a. Are the details specific or too general?
   b. Is there a sufficient number of different details?
   c. What details are missing?
3. Does the paragraph have a concluding sentence? Explain.

Kinds of Paragraphs

Information is organized according to the purpose of your writing. In Chapter 1 (page 13, you learned that your purpose may be narrative, descriptive, expository, or persuasive. In this textbook, you will learn to organize information according to the specific characteristics of the paragraphs in the following chart. Each paragraph serves a specific purpose and has its own unique format and characteristics for the topic sentence, the body, and the concluding sentence.

KINDS OF PARAGRAPHS				
PARAGRAPH TYPE	PURPOSE	CHARACTERISTICS OF THE TOPIC SENTENCE	CHARACTERISTICS OF THE BODY AND SUPPORTING DETAILS	EXAMPLES OF TOPIC SENTENCES
Narrative	Tells a story about a specific incident or event of significance	-Identifies the event and/or the significance of the event	-Chronological order -Action verbs in past tense -Written in first or third person -Words convey mood, feeling, significance -Vivid images create the event in the reader's mind	Temporary paralysis left me feeling pathetically helpless.
Descriptive	Creates a vivid picture of the appearance or nature of a person, place, thing, or idea	-Identifies the subject that will be described -Includes a point of view, emotion, or feeling toward the subject	-Spatial, chronological, or emphatic organization -A dominant impression -Vivid imagery through adjectives, verb, adverbs -Sensory descriptions	Dusty Harry is a coal miner who will never be forgotten.
Process	Explains how to do, make, or repair something; explains how something was already done	-Clearly states the process -Uses the word *steps* or *stages* -May identify the number of steps/stages involved	-Chronological order -Individual steps clearly defined -Use of transition words -Secondary details to explain each individual step -The word *you* can be used to address the reader	Five steps can be learned to increase your opportunity to win a scholarship.
Comparison	Shows the similarities between two subjects	-Mentions both subjects -Indicates the subjects will be compared -Focuses on similarities	-Point-by-point method or block method to present the details -Equal development of subtopics for both subjects -Transition words between subjects	ADD and ADHD, two disorders frequently diagnosed in children, have many similarities.
Contrast	Shows the differences between two subjects	-Mentions both subjects -Indicates the subjects will be contrasted -Focuses on differences	-Point-by-point method or block method to present the details -Equal development of subtopics for both subjects -Transition words between subjects	Childhood and adult diabetes are quite different.

(Continue on page 64)

KINDS OF PARAGRAPHS				
PARAGRAPH TYPE	PURPOSE	CHARACTERISTICS OF THE TOPIC SENTENCE	CHARACTERISTICS OF THE BODY AND SUPPORTING DETAILS	EXAMPLES OF TOPIC SENTENCES
Examples	Uses examples to explain a statement or a point of view	-Statement that requires details to be fully understood	-Examples presented in emphatic (order of importance or emphasis), spatial, or chronological order -Two to four examples presented as subtopics -Secondary details follow subtopics -Transition words between examples	Students will gain the most benefits by an increase in student fees next year.
Classification	Explains a subject by breaking it into categories or groups	-States the subject clearly -May use words such as *categories, groups, types,* or *kinds*	-Each category or group developed with secondary details -Similar or dissimilar characteristics presented	Doctors now treat three kinds of diabetes.
Definition	Defines and clarifies the meaning of a term	-States the term to be defined -May include a basic definition	-Emphatic order (order of importance) for the details -Ways to expand the basic definition: anecdotes, analogies, synonyms, examples, negatives, or categories	*Tsunami* is a Japanese word that puts fear in the hearts of coastal dwellers.
Cause/Effect	Tells causes (reasons) or effects (outcomes) of a specific event or situation	-Indicates a cause-effect relationship -May use a signal word such as *causes, reasons, effects, outcomes*	-Chronological, spatial, or emphatic order for details -May include more than one cause or effect	Radiation waves create the greenhouse effect.
Summary	Gives the highlights and key points of an article or an essay	-Gives the name of the article or essay -Gives the author's full name -States the thesis	-Chronological or emphatic order -Each main idea is introduced with the author's last name and a present tense verb -Includes main ideas and only a few key details -Uses writer's personal words	In "Making a Man out of a Boy," Rachel Walters mocks the rituals that men follow in order to prove their manhood.

Writing a Cover Letter

Are you interested in finding a part-time job now or in the near future? If you are, you may need to compete with other people interested in the same job. So, how does one complete for an interview and then for a job if the initial process of applying for a job is done solely on paper without any personal contact with the employer? The answer is that you need to sell yourself on paper by using your writing skills to persuade an employer that you are the right candidate to fill the position. Most job postings require a resume or an information sheet with personal information. A cover letter on top of the resume is an excellent way to impress the employer before you have the opportunity to meet in person.

The steps for writing a cover letter are as follows:

1. Examine the job description or classified ad carefully. Highlight the qualities and skills that are required.
2. Create two headings on a piece of paper: job-related skills and personal qualities. Categorize all the skills and qualities found in the job description under these two categories. Across from each skill, jot down skills or experiences you have for each item. Across from the personal qualities, jot down your qualities. Also try to "read between the lines" to determine related qualities the employer would likely wish to see in an employee. Add these to your list. (See page 67.)
3. Use a standard business letter format for your cover letter. Refer to the format shown in the sample letter on page 68. Include your address, the date, the inside address, a salutation or greeting, the body of the letter, and a closing.
4. Write the first draft, which should consist of four short paragraphs. Dedicate each paragraph to a specific topic or focus.

   Paragraph 1: Identify the position and how you learned about the job.

   Paragraph 2: Briefly refer to the job-related skills and experiences you have that qualify you for the job.

   Paragraph 3: Discuss the personal qualities that make you a worthy, desirable employee.

   Paragraph 4: Briefly state your availability, interest in an interview, and contact information.
5. Revise the draft. Look for ways to strengthen the content. Check the sentence structure, grammar, and spelling. Type the letter if possible.
6. Sign the letter, make a copy, and drop the original letter in the mail.

The following classified ad demonstrates the first four steps for writing a cover letter.

HELP WANTED: Perfect job for the right person. Help needed organizing creative educational and recreational programs for pre-teens. Job requires giving feedback/suggestions on current programs; helping design and market new programs. Fifteen hours a week. Flexible hours to fit your schedule. Hourly wage begins at $19/hr. Benefit package available after 3 months. You must be motivated, goal-oriented, self-directed, and a team-player. Prefer experience working with diverse populations and familiarity with interests of pre-teens. Apply to Wishful Thinking, 7777 Lucky Lane, Somewhere, OR 97405. No phone calls.

Step 1

Examine the job description. Highlight the qualities and the skills required. The words and phrases in italics indicate significant qualities and skills that need to be discussed in the cover letter.

HELP WANTED: Perfect job for the right person. Help needed ***organizing creative educational and recreational programs for pre-teens.*** Job requires ***giving feedback/suggestions*** on current programs; helping ***design and market new programs.*** Fifteen hours a week. Flexible hours to fit your schedule. Hourly wage begins at $19/hr. Benefit package available after 3 months. You must be ***motivated, goal-oriented, self-directed, and a team-player.*** Prefer ***experience working with diverse populations and familiarity with interests of pre-teens.*** Apply to Wishful Thinking, 7777 Lucky Lane, Somewhere, OR 97405. No phone calls.

Step 2

Categorize the qualifications in the ad under two categories: job-related skills and personal skills. Jot down skills or experiences you have for each item. Add any other items to the list that you believe will interest the employer. Assume for this example that you have worked for two years as an aide in the after-school program at the YMCA. Ideas added to the lists are shown in italics.

With your compiled list of skills and qualities, you will have ample details to use to write a cover letter. Your list of skills and abilities will also become the beginning organizational structure for the paragraphs in the body of your cover letter.

JOB-RELATED SKILLS	MY SKILLS AND QUALIFICATIONS
organize educational programs	after-school program at YMCA
organize recreational programs	after-school programs at YMCA
work with pre-teens	have a pre-teen son
provide feedback on programs	curriculum planning with teachers
provide suggestions on programs	after-school program at YMCA
design new programs for pre-teens	after-school program at YMCA
market new programs	school newsletter, public speaking
experience working with diverse populations	after-school program at YMCA
familiarity with interests of pre-teens	after-school program at YMCA
computer skills	Microsoft Word and Word Perfect
advertising/graphic skills	design school and church newsletters
communication skills	speech class, public speaking

PERSONAL QUALITIES	MY QUALITIES
motivated	highly motivated, ambitious
goal-oriented	set goals, manage time well
self-directed	can work independently
team player	share ideas, communicate effectively, attend meetings
respectful of others	courteous, compassionate
sensitive to different needs	sensitive to others' needs and feelings
creative	enjoy innovation, not afraid to try new things
organized, detail-oriented	very organized, good with details, follow through

Step 3

Use a standard business letter format, as shown below:

STANDARD BUSINESS LETTER FORMAT

The heading gives your street address, city, state, ZIP code, and the date. Notice the use of commas.

211 Elkhorn Drive
Sutton, OR 97401
December 12, 2001

The inside address gives the employer's name or the name of the department, the company name, the street address, the city, state, and ZIP code. Notice the punctuation.

Personnel
Wishful Thinking
7777 Lucky Lane
Somewhere, OR 97405

The salutation is the greeting. Use the person's name if you know it. If you do not know it, you may address the letter by the person's position. Use a colon after the name.

Dear Personnel Director:

The body of the letter consists of individual paragraphs that provide the necessary information. Limit each paragraph to developing one idea.

Body of the letter:

A standard closing is the word *sincerely*. Place your signature under the closing. Type your name under the signature.

Sincerely,

Randy Sweeting

Step 4

Write the first draft. Each paragraph should focus on one idea. Though the order may vary, the topics for the paragraphs that were recommended on page 65 are used in the sample letter. Refer to your categories of information as guides in writing the paragraphs.

211 Elkhorn Drive
Sutton, OR 97401
December 12, 2001

Personnel
Wishful Thinking
7777 Lucky Lane
Somewhere, OR 97405

Dear Personnel Director:

I am applying for the position working with pre-teen programs. I saw the ad in *The Daily News* on December 9 and was immediately attracted to this job.

As you will see from my resume, I have many job-related skills that qualify me for this job. I have worked as an after-school aide for the YMCA program for two years. My responsibilities include organizing materials for activities, planning with the teachers, organizing field trips, and doing some basic record-keeping for the program. The successful Math Through Basketball program is one of my innovations. I also have experience with design work, marketing, writing newsletters, and public speaking. I have computer skills and am comfortable with both Word and Word Perfect. I use graphics programs as well.

I believe I am an excellent candidate for this job. I am highly motivated and ambitious. set goals well, meet deadlines, and manage my time efficiently. I am self-directed and can work independently. However, I am also a good team player who likes to share ideas, communicate in a positive manner, and participate in meetings and planning sessions. I am respectful, courteous, and sensitive to the needs of diverse populations. I enjoy the opportunity to be creative and am not afraid to try new things. I am attentive to details and am well organized. I truly love working with pre-teens and believe they need programs to help them grow in positive ways.

I am very interested in interviewing for this job. I am available to begin work immediately. I can be reached at (541) 555-1212 during the days or evenings.

Sincerely,

Randy Sweeting

Step 5

Revise your draft. Look for ways to strengthen the content. Add information if the letter seems underdeveloped and does not convince the reader that you are an excellent candidate for this job. Delete information if the letter seems too wordy or points seem redundant. Look for ways to combine sentences to be more concise. Check the letter for correct grammar, sentence structure, and spelling. Type a final version.

Step 6

Sign the letter. Make a copy for your files. If a resume is required, include a resume with your cover letter. (Check with your career center on campus to learn how to write a resume.) Address the envelope and drop it in the mail. All that is left to be done is to wait for the call to schedule an interview!

WRITING ASSIGNMENT: WRITE A COVER LETTER FOR A JOB

1. Select a classified ad for employment from a local newspaper. Try to find a job position that interests you even if you are not currently seeking employment. This writing assignment will be easier to complete if you select an ad that requires a variety of job-related skills and qualifications.
2. Complete the first four steps for writing an effective cover letter. For the sake of this assignment, if the advertisement does not list an address, create a fictitious inside address for your letter.
3. Ask a friend, classmate, or tutor to read your draft and provide you with suggestions for improving the letter. Your instructor may also want to provide comments on your draft.
4. Complete Step 5. Revise your cover letter by making any changes that you feel strengthen your letter. Turn the following items in to your instructor for comments, feedback, and possibly grading:
   - The classified advertisement from the newspaper
   - The draft(s) of your cover letter
   - The revision and final version of your cover letter
5. If you are currently seeking employment and the job is suited to your interests, school schedule, and other preferences, complete Step 6. Mail the cover letter to the employer and notify the class after you hear the results.

Grammar and Usage Tips

Study each tip with its accompanying examples and explanations. Complete the exercises following each tip. After you have completed an exercise, carefully check your work with the answer keys in Appendix A and record your number of errors for each exercise. Review the tip and examine the correct answer. In the margins of each exercise, jot down questions that you would like to ask your teacher regarding the skills.

Be sure that every sentence has a subject. The subject will be a noun or a pronoun that tells who or what performs the action of the sentence. The subject is never found inside a prepositional phrase. The subject often, but not always, appears before the verb in the sentence.

Noun Review

A **noun** names a person, place, thing, or idea. Nouns can be placed throughout a sentence. When nouns tell who or what performs the action of the sentence, the noun functions as the **subject** of the sentence. The following underlined words are nouns, and they are working as subjects of the sentences:

> People respond to praise in many different ways.
>
> Benjamin Franklin was well known for his philanthropy.
>
> North Carolina experienced two horrendous hurricanes within a two-week period.
>
> Bribes in some countries are acceptable business practices.
>
> Creativity involves innovative thinking and the courage to be different.

Prepositional phrases begin with prepositions and end with nouns or pronouns. The nouns and the pronouns inside the prepositional phrases can never be the subjects of sentences. Since prepositional phrases are considered "sentence extras" and do not contain the subjects (or the verbs) of the sentence, ignore them in sentences when you are analyzing sentences for their subjects or verbs. In the following examples, prepositional phrases are placed inside parentheses and are crossed out as a reminder that the subject never appears inside a prepositional phrase. (Refer to the list of prepositions in Chapter 1 on page 37 as needed.)

Stress (~~in adults~~) can lead to tension headaches, cluster headaches, or migraines.

People (~~with migraines~~) should consult a doctor for treatment.

The muscles (~~around the scalp~~), (~~in the back~~) (~~of the neck~~), and (~~throughout the shoulder area~~) tighten (~~in stressful situations~~) and trigger a pounding sensation.

Pronoun Review

Pronouns are words that replace nouns. The term **pronoun case** refers to the way pronouns function in a sentence. The three pronoun cases are **subjective, objective,** and **possessive.**

PRONOUN CASES		
PRONOUN CASE	PRONOUNS	FUNCTION
Subjective	I, we, you, he, she, it, they	1. As subjects of sentences *We* arrived early for the lecture. 2. As predicate pronouns after a linking verb It was *she* who called the doctor.
Objective	me, us, you, him, her, it, them	1. As objects of a prepositional phrase I studied (with *them*) for an hour. 2. As direct objects I called *her* at midnight. 3. As indirect objects We gave *them* recognition pins.
Possessive	my, our, your, his, her, its, their mine, ours, yours, his, hers, its, theirs	1. Modify nouns I presented *my* project yesterday. 2. Show possession without modifying other nouns This notebook is *yours*.

Subject pronouns work as subjects of sentences to tell who or what performs the action of the sentence. Personal pronouns, indefinite pronouns, most relative pronouns, and demonstrative pronouns can work as subjects of sentences.

<table>
<tr><th colspan="5">SUBJECT PRONOUNS</th></tr>
<tr><td>Personal Pronouns</td><td colspan="4">I, you, he, she, it, we, they</td></tr>
<tr><td rowspan="7">Indefinite Pronouns</td><td>anyone</td><td>anybody</td><td>anything</td><td>everyone</td></tr>
<tr><td>everybody</td><td>everything</td><td>someone</td><td>somebody</td></tr>
<tr><td>something</td><td>one</td><td>no one</td><td>nobody</td></tr>
<tr><td>nothing</td><td>each</td><td>another</td><td>either</td></tr>
<tr><td>neither</td><td>some</td><td>both</td><td>few</td></tr>
<tr><td>many</td><td>several</td><td>all</td><td>any</td></tr>
<tr><td>none</td><td>most</td><td>more</td><td></td></tr>
<tr><td>Relative pronouns</td><td colspan="4">who, which, that</td></tr>
<tr><td>Demonstrative Pronouns</td><td colspan="4">this, that, these, those</td></tr>
</table>

The words that are underlined are subject pronouns.

> I had never done a live interview and had never written an article based on geology.
>
> You can create an expansive compact disk library without leaving the privacy of your home.
>
> They can be fortified with extra vitamins and even vaccines.
>
> Anyone is eligible to apply for the scholarship.
>
> Some of the traits are seen in both men and women.
>
> Neither wants to compromise or fail.
>
> Who is interested in learning about mutual funds?
>
> Which is the best resource to use?
>
> These are my favorite earrings.

Some pronouns cannot be used as subjects of sentences. Pronouns that cannot work as subjects are called **object pronouns.** Using an object pronoun as a subject of a sentence creates a pronoun error. Notice in the following examples how the pronoun errors are corrected by using the correct subject pronouns.

> ~~Her~~ She and I will present our project to the class on Friday.
>
> ~~Him~~ He and Ramona interviewed two geologists for their research paper.
>
> My roommate and ~~me~~ I decided to redecorate our dorm room.

Likewise, pronoun errors will occur if subject pronouns are used inside prepositional phrases. Notice in the following examples how the pronoun errors are corrected by using object pronouns instead of subject pronouns inside the prepositional phrases.

1. (Between him and ~~I~~ me), a strong bond of friendship has formed.
2. (With the support) (of ~~he~~ him and her parents), Maria was able to attend college this year.

EXERCISE 2.1 Identifying Subjects

Score: ______

Each of the following sentences has one subject. The subject is a noun or a pronoun. Identify and underline the subject in each sentence.

Example: The construction **crew** worked diligently to finish the house on time.

1. The toothed whales have teeth instead of baleen.
2. Many web site addresses begin with the letters *www*.
3. The hurricanes clocked winds over 80 miles per hour.
4. For many weeks, the winner of the election was unknown.
5. Hepatitis can be contracted by eating contaminated food or drinking contaminated water.
6. Cluster headaches often begin with a sharp, sudden burning pain behind or around the eye.
7. The reader is able to follow the writer's development of the topic sentence.
8. I drafted a series of questions for the interview.
9. The federal government collects taxes to pay for government transfer payments.
10. Neither of the contestants knew the correct answer.

EXERCISE 2.2 Identifying Subjects and Prepositional Phrases

Score: ______

Mark the prepositional phrases with parentheses. Refer to the list of prepositions on page 37 of Chapter 1 if necessary. Draw one line under the noun or the pronoun that is the subject of the sentence. Remember that the subject can never be found inside a prepositional phrase.

Example: All (of the volunteers) were hypnotized (on stage).

1. Parent rage at youth sports events is occurring at an alarming rate.
2. Three forms of the flu virus are common in the United States.
3. The muscles around the scalp, in the back of the neck, and throughout the shoulder area tighten in stressful situations.
4. Each of the following paragraphs has problems with coherence.
5. Two kinds of federal taxes are the most significant sources of federal tax revenue.
6. The television show focuses on inspirational personal stories.
7. On a separate piece of paper, you can list all your qualifications.
8. In two hours, we will see a solar eclipse.
9. Lack of eye contact with the speaker signals boredom.
10. This report demonstrates the value of our new product.

TIP 2 **To add sentence variety and to avoid wordiness, combine two sentences that have the same verb into one sentence with compound subjects (two or more subjects). Both subjects usually appear before the verb in the sentence.**

In the following examples, individual sentences are combined into one sentence that has compound subjects. The subjects are underlined with one line; the verbs are underlined with double lines. Notice how the verb changes to match the compound (plural) subjects.

Individual sentences with single subjects:

Corn is a staple crop in many countries. Rice is a staple crop, too. Wheat is also a staple crop.

Combined by using compound subjects:

Corn, rice, and wheat are staple crops in many countries.

Individual sentences with single subjects:

A topic sentence is present in your paragraph. The body is present in your paragraph. A concluding sentence is present in your paragraph.

Combined by using compound subjects:

A topic sentence, the body, and a concluding sentence are present in your paragraph.

Individual sentences with single subjects:

Serena Williams demonstrates power and grace on and off the courts.

Vanessa Williams demonstrates power and grace on and off the courts.

Combined by using compound subjects:

Serena and Vanessa Williams demonstrate power and grace on and off the courts.

EXERCISE 2.3 Singular and Compound Subjects

Score: ______

Mark the prepositional phrases with parentheses. Underline the subject(s) once. Remember that subjects cannot be inside a prepositional phrase.

Example: (At our college), scholarships, grants, and loans are available for students.

1. Residential areas, schools, and hospitals were evacuated.
2. Examples, facts, definitions, and reasons may be used in the body of a paragraph.
3. Tempers frequently flare at intersections and on freeways.
4. The geologists from the U.S. Geological Survey Team monitored the mountain.
5. The date should appear under the line with the city, state, and ZIP code information.

6. The quantity and quality of supporting details are important.

7. They live under the same roof and share the family responsibilities.

8. Nuclear families and extended families exist in many countries.

9. Fidgeting, doodling, and daydreaming signal a lack of interest in the speaker or the topic.

10. Sturdy shoes, a backpack, and a supply of food are essential for the hiking event.

TIP 3 **Be sure that every sentence has a complete verb. Verbs are words that express action or a state of being of the subject. Three kinds of verbs can be used in sentences: action verbs, linking verbs, or verb phrases. Verbs are never found inside prepositional phrases.**

Action Verbs Review

An **action verb** expresses the action done by the subject. After you have identified the subject, ask yourself, "What is the subject doing?" or "What has the subject done?" If the answer is expressed by a word that shows action, the sentence has an action verb. In the following examples, the action verb is underlined with two lines. Notice how the verb is directly related to the action done by the subject. Remember, the verb can never be found inside a prepositional phrase.

subject verb
Neither wants to compromise or fail.

Many web site addresses begin with the letters *www.*

Sentences in the body of a paragraph expand the main idea of the paragraph.

I drafted a series of questions for the interview.

We walked between the pond and the rose garden.

The hurricanes clocked winds over 80 miles per hour.

In the previous examples, the verbs *wants, begin,* and *expand* express action that is happening in the present. These are called **present-tense verbs.** With present-tense verbs, notice how the verb forms vary for singular and plural subjects. When the subject is singular, the verb has an *-s* or an *-es* suffix. When the subject is plural, the verb does not have an *-s* or an *-es* suffix.

Singular Subjects and Verbs	**Plural Subjects and Verbs**
Neither wants to compromise.	The administrators want to compromise.
The address begins with a number.	The addresses begin with a number.
This sentence expands the idea.	The sentences expand the idea.

The verbs *drafted, walked,* and *clocked* express action that has already taken place. These are **past-tense verbs.** The simple past tense of many verbs is made by using an *-ed* suffix. Other verbs, called **irregular verbs** use other verb forms for the past tense. The following examples show regular and irregular verbs in simple past tense. (Verb tenses will be discussed in greater detail in Chapter 5.)

Regular Verbs in Past Tense	**Irregular Verbs in Past Tense**
The car stalled on the track.	The car ran well for ten laps.
The mechanics tried to cool the engine.	The mechanics felt frustrated.
The driver managed to place third.	The driver spoke to the media.

At first glance at the preceding examples, you might have mistaken the words *cool* and *place* to be the verbs in the sentences. Notice, however, that the word *to* precedes each of these words. The result is an **infinitive,** the base form of a verb. An infinitive does not show a verb tense. An infinitive is never the action of a sentence. Like prepositional phrases, infinitives can be ignored when you analyze a sentence to find its subject and verb. In the following examples, infinitives are placed inside brackets and crossed out as a reminder that they do not function as the verb of the sentence.

The mechanics tried [~~to cool~~] the engine.

The driver managed [~~to place~~] third.

The administrators want [~~to compromise.~~]

The players wanted [~~to request~~] a ruling on the play.

The dogs prefer [~~to eat~~] fresh, ground meat and table scraps.

Sammy Sosa and Mark McGwire hope [~~to break~~] their own home run records this year.

EXERCISE 2.4 Identifying Action Verbs

Score: ______

Place parentheses around the prepositional phrases. Place brackets around the infinitives. Underline the subjects once and the action verbs twice. Remember that action verbs express the action done by the subject.

Example: An armadillo apparently hoped [to find] food (in our backyard).

1. A foot of rain flooded the coastal towns.
2. A person with an internal locus of control feels in charge of his or her life.
3. We rode with them for the next three hundred miles.
4. People respond to praise in many different ways.
5. The public safety officials wanted to evacuate the entire area.
6. The plant supervisor requested a meeting with the union to discuss several problems.
7. Neither of the contestants knew the correct answer.
8. Lack of eye contact during an interview signals a lack of confidence and shyness.
9. Preschool children need vaccinations to prevent childhood diseases.
10. During the test, I remembered to develop each answer with sufficient details.

Linking Verbs Review

Linking verbs show a state of being, existence, or a condition of the subject. They express no action. If you are not able to locate an action verb in a sentence, look for a linking verb. The following verbs are linking verbs; they link the subject to the remaining words in the sentence.

linking verb

Your apartment is spacious and clean.

LINKING VERBS	
PRESENT TENSE	PAST TENSE
am is are	was were
feel taste sound look smell	felt tasted sounded looked smelled
become appear grow seem remain	became appeared grew seemed remained

Notice in the following sentences that there are no action verbs, but there are linking verbs. The linking verb forms a bridge to link the subject to the remainder of the sentence. The linking verbs shown below are in present tense or past tense.

Present Tense	**Past Tense**
I am Mark's oldest sister.	The lights were on sale last weekend.
They are members of the crew.	He felt feverish and weak after the race.
This plan sounds too good to be true.	She became a well-known songwriter.
The turkey smells delicious.	The audience grew impatient.

EXERCISE 2.5 Identifying Linking Verbs

Score: ________

Place parentheses around the prepositional phrases. Place brackets around the infinitives. Underline the subjects once and the linking verbs twice. Remember that linking verbs link the subject to the remainder of the sentence.

Example: All (of the receipts) (for the trip) are (in the box) and ready [to enter] (into the books.)

1. The young children grew restless during the long concert.
2. Anyone is eligible to apply for the scholarship.
3. Three forms of hepatitis are common in the United States.
4. The comet appears once every one hundred years.
5. Detergent, floor wax, mops, and air freshener are on sale at Mickey's Market.
6. The fresh bread from the bakery across the street smells wonderful.

7. Homemade vegetable soup tastes good on a cold winter day.

8. Scientists were eager to study the effects of genetically altered food.

9. Many ridiculous and outdated laws remain on the books in some states.

10. Lately, you seem to be unhappy and under a lot of stress.

Verb Phrases Review

Verb phrases consist of two or more verbs that work together to show the action done by the subject. A verb phrase consists of a **helping verb** plus a **main verb,** which may have suffixes (endings such as *-s, -ing,* or *-ed*). Verb phrases show different time periods during which the action in the sentence occurred, started, or ended.

The following words can work as helping verbs in verb phrases. Notice that some of the helping verbs also work as linking verbs when they are not attached to a main verb in a verb phrase.

HELPING VERBS					
am	is	are	was	were	been
do	does	did	has	have	had
can	will	shall	could	should	would
may	might	must			

In the following sentences, the subjects are underlined once and the complete verb phrase (helping verb and main verb) twice.

Both parents and teachers had praised the new curriculum.

Many athletes will arrive for the ceremony one day early.

They can consume large amounts of food each day.

Many students are enrolling in the new ethnic studies course.

Residents were fleeing from the forest fire.

Several airline pilots had seen strange lights in the sky.

Sometimes **adverbs** may appear between a helping verb and a main verb to modify or describe the verb. Many, but not all, adverbs end with an *-ly* suffix. *Quickly, frequently,* and *secretly* are examples of adverbs with the *-ly* suffix. *Not* and *never* are other examples of adverbs in the following sentences. When you mark verb phrases in sentences, skip over the adverbs; mark only the helping verbs plus the main form of the verb. (Review adverbs in Chapter 1 if necessary.)

The child had *quickly* gone home.

Flights can *frequently* depart during the early morning hours.

Three of the ticket holders were *secretly* recording the concert.

I was *not* thinking clearly.

Your sales will *never* increase with that attitude.

The following list of adverbs that do not end in *-ly* frequently appear between a helping verb and a main verb.

almost	never	not	often	quite	seldom	very

His pessimistic attitude has *often* caused problems at work.

The rash can *seldom* spread from one person to another.

Mr. Engles may *never* find his lost puppy.

Grammar and Usage Tip 3 states that every sentence must have a complete verb. This means that verb phrases must appear with both a helping verb and a main verb. An incomplete verb will cause a fragment, a common writing error. The following rules will help you write complete verbs:

1. **A main verb with an *-ing* suffix must always have a helping verb.** Failure to include the helping verb will result in an incomplete verb, and thus a fragment. Notice how the verb error can easily be corrected by adding the appropriate helping verb or by replacing the *-ing* suffix with a present-tense or past-tense form of the verb.

   Fragment: The driver looking for directions to the university.

   Correct: The driver was looking for directions to the university.
   The driver looked for directions to the university. (past tense)
   The driver looks for directions to the university. (present tense)

2. **A main verb with an *-ed* suffix sometimes requires the helping verbs *has, have,* or *had* (past perfect tense).** Failure to include the helping verb results in a fragment. Other times, however, a main verb with an *-ed* suffix forms the simple past tense that does not use a helping verb. Carefully proofread sentences with a verb with an *-ed* suffix to determine whether the verb is an incomplete verb phrase or a verb in simple past tense.

   Simple Past Tense: The lake reflected the peaks of the mountains.

   Verb Phrase: Fuel from speedboats has contaminated the water.

EXERCISE 2.6 Identifying Verb Phrases

Score: ______

Place parentheses around the prepositional phrases. Place brackets around infinitives. Underline the subject once and the complete verb phrase twice.

Example: I am going [to call] the customer service department (about the delivery date).

1. The topic sentence should capture the reader's attention.
2. Sentences in the body of the paragraph should not stray from the main idea.
3. The sisters were hoping to win at Wimbledon.
4. Some species of whales have been on the brink of extinction for many years.
5. Technology has created new concerns about copyright infringements.
6. The movie industry will never sanction duplication of movies over the Internet.
7. International companies must understand the cultural practices of other countries.
8. The prosecution has listed the evidence in chronological order.
9. The tourists from Switzerland had planned to visit Washington, D.C.
10. His temporary manager had treated him badly.

TIP 4 **For sentence variety and to avoid wordiness, combine two sentences that have the same subject into one sentence with compound verbs. The term *compound verb* is used when the subject of the sentence performs two or more actions.**

The following groups of sentences are wordy. Notice how the sentences can be combined into one sentence with **compound verbs.** The compound verbs come after the subject and express the actions done by the subject. When marking the compound verbs in sentences, underline all of the verbs, or all of the words that show the action done by the subject.

Individual sentences with single verbs:

Our web site creates road directions for you.

The web site also provides a map of the route.

[What two things does the web site do? It *creates* road directions. It *provides* a map of the route. You can combine these two sentences.]

Combined sentence using compound verbs:

Our web site creates road directions for you and provides a map of the route.

Individual sentences with single verbs:

The program estimates the travel time.

The program gives the distance between cities.

[What two things does the program do? It *estimates* travel time, and it *gives* the distance between cities. You can combine these two sentences.]

Combined sentence using compound verbs:

The program estimates the travel time and gives the distance between cities.

Two or more verb phrases are also considered compound verbs. When both main verbs use the same helping verb, sometimes the second helping verb is not stated, the helping verb is implied or assumed to be included in the verb phrase. The following sentence with compound verb phrases can be shortened by removing the second helping verb. In this compound verb situation, the second verb phrase is still considered to be a complete verb.

Tina had planned her trip weeks in advance and had used the web site for directions.

Tina had planned her trip weeks in advance and used the web site for directions.

EXERCISE 2.7 Identifying Compound Verbs

Score: ______

Place parentheses around the prepositional phrases. Place brackets around the infinitives. Underline the subject once and the compound verbs twice.

1. Baleen hangs inside whales' mouths and sifts food from the water.

2. Roller coasters at theme parks, carnivals, and fairs draw large crowds and provide fun for thrill-seekers.

3. The writer does not wander from the topic or include unrelated information.

4. Sunburn ointment can reduce the burning sensation on your skin and prevent blisters.

5. Sarina was pruning the roses and the bushes and fertilizing all the plants.

6. An underdeveloped paragraph lacks sufficient details and fails to explain the main idea.

7. An effective speaker acknowledges and respects differing points of view.

8. The music industry will find ways to stop the abuse and force compliance of copyright laws.

9. Biotech farming can increase food production and improve the quality of crops.

10. At work, I set goals well and manage my time efficiently.

TIP 5 **Avoid fragments by checking that each sentence has a subject, has a complete verb, forms a complete thought, and can stand by itself and make sense. A fragment is only part of a complete sentence that poses as a complete sentence. One or more parts of the sentence are missing.**

An independent clause is a group of words that has a subject and complete verb and can stand on its own as a sentence. A simple sentence is an independent clause standing by itself as a sentence. One way to avoid writing fragments is to write error-free independent clauses or simple sentences.

Fragments

Many kinds of **fragments** can mar your writing. One kind of fragment occurs when a group of words that pose as a sentence lacks a subject or a complete verb, or does not form a complete thought. The following examples show this kind of fragment error:

Lacks a subject: (Without a care) (in the world) traveled (from one city) (to another) (for a year)

[Who traveled from one city to another? The subject is missing.]

Lacks a verb: Too many drivers (on the busy freeways) (of America) (without car insurance).

[What do the drivers on the freeways do? The verb is missing.]

Lacks a complete verb: Scientists experimenting (with new ways) [to increase] crop yields.

[Verbs that end with an *-ing* suffix must have a helping verb to be complete.]

Lacks a complete thought or ability to stand alone: When parents take the time [to safeguard] their homes.

[This is not an independent clause because of the word *when*. A clause that is not an independent clause creates a fragment if it tries to stand on its own.]

You can correct fragments created by the above errors by using these methods:

1. *Add the missing subject:*

   (Without a care) (in the world), **the young graduate** traveled (from one city) (to another) (for a year).

2. *Add the missing verb:*

   Too many drivers (on the busy freeways) (of America) **drive** (without car insurance).

3. *Add the missing helping verb to complete the verb phrase:*

   Scientists **are** experimenting (with new ways) [to increase] crop yields.

4. *Remove the word or words that make the thought incomplete. Add words to make the thought complete:*

   Conscientious
   ~~**When**~~ ^ parents take the time [to safeguard] their homes.

Independent Clauses/Simple Sentences

An **independent clause** is a group of words that has a subject, has a complete verb, forms a complete thought, and can stand by itself and make sense. When an independent clause stands by itself without any other clauses, it is called a **simple sentence.** Simple sentences as well as independent clauses may have compound subjects and/or compound verbs.

To avoid fragments, ask yourself these questions:

1. Is there a subject?
2. Is there a complete verb?
3. Does the clause form a complete thought?
4. Can the sentence stand by itself and make sense?

All of the following independent clauses are simple sentences. They have at least one subject and one complete verb, form a complete thought, and can stand by themselves and make sense.

one subject one verb
Muscles tighten in the neck, in the back, and across the shoulders during stressful situations.

one subject one verb
Anyone is eligible to apply for the scholarship.

one subject one verb
The judge is announcing the finalists at 2:00 P.M.

compound subject one verb
Millions of stars and two meteorites appeared in the dark sky.

one subject compound verb
The golf fans cheered for Tiger and applauded loudly at the end of each hole.

EXERCISE 2.8 Identifying Simple Sentences and Fragments

Score: ______

On each line below, write **S** if the group of words forms a simple **sentence.** Write **F** if the group of words is a **fragment**.

Examples: **S** The young child was hoping for a miracle.

F The young child hoping for a miracle.

______ 1. The pilot and the copilot of the 747 jet have worked together for nine years.

______ 2. International flights arriving and departing from the airport every hour of every day.

______ 3. Between the late night flights and the early morning flights.

______ 4. Flight attendants must adjust to varied sleep patterns.

______ 5. Consumers demanding more and more accountability and reliability from airlines.

______ 6. Weather conditions delay flights or cause cancellations.

______ 7. Meals on airplanes are practically nonexistent.

______ 8. Soft drinks, juices, and other beverages along with pretzels on most domestic flights.

_________ 9. Crammed into the narrow seats with little leg room or arm room.

_________ 10. Flying to destination is almost always faster than traveling by car or by train.

EXERCISE 2.9 Combining Sentences

Score: _______

On separate paper, rewrite the following paragraph. Do not change the topic sentence or the concluding sentence. Within the body of the paragraph, combine sentences to create sentences with compound verbs. Combine the verbs by using the conjunction *and* or the conjunction *or.*

> The Chinese still favor their *bu xie*, cloth slip-on shoes. The shoes are soft and cool. The shoes do not pinch their feet. The shoes are inexpensive. The shoes cost an equivalent of one dollar. Some Chinese wear Italian-style leather shoes. Some Chinese walk around in Nike sneakers and their knock-offs. However, the traditional Chinese cloth shoes are still frequently worn with business suits. The traditional Chinese cloth shoes are still frequently used by construction workers instead of steel-toed construction boots. Though shoes with support and more durability seem to make more sense, many Chinese continue to favor their traditional *bu xie*.
>
> [Adapted from: Associated Press, " . . . Chinese Eschew the Newer Shoes," *Register Guard*, August 4, 2000, p.A11.]

Grammar and Usage Tips Summary

TIP 1 Be sure that every sentence has a subject. The subject is never found inside a prepositional phrase.

TIP 2 Use compound subjects when two or more subjects perform the same action.

TIP 3 Be sure that every sentence has a complete verb. Verbs may be action verbs, linking verbs, or verb phrases. An infinitive is not the verb in a sentence.

TIP 4 Use compound verbs when the subject of the sentence performs more than one action.

TIP 5 Avoid fragments by checking that each sentence has a subject, has a complete verb, forms a complete thought, and can stand by itself and make sense. A simple sentence is one independent clause. A fragment is only part of a complete sentence.

CHAPTER 2 • Writing Effective Paragraphs • Proofreading and Editing Exercises

Proofreading 1

Carefully read the following paragraph, in which each sentence is numbered. On the numbered lines below the paragraph, indicate whether the group of words for each number is a sentence or a fragment. Write **S** to indicate the words form a complete **sentence**. Write **F** to indicate the words form a **fragment**, or only a portion of a complete sentence.

AZORES

[1]Few people know about the beauty and the simplicity of the Azores. [2]The Azores archipelago is a group of nine volcanic islands between the American and the European continents. [3]The natural powers of nature basically formed these islands. [4]Powerful earthquakes, volcanic eruptions, and the grinding ocean shaped these groups of islands. [5]Many volcanic craters with blue lagoons. [6]The islands with fertile volcanic soil, warm Gulf Stream winds, and plentiful rain. [7]The hillsides are lush and green, with a wide variety of vegetation. [8]With few inhabitants, the natural environment unspoiled by the modern world. [9]Vehicles are scarce. [10]Most dairy farmers deliver their products to the markets on mules. [11]These nine volcanic islands, however, attract more and more tourists every year. [12]Azoreans not interested in a massive tourist industry for their small, unspoiled group of islands. [13]They do not want to lose the beauty and the simplicity of their natural environment or peaceful islands.

[Adapted from: Barry Hatton, "The Azores," *Register Guard*, 11-7-1999, p. 4H.]

1. ____________ 6. ____________ 11. ____________
2. ____________ 7. ____________ 12. ____________
3. ____________ 8. ____________ 13. ____________
4. ____________ 9. ____________
5. ____________ 10. ____________

Proofreading 2

Proofread the Writing Warm-Up 2 you wrote at the beginning of the chapter. Read each sentence carefully to be sure it has a subject and a complete verb and can stand on its own. This chapter discusses only simple sentences. Many of your sentences may be compound or complex sentences, which are types of sentences covered in Chapters 3 and 4. For now, do the best that you can to proofread, edit, and revise your writing warm-up.

Follow these steps to prepare your final writing sample:

1. Reread your writing warm-up. Revise by making any changes that will strengthen your writing.
   - Could the topic sentence be stronger and more to the point?
   - Are the sentences in the body of the paragraph arranged in a logical manner?
   - Do you have enough supporting details?
   - Does each sentence make sense?
   - Is there an effective concluding sentence?
2. Edit the revision. Use a different colored pen to add or delete words or punctuation in the revision. Make changes that will strengthen your writing.
   - Does every sentence begin with a capital letter and end with a period (or a question mark)?
   - Are words spelled correctly?
   - To the best of your knowledge at this time, are sentences properly punctuated?
3. In the upper right-hand corner of your paper, write a heading. The heading should have your name, the name of the class, the name of the writing assignment (Writing Warm-Up 2), and the date.
4. Rewrite or retype the sample writing.
5. Follow your instructor's directions. You may be asked to turn in all your drafts to your instructor, or you may be asked to keep the drafts in a cumulative portfolio.

Internet Enrichment

Log onto the web site for this textbook for additional exercises and links for the following topics:

Topic Sentences
Unity, Coherence, and Adequate Development
Subjects in Simple Sentences
Verbs in Simple Sentences
Avoiding Fragments

Go to: http://college.hmco.com. Click on "Students." Type *Paragraph Essentials* in the "Jump to Textbook Sites" box. Click "go," and then bookmark the site. Click on Chapter 2.

CHAPTER 2 • Grammar and Usage Review

Name ______________________

Date ______________________

Sentence Work

In the following sentences, mark the prepositional phrases with parentheses and the infinitives with brackets. Underline the subjects once and the complete verbs twice.

1. She has never understood the rules of football.

2. Sentences in the body of the paragraph expand the main idea of the paragraph.

3. Too many trucks, cars, and buses cause congestion during peak hours of the day.

4. Allergy sufferers are often allergic to pollens, dust, and mold spores.

5. We rode with them on the train for nine hours and talked the entire way.

6. Within a few hours, I had written the article to my satisfaction.

7. In the third paragraph, you can list your personal qualities and accomplishments.

8. You will increase your chances for an interview by using these steps.

9. Millions of people access the Internet on a daily basis.

10. Young viewers' interest in the new television show has surprised many people.

11. Sometimes it is difficult to tell the difference between fog and smog.

12. Several community groups bid for the contract to clean up the stadium after games.

Proofreading and Editing

Proofread the body of the following cover letter for a job. Use any method to correct fragments or subject pronoun errors. Write the corrections above the errors.

I am responding to your job posting in the *Star Tribune* on June 14, 2001. My work experiences and training qualify me for the position you have available.

I have worked part-time in the car industry for seven years. I was the parts assistant manager at Tom's Auto Supply Store for four years. Then three years as the office manager. I am familiar with sales, repairs, and customer service. Familiar with most kinds of cars and always do my own repair work.

I enjoy working with cars and with people. I have good communication skills. I am polite, punctual, and reliable. You can trust me with your individual customers and your larger accounts. I learn quickly. No problem learning about the tires you carry, the warranties, or the services. I work well with others and like to be a part of a team.

References included. I would like the chance to talk with you more about this job.

CHAPTER 3

Narrative Paragraphs

The topic sentence introduces a significant, specific event and a controlling idea.

The body tells a story in chronological order. Use vivid descriptive words and action verbs in past tense.

The concluding sentence echoes the topic sentence.

Topic sentence ....

Unity + Chronological Order + Adequate Development ....

Concluding sentence ....

In Chapter 3 you will learn about the following:

1. First- and third-person narratives
2. The structure of a narrative
3. The writing process for narratives
4. Three additional grammar and usage tips

WRITING WARM-UP 3

Write a narrative about a significant, specific event in your life in which you felt a sense of pride, accomplishment, or achievement. Write the story in first person, that is from your point of view, using the word *I* or *we* throughout the story. Use past-tense verbs to indicate that the story occurred in the past.

The Narrative Paragraph

To narrate means to tell or give an account of an event that has already occurred. A **narrative** is a story, usually about a significant event that has happened to you, the writer, or to someone you know. The purpose of a narrative is to inform, entertain, make a specific point, or evoke a certain emotional response from the reader. Above all, a narrative, like good storytelling, should capture the reader's interest with clearly defined characters, setting, and a time frame. The details should create images in the reader's mind so the reader can "see the events" unfold. Action verbs help move the story along and keep the reader involved in the event.

First-Person Narrative

In writing a first person narrative, you tell a story about a specific event that happened in your life, an event that left a lasting impression or emotional memory. Your goal is to convey the feelings or emotions of that situation clearly and vividly and evoke the same emotional response from your reader.

3.1 What do you think?

Read the following narrative and respond to the questions that follow. Write your answers on separate paper.

Scared Stiff

My heart never raced as fast as it did when I was cornered in a voodoo shop in Brazil. Three of my high school friends and I decided to wander around downtown São Paulo to kill time and "be cool." We chose to window shop on an unfamiliar side street. The third shop window we passed startled us; it was a voodoo or *macumba* shop. I had grown accustomed to seeing remains of *macumba* rituals at the intersections of neighborhood streets, so I wasn't really surprised to discover that *macumba* shops existed to sell items for the various white and black magic rituals. All the foreign objects that cluttered the dusty shelves and hung from the ceiling intrigued me. One of my friends noticed my interest and dared me to go inside. I stood up to the challenge, but my heart pounded and my stomach churned. A little bell rang when I opened the big wooden door and walked into the musty smelling store. I noticed many kinds of candles, colored cloths, animal feathers, bells, beads, and other trinkets inside the glass cases. I wandered to the back of the store and looked up. Right in front of my eyes, no more than twelve inches away, hung several shrunken heads. My head spun, my knees shook uncontrollably, and I thought I was going to throw up right there on the dusty counter and in front of any spirits lingering around the shop. Suddenly, I felt a presence behind me. For a brief moment, I felt a sense of relief because I thought one of my friends had finally ventured in. Then an eerie, chilling feeling crept up my spine and swept over me. Somehow I knew that more than one person was behind me and that they were not my friends. The two shop owners moved uncomfortably close to me. One gently touched the top of my head and ran his hand down my long, blond hair. He said I was a goddess. They stepped closer and closer and finally asked what I wanted to buy from their store. My heart pounded even faster. I almost started to cry. I attempted a phony smile. I didn't know what to do. One of my friends knocked on the window. I used that as an excuse to flee without so much as a good-bye or a thank-you. I knew from that moment that curiosity and dares are not strong enough reasons to wander into places where I do not belong.

1. What emotional response do you think the writer wants to evoke from you? Was she successful? Explain.
2. In a narrative, you should clearly define the character, a specific setting, and a specific time frame. Answer each of the following questions.
   a. In this narrative, does the story focus mainly around one character?
   b. Is the setting specific? Where does the story take place?
   c. Is the time frame specific? When does the story occur? How much time passes before the main action of the narrative occurs?
3. A well-written narrative should capture your interest. Does this narrative capture your interest? Explain your answer.
4. The narrative begins with the main idea and several sentences that provide you with background information. Answer the following questions.
   a. Where does the action part of the story begin?
   b. Does the action move along or does the narrative seem slow? Explain your answer.
5. List descriptive words or action verbs that create strong images and emotional responses from you.

Third-Person Narrative

In writing a third-person narrative, you tell a story about a specific event that happened to another person. A third-person narrative may be about an event you personally witnessed, or it may be an account of an event you know about from reading or from the media but did not personally experience. Throughout a third-person narrative, use the pronoun *he, she,* or *they*. You become the observer who reports the story but does not refer to yourself in the story. As with a first-person narrative, the story should make a specific point and evoke an emotional response from your reader. The character, the setting, and the time frame should be specific.

3.2 What do you think?

Read the following narrative and respond to the questions that follow. Write your answers on separate paper.

Greg

Cancer can hit people whom you least expect to get sick. My cousin Greg was a good kid. He never did anything wrong. He was 22 years old and hardly ever drank alcohol. He was focused on school and getting his work done on time. He attended Salisbury State and was studying to be a meteorologist. When he wasn't studying, he would often go surfing. He loved the water, the hot weather, and Ocean City. One day Greg found a lump under his arm, but he did not think much of it. After a week or so, he decided to tell his mother, who is a nurse. My aunt told him to go to see a doctor. He got an appointment for a week later. The doctor wasn't sure what the lump was, so the doctor thought it was best to remove it. He scheduled surgery, a surgery Greg never got, for the day before Thanksgiving. Greg stayed at my house because he had no heat in his house. On the morning of November 18, 1999, my mother went to check on Greg. She found Greg on the floor rolling around with stomach pain. My mother immediately took him to the hospital and then called my aunt to tell her so she could come down. When the doctor came out to talk to my aunt, he told her that they were running some tests and would let her know the results soon. The x-rays showed that Greg had tumors completely covering his liver and one of his kidneys. They put him on a dialysis machine. Then the other test results came back; Greg had cancer. The doctors ran more tests, which took a couple of days. Greg remained on the dialysis machine. The tests came back on Thanksgiving Day. Greg had widespread skin cancer and had only a few weeks to a few months to live. The doctors transferred Greg to Baltimore. By now the cancer had gone to his head, and he could not see. The doctors said they could keep him on dialysis, but that would only prolong his life and put him through more pain, or they could just let the cancer take its course. Early Monday, November 29, 1999, my cousin was done with his pain and suffering. Cancer not only affects the individual, but it affects family and friends as well. This sickness came as a very unpleasant surprise for my entire family.

Lindsay R. Allen
Wor-Wic Community College
Salisbury, Maryland

1. What emotional response do you think the writer wants to evoke from you? Is she successful? Explain.
2. In a narrative, you should clearly define the character, a specific setting, and a specific time frame. Answer the following questions.
   a. In this narrative, does the story focus mainly around one character?
   b. Is the setting specific? Where does the story take place?
   c. Approximately what length of time is involved in the main action of the narrative?
3. A well-written narrative should capture your interest. Does this narrative capture your interest? Explain your answer.
4. Where does the action part of the story begin?
5. Does the action move along or does the narrative seem slow? Explain your answer.
6. List descriptive words or action verbs that create strong images and emotional responses from you.
7. Does the concluding sentence evoke an emotional response from you? Explain.

The Structure of a Narrative

In Chapter 2, you learned that a paragraph is a well-organized series of sentences that develops one main idea about a specific topic the writer wishes to convey to a reader. The topic sentence, which has been narrowed, states the main idea of the paragraph (the controlling idea). The body of the paragraph provides the reader with carefully selected supporting details that develop and support the topic sentence with the controlling idea. A concluding sentence signals the end of the paragraph. Use this standard paragraph structure for the narratives that you write.

Developing the Topic Sentence

Use the following guidelines to write an effective topic sentence with a controlling idea that reveals your point of view, opinion, or attitude toward the subject of your paragraph.

1. Clearly identify a specific topic for your narrative. In order to stay within the scope of a paragraph, use one setting and one event that occurs in a relatively short time frame.
2. Use the topic sentence to show the reader the purpose or the intent of your paragraph by providing a glimpse or a hint about the significance of the event or the emotion you experienced. Is the controlling idea (your point of view, opinion, or attitude toward the subject) clear to your reader? Will your reader be able to predict the subject of the paragraph and possibly some of the details?

3. Reword or revise the topic sentence to attract the reader's interest. An effective topic sentence entices the reader to continue reading.

3.3 What do you think?

Answer yes or no to the following questions for the following topic sentences that are from previous narrative paragraphs.

1. *My heart never raced as fast as it did when I was cornered in a voodoo shop in Brazil.*

   a. Is the topic specific rather than broad or general?

   ____

   b. Does it give the impression that the paragraph will take place in one setting? ____________

   c. Does it give the impression that the story will cover a relatively short time frame? ____________

   d. Do you get a glimpse or a hint about the significance of the event to the writer?____________

   e. Do you get a glimpse or a hint about the emotions that might be evoked?____________

   f. Can you predict the kinds of details that might be in the paragraph? ____________

   g. Did the topic sentence capture your interest? ____________

   Were you enticed to read the paragraph to learn more about the topic? ____________

2. *Cancer can hit people whom you least expect to get sick.*

   a. Is the topic specific rather than broad or general? ____________

   b. Does it give the impression that the paragraph will take place in one setting? ____________

   c. Does it give the impression that the story will cover a relatively short time frame? ____________

   d. Do you get a glimpse or a hint about the significance of the event to the writer? ____________

   e. Do you get a glimpse or a hint about the emotions that might be evoked? ____________

   f. Can you predict the kinds of details that might be in the paragraph? ____________

   g. Did the topic sentence capture your interest? ____________

Developing the Body of the Paragraph

Use the following guidelines to develop the body of your paragraph and the controlling idea stated in your topic sentence.

1. Create *unity* by selecting a sequence of events that develops or supports the topic sentence.
   - Eliminate details that are insignificant or nonessential to the telling of the story. Each sentence in the body of the paragraph should be essential to the telling of the story.
   - Do not sidetrack from the main sequence of action in the story. Eliminate sentences that do not contribute to the development of the controlling idea.
   - Do not mix first person (*I* or *we*) and third person (*he*, *she*, or *they*).
2. Create *coherence* by writing the sequence of events in chronological order, which means that the story will be told in the order in which the individual actions occurred.
   - If you need to give brief background information before beginning the main sequence of action, place the background information after the topic sentence.
   - Generally, you should avoid shifts in time. Strive to tell the story without jumping back in time after you begin the main action of the narrative.
3. Use transition words and conjunctions that show time and create coherence.

COMMON TRANSITION WORDS FOR NARRATIVES					
after	afterward	at last	at the same time	as	as soon as
as long as	before	during	finally	first	furthermore
in the meantime	later	meanwhile	next	once	second
since	subsequently	then	third	until	when
whenever	while				

4. Use verbs in the simple past tense to show that the event or the story has already taken place. (See the Grammar and Usage Tips at the end of this chapter.)
5. Select descriptive words to create a strong visual image for the reader. Your goal is to re-create the event for the reader by activating his or her imagination. Use a thesaurus or a dictionary to locate precise words to express your ideas and emotions clearly to the reader.

- ☼ Keep the story moving by using action verbs instead of linking verbs. For example, saying *I wandered to the back of the store* is more effective than saying *I was in the back of the store.* Remember that a reader will lose interest in the story if the controlling idea is not developed at a reasonable pace.
- ☼ Create a vivid image of the story by selecting words that create a "movie in the mind of the reader." Carefully select adjectives and adverbs that describe the details and the action as precisely as possible. Your goal is to re-create the situation, the emotions, and your overall impressions for your reader.
- ☼ Select words that are consistent with the emotion or the mood of the paragraph. Avoid using words that convey a different or an opposite impression. For example, in the story about the voodoo shop, saying that *a warm feeling swept over me* would be inconsistent with the emotion of fear. Using the words *an eerie, chilling feeling crept over me* is consistent with the purpose of the paragraph and contributes to the development of the controlling idea that is stated in the topic sentence.

6. Include *adequate development* in your paragraph by selecting sufficient details to develop the story and re-create the experience for your reader.
    - ☼ Too few details will distance your reader from the experience, its significance, and the emotions that you want to convey. The reader will not understand or have an adequate sense of the character, the setting, the time frame, or the significance of the narrative.
    - ☼ Excessive details clutter the story, slow the story down, distract your reader, and weaken the emotional response and interest in the story.

3.4 What do you think?

Read the following narrative and respond to the questions that follow. Write your answers on separate paper.

My Father's Advice

Being lost for hours as a child in the woods is frightening. When I was seven, my best friend and I went out to cut firewood with our fathers. We wanted to do some exploring, so my father told us that there was a beaver dam at the bottom of the draw and that we could investigate. As we came upon the beaver dam, we were so thrilled and mesmerized that we lost track of the time. The sky was darkening, so we unwillingly started walking back, only to realize that in all of our excitement, we had lost track of where we were and where the path was to return us to our fathers. We stopped and listened to see if we could hear the sound of the chainsaws. We heard nothing but all the intimidating sounds of the great outdoors. I remembered one thing that my father had always told me: If I ever got lost in the woods, I should find a river or a creek and follow it downstream, and I would eventually come to a road. We walked along the stream for what seemed like hours before we finally found a road. We walked along the road until we came to the main road that we had traveled earlier in the pickup. I remembered that there was a little store just up the road. When we reached the store, the elderly couple who owned the store gave us something to eat and drove us back to the landing. Our fathers were just loading up the wood and the chainsaws. They were shocked when they saw us get out of the couple's car. That frightening experience in the woods taught me a very valuable lesson. Listening to my father's advice may actually have saved my life that day in the woods.

Kevin Peacher
Lane Community College
Eugene, Oregon

1. Does this paragraph have unity? Does each sentence contribute to the development of the topic sentence? Should the writer delete any sentences? Explain your answer.
2. Does the paragraph have coherence? Is the sequence of events in chronological order? Explain your answer.
3. List transition words that the writer uses to achieve coherence and develop the story chronologically.
4. Does the writer use verbs effectively? Are all the verbs in past tense? Does the writer use action verbs?

   Does the action move along at an appropriate pace? Explain your answer and include examples.
5. Does the choice of wording activate your imagination so you sense what the experience was like for a child? Explain your answer.
6. Is there adequate development? Is the number of details sufficient, too few, or excessive? Explain your answer.

3.5 What do you think?

Read the following narrative and respond to the questions that follow. Write your answers on separate paper.

Providing Life for a Child

In August of 1998, I made a decision that changed the life of a child in a poor country. I was at a Christian gathering in Atlanta, Georgia. Inside one of the rooms where a band was playing, I saw a display for Compassion International. This organization's goal is to give food, education, clothing, and health care to poor children around the world. As my eyes gazed at the table, I observed cream-colored papers neatly folded with the words "My Child of Compassion" sketched in chocolate-brown ink. My shaking hands carefully peeled the brochure open. A picture of a pale, heartbreaking face popped out at me. The gorgeous black hair on the young girl surrounded her soft, oval face. Her licorice eyes whispered her poor state of living conditions. Her frail, worn-out body yearned for tender loving care. My heart skipped a beat; I had to save this child's life! Eagerly, I picked up a pen and filled out the information on the form. Twenty-four dollars a month was all it would take to provide this girl with the health care and the attention she deserved. Finally, her parents would have hope of seeing their daughter grow up healthy. As the intern from Compassion International gave me the information for sponsoring this gift from God, my face beamed with joy. Somewhere, I was making the wish of this little girl's hope of breathing one more day come to life.

Tracey Thomas
Carroll Community College
Westminster, Maryland

1. Does this paragraph have unity? Does each sentence contribute to the development of the topic sentence? Should the writer delete any sentences? Explain your answer.
2. Does the paragraph have coherence? Is the sequence of events in chronological order? Explain your answer.
3. List the transition words the writer uses to achieve coherence and develop the story chronologically.
4. Does the writer use verbs effectively? Are all the verbs in past tense? Does the writer use action verbs? Does the action move along at an appropriate pace? Explain your answer and include examples.

5. Does the choice of wording activate your imagination so you can sense the writer's experience of making the decision to sponsor a child? Explain your answer.
6. Is there adequate development? Is the number of details sufficient, too few, or excessive? Explain your answer.

Developing the Concluding Sentence

Use the following guidelines to bring your paragraph to an end.

1. Write a concluding sentence that echoes the topic sentence. A concluding sentence that varies too much from the topic sentence often signals that you got sidetracked and that the paragraph lacks unity and coherence.
2. Use the same emotion and sense of significance that you stated in the controlling idea and expressed throughout the paragraph.
3. Check that your concluding sentence comfortably flows from the body of the paragraph and does not give your reader the sense that it was tacked on as an afterthought.

3.6 What do you think?

Read the topic sentences and the concluding sentences for the three narratives you have just read. Explain whether you think the concluding sentence is effective. Be specific. If you think the sentence is not effective, suggest an alternative concluding sentence.

1. Topic Sentence: My heart never raced as fast as it did when I was cornered in a voodoo shop in Brazil.

   Concluding Sentence: I knew from that moment that curiosity and dares are not strong enough reasons to wander into places where I do not belong.

   I think ______________________________

   ____

   ____

2. Topic Sentence: Being lost for hours as a child in the woods is frightening.

   Concluding Sentence: Listening to my father's advice may actually have saved my life that day in the woods.

   I think ______________________________

   ____

   ____

3. Topic Sentence: In August of 1998, I made a decision that changed the life of a child in a poor country.

   Concluding Sentence: Somewhere, I was making the wish of this little girl's hope of breathing one more day come to life.

   I think ____

   ____

   ____

The Writing Process for Narratives

Step 1: Generate ideas.

Everyone has a wealth of experiences that can be used as the topic of a narrative. The following topics will help you generate possible ideas for your narrative paragraph. Place a star next to ideas you may want to develop.

1. A personal experience that was exciting, scary, funny, humiliating, sentimental, inspiring, or motivational
2. A family story that has been passed down through the generations
3. A memory of a transition or time of change, such as an experience moving, a job interview, getting hired or fired, an engagement, graduation, getting your license, leaving home, or entering the military
4. A first-time event, such as skiing, driving a car, flying, bungee jumping, seeing an ocean/volcano/snow, getting a speeding ticket, going on a blind date, or getting caught doing something inappropriate
5. A personal experience in which you learned a valuable lesson
6. A story related to a specific emotion: joy, pride, jealousy, embarrassment, helplessness, faith, friendship, remorse, disgrace, awe, or anger
7. An unusual adventure, such as a rafting trip, climbing a volcano, scuba diving, entering a foreign country, participating in a search and rescue mission, or skydiving

List other possible ideas that came to mind as you read the above list or as you reread some of the previous narrative paragraphs in this chapter:

3.7 What do you think?

Brainstorming is the process of listing as many ideas for a writing topic as possible. During the process of brainstorming, do not evaluate, accept, or discard ideas; instead, simply list them quickly and evaluate them later. On separate paper, write headings for the following four topics that are from the introductory list of possible topics for a narrative. Under each heading, list as many events or incidents in your life that you could possibly use for a narrative.

A funny incident	**Different emotions**
The first time I . . .	**An unusual adventure**

Step 2: Get a focus.

After you select a general topic, your next step is to focus the topic and make it specific. Narrowing the topic for a narrative involves finding a starting point and a finishing point for your story. Many events lead up to your story and many events follow the main part of your story. The goal is to focus the paragraph on the key time frame when the action you wish to describe took place.

For example, in the narrative "Scared Stiff" on pages 94–95, the writer and her friends were involved in activities prior to wandering downtown to kill time. However, the story would have dragged on too long and the reader might have lost interest if the writer had included all of the events of the day leading up to the window shopping at a voodoo shop. Instead, the writer decided that the reader did not need to know the information prior to the event. Invariably, conversations and other events followed the exit from the voodoo shop. Again, the writer decided to end the main action part of the story by fleeing from the shop. Continuing to tell "what they did next" would have diluted the drama and the emotions of the story.

The following guidelines can help you focus the topic of your narrative:

1. Limit the main action of the story to one setting. For example, "Scared Stiff" takes place in a voodoo shop in Brazil. "My Father's Advice" takes place in the woods.
2. Limit the time frame. Sometimes the situation of the story occurred in a matter of minutes or at the most a few hours. Extending the time frame to a day or longer may move the narrative paragraph outside the range or scope of a paragraph. For example, "Scared Stiff" occurs within a five-minute time frame. "My Father's Advice" occurs within a time frame of several hours.

Focusing the topic also involves paying attention to your audience and the purpose of your paragraph. For your narrative paragraph, the audience is your classmates and your instructor. Your purpose is to tell a story and let your reader know its significance to you. Your purpose is also to evoke feelings or emotions from your reader that are similar to the ones you experienced at the time of the event.

Keep in mind that the writing process involves revisions throughout the various steps of writing. If you find yourself moving unnecessarily from one location to another when you write your first draft, seek ways to limit the main action of the narrative to only one location. If you find the story encompasses a time frame longer than a few hours, examine whether the longer time frame is essential to the story. If it can be shortened, seek ways to delete the events that lead up to or follow the main action of the paragraph.

Step 3: Gather and organize your information.

Once you select and focus your topic, the next step is to gather information and details for your paragraph, organize them chronologically, and then write a strong topic sentence.

Clustering

Clustering is an excellent technique for organizing details on paper. Write your narrowed topic in the center of your paper. Begin the details in your cluster in the upper left-hand corner of your paper. Use words, phrases, or short sentences to indicate the starting point of your story. Continue adding the sequence of events in a chronological order, writing them in a clockwise direction. Add all the details that come to your mind. You can eliminate unnecessary details later.

For example, a cluster for "My Father's Advice" may have looked like the following cluster. Notice that all of the details in the cluster were not used in the final paragraph.

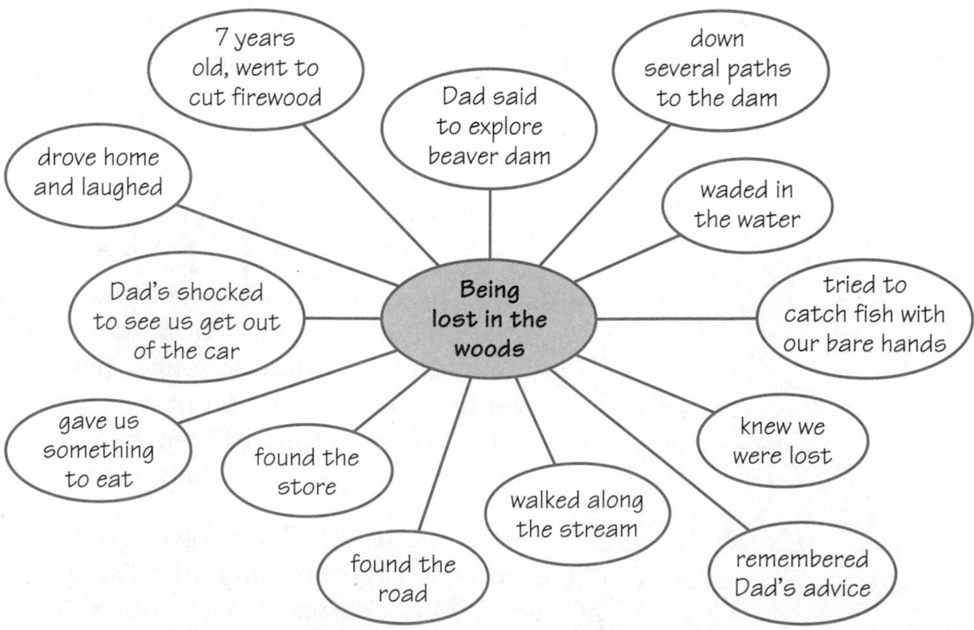

Developing the Topic Sentence

At this stage in the writing process, you have selected a topic, narrowed the topic to reflect your audience and purpose, gathered ample ideas that may work as details for your paragraph, and organized them in a cluster. You now have a much stronger sense of the direction you can move with this narrative. Using all of this preliminary information, it is time to draft a strong topic sentence.

Your **topic sentence** needs to clearly state the controlling idea for your paragraph in a direct and powerful way. Recall the following key points about topic sentences:

1. The topic sentence should state a specific, narrowed main idea.
2. The topic sentence should get right to the point so the reader clearly understands your purpose and senses the emotions, the significance, or the type of incident that will be developed in the paragraph.
3. The topic sentence should capture the reader's interest. Your choice of words and the way you state the controlling idea need to intrigue the reader and create a desire in the reader to read the paragraph for more details.
4. The topic sentence is usually placed at the beginning of the paragraph to help the writer and the reader stay focused on the topic.

Writing a powerful topic sentence often involves writing several possible topic sentences and then revising and refining one of the sentences. Because the topic sentence controls the content of the paragraph, spend ample time writing, rewording, revising, and refining your topic sentence. Do not settle too quickly on a topic sentence. Select a topic sentence to use only after you have experimented with several possibilities and have created one that truly meets with your satisfaction.

One student wanted to write about a Vietnam veteran named Charles. The student wrote and reworded the following topic sentences before an effective topic sentence (# 6) emerged:

1. Charles visited the Vietnam Memorial for the first time in September.
2. Charles was not sure he wanted to visit the Vietnam Memorial near his home in Washington, D.C.
3. Charles had strong ~~feelings~~ reservations about ^visiting the Vietnam Memorial.
4. Charles had stronger feelings about the Vietnam Memorial than most people ~~had~~ could comprehend.

5. The Vietnam Memorial triggered more feelings for Charles than most people could comprehend.
6. The Vietnam Memorial represented more to Charles than most people can ^ever begin to^ comprehend.

Step 4: Write the rough draft.

Remember, a rough draft is exactly that: rough. A rough draft is the starting point for later revisions and editing. It is your first attempt to move your ideas from your head and your planning sheet onto paper in paragraph form.

Use the following suggestions for writing your rough draft:

1. Double space your work so you have space on the paper to add words or phrases or make minor revisions even as you write the rough draft.
2. If you know how to use a computer and type at a rate that allows your ideas to flow, write the rough draft on the computer. Revising and editing are easier to do on a computer. If your typing rate slows you down, or if you are not comfortable composing on the computer, handwrite the rough draft and then type it on the computer later.
3. Focus mainly on getting your ideas on paper. Do not be concerned at this time with grammar, spelling, or sentence structure. During this step, you want your ideas to flow as smoothly as possible so you can capture your thoughts without hesitation.
4. Use your cluster as a guide. Since the cluster is done in chronological order, it can guide the order of the information in your paragraph. Recognize, however, as you write your draft, you can insert additional key ideas that are not on your cluster. Also, you may find that some ideas on the cluster can be deleted because they do not seem to belong in the paragraph.

Step 5: Revise, revise, revise.

Revising is the process of carefully reading what you have written, thinking about your purpose and the information you want to communicate, and then making changes to improve and strengthen your paragraph. During the revision step, ask yourself, "Can I revise further to strengthen the paragraph in other ways?" The answer is almost always "yes."

Methods for revising will vary from one person to another and one assignment to another, but here are some possible stages of revision:

1. Evaluate the effectiveness of the topic sentence and the concluding sentence. The topic sentence should indicate the topic, provide the reader with clues about the event, significance, and/or emotion, get right to the point, and capture your reader's interest. The concluding sentence should echo the topic sentence; if the concluding sentence does not reflect the same topic, emotion, and significance of the topic sentence, you need to revise it further.
2. Evaluate your effective use of the three elements of the body of a paragraph: unity, coherence, and adequate development. Revise as needed.
3. Evaluate your use of transition words. Do you use appropriate transition words to connect the events and show the reader the coherence of the story?
4. Evaluate your effective use of words. Can you use more effective action verbs? Do you need to include more descriptive language, such as more adjectives or adverbs? Do the words in the paragraph really say what you want to say and convey the emotions and impressions you want to convey?
5. Evaluate the effectiveness of your sentences. Can you combine some sentences more effectively?
6. Use the checklist in Chapter 1 (page 26) to identify other elements in your paragraph that can be strengthened.

Feedback from your peers, friends, or writing tutors is valuable during the revision process. Give the checklist above and your paper to someone whose opinion you value. Listen carefully and objectively to his or her suggestions; consider ways to incorporate the feedback that will strengthen your paper. You can also use Step 5 on the Planning Sheet (page 117) to obtain feedback from a classmate. If you prefer your wording or organization after carefully considering other people's suggestions, you are the final decision-maker.

In the following paragraph, the writer revised the paragraph by evaluating the structure of the paragraph. She made changes with the topic sentence, the body of the paragraph, and the concluding sentence. She carefully checked the unity, coherence, and adequate development in the paragraph. She also focused her attention on the wording and sentence structure. She experimented with alternative ways to express her ideas and feelings more precisely.

3.8 What do you think?

Read the following paragraph, paying close attention to the revisions. On separate paper, answer the questions that follow the final revision.

One Mysterious Night

I will never forget the mysterious night I experienced long ago.
~~It all happened so long ago, but I hope to never forget one mysterious~~
A strange
~~night~~. ~~The~~ sound ~~is what~~ enticed me to go outside. The minute I
stepped out, my mind raced for some explanation. I thought of aircraft,
machinery, autos, even the many sounds of the mountains and timbers.
definitely such sounds
Nothing matched. ~~It was definitely something~~ I had never heard before.
by the creek about
One of my dogs was tied ~~out~~ fifty feet from the house ~~by the creek~~.
darted
On impulse, wanting to have him with me, I ~~walked~~ over to him.
When I turned around to start back to the house, a ~~strobe-~~bright
strobe
blue-green, iridescent, shimmering light covered the ground between
the creek and the house. It was not a beam coming down from the
mass of illuminating, shimmering light.
sky, but a fifty-foot square ~~hunk of light, illuminating and shimmering~~.
Strange feelings, not of fear,
~~It is hard to explain the feelings that went through my body. It was not~~
~~fear~~, but more like ~~strange~~ chills, almost like the ground was dropping
, shot through my body.
out from under me. The dog and I just stood there awestruck. Then,
my body was vibrating.
the light disappeared. When we got back to the house, ~~vibrating at this~~
~~point~~, I grabbed the double-barreled shotgun that was just inside the
door. I took one look at it and had to smile. What was I going to do
with this shotgun? I had my suspicions at that point as to what was
After several minutes of thoughts racing through my head,
going on. ~~I don't know how long I spent with my thoughts until~~ my
curiosity took over. Once again I went outside to have a look. This
time the same light caught my eye in the timbers. The light was below
the canopy of the trees, in a long rectangle with no visible beam
shimmered
coming down. It ~~was just shimmering~~, and then it vanished. To this
the lights were that I saw.
day, not one person can tell me what ~~it was~~. All I know is that ~~it is~~
the night of the mysterious lights
~~an experience~~ I will never forget.

Kathleen Maddux
Lane Community College
Eugene, Oregon

1. Does the topic sentence capture your interest? Why or why not?
2. What emotion does this paragraph convey to you?
3. List four or more words or expressions in the paragraph that you feel support or develop this emotion in the paragraph.
4. Does the story move along at an effective pace? Explain your answer.
5. Using descriptive words, such as adjectives and adverbs, and using descriptive action verbs help the reader create a strong visual image of the story as it unfolds. List adjectives, adverbs, and action verbs in the paragraph that helped create a visual image of this story in your mind.

3.8 What do you think?

With a partner or on your own, suggest a topic sentence with a controlling idea for the following paragraph. Then evaluate the concluding sentence to see if it echoes your topic sentence, and revise it if you wish. You may write any suggestions directly above or below the concluding sentence. After you have worked with the topic sentence and the concluding sentence, answer the questions that follow the paragraph. Write your answers on separate paper.

A Strange Expression

Topic sentence: ______________________________

I was on the phone one day with one of the taxicab licensing examiners, inquiring about the result of my test taken two days earlier; unfortunately, he told me that I had not passed the test and I should take the test again. I was upset, as every person would be when he or she has failed. I hesitantly replied, "Thank you very much, sir." He then swiftly answered, "You bet," and hung up the phone. I was amazed when I heard the expression *you bet* because I thought it had something to do with wagering. The expression seemed irrelevant to our conversation. I kept thinking about the expression and trying to figure out what he meant, but I could not. The expression kept troubling me because I am a guy, who, for some reason, feels uncomfortable with things that puzzle me until I get some sort of answer. Luckily, in the middle of last quarter, I decided to take the matter to my English teacher. He explained that *you bet* simply means *of course* or *sure*. From that day onward, if I come across a strange phrase or expression, I am not bothered anymore because I learned that when words are put into a phrase, the original meaning can completely change.

Taman Khakal
Bellevue Community College
Bellevue, Washington

1. Does this paragraph have *unity?* Explain your answer.
2. Does this paragraph have *coherence?* Explain your answer.
3. Does this paragraph have *adequate development?*
4. Learning another language is often difficult; expressions or idioms that are used on a daily basis make English a difficult language to learn. List the details in the paragraph that show the student's reaction to the expression *you bet.*
5. What is the main purpose or point this writer wants to make for the reader?
6. What emotion does this paragraph evoke from you?

3.9 What do you think?

The writer in the following paragraph did an excellent job of getting her ideas on paper. For the first revision, the writer focused on deleting information that was nonessential to the development of the narrative. To create a sharper focus on the grandmother, she deleted first-person statements that used the word *I.* She created a stronger topic-sentence by moving one sentence. She combined other sentences. Read the original paragraph, compare it to the revision, and then answer the questions that follow the revised paragraph. Write your answers on separate paper.

My Grandmother

Convert to a topic sentence.

She had gone out on the porch without any cause and glanced at the road like she was waiting for somebody.

She came into the kitchen holding the letter in her hands and cautiously put it on the mirror where she kept the pictures of her children and her grandchildren. She continued to make lunch, frequently glancing at the letter. She returned to the letter when all her chores were done because she could not read the letter in a hurry. ~~At this point, I understood her behavior in the past days. I understood why~~ she had gone out on the porch without any cause and glanced at the road like she was waiting for somebody. ~~She had waited for this letter~~ for the last two weeks. She sat in her favorite chair near the window, straightened her apron and long brown skirt, and checked the buttons on her always snow-white, starched blouse. She carefully took the envelope and held it with maximum attention like it was rare china. ~~I recalled in that moment that these hands could do all kinds of work. Indeed, during hard work, they were strong and sinewy. At the same time, I have never seen more adept hands than hers. For example, her fingers moved faster than bird wings while she was picking berries from plants, and while she was sewing or knitting. They were always white, warm, and smelled sweet like the biscuits she often baked. Now~~ her fingers touched the envelope as if they

Delete references to first person (I).

wanted to guess its contents. At last, she opened it, took a breath, and started to read. Her eyes began to shine happily, narrowed, and blinked frequently because of tears. A net of tiny wrinkles covered her face. ~~Now she began to look like that smiling girl putting on the old fashioned dress in the old picture I saw once in my grandmother's photo album. It was my grandmother many years ago but in the same happy and exciting moment. Now I saw their similarities. In happiness, they have the same expression. In two minutes, I realized she had passed to another part of the letter.~~ Her eyes stopped blinking and became wider. Her eyebrows flew together. Her lips moved slowly, pronouncing the words to understand better their meaning. Her back, stretched before, folded forward like the gravity she suddenly felt. She unbuttoned the upper button of her blouse as if there was not enough air. One hand nervously fingered the tip of her apron. The other hand that held the letter was shaking more than before. ~~I was so sorry for her. In this moment, I wanted to protect her from the whole world, but I could not.~~ My grandmother lifted her wet eyes and looked for a while through the window at the bending of the fragile birch in the hard wind. She carefully put the letter on the mirror and stood silently for a moment. Her soul stormed like the weather and felt the severe torments like that thin but flexible tree.

Keep the focus on the main action

Do not mix first and third person.

Irena Buynova
Bellevue Community College
Bellevue, Washington

My Grandmother

For two weeks my grandmother had frequently gone out on the porch and glanced down the road like she was waiting for someone. Finally, one day she came into the kitchen holding a letter in her hands. She put the letter on the mirror where she kept the pictures of her children and her grandchildren and continued to make lunch, frequently glancing at the letter. She returned to the letter when all her chores were done because she could not read the letter in a hurry. She sat in her favorite chair near the window, straightened her apron and long brown skirt, and checked the buttons on her always snow-white, starched blouse. She carefully took the envelope and held it with maximum attention like it was rare china. Her fingers touched the envelope as if they wanted to guess its contents. At last, she opened it, took a breath, and started to read. Her eyes began to shine happily, narrowed, and blinked frequently because of tears. A net of tiny wrinkles covered her face. Her eyes stopped blinking and became wider. Her eyebrows flew together. Her lips moved slowly, pronouncing the words to understand better their meaning. Her back, stretched before, folded forward like the gravity she suddenly felt. She unbuttoned the upper button of her blouse as if there was not enough air. One hand nervously fingered the tip of her apron. The other hand that held the letter was shaking more than before. My grandmother lifted her wet eyes and looked for a while through the window at the bending of the fragile birch in the hard wind. She carefully put the letter on the mirror and stood silently for a moment. Her soul stormed like the weather and felt the severe torments like that thin but flexible tree.

1. Do you prefer the topic sentence of the first paragraph or the second paragraph? Why?
2. Is the story told in chronological order?
3. List transition words that are used to achieve coherence.
4. Do you have a clear picture of Grandmother in your mind? Why or why not?
5. Approximately how much time passes during the main action of the story? Is this an appropriate or inappropriate amount of time for a narrative paragraph? Explain.
6. Sometimes a concluding sentence does not echo the topic sentence closely, but it still works as a conclusion to the story. Do you think the concluding sentence is effective or not? Explain your answer.
7. Does the draft or the revised paragraph have a greater emotional impact on you? Why?
8. What do you think the contents of the letter were?

Step 6: Proofread and edit.

After you complete one or more revisions, your attention now needs to focus on the mechanics of your writing. **Proofreading** requires careful and accurate reading of the individual words and sentences in your paragraph. Get into the habit of reading each sentence out loud to increase your proofreading accuracy. **Editing** involves correcting any errors you identify during the process of proofreading. During the process of proofreading, pay close attention to spelling, punctuation, and sentence structure.

Use the following checklist to guide you through the proofreading and editing of your narrative.

1. Check that every sentence has a subject and a complete verb.
2. Check that you used subject and object pronouns correctly. (Refer to Chapter 2, pages 72–74.)
3. Correct any fragments by adding the missing subjects, verbs, or words to form a complete thought.
4. Consider greater sentence variety by including some sentences with compound subjects or compound verbs.
5. Check that all the verbs are in past tense.
6. Check the spelling of all words.
7. Check that each sentence begins with a capital letter and ends with a period or a question mark.
8. Check that you used descriptive words (adjectives and adverbs) correctly and effectively.

Step 7: Prepare the final version of your narrative.

For the final version of your narrative, use the format shown in Chapter 1, page 28, unless your instructor specifies another format to use. On the top of your paper, write a heading that includes your name, the name of the course and the instructor, the name of the assignment, and the date.

For easy reference, give your narrative a title. Then, if possible, type your final paragraph. Papers that are typed are usually easier to read and have a neater appearance. Use double spacing between lines. Use a 12 point font. Type each sentence carefully. Check that you have incorporated all the editing changes made in Step 6.

By using this seven-step approach to writing, you should have a finished product that reflects your very best quality of work. The time you have spent writing, revising, and refining will be reflected in your final version.

WRITING ASSIGNMENT

Use the steps of the writing process to write a narrative paragraph.

Complete each of the following steps for writing a narrative paragraph. Unless your instructor indicates a different approach, use the Narrative Planning Sheet on page 117 for each step of the writing process.

Step 1: Gather ideas.
Select a topic for your narrative paragraph. Refer to the brainstorming ideas on pages 104 and 105. Write the topic on the Planning Sheet. If you need additional ideas, consider one of the following:

a humbling experience	a desperate act	a memorable holiday
the birth of a child	an ambulance ride	giving roadside help
an act you regret	a haunting experience	being the butt of a joke
a disastrous party	a hospital visit	a moment of glory
an act of generosity	putting a pet to sleep	experiencing someone's death
a careless accident	an April Fool's prank	getting locked in
visiting a kindergarten	winning a game	defying a parent or authority figure

Step 2: Get a focus.
Focus the topic for your paragraph. Answer the questions for Step 2 on the Planning Sheet.

Step 3: Gather and organize your information.
On separate paper, create a cluster to show the different details you plan to include in your paragraph. Begin near the top of the cluster. List the details in chronological order and in a clockwise direction around the center of the paper. Then, write several topic sentences to consider for the paragraph. Select the topic sentence that works best as a controlling idea for your narrative.

Step 4: Write a rough draft.
Write your rough draft. Answer the question for Step 4 on the Planning Sheet.

Step 5: Revise, revise, revise.
Use the checklist on page 109 to guide the revision process. On the Planning Sheet, use the Partner Feedback form to get feedback from one of your classmates. Revise your paragraph.

Step 6: Proofread and edit.
Use the checklist on page 115 to guide the proofreading and editing process. Answer the question for Step 6 on the Planning Sheet.

Step 7: Prepare the final version of your paragraph.
Use the guidelines provided by your instructor or the guidelines on page 115. If your instructor does not ask you to turn in your prewriting materials and drafts, save them in a file.

NARRATIVE PLANNING SHEET

Name______________________________

Step 1: Write your topic for a narrative paragraph:

____

Step 2: Show your plans for focusing your topic:

What is the one specific setting for your narrative? ______________________________

How long is the time frame for the main action of your paragraph? ______________________________

What emotions do you want to evoke in the reader, or what impression do you want to create in the reader's mind? ______________________________

____

Step 3: On separate paper, create a cluster to show possible details for your paragraph. Attach your cluster to this Planning Sheet.

Write several possible topic sentences for your paragraph.

Option 1: ______________________________

____

Option 2: ______________________________

____

Option 3: ______________________________

____

Place a star next to the topic sentence you prefer.

Step 4: When did you finish writing the rough draft? ______________________________

Step 5: Revise, revise, revise. Save all your revisions. Ask a partner to read your latest revision and to answer the following questions.

PARTNER FEEDBACK FORM

1. Is the topic sentence specific, to the point, and interesting? Explain. ______________________

____

____

2. Does every sentence support the controlling idea? Is there unity? Explain. ______________

____

____

3. Are the details in chronological order? Explain. ______________________________

____

____

4. List any transition words. Does the writer use them effectively? Explain. ______________

____

____

5. Is there adequate development? What details can be deleted? What additional details might be added? Explain. ____

____

____

6. Are there enough descriptive words to create an image of the event in your mind? ________

____

____

7. Does the concluding sentence echo the topic sentence? ______________________

____

8. What mechanical errors did you notice that the writer will need to correct? ____________

____

____

Partner's name ______________________________

Step 6: Proofread and edit. Save the drafts that show your proofreading and editing work. Write the date you completed this step: ______________________________

Step 7: Prepare the final version of your narrative paragraph.

Grammar and Usage Tips

Carefully read the three new grammar and usage tips. Complete the exercises following each tip. After you have completed the exercises, carefully check your work with the answer keys in Appendix A and record your number of errors for each exercise. Review the tip and examine the correct answer. In the margins of each exercise, jot down questions that you would like to ask your instructor regarding the grammar and usage points covered.

Use simple past-tense verbs in narrative paragraphs. For regular verbs, add an *-ed* suffix to the main form of the verb to make the simple past tense. For irregular verbs, use the past tense form of the verb, which does not use an *-ed* suffix.

Verb Tenses

Verb tenses tell when an action occurs, occurred, or will occur within a given sentence. Verb tenses also indicate whether the action or the state of being is continued or completed. There are three simple verb tenses:

Simple Present Tense: I *plan* to write my narrative rough draft today.

Simple Past Tense: I *planned* to write my narrative rough draft yesterday.

Simple Future Tense: I *will plan* to write my narrative rough draft this weekend.

Simple past tense expresses an action that has already taken place and is completed. The simple past tense of a verb is formed with one word. In most situations, the simple past tense should be used in narrative writing because the action has already taken place and is completed. A sentence with compound verbs, such as in the last sentence in the following examples, has two or more action verbs in simple past tense. Each of the action verbs shown in bold print in the following sentences are in simple past tense.

The foreign objects **intrigued** me.

My shaking hands carefully **peeled** open the brochure.

We **stopped** and **listened** for the sound of the chainsaws.

Simple Past Tense of Regular Verbs

Regular verbs are action verbs that use a set pattern to form the past tense. The past tense is formed by using the *-ed* suffix. As you will notice in the following list of action verbs and their past tenses, minor spelling changes occur when the *-ed* suffix is added to some words. A final *e* on the end of a word may be dropped before the *-ed* suffix is added, or the final consonant of a word may be doubled before the *-ed* suffix is added. Consult a dictionary or a spell checker if you are uncertain of the correct spelling of a regular verb in the simple past tense.

Present Tense	Simple Past Tense
anchor	anchored
bounce	bounced
strap	strapped
hum	hummed
enjoy	enjoyed
name	named

Simple Past Tense of Irregular Verbs

Irregular verbs are action verbs that do not use the set pattern of an *-ed* suffix to form the past tense. As you will notice in the following list of irregular verbs, some irregular verbs form the past tense by using a new word with a spelling that is different from the present-tense verb; others use the same word for both the simple present and the simple past tenses.

Present Tense	Simple Past Tense	Present Tense	Simple Past Tense
choose	chose	beat	beat
break	broke	burst	burst
catch	caught	cast	cast
dig	dug	cost	cost
freeze	froze	cut	cut
flee	fled	hurt	hurt
lead	led	put	put
swim	swam	quit	quit
think	thought	shut	shut

In Appendix B you will find a comprehensive list of the past tense for irregular verbs. Refer to the list or to a dictionary when you are uncertain of the past tense of an irregular verb. When you consult a dictionary, begin by locating the word and the definitions for the word as a present-tense verb. Immediately following the label that indicates the word works as a verb, the past tense form of the word appears. Carefully check the spelling of the past tense of irregular verbs.

EXERCISE 3.1 Using Simple Past-Tense Verbs

Score: ______

Circle the correct past-tense verb in the following sentences. Consult the list of past-tense verbs in Appendix B if needed.

1. We (chose, choose) to window shop on an unfamiliar street.
2. A little bell on the shop door (rang, rung).
3. Several shrunken heads (hung, hanged) from the ceiling.
4. My head (spun, spinned) and my knees (shaked, shook).
5. The clock (struck, striked) midnight.
6. We (shutted, shut) the door behind us and (swore, sweared) never to return.
7. He (paid, payed) the parking ticket.
8. The crows (stealed, stole) all the food from our grocery bags.
9. They (slitted, slit) the bags and scattered the contents.
10. After dinner, he (ground, grinded) the coffee beans and made fresh coffee.

EXERCISE 3.2 Writing Past Tenses for Irregular Verbs

Score: ______

Without referring to the list of verbs in Appendix B, write the past tense for each of the following irregular verbs. After you have completed this exercise, check your answers with the list of verbs in Appendix B.

1. ride ______	2. buy ______	3. bite ______
4. bend ______	5. spread ______	6. sweep ______
7. weep ______	8. set ______	9. fight ______
10. lay ______	11. rise ______	12. creep ______
13. broadcast ______	14. keep ______	15. speed ______

16. sting ________	17. swing ________	18. lend ________
19. draw ________	20. feel ________	21. cling ________
22. bear ________	23. lie ________	24. sling ________
25. shake ________	26. know ________	27. shoot ________
28. take ________	29. drink ________	30. bleed ________

For sentence variety, combine two independent clauses to form compound sentences. Three methods can be used to combine independent clauses; use the appropriate punctuation between the independent clauses.

Three Methods for Creating Compound Sentences

Writing that consists solely of simple sentences tends to bore the reader, move more slowly, and become wordy. Compound sentences add variety and sophistication to your writing. Knowing how to combine simple sentences to make compound sentences provides you with more options for expressing your ideas clearly. The following chart shows the three methods that you will learn to make compound sentences.

THREE METHODS FOR MAKING COMPOUND SENTENCES		
INDEPENDENT CLAUSE	+	INDEPENDENT CLAUSE
Subject + Verb + Complete Thought	connector	Subject + Verb + Complete Thought
1. Coordinating Conjunctions*	2. Semicolon	3. Semicolon + conjunctive adverb + comma
, and *, but* *, for* *, nor*	*;*	*; nevertheless,* *; therefore,*
, or *, so* *, yet*		*; however,* *; in addition, etc.*

*An acronym can be used to remember these coordinating conjunctions: FANBOYS. Each letter of this acronym represents one of the coördinating conjunctions.

Independent Clauses

An **independent clause** is a clause that has a subject and a complete verb, forms a complete thought, and can stand by itself as a sentence. An independent clause is a simple sentence; a compound sentence is a sentence in which two independent clauses are joined.

SIMPLE SENTENCES	COMPOUND SENTENCE
Simple Sentences = Two Independent Clauses	Two Independent Clauses Joined
Thirty students enrolled in the course. Only nineteen students remained at the end of the term.	Thirty students enrolled in the course, **but** only nineteen students remained at the end of the term.
Record rain fell overnight. Roads were closed due to mudslides.	Record rain fell overnight; roads were closed due to mudslides.
Cindy is transferring to the university. She wants to take transferrable courses.	Cindy is transferring to the university; **therefore,** she wants to take transferrable courses.

Conjunctions are connectors, or words that join two or more words, phrases, or clauses. Two kinds of conjunctions can join independent clauses: coordinating conjunctions and conjunctive adverbs.

Method 1 to Form Compound Sentences

Join two independent clauses with a comma and a coordinating conjunction. Seven words can serve as coordinating conjunctions: *and, but, for, nor, or, so,* and *yet.* Conjunctions must be selected carefully to show the appropriate relationship between the two clauses. The following chart shows the meanings of each conjunction.

COORDINATING CONJUNCTIONS		
COORDINATING CONJUNCTION	FUNCTIONS	EXAMPLES
And	-shows clauses of equal value -adds information -means "in addition to" or "along with"	My youngest sister is a nurse, **and** my oldest sister is a veterinarian. I attended all the lectures, **and** I completed my term paper. I bought a new computer, **and** I signed up for an email account.
But	-shows an opposite idea, a contrast, or a difference -means "except" or "however"	I wanted to attend your wedding, **but** I could not afford the airfare. The incident occured on Saturday, **but** no one heard about it until Monday. My taxes are due in a few days, **but** I do not have time to complete the forms.

(Continue on page 124)

COORDINATING CONJUNCTIONS		
COORDINATING CONJUNCTION	FUNCTIONS	EXAMPLES
For	-shows how the action of the first clause occurs because of the action of the second clause -shows a reason or cause -means "because"	Robert could not order a transcript, **for** he had forgotten his identification. Maurice is transferring to Chicago, **for** his fiancee has accepted a job with a newspaper there. I did not receive the magazine, **for** my subscription had expired.
Nor	-joins two negative ideas -means "not"	My study partner is not supportive, **nor** is he interested in helping me with my research paper. I cannot find a job, **nor** can I find a place to live. The students could not get enough signatures on the petition, **nor** could they find enough volunteers.
Or	-shows a choice between two options or possibilities	I could pick up the groceries, **or** you could stop on your way home. Professor Wilson will be in his office, **or** he will leave the information posted on his door. We can go to the mall, **or** we can skateboard in the park.
So	-shows that the action of the first clause causes the action of the second clause to occur -means "therefore"	I studied until four o'clock in the morning, **so** I am tired. My mother knows sign language, **so** she offered to interpret for a deaf woman in the grocery store. I was sorry for my rude comments, **so** I apologized.
Yet	-shows that one action occurs in spite of the other action -means "however," "nevertheless," or "but still"	Walking and running are good cardiovascular exercises, **yet** many people fail to make time for exercise. The bus is an inexpensive form of transportation, **yet** few students ride the bus to school. Smoking causes health problems, **yet** millions of people continue to smoke.

Conjunctions Can Join Two Words or Phrases

Some coordinating conjunctions can also be used to join two words or two phrases. When two words or two phrases are joined with a coordinating conjunction, do not use a comma.

The lanterns **and** the flashlights provide campers with light at night.

The flowers sat on her desk **yet** did not attend her attention.

My rent **but** not my car payment is due on the first of each month.

Citations **or** warnings are frequently issued on that stretch of the freeway.

Conjunctions Can Join Three or More Words in a Series

When the conjunction *and* or *or* is used to join three or more words or phrases in a series, use a comma before the conjunction. The following examples show commas between words or phrases that appear in simple sentences.

The woman on the bike was obviously upset, angry**, and** belligerent.

One of the Blue Angel jets dove for several feet, leveled out**, and** regained altitude.

You can order salmon, shark**, or** oysters on the special seafood menu.

The Conjunction *Nor*

The coordinating conjunction *nor* works differently than the other conjunctions. When two independent clauses are joined with the conjunction *nor,* the subject and verb pattern in the second clause is inverted. The negative *not* in the second clause is replaced with the conjunction *nor,* which has the same meaning as *not.*

Simple Sentences: I could **not** find the map. I could **not** use my pocket compass.

Compound Sentence: I could **not** find the map**, nor** could I use my pocket compass.

Simple Sentences: The teacher would **not** tolerate tardiness. He would **not** accept late papers.

Compound Sentence: The teacher would **not** tolerate tardiness**, nor** would he accept late papers.

The Conjunction *For*

The word *for* can work as a preposition to begin a prepositional phrase, or it can work as a conjunction to form a compound sentence. When you are editing your work and see the word *for* in a sentence, analyze the sentence carefully to determine whether the word is beginning a prepositional phrase or connecting two independent clauses. When *for* is used as a conjunction to connect two independent clauses, it has the same meaning as the word *because.*

Conjunction: The police arrived, **for** the child had dialed 911.

Conjunction: The city council members voted to adjourn, **for** they had discussed all the agenda items.

Preposition: All items (**for** the next council meeting) need to be received by Monday.

Preposition: The minutes (**for** today) will be sent to you via email.

EXERCISE 3.3 Writing Compound Sentences

Score: ______

Combine the two simple sentences to form a compound sentence. Use an appropriate coordinating conjunction to join the two clauses. Remember to place a comma before the conjunction. Check that a complete subject and verb are on each side of the coordinating conjunction. Write your sentences on separate paper.

Example: The phone rang. I could not get to the phone in time to answer it.

The phone rang**, but** I could not get to the phone in time to answer it.

1. I could not move. I could not cry out for help.
2. I crouched down behind the bushes. I started to pray.
3. The bear picked up my scent. He did not head in my direction.
4. He brushed against the tree to scratch his back. I was still too frightened to move.
5. He worked his way toward the river. He was hungry and wanted to catch some fish.
6. The bear was out of sight. He might still return.
7. I could sit quietly for a few more minutes. I could move slowly to my car.
8. I decided to ease my way toward my car. The car would be safer than staying out in the open air.
9. I unlocked the car door. I got in.
10. From the car, I could see the bear down by the river. I had no desire to get a closer look.

EXERCISE 3.4 Using Commas Score: ______

Proofread the following sentences for comma errors. Add commas if they are missing. Cross off commas that are used incorrectly. Write **C** next to the sentences that are **correct**.

1. A young woman straddled her surfboard and scanned the ocean, for a sign of the perfect wave.
2. Two weeks of women's surfing competition started and fifty women came to compete.
3. The women wore body suits, and board shorts but their attire was fashionable.
4. Five years ago, less than five percent of the surfers were women but now women make up twenty percent of the 1.5 million active surfers in the World Surfing Association.
5. The popularity of surfing among women has steadily increased, yet many people still see surfing as a man's sport.
6. Acceptance of women surfers has increased, yet their monetary awards are still less than those of their male counterparts.
7. Promoters of the sport, and sponsors of surfing competitions tend to support the male surfers but such favoritism may change in the near future.
8. Female surfers will not accept a lower status, for long nor will they accept the status quo quietly.
9. Marketing experts, clothes designers and surfing schools are paying more attention now to female surfers for the women have money to spend on the sport.
10. Surfing champs in southern California attract as many fans as movie stars.

Method 2 to Form Compound Sentences

A second method to form compound sentences involves the use of a semicolon. A semicolon replaces the period between the two independent clauses. Use a semicolon to form a compound sentence only when the two independent clauses are closely related, and the relationship between the two clauses is clear.

Simple Sentences:	Three hundred families in Bitterroot Valley vacated their homes.
	More than ninety wildfires blazed out of control in the nearby mountains.
Compound Sentence:	Three hundred families in Bitterroot Valley vacated their homes**;** more than ninety wildfires blazed out of control in the nearby mountains.
Simple Sentences:	The safety of the fire crews is a grave concern. They are overworked and have no backup relief.
Compound Sentence:	The safety of the fire crews is a grave concern**;** they are overworked and have no backup relief.

Method 3 to Form Compound Sentences

A third method to form compound sentences also uses a semicolon. With this method, however, the semicolon is followed by a **conjunctive adverb** and a **comma**. The conjunctive adverb provides the reader with a clearer understanding of the relationship between the two clauses. For this reason, conjunctive adverbs are also referred to as *transitional words*. In the following examples, notice the use of the semicolon before the conjunctive adverb and the use of a comma after the conjunctive adverb. The conjunctive adverbs are in bold print.

Simple Sentences:	Resources have been stretched thin. We have asked reinforcements from other counties and other states to join the fire lines.
Compound Sentence:	Resources have been stretched thin**; consequently,** we have asked reinforcements from other counties and other states to join the fire lines.
Simple Sentences:	Several of the smaller fires have been contained. New lightning strikes ignite new fires.
Compound Sentence:	Several of the smaller fires have been contained**; however,** new lightning strikes ignite new fires.

Conjunctive adverbs must be selected carefully to show an accurate relationship between the two clauses. See the chart of conjunctions in Chapter 2 (pages 54–55) and use the following chart to learn the meaning of any unfamiliar conjunctions.

CONJUNCTIVE ADVERBS AND TRANSITIONAL PHRASES			
CONJUNCTIVE ADVERB	MEANING	CONJUNCTIVE ADVERB	MEANING
accordingly	consequently, thus	indeed	in fact
additionally	also, in addition	later	next in time
afterward	later	likewise	also, furthermore
also	in addition	moreover	furthermore, in addition
as a result	consequently	nevertheless	however, nonetheless
besides	in addition, moreover	next	following in time
consequently	as a result, therefore	nonetheless	however, nevertheless
contrarily	on the other hand	on the other hand	however
earlier	before in time	otherwise	in contrast, contrarily
finally	at last, lastly	second	in time sequence
first	beginning of a sequence	similarly	also, likewise, thus
for example	for instance	still	however, furthermore
for instance	for example	subsequently	after, consequently
fortunately	luckily	suddenly	abruptly, quickly
furthermore	in addition, moreover	then	after, next in time
hence	therefore, as a result	therefore	consequently
however	but	third	in time sequence
in fact	for example	thus	therefore, consequently
in addition	also	unfortunately	sadly, unluckily
in conclusion	finally		

Simple Sentences: You will need to pay taxes on your lottery winnings.

The final earnings will still provide you with a comfortable income.

Relationship: contrast

Compound Sentence: You will need to pay taxes on your lottery winnings**; however,** the final earnings will still provide you with a comfortable income.

Other Functions of Transitional Words

1. The transitional word or conjunctive adverb may appear as an introductory word at the beginning of a sentence. When a transition word introduces a sentence, use a comma after the introductory word. If the sentence is closely related to the preceding sentence, a semicolon can be used to join the two sentences to form a compound sentence.

   Simple Sentences: I sent out several dozen applications. Finally, I was called for an interview.

   Compound Sentence: I sent out several dozen applications**;** **finally,** I was called for an interview.

2. Many transitional words (adverbs) can also appear within independent clauses; in such cases, the transitional words interrupt the flow of the sentence. Use a comma before and after such a sentence interrupter. In the following examples, notice that the adverb does not join two independent clauses; a subject, a complete verb, and a complete thought do not appear before and after the adverb.

   The accountant, **however**, wanted to check the figures one final time.

   The questions are routine but, **nevertheless**, important to the employer.

EXERCISE 3.5 Simple and Compound Sentences Score: ______

Read each of the following sentences with independent clauses. On the line, write **S** for **simple** sentence with one independent clause and **C** for **compound** sentence with two independent clauses.

______ 1. One in three working wives in America now earns more income than her spouse; consequently, family dynamics are changing in America.

______ 2. This economic trend is more common among highly educated women; interestingly, in the 1990s, one-fifth more women than men graduated from American colleges and universities.[1]

______ 3. As a result, traditional gender roles in the family are changing, and sociologists notice a change in expectations on the home front.

______ 4. Men in role-reversal situations now assume more responsibilities with housework, provide more hours of child care, and participate more actively in their children's schools and recreational programs.

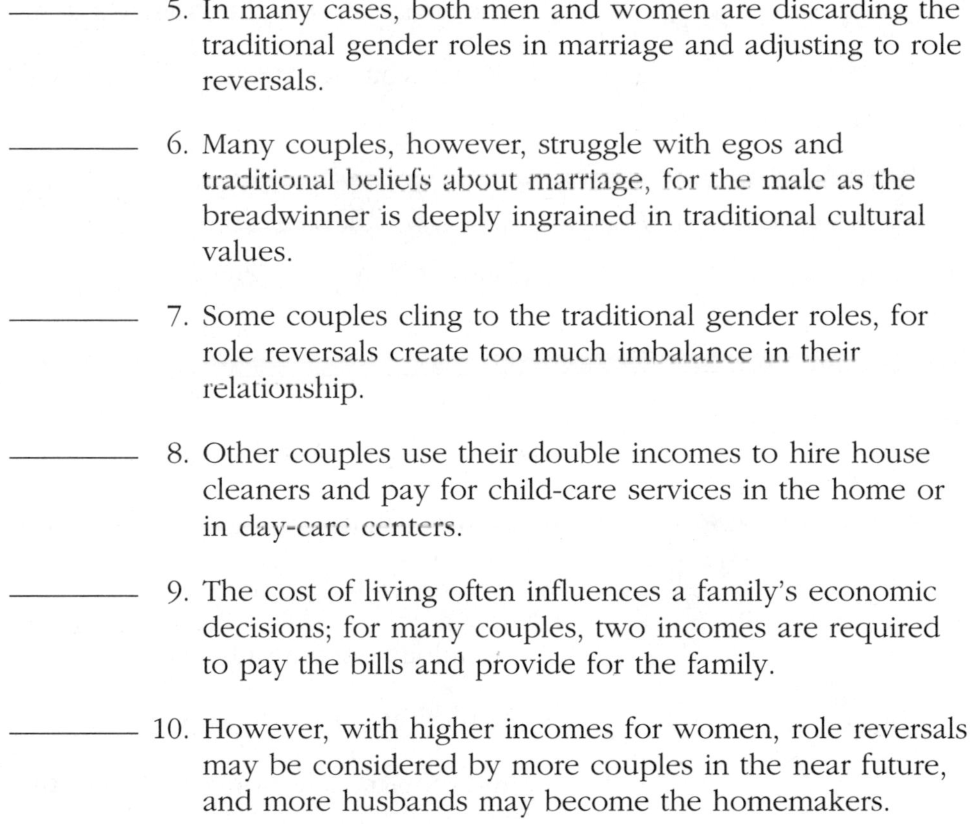

_______ 5. In many cases, both men and women are discarding the traditional gender roles in marriage and adjusting to role reversals.

_______ 6. Many couples, however, struggle with egos and traditional beliefs about marriage, for the male as the breadwinner is deeply ingrained in traditional cultural values.

_______ 7. Some couples cling to the traditional gender roles, for role reversals create too much imbalance in their relationship.

_______ 8. Other couples use their double incomes to hire house cleaners and pay for child-care services in the home or in day-care centers.

_______ 9. The cost of living often influences a family's economic decisions; for many couples, two incomes are required to pay the bills and provide for the family.

_______ 10. However, with higher incomes for women, role reversals may be considered by more couples in the near future, and more husbands may become the homemakers.

[[1]Adapted from: Amy Goldstein, *Washington Post,* Feb. 29, 2000.]

EXERCISE 3.6 **Punctuating Compound Sentences** Score: _______

Mark the prepositional phrases with parentheses and the infinitives with brackets. Underline the subjects once and the verbs twice in the following compound sentences. Add the correct punctuation between the two independent clauses.

Example: The women's rights movement has a long history**;** changes began (in 1848).

1. In early American history, women did not publicly demand suffrage that changed in 1848.
2. Women publicly demanded their rights in 1848 in fact they organized a Women's Rights Convention and adopted twelve resolutions for equal rights.

3. The press ignored the women's demands in addition opponents pelted women's rights advocates with rotten fruit and chastised them.
4. By 1900, women suffragists became more vocal and more aggressive with their demands yet the men in power still ignored and ridiculed their demands.
5. Consequently, women started to march in the streets and to voice stronger demands for their equal rights twenty years later, they won the right to vote.
6. Women were happy to win the right to vote but there were other inequities to confront.
7. Many women wanted access to education, the military, politics, and employment opportunities but many men and even some women tried to stop the feminist movement and to maintain the status quo.
8. In the 1960s, a powerful activist surfaced to add momentum to the women's struggle for equality Gloria Steinen was her name.
9. The feminist movement in the 1960s fought many forms of gender discrimination as a result women today earn higher wages and have greater access to education, employment opportunities, military positions, and women's sports programs.
10. The women's rights movement throughout the last century fought and won many rights for women however the fight for gender equality continues in the courts, in the media, and at the ballot box.

Use appropriate punctuation between two independent clauses to avoid creating the two kinds of *fused sentence:* run-on sentences and comma splices. A *run-on sentence error* occurs when a compound sentence has no punctuation between the independent clauses: A *comma splice error* occurs when a comma appears between the two independent clauses.

Run-On Sentences

A **run-on sentence** lacks punctuation between the two independent clauses. In the following examples of run-on sentences, the arrows and the abbreviation RO show the point at which the run-on sentence error occurs due to the lack of punctuation.

> independent clause
> In early American history, women did not publicly demand suffrage ↓RO that changed in 1848.
> independent clause

> independent clause
> Consequently, women started to march in the streets and voice stronger demands for their equal rights ↓RO twenty years later, they won the right to vote.
> independent clause

> independent clause
> In the 1960s, a powerful activist surfaced to add momentum to the women's struggle for equality ↓RO Gloria Steinem was her name.
> independent clause

Identifying Run-On Sentence Errors

To identify run-on sentences, analyze the subject-verb patterns in sentences. When one subject-verb pattern forms a complete thought, the end of the clause should be punctuated before the next subject-verb pattern begins. Use the following method to proofread for run-on sentence errors:

1. Locate the end of the first subject-verb pattern and its complete thought. Place an imaginary period at that point.
2. Look to see whether the remaining words form a new sentence that is complete with its own subject, complete verb, and complete thought.

In a run-on sentence error, you should be able to identify two separate sentences that can stand alone as simple sentences. You should also be able to identify the point at which the two separate sentences connect to form a compound sentence. The following example shows two independent clauses that run together to form a run-on sentence error (RO):

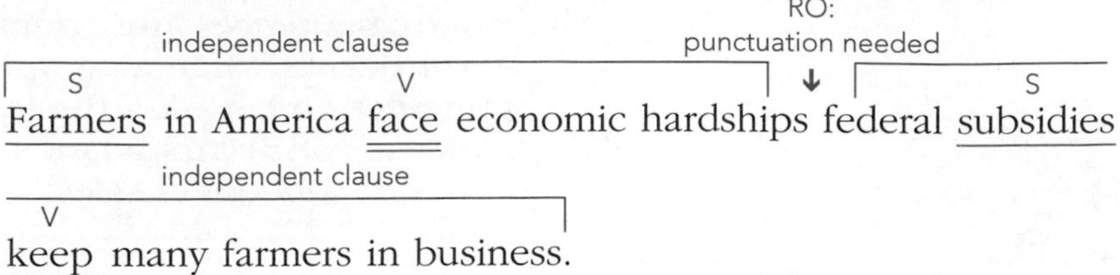

Correcting Run-On Sentence Errors

After you identify a run-on sentence error, use any one of the following four methods to correct the error:

1. Add a period at the end of the first independent clause and capitalize the first word of the second independent clause. Instead of a compound sentence, you will have two simple sentences.

   In early American history, women did not publicly demand suffrage**.** That changed in 1848.

2. Add a comma and a coordinating conjunction *(and, but, for, nor, or, so, yet)* between the two independent clauses.

   In early American history, women did not publicly demand suffrage**, but** that changed in 1848.

3. Add a semicolon between the two independent clauses.

   In early American history, women did not publicly demand suffrage**;** that changed in 1848.

4. Add a semicolon and a conjunctive adverb followed by a comma between the independent clauses.

   In early American history, women did not publicly demand suffrage**; however,** that changed in 1848.

Note that you cannot add a comma between two independent clauses to correct a run-on sentence error. A comma will replace one sentence error with another sentence error, the comma splice error.

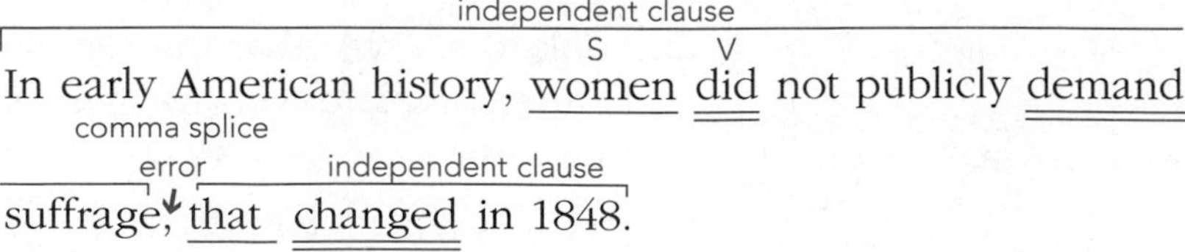

EXERCISE 3.7 **Identifying and Correcting Run-On Sentence Errors** Score: ______

Read the following sentences carefully. For sentences with run on sentence errors, use any one of the four methods to correct the error. Write a **C** next to the sentences that are **correct** and do not have any run-on sentence errors.

1. Not all women enjoy working outside of the home some prefer to remain at home with their children.
2. Many children, however, gain valuable social skills from child-care centers and preschools.
3. Children learn to work in small groups, to share their toys, and to get along with each other they also learn to handle their emotions, in new ways.
4. For some children, separation from their parents is difficult they cry and throw temper tantrums in the initial separation process.
5. Young fathers nowadays do more than play ball with their children.
6. Many fathers provide emotional support and teach children valuable social skills.
7. Many children look to their fathers for one kind of advice they turn to their mothers for other kinds of advice.
8. Communication between parents and children is more open than in previous generations unfortunately, communication during the teenage years continues to be difficult.
9. Generation gaps have always existed our parents would acknowledge this fact.
10. Healthy children feel safe, loved, and protected parents contribute greatly to the physical, social, and emotional health of their children.

Comma Splice Errors

A **comma splice error** occurs when a comma is used in a compound sentence to connect two independent clauses. The following examples show comma splice errors.

independent clause | comma splice error | independent clause

Generation gaps have always existed, each generation struggles to close the gap.

comma splice error

independent clause

Healthy children feel safe, loved, and protected, parents contribute greatly to the physical, social, and emotional health of their children.

independent clause

Use of Commas

When you proofread sentences for comma splice errors, remember that commas serve many different functions. Commas are used between three or more words in a series. Commas are used with some adverbs that interrupt the flow of the sentence. Commas are also used before coordinating conjunctions to form compound sentences. The commas in the following sentences are essential and do not create comma splice errors.

interrupter

Generation gaps, however, have always existed.

words in a series

Healthy children feel safe, loved, and protected.

independent clause — coordinating conjunction

Open communication exists with younger children, but it is hard to maintain with teenagers.

independent clause

Identifying Comma Splice Errors

Identify comma splice errors by analyzing the subject-verb patterns in sentences. When one subject-verb pattern forms a complete thought and it is joined to a second complete thought by a comma, a comma splice error occurs. When you edit your work, use the following method to identify comma splice errors:

1. Locate the end of the first subject-verb pattern and its complete thought. If there is a comma at the end of the thought, replace the comma with an imaginary period.
2. Look to see whether the remaining words form a new sentence with its own subject, complete verb, and complete thought. In a comma splice error, you should be able to identify two separate sentences on each side of the comma that joins the two sentences.

Notice in the following comma splice error that one independent clause (or one simple sentence) appears on each side of the comma.

comma splice error

independent clause — independent clause

Generation gaps have always existed, each generation struggles to close the gap.

Correcting Comma Splice Errors

After you identify a comma splice error, use any one of the following four methods to correct the error:

1. Replace the comma with a period to make two simple sentences. Remember to capitalize the first word of the second sentence.

   Generation gaps have always existed. Each generation struggles to close the gap.

2. Keep the comma and add a coordinating conjunction (*and, but, for, nor, or, so, yet*) between the two independent clauses.

   Generation gaps have always existed, so each generation struggles to close the gap.

3. Add a semicolon between the two independent clauses.

   Generation gaps have always existed; each generation struggles to close the gap.

4. Add a semicolon and a conjunctive adverb followed by a comma between the independent clauses.

   Generation gaps have always existed; consequently, each generation struggles to close the gap.

EXERCISE 3.8 Identifying and Correcting Comma Splice Errors

Score: ______

Read the following sentences carefully. For sentences with comma splice errors, use any one of the four methods to correct the error. Write **C** next to the sentences that are **correct** and do not have any comma splice errors.

1. The House of Representatives voted to increase the minimum wage by one dollar an hour, the increase will be phased in by the year 2002.

2. The increase will have an immediate impact on thousands of families, for it will equal a $2,000 raise for full-time workers.

3. The average pay for corporate chief executives has risen nearly 750 percent since 1980, however, the average worker has seen only a 68 percent pay increase since 1980.

4. Opponents of the bill, however, are concerned about the impact on businesses and industry, so they want a special tax relief bill for businesses and industry.

5. About 4 million workers in America are paid the minimum wage, all four million are not full-time workers.

6. The concept of minimum wage began in October 1938, the minimum wage then was 25 cents.

7. Workers do not receive minimum wage increases every year, in fact, a trend of annual raises in minimum wages occurred only during 1974 to 1976 and 1978 to 1981.

8. The longest time period without a raise in minimum wage occurred between 1981 and 1990, so the minimum wage of $3.35 lasted for nine years.

9. The latest minimum wage increase is the largest in American history, the increase typically varies from ten cents to forty cents.

10. Many Americans, undoubtedly, will welcome their larger paychecks at the end of the month, but larger paychecks may actually lead to more money deducted for taxes.

[*Associated Press,* "House OKs Minimum Wage," March 10, 2000.]

Grammar and Usage Tips Summary

TIP 6 Use simple past tense verbs in narrative paragraphs. Use an *-ed* suffix for regular verbs; use the correct past tense form for irregular verbs.

TIP 7 For sentence variety, combine two independent clauses to form compound sentences. Join the independent clauses by using a comma and a coordinating conjunction, a semicolon, or a semicolon followed by a conjunctive adverb and a comma.

TIP 8 Use appropriate punctuation between two independent clauses to avoid creating fused sentences. Run-on sentences and comma splice errors are two kinds of fused sentences. Fused sentences can be corrected by using correct punctuation and logical conjunctions between the two independent clauses.

CHAPTER 3 • Narrative Paragraphs • Proofreading and Editing Exercises

Proofreading 1

Work with a partner or by yourself to proofread and edit the following paragraph. Add missing punctuation and correct any errors with simple past tense verbs. Use any method to correct run-on sentences and comma splice errors. Write the corrections above the errors.

Camping at the Coast

Not all camping trips are a wonderful experience. Shortly after my husband and I were married, we decide to retreat to the coast for our first camping trip together. We envisioned five leisurely days sleeping in our tent, sitting around a campfire, and cooking over an open stove. We packed the car with our tent, sleeping bags, food, campfire pans, lanterns, and clothes. We drive two hours to the coast. Within a short amount of time, we locate a perfect campsite near the edge of a river. We unload our supplies, set up the tent, and decided to explore suddenly, my husband started tearing everything apart looking for his wallet. We could not go anywhere without gas, all of our money was in his wallet. He grew pale. He then remembers that he left his wallet at home. Fortunately, I had an extra gas card in the glove compartment. The only option was to drive home to retrieve the wallet. We got in the car we trust that no one would come into our campsite to steal our gear. The round trip was long and our tempers were short. Our spirits were coming out of the slump we entered the park and turned into our campsite. Within the flash of a second, our hearts sank. We were stunned. We stare at our campsite in total disbelief. The entire campsite was ransacked. Food was scattered all over the ground paper bags were torn apart. The contents were strewn everywhere. I screamed I cried I cursed. What else could go wrong on our camping trip? The camp guard responded to my distress calls but then he proceeded to laugh in my face. He told me that some mighty vicious crows hover in the tall trees just waiting for dumb campers to leave food visible and accessible. They had a hearty party and left very little for us. Then a real cloud burst. Within minutes, we were drenched. We took cover in the tent only to find out that it was not waterproofed yet. Everything in the tent, including our clothes, our sleeping bags, and our pillows, were soaking wet. We looked at each other and realized there was only one option. We opened the trunk, threw every soggy, wet, muddy thing inside and started our two-hour journey home. Camping may sound exciting and relaxing but I can easily testify that camping can be downright miserable frustrating and enormously disheartening.

Proofreading 2

Carefully proofread the following sentences in bold print for errors. Use any method to correct the errors that you find. Write your corrections above the errors. Be sure to carefully check the verb tenses, punctuation, and sentence structures. Use any method to correct fragments, run-on sentences, and comma splice errors.

The Veteran

The Vietnam Memorial represented more to Charles than most people can ever begin to comprehend. **For many months, Charles full of apprehension about visiting the massive marble monument in Washington, D.C.** Would the memorial revert him to the battlefields? Would the haunting memories return every night? **One day in September. Charles decided to face his fears and visit the memorial.** He hoped deep in his heart that the memorial would become a part of his healing process and a sign that other Americans recognize the sacrifices, physical pain, and emotional scars that American soldiers endured in Vietnam for their country. **He slowly put on his fatigues, slipped his feet into his combat boots, and pinned his medals on his shirt. He hitched a ride to the memorial. Within minutes, he stood at the beginning of the black, marble wall. A glazed look washed over his face he saw the thousands of names inscribed on the wall.** His leathery hand, missing two fingers, hesitantly touched the wall. Keeping his hand on the wall so his fingers crossed over names as he walked slowly down the sidewalk, he felt a steady stream of tears roll down his face. **The tears were tears of pain. Tears of pride. He felt no need to hide his emotions, he let the tears continue to roll down his face and drop onto his shirt. He felt the smooth marble but he couldn't bring himself to read any of the names.** He already knew some of the names that were on the wall. As he moved farther and farther down the sidewalk, the wall grew taller and taller. **His emotions grew with the wall.** As he stood at the apex of the wall, he crumbled to his knees, closed his eyes, and openly sobbed. **His broad shoulders heav-**

ing up and down. His entire body shook uncontrollably. Another veteran in a wheelchair rolled up beside him and gently placed his hand on Charles' back. Charles opened his eyes and found himself looking at a delicate bouquet of flowers that had been placed at the base of the wall. As he glanced to his side, he saw the metal frame of a wheelchair. **In a flash of a moment, he felt gratitude. His name was not on the wall. He was only missing two fingers. He had the will to move forward with his life.**

Proofreading 3

Use the proofreading checklist on page 115 to proofread and edit your Writing Warm-Up 3. Revise your work. Turn in your original Writing Warm-Up 3 and your revision.

Internet Enrichment

Log on to the web site for this textbook for additional exercises and links for the following topics:

Narrative Paragraphs
Clustering
Simple Past-Tense Verbs
Compound Sentences
Comma Splice Errors
Run-On Sentence Errors

Go to: http://college.hmco.com. Click on "Students." Type *Paragraph Essentials* in the "Jump to Textbook Sites" box. Click "go," and then bookmark the site. Click on Chapter 3.

CHAPTER 3 • Grammar and Usage Review

Name ______________________

Date ______________________

Simple and Compound Sentences

Read the following sentences carefully. Identify the subject-verb pattern or patterns. Write **S** if the sentence is a **simple** sentence. Write **C** if the sentence is a **compound** sentence.

________ 1. In Las Vegas, a city of glitter and gaudiness, weddings can be quite bizarre.

________ 2. Couples can dress in intergalactic attire and get married aboard a replica of the starship USS Enterprise.

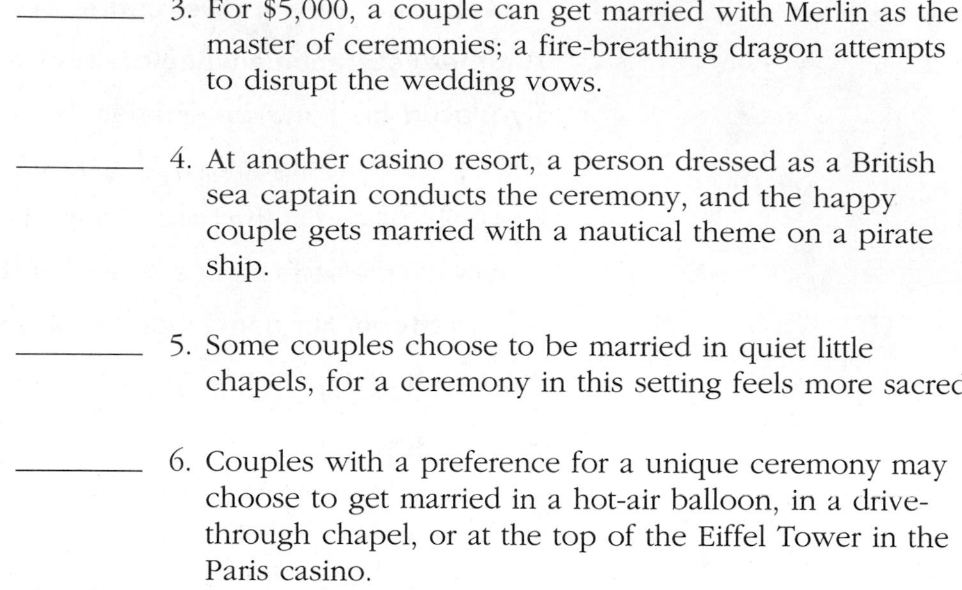

_______ 3. For $5,000, a couple can get married with Merlin as the master of ceremonies; a fire-breathing dragon attempts to disrupt the wedding vows.

_______ 4. At another casino resort, a person dressed as a British sea captain conducts the ceremony, and the happy couple gets married with a nautical theme on a pirate ship.

_______ 5. Some couples choose to be married in quiet little chapels, for a ceremony in this setting feels more sacred.

_______ 6. Couples with a preference for a unique ceremony may choose to get married in a hot-air balloon, in a drive-through chapel, or at the top of the Eiffel Tower in the Paris casino.

Proofreading and Editing

Proofread the following sentences for punctuation errors. Use any method to correct the errors.

1. My daughter enjoys tap dancing ballet dancing and gymnastics she loves to perform before an audience.

2. I will never forget one of her recitals, nothing seemed to go according to the plan.

3. First, she missed her cue to get on stage the director had to call her name and tell her to come out from behind the curtain.

4. She rushed on the stage, and tripped over her own feet she looked stunned.

5. The audience laughed my daughter's face turned red and tiny tears flowed down her face.

6. Finally, she gained her composure and started to dance however the audience once again started to laugh.

7. A long piece of toilet paper hung from the back of her costume, fortunately, she did not notice the addition to her costume.

8. Her gracefulness, and her personality captured the audience's approval she received hearty applause and a standing ovation.

CHAPTER 4

Descriptive Paragraphs

The topic sentence introduces a specific person, place, thing, or event and states a central impression (the controlling idea).

The body provides a vivid, mental picture of the subject. Well-chosen descriptive details develop the central impression.

The concluding sentence restates or echoes the central impression or concludes the paragraph with one strong, final impression.

Topic Sentence ....
Unity + Coherence + Adequate Development ....
Concluding Sentence ....

In Chapter 4 you will learn about the following:

1. Objective and subjective descriptive paragraphs
2. The structure of a descriptive paragraph
3. The writing process for descriptive paragraphs
4. Four additional grammar and usage tips

WRITING WARM-UP 4

Write a description of an item in your home or your place of work that you use on a regular basis. State the item in the topic sentence and give the reader a sense of your attitude or feeling toward the item. Then proceed to describe the item with as much attention to detail as possible.

The Descriptive Paragraph

Descriptive writing is an essential element in many forms of paragraphs. The use of vivid, precise, descriptive words enriches and enhances any paragraphs that you write. In a narrative, for example, descriptive writing creates a powerful image in the mind of your reader and evokes emotions that are compatible with your topic sentence. Longer pieces of writing, such as an essay, often contain descriptive writing to help make ideas and supporting points clear. While descriptive writing is incorporated in many other kinds of paragraphs and longer forms of writing, this chapter focuses on descriptive paragraphs that stand on their own. The purpose of a descriptive paragraph that stands on its own is to focus the reader's attention on specific details in order to form a strong image of a person, place, object, or event. The purpose may be to entertain the reader, or it may be to inform the reader about a technical topic, such as a piece of equipment.

When you write a descriptive paragraph, you provide your reader with a vivid mental picture of a specific person, place, object, or event. Through your use of details, you convey a **central impression,** which reveals your specific attitude, opinion, or feeling about your topic. The mental picture and the central impression in your writing are not limited to how things look. When appropriate for your topic, you can make your descriptive paragraph come alive by including sensory details associated with sight, sound, smell, taste, and touch. Your main goal with descriptive writing is to select details that clearly and effectively develop or support the central impression you wish to convey to your reader.

Subjective and Objective Description

Descriptive writing with a central impression that evokes an emotional response from the reader is called **subjective description.** In subjective descriptive writing, your goal is to select words that trigger a specific image and emotional response from your reader. You want your reader to feel and experience the central impression in a personal, or subjective, way. The focus in this chapter is on subjective description.

Objective description, another form of descriptive writing, appears in many of your textbooks and college writing assignments. Objective description, which is impersonal, excludes personal feelings and experiences. Instead, it describes a person, an object, or an event without emotional appeal or an emotional central impression. Objective descriptive writing is *technical writing*. Manuals for equipment or machinery, workplace procedures, or operational policies are prime examples of technical writing. The purpose of objective description is to provide the reader with essential information and an impersonal description of an item and its functions.

The following descriptions about an automatic watering system show the differences between objective description and subjective description. Subjective words appear in italics.

OBJECTIVE DESCRIPTION: Impersonal/No Emotional Central Impression

The Water Wizard is an automated watering cycle system for home landscaping. The complete system mounts on a wall and requires 6 inches by 4 inches of wall space. Two program cycles, Program A and Program B, initiate two separate watering cycles. Each watering cycle opens and closes one to six separate valves. Each program is independent of the other, so different watering days and watering times can be set for each of the valves in each of the programs. The Water Wizard allows homeowners to select the best watering cycles and sequences for their landscape.

SUBJECTIVE DESCRIPTION: Positive Central Impression

The Water Wizard is an *incredible* watering cycle system for home landscaping. This *compact* and *user-friendly* system mounts *easily* on a wall and requires *only* a small amount of wall space. The system has two separate programs and six separate valves so users can *personalize* the system to reflect the watering needs *in their area and with their landscaping.* To make the process *easy* to program, a *large-print* screen guides the user through the steps. The entire system is *well designed* and *convenient.* The large, white dial, which is used to set the program, can first be set on Program A. The user can then select the starting time, the days of the week, and the amount of watering minutes for six different sprinkler heads in *his* or *her* yard. In addition, the user can set a second watering time by using Program B. *Homeowners do not need mechanical or computer skills* to program and use this *wonderful* home watering system. *Beautiful gardens and rich, lush lawns* will *adorn* the property of homeowners who use the Water Wizard.

SUBJECTIVE DESCRIPTION: Negative Central Impression

The Water Wizard is one of the *most frustrating* gadgets in my entire home. This tiny white box mounted on my garage wall is *doing nothing more than taking up wall space.* The big, *ugly* white dial on this gadget has yet to program the sprinklers to go on at the selected times. When I try to program the system, a tiny lime-colored screen starts flashing the letters A and B at me; some *small, blurred, hard-to-read directions, for some unknown reason, emphatically* appear on the screen every few seconds. Small, gray arrows on the far left side of the screen point to one of the numbers one through six. An arrow pointing up and down flashes *impatiently*, waiting for *some unknown* command to be entered into the system. Three round buttons on the bottom of the system are *a total mystery*. When each is pushed, the *only* thing that happens is a new screen appears with more flashing arrows and blinking lights. After *numerous attempts* at programming this *useless white box*, and after the *ugly*, white dial was placed on *Run*, a week later my sprinklers came on once, and *that was during a barbecue party*. The engineers of this *"clever" little device* did not program it in a way *an average, intelligent person can understand*. Needless to say, the *only miracle with this miracle gadget is that it is still taking up wall space*.

The Structure of a Descriptive Paragraph

The structure of a descriptive paragraph consists of the same key elements that are used in a narrative and in all other paragraph forms: a topic sentence with a controlling idea, a body with supporting details, and a concluding sentence. The following points serve as guidelines for developing the structure of a descriptive paragraph.

Developing the Topic Sentence

Use the following guidelines to write an effective topic sentence with a controlling idea (a central impression) that reveals your point of view, opinion, or attitude toward the subject of your paragraph.

1. Clearly identify a specific person, place, thing, or idea to use as the topic of your paragraph.
2. Select a central impression (your controlling idea), which expresses your attitude, opinion, or feeling toward the topic. If your descriptive paragraph lacks a central impression, it will lack unity.
3. Limit the scope of your topic and your topic sentence. Select a specific time frame for your description. Perhaps it is a specific time of the day, week, or season of the year. For example, the description of a forest at night will vary considerably from a description of a forest during the day; a forest during the fall season when the leaves change colors will vary considerably from a forest during a snowstorm. Your limited time frame may or may not be stated in your topic sentence, but it should be clear in your mind and reflected in the body of your paragraph if it is not stated in the topic sentence.
4. Experiment with different ways to express the topic and the central impression by writing several possible topic sentences. Reword or revise one or more of the topic sentences until an effective, powerful topic sentence emerges. Because the topic sentence plays the key role of controlling the content of the paragraph, spend ample time developing your topic sentence.

4.1 What do you think?

Which of the following are effective topic sentences for a descriptive paragraph? In class or with a partner discuss each of the topic sentences.

1. Clayton is a survivor.
2. Mrs. Manning, my childhood piano teacher, could scare any child into learning to play the piano.
3. The mountain peaks are tall and majestic.
4. The Delta Ponds are next to the shopping center.
5. Construction of subdivisions continues at a rapid pace.
6. The dilapidated house with a junkyard in front is a neighborhood eyesore.

4.2 What do you think?

Work with a partner or on your own. Read the following descriptive paragraph carefully. On separate paper, answer the questions that follow the paragraph.

Grandmother's Picture

One picture that I have of my grandmother in the courtyard of our home reminds me of what my grandmother was like. In the picture, she is sitting beside and almost dwarfed by a huge birthday cake with lighted candles. Her face is stern and unsmiling. Her lips are shut firmly, revealing the Confucian beliefs that society and legend taught her. She is small and delicately boned with skin that is wrinkled but soft brown. Her white hair is neatly pulled back with a metallic hairpin called a *be nyou.* I always teased her about wearing a short chopstick in her hair. She always wore, whether with a housedress or her best-occasion *hanbok,* her white cotton apron. It is trimmed with handmade tatting, which she continued to make as long as her eyesight allowed. She wore her apron through all the years when she had the role of taking care of five grandchildren from birth to adulthood, and she wore the apron as she did years of house chores. She softly holds her hands with swollen knuckles in her lap. Her hands show her many years of harsh life.

Nicole Lee
Bellevue Community College
Bellevue, Washington

1. Which sentence is the topic sentence?
2. What is the central impression the writer wants to express? Is the central impression expressed in the topic sentence? Explain.
3. Frequently, writers experiment with several different topic sentences for a paragraph before finding an effective topic sentence that clearly introduces the specific topic and expresses the central impression. Write an alternative topic sentence for this paragraph.

Developing the Body of the Paragraph

Use the following guidelines to develop the body of your paragraph and the controlling idea stated in your topic sentence.

1. When writing a descriptive paragraph, stay focused on the topic and limit the time frame. Do not get drawn into telling a story. Observe the subject from a stationary perspective. Focusing on your subject is much like looking through the lens of a camera; the description recounts what you see through the eye of the camera without a story or a plot.

2. Strengthen the *central impression* (the controlling idea) of your paragraph by carefully selecting descriptive words that create strong, vivid images in your reader's mind. Use a dictionary or a thesaurus to locate effective nouns, verbs, adjectives, and adverbs to use in your descriptive writing. Avoid using vague, meaningless, nondescriptive words.

3. Include *sensory details* that describe more than what you see. Depending on your topic, your descriptions may include sounds, tastes, smells, and tactile (touch) sensations. For example, an item such as a couch may be described through a variety of sensory details: squeaky, musty, pink, threadbare, perfumed, soft, velvety, coarse, prickly, cool, silky, sticky, or grimy. In another example, sensory details could be used to describe mud: brown, foul-smelling, rancid, stinky, malodorous, stagnant, disease-bearing, bug-infested, slimy, cold, gooey, lumpy, slippery, soothing, sensuous, therapeutic, invigorating, revitalizing, rejuvenating, or warm.
4. Create *unity* by selecting descriptive details that are consistent with the central impression in your topic sentence. Each sentence in the body of your paragraph needs to support the topic sentence. Eliminate any sentences or details within sentences that detract from your topic sentence, weaken your central impression, or wander beyond the scope, time frame, or physical boundaries of your paragraph.
5. Create *coherence* by using a logical method to sequence your details. You have a number of options for your descriptive paragraph. The first option, spatial order, is the most common organizational pattern used to develop coherence in a descriptive paragraph.

Spatial Order: Organize the details in the order that they appear in space. In other words, present the details in the order that your eye would move. This may be from left to right, from top to bottom, from outside to inside, or from close to far. Avoid jumping randomly from one point in space to another.

Emphatic Order (Order of Importance): Organize the details in the body of a descriptive paragraph according to their order of importance, specificity, or complexity. Deductive and inductive order, which are opposite organizational patterns, may be used for descriptive paragraphs.

With **deductive order**, after the topic sentence, the body of the paragraph begins with the most important sentence, the most general sentence, or the sentence with the strongest impression. The details are then presented in the order of most important to least important, most complex or detailed to least complex or least detailed. The body of the paragraph ends with the least significant or smallest detail of the paragraph.

The order of details in **inductive order** is the reverse of the deductive order. To use inductive order, begin your paragraph with the least significant or least complex detail. Progress through the paragraph by presenting details with increasing importance or complexity. The topic sentence, which has the main idea and the central impression, is saved for last. Inductive order can be used when you want to build suspense or drama in a descriptive pattern.

Chronological: Develop your topic through a description of brief, generalized movements or actions that occur chronologically over a short time frame. Select actions that demonstrate the character, personality, or mannerisms of your subject. Avoid developing the action into a narrative.

6. Use *transition words* and conjunctions that show spatial, emphatic, or chronological order.

COMMON TRANSITION WORDS FOR DESCRIPTIVE PARAGRAPHS					
above	below	behind	beside	in front of	in the distance
near	next to	on	on the left	on the right	under
a more significant . . .		a less significant . . .	a smaller . . .	a more complex . . .	
(Also see the transitions in Chapter 3, page 99 for chronological order.)					

7. Include *adequate development* in your paragraph by selecting a sufficient number of different details to develop the central impression clearly and vividly in your reader's mind. Check that each detail contributes to the development of your attitude, opinion, or feeling toward the subject.

4.3 What do you think?

Work with a partner or on your own. Read the following descriptive paragraph carefully. On separate paper, answer the questions that follow the paragraph.

My Wicked Piano Teacher

Mrs. Manning, my childhood piano teacher, could scare any child into learning to play the piano. Her plump little body greeted every student at the door of her humble home. With a stern look always painted on her face, her powerful, pudgy hands would grab her pupil's arm as she ushered the frightened child directly toward the piano bench. She barked at the unfortunate soul who sat on the bench to play different scales and then used her skinny, wooden pointer with a gold tip to poke the fingers that missed the correct keys. Abruptly, she would slap a page of sheet music on the music holder and command her pupil to play with love and passion. The fat that hung from her arms wiggled and shook every time she slapped the rhythm of the tune on top of the piano. She would often tilt her head back, point her chin toward her pupil, and then peer from the bottom of her bifocals. She never held back frowns to show her displeasure with the sounds that came out of the piano. Sometimes her head shook back and forth so violently that it was a miracle that the tight bun nailed to the back of her head stayed in place. At the end of the lesson, she moved out of her typical character and softened up. She always gave her pupil a piece of candy, a hug, and told him or her that someday she would see that student give an outstanding performance at her annual piano recital. She was right. Every one of her frightened pupils learned to play the piano well enough to be in the annual piano recital.

1. The subject, Mrs. Manning, has been narrowed or restricted to a specific setting and time of day. What specific setting and time of day are used in the paragraph?
2. What is the central impression the writer wants to express toward Mrs. Manning? List words from that paragraph that develop this central impression.
3. Does the paragraph have unity? Explain your answer.
4. How does the writer develop coherence in the paragraph?
5. In your opinion, does the paragraph have adequate development? Explain your answer.

4.4 What do you think?

Read the following descriptive paragraph carefully. On separate paper, answer the questions that follow the paragraph.

The Moorea Lagoon

The Moorea Lagoon is filled with visions from a wild imagination. After experiencing the spectacular beauty of the white surf breaking as it meets the coral reef, my breath is taken away by the crystal clear, multicolored water of the lagoon. The mysteriously exotic mountains look down upon everything beneath them while at the same time they reach for the sky. The air is like breathing sweet pleasures in dreams, as if the breeze is intertwined with exotic flowers of the island. I know without a doubt that I am truly in the South Pacific, far from anything remotely familiar. The endless warm sand of the white beach beneath my feet touches my soul as the water reaches out to tempt me into the lagoon. Yielding to its plea, I am drawn into a world of exquisite beauty. All the colors in the capacity of thought are mingled among the coral. As I swim through the walls of lace, fans, castles, and shapes that are not even imaginable, instantly an empty space is filled with combinations of shapes and colors as the schools of fish appear. Some fish are curious, and some are not. Some come near and nudge, poke, or nibble on me; others swim by me as if I am a normal part of the sea. Surrendering to the total sensation, I follow and swim among them in fascination through a maze of beauty in their world.

Kathleen Maddux
Lane Community College
Eugene, Oregon

1. Which sentence is the topic sentence?
2. What is the central impression for the paragraph? List specific words, phrases, or details that develop the central impression.
3. Does this paragraph have *unity*? Explain your answer.
4. How does the writer develop *coherence*? What sequence does the writer use to organize the details in the body?
5. Does the paragraph have *adequate development*? Explain your answer.
6. Why do you think the writer chose to write this descriptive paragraph in present tense?

Developing the Concluding Sentence

Use the following guidelines to bring your paragraph to an end.

1. Check that your concluding sentence echoes the topic sentence. It should echo or emphasize the topic and the central impression (the controlling idea) that are stated in your topic sentence.
2. Compare your topic sentence to the concluding sentence. With the exception of the inductive approach, if the two sentences are considerably different, and thus do not echo each other, you wandered off course from your topic and your controlling idea. Check your paragraph carefully for unity and coherence. Remember, however, that when you use an inductive approach, the concluding sentence *is* the topic sentence, so the paragraph does not have two separate sentences to compare or to echo each other.

4.5 What do you think?

Work with a partner or on your own. Read the following descriptive paragraph. Write a topic sentence with a central impression that echoes the concluding sentence. Then, on separate paper, answer the questions that follow the paragraph.

Father-in-Law

Topic sentence: ______________________________

My father-in-law was not a tall man compared with average American men. His arms and legs were not fat or big. Only his waist was huge compared to the other parts of his body. His waist looked liked a stuffed cushion. He loved to drink, which may have contributed to his waistline. His face was always gentle like a typical grandpa. His wavy hair was shiny white and gray, but he was not at all bald. His hairstyle reminded me of a movie star's hairstyle, which is called "romantic gray." He must have been a very handsome man when he was young. He had a wide forehead. When my son played with him, he would bump his forehead against my son's forehead. His eyes, which I could see through his glasses, became very sharp when he discussed politics with his son. He told me he had read most of the books in the neighborhood library. His eyes showed his high level of intelligence. His mind was active even in his later years. I was surprised by his tremendous knowledge. From his mouth, all different kinds of stories would come. His voice was deep and low. He always wore long-sleeved, button-down shirts and chino pants, which were always ironed neatly. He often looked like an early-age yuppie. My father-in-law was a warm-hearted person and a good grandfather for my sons.

Mariko Boyle
Bellevue Community College
Bellevue, Washington

1. What did you write for a topic sentence?
2. Does the writer develop coherence chronologically, spatially, or emphatically? Do you think this method for organizing the details is effective? Explain.
3. Is the concluding sentence effective? Explain your answer.

The Writing Process for Descriptive Paragraphs

Step 1: Generate ideas.

Descriptive paragraphs describe a specific person, place, thing, or event that can be developed by using a central impression. To generate ideas for a descriptive paragraph, you can **brainstorm** to identify interesting people, places, things, or events to describe. Scanning through your life and your personal experiences is one of the best ways to brainstorm for topics. Descriptive paragraphs, however, do no need to be limited to personal experiences. As long as you give proper credit, you can use the Internet, the library, television, and other forms of media can be used as sources for details about a topic that is outside your personal experiences. For example, a descriptive paragraph can be about a famous person, a historical place, a specific product or object, or a specific place or event you have read about or heard about.

Brainstorming

When you brainstorm, list every idea that comes to your mind; you can sort, discard, or accept topics later. Read the question on the left. Quickly write down possible ideas in the box at the right. Move through the questions, listing as many possible answers as you can in a 5- to 15-minute period of time.

Who do you know who is interesting, funny, unique, or unusual?	
Who do you know who is colorful or controversial?	
Who is significant to you?	
Who is your hero? Whom do you admire?	

(Continue on page 154)

Where have you been that made you feel happy, content, grateful, or appreciative?	
Where have you been that made you feel melancholic, pensive, reflective, or stunned?	
Where would you like to visit? Where would you never like to visit again?	
What do you own or want to own that is an antique, a treasure, or rare?	
What do you own or use that is sentimental, sacred, or cherished?	
What do you own that is funny, odd, colorful, trashy, or entertaining?	
What product would a reader like to know more about?	
What piece of equipment, machinery, or technology do you know how to use well?	
What ceremony have you participated in or observed?	
What event have you observed that was sacred, solemn, or serious?	
What event attracts people's interest because it is gaudy, exotic, disturbing, or dangerous?	
What historical event interests you?	

Step 2: Get a focus.

After you select a general topic, your next step is to focus the topic and make it specific. Narrowing the topic for a descriptive paragraph involves specifying the time frame, the setting, and the point of observation. You can use the following guidelines to focus your topic:

1. Identify a specific time frame. What time of the day do you have in mind for the description? What is the month, the season, or the year?
2. Identify a specific setting. Where is the location? Were you personally present as an observer or is the description based on information that you learned from means other than personal experience?
3. In your paragraph, decide if you will be observing and describing the subject from a stationary position or if you will be in motion, moving toward the subject, away from it, or around it.

Step 3: Gather and organize your information.

For Step 3 in the writing process, gather as many different details as possible that relate to your topic. Usually, you will gather more details than you will actually use in the paragraph. Gathering a wide variety of details provides you with an opportunity to see your subject from more than one perspective. You will then be in a better position to select an appropriate central impression and to develop your topic sentence.

Clustering

Clustering is an effective technique to generate possible details for your descriptive paragraph. Unlike a cluster for a narrative that shows a chronological order of detail, a cluster for a descriptive paragraph shows a random order of detail. Jot down a wide variety of details, scattering the details randomly around the center of the cluster. The cluster on page 156 shows a variety of details written about a subject named Clayton.

Selecting a Central Impression

After you create a cluster, examine all the details in your cluster to see whether a central impression, such as an opinion, an attitude, or a specific feeling, emerges. If a central impression does not immediately emerge, spend time thinking further about your attitude or feeling toward the subject. Are your feelings negative, positive, or neutral? Strive to state clearly and specifically how you feel about the subject; the result will be your central impression.

In the first cluster on the following page, the writer could have selected a central impression that focused on Clayton's interests, hobbies, and skills. Instead, the writer selected a central impression that focused on Clayton's strengths as a cancer survivor. Notice how the writer deleted details that did not develop the central impression in the second cluster. The remaining details, plus other details the writer may add while writing the draft, will be used to develop the central impression of the paragraph.

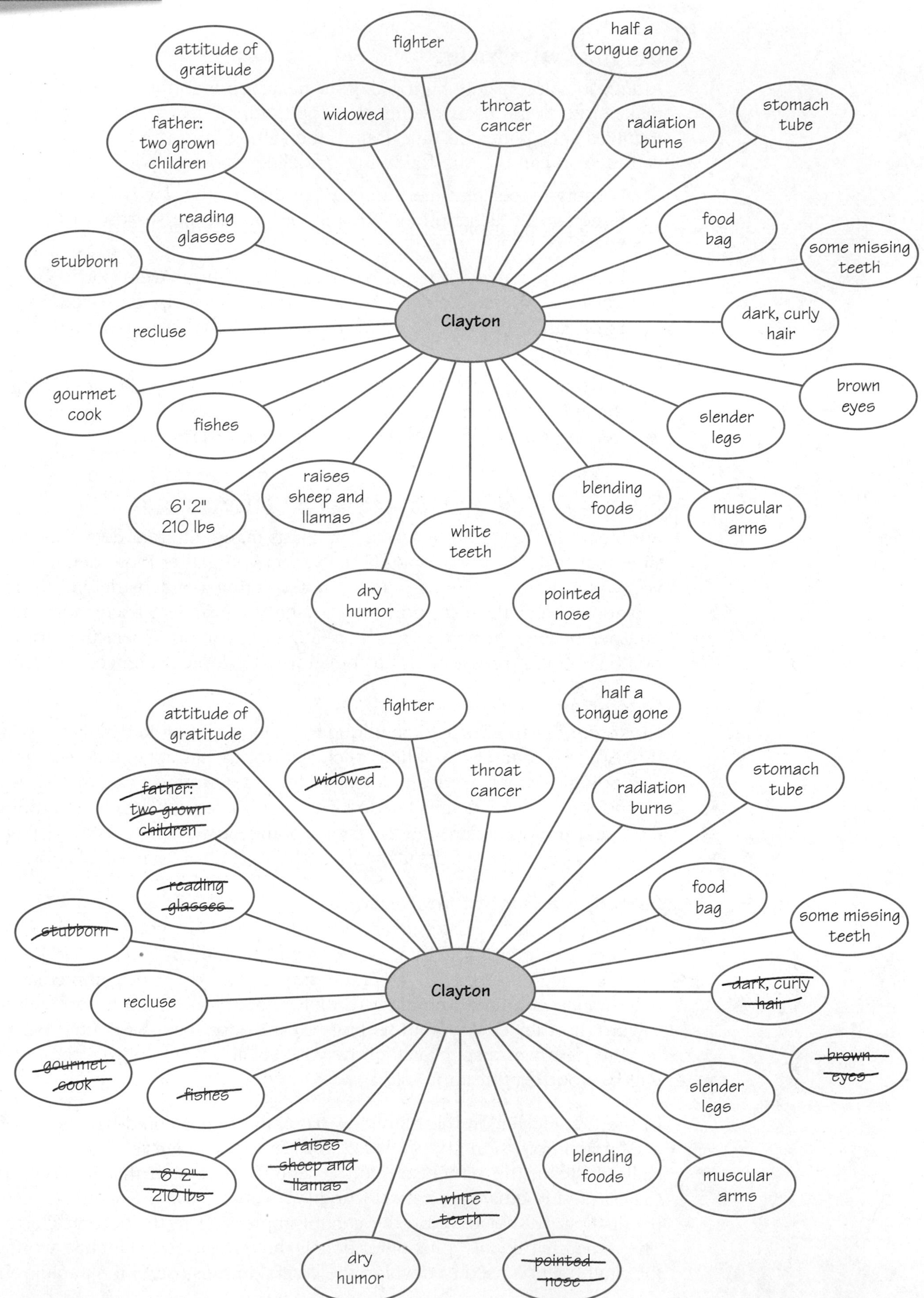
Clayton
attitude of gratitude
fighter
half a tongue gone
widowed
throat cancer
radiation burns
stomach tube
father: two grown children
reading glasses
food bag
stubborn
some missing teeth
recluse
dark, curly hair
gourmet cook
brown eyes
fishes
slender legs
raises sheep and llamas
6' 2" 210 lbs
blending foods
muscular arms
white teeth
dry humor
pointed nose
Clayton
attitude of gratitude
fighter
half a tongue gone
~~widowed~~
throat cancer
radiation burns
stomach tube
~~father: two grown children~~
~~reading glasses~~
food bag
~~stubborn~~
some missing teeth
recluse
~~dark, curly hair~~
~~gourmet cook~~
~~brown eyes~~
~~fishes~~
slender legs
~~raises sheep and llamas~~
~~6' 2" 210 lbs~~
blending foods
muscular arms
~~white teeth~~
dry humor
~~pointed nose~~

Writing the Topic Sentence

Once you determine your central impression, write a strong topic sentence that introduces your topic and expresses your central impression. The topic sentence controls the remainder of the paragraph, so experiment with different topic sentences until you come up with one that captures the reader's interest, names the topic, and clearly expresses the central impression you want to convey. In the following topic sentences, a strong topic sentence finally emerges when the writer creates sentence #6:

1. Clayton is a survivor.
2. Clayton's personal strength made him a survivor.
3. Clayton is a survivor because of his personal strength.
4. My friend Clayton overcame the odds to become a survivor.
5. My friend Clayton fought cancer and won.
6. My friend Clayton has incredible courage and a powerful will to live.

Step 4: Write the rough draft.

The rough draft is your first attempt to organize your information and your ideas on paper. The rough draft is only the starting point to get your ideas from your head onto the paper.

In the following rough draft, the writer started with her topic sentence and then proceeded to use details from her cluster to develop the body of the paragraph. The writer incorporated new details into the paragraph and used some of the physical descriptions to strengthen the visual image of Clayton in the reader's mind.

Clayton

My friend Clayton has incredible courage and a powerful will to live. He lives with a feeding tube protruding from his stomach. Twelve times a day, he slips out of sight to feed his tube. His long, muscular arms reach above his head to hang a food bag. The food bag holds potent concoctions of juices that are loaded with vitamins and minerals. He researched the foods rich in antioxidants and started blending his own high-potency formulas that would return his 6'2" frame to its original strength and boost his immune system. His dark brown eyes look up at the feeding bag, and he smiles, knowing he will win the battle with tongue and throat cancer. Half of his tongue has been cut away, and he lost part of the roof of his mouth. He knows he will eventually return to eating solid foods. His right arm is scarred from surgery that removed arteries and skin to reconstruct his neck. Radiation treatments darkened the sides of his face. He flashes a smile and shows his white teeth. His own courage and will to survive cloak him with an air of gratitude and pride.

Step 5: Revise, revise, revise.

Step 5 of the writing process provides you with several opportunities to strengthen, refine, and improve your paragraph. The following questions can guide you through the revision process, which often occurs in several stages:

1. Paragraph Structure

   Does the topic sentence clearly state a specific subject and a central impression?
   Does the topic sentence capture the reader's attention?
   Does the concluding sentence echo the topic sentence or reflect the central impression?

2. Essential Paragraph Elements

   Does the paragraph have unity? Does every sentence support the central impression?
   Does the paragraph have coherence? How are the details organized in the body?
   Do the ideas in the paragraph flow together smoothly and logically?
   Does the paragraph have adequate development? Are there enough different details to create a strong image of the subject and develop the central impression?

3. Effective Choice of Words

   Do the words you use evoke an emotional response from your reader?
   Do the nouns, verbs, adjectives, and adverbs you use create a clear description?
   Do the sensory details you use develop the central impression?

With each revision, your paragraph should be stronger, clearer, and more effective. After using the revision questions to guide the revision process, the writer made the following changes to her paragraph:

Clayton

My friend Clayton has incredible courage and a powerful will to live.

He knows he can win the battle against tongue and throat cancer.

the doctors located they cut away and discarded
After ^ the tumor in his throat, ^ ~~was located~~ half of his tongue and a

They pulled his
section of the roof of his mouth. ~~had to be~~ ^ ~~cut away~~. ~~His~~ back teeth

~~were removed~~ for radiation treatment; burns from the radiation

scarred and darkened Chewing and swallowing are impossible,
treatments ~~left~~ the sides of his face. ~~darkened and~~ ^ ~~scarred~~. ~~He cannot~~

~~chew or swallow~~ so he lives with a feeding tube protruding from his stomach. Twelve times a day, he slips out of sight to pour potent concoctions of juices that are loaded with vitamins and minerals into his ~~tube.~~ feeding bag. He researched the foods rich in antioxidants and started blending his own high-potency formulas that would return his 6′2″ frame to its original strength and boost his immune system. His long, muscular arms reach above his head to hang the soft plastic food bag. His right ~~arm~~ hand, scarred from surgery that removed arteries and skin to reconstruct his neck, straightens the tube. His long, slender fingers fiddle with the dial to adjust the flow of the liquids. His dark brown eyes ~~look up~~ glance up confidently at the feeding bag, and he flashes a smile, knowing that his efforts to return to health will pay off. His own courage and will to survive cloak him with an air of gratitude and ~~pride.~~ courage.

Step 6: Proofread and edit.

Use the following checklist to proofread and edit:

1. Does every sentence have a complete subject and a complete verb and form a complete thought?
2. Do you avoid using fragments, run-on sentences, or comma splices?
3. Does the paragraph have good sentence variety? Are there simple, compound, and complex sentences in the paragraph? (Complex sentences are discussed at the end of this chapter.)
4. Do you punctuate all sentences correctly?
5. Do you use correct spelling for all words?
6. Do you use verbs, adjectives, and adverbs correctly?

Step 7: Prepare the final version of your descriptive paragraph.

Use the standard format on page 28 in Chapter 1 to prepare the final version of your descriptive paragraph. This format includes a heading, an optional title, and the final version of your paragraph typed or handwritten with double spacing.

WRITING ASSIGNMENT

Write a descriptive paragraph about a specific person, place, thing, or event. Your paragraph should be able to stand by itself as a complete paragraph with a topic sentence, a body, and a concluding sentence.

Complete each of the following steps for writing a descriptive paragraph. Unless your instructor indicates a different approach, use the descriptive planning sheet on page 161 for each step of the writing process.

Step 1: Generate ideas.
Select a topic for your descriptive paragraph. You may select one of the ideas from your brainstorming lists on pages 153–154, or you may add new ideas to the list. If you need additional ideas, consider one of the following:

a local politician	a former teacher	an agent of the Internal Revenue Service (IRS)
a childhood idol	a favorite athlete	a political, military, or religious leader
a peacemaker	a peaceful place	a club or a restaurant
a midway at a fair	a mortuary	a haunted house or mansion
a castle	a waterfall	an antique object (spinning wheel, etc.)
a cave or a cavern	a coin collection	a specific animal

Step 2: Get a focus.
Focus the topic for your paragraph by narrowing the topic, identifying the specific time frame and setting, and deciding on the position of your observation. Answer the question for Step 2 on your Planning Sheet.

Step 3: Gather and organize your information.
On a separate piece of paper, create a cluster of possible details to use in your descriptive paragraph. Then decide what central impression you want to express about your topic. Use the topic and the central impression to write several possible topic sentences. Draft a topic sentence that expresses your idea clearly and captures your reader's attention and interest. Complete Step 3 on the Planning Sheet.

Step 4: Write a rough draft.
Write a rough draft that begins with your topic sentence, includes your descriptive details in the body of the paragraph, and ends with a strong concluding sentence. Answer the question for Step 4 on the Planning Sheet.

Step 5: Revise, revise, revise.
Revise one or more times to strengthen your paragraph. Use the revision suggestions on page 158 to guide your revision process. Save each of your revisions. Share your revised draft with a partner and ask your partner to complete the feedback questions on the Planning Sheet.

Step 6: Proofread and edit.
Use the checklist on page 159 to guide you through the proofreading and editing step. Answer the question for Step 6 on the Planning Sheet.

Step 7: Prepare the final version of your paragraph.

DESCRIPTIVE PARAGRAPH PLANNING SHEET

Name ____________________________

Step 1: Write the subject of your descriptive paragraph: ____________________________

Step 2: Show how you focused the topic by answering the following questions:

What is the specific time frame? ____________________________

What is the specific setting? ____________________________

Where will you be positioned to observe the subject? ____________________________

Step 3: On separate paper, create a cluster of possible details for your paragraph. Attach your work to this Planning Sheet.

What is the central impression you want to create? ____________________________

Write several possible topic sentences.

Option 1: ____________________________

____

Option 2: ____________________________

____

Option 3: ____________________________

____

Option 4: ____________________________

____

Place a star next to the topic sentence you prefer.

Step 4: When did you complete this rough draft? ____________________________

Step 5: Revise, revise, revise. Save all your revisions. Show your revised draft to a partner. Ask the partner to answer the following questions. When you receive the feedback, use your partner's comments for further revisions of your paragraph.

PARTNER FEEDBACK FORM

1. Does the paragraph have an effective topic sentence? Explain: ______________________

____

____

2. What is the central impression? ______________________

Do all the details in the body of the paragraph support and develop the central impression? Explain. ______________________

____

____

____

3. Does the paragraph have coherence? Would you suggest reordering or rearranging the details another way? Explain. ______________________

____

____

____

4. Does the writer use well-chosen descriptive details to develop the central impression? Explain by giving specific examples. ______________________

____

____

5. Is the concluding sentence effective? Does it echo the topic sentence? Explain.

____

____

6. Did you notice any errors that the writer will need to correct during the proofreading and editing step? Highlight the errors or mark them with a pencil to draw the writer's attention to them.

Partner's name ______________________

Step 6: Proofread and edit. Save the drafts that show your proofreading and editing work.

Write the date you completed this step: ______________________

Step 7: Prepare the final version of your descriptive paragraph.

Grammar and Usage Tips

Carefully read the four new Grammar and Usage Tips. Complete the exercises following each tip. After you complete the exercises, check your work with the answer keys in Appendix A and record your number of errors for each exercise. Review the tip and examine the correct answer. In the margins of each exercise, jot down questions that you would like to ask your instructor regarding the grammar and usage points covered.

Write complex sentences with subordinate conjunctions to achieve greater sentence variety in your writing. Complex sentences have one independent clause and one or more dependent clauses. Dependent clauses must be attached to an independent clause to avoid becoming a fragment.

Independent and Dependent Clauses

An **independent clause** can stand by itself as a complete sentence. Every independent clause has a complete subject and a complete verb and forms a complete thought. The following statements are all independent clauses. The subjects are underlined once; the complete verbs are underlined twice.

A new screen appears with more flashing arrows.

The endless warm sand of the white beach beneath my feet touches my soul.

We returned to the scene of the crime.

I will stay late to compile the data.

A **dependent clause** has a subject and a complete verb, but it does not form a complete thought. Every dependent clause needs to be attached to an independent clause; it cannot stand on its own as a sentence. If a dependent clause poses as a complete sentence, the result is a fragment.

If someone walked up to you and made the following statements, you would likely wait for the person to finish the thought. Each of the following statements is a dependent clause. Since the clauses are punctuated as sentences, they are fragments, not sentences.

When I push each button.

After all of the reporters had left.

As the water reaches out to tempt me into the lagoon.

Unless you want me to wait until tomorrow.

Complex Sentences

Complex sentences have one independent clause and at least one dependent clause. Each clause has its own subject and verb pattern. Notice in the following complex sentences that the dependent clause may appear before or after the independent clause. A comma is used at the end of a dependent clause when the dependent clause appears before an independent clause.

Dependent Clause — comma — Independent Clause

When I push each button, a new screen appears with more flashing arrows.

Independent Clause — no comma — Dependent Clause

A new screen appears with more flashing arrows **when I push each button.**

Dependent Clause — comma — Independent Clause

After all of the reporters had left, we returned to the scene of the crime.

Independent Clause — no comma — Dependent Clause

We returned to the scene of the crime **after all of the reporters had left.**

Subordinate Conjunctions

Subordinate conjunctions are words that begin dependent clauses. They show a relationship between the dependent and the independent clauses. A subordinate conjunction may show *time, place, frequency, manner* or *condition, cause-effect, purpose, concession,* or *comparison/contrast.* The following chart shows common subordinate conjunctions that begin dependent clauses. Note that some subordinate conjunctions consist of two or three words.

SUBORDINATE CONJUNCTIONS			
after	even though	provided that	when
although	if	since	whenever
as	in order that	so long as	where
as if	in that	so that	whereas
as long as	less than	than	wherever
as soon as	more than	though	whether
as though	no matter how	till	while
because	now that	unless	
before	once	until	

EXERCISE 4.1 Identifying Dependent Clauses

Score: ______

Work with a partner or on your own. Draw a box around all the dependent clauses. Circle the subordinate conjunction that signals the beginning of the dependent clause.

Example: Though power brownouts are common in some areas, we seldom get them here.

1. Although the power was off, the generators worked.
2. The electricity went off because a construction crew accidentally cut the power line.
3. The electricity will be turned back on as soon as the power company repairs the line.
4. While the power was off, many people lit candles and used flashlights.
5. Before the power was turned on, hundreds of customers had called the power company.
6. After the power company repaired the line, all the digital clocks in the house needed to be reset.
7. Even though some homes use solar energy, most homes rely on electricity.
8. Whenever power lines go down, hospitals automatically activate emergency generators.
9. If you are in your home during a power outage, just be patient.
10. When you are without electricity, a flashlight or candles are an excellent source of light.

EXERCISE 4.2 Punctuating Compound and Complex Sentences

Score: ______

Some of the following sentences are missing proper punctuation between clauses. Add the missing commas or semicolons in the following sentences. Write **C** if the sentence is **correct** as is.

Example: Because technological advances make acquisition of new data possible scientists are able to make new discoveries about the universe.

Because technological advances make acquisition of new data possible, scientists are able to make new discoveries about the universe.

1. Astronomers have discovered ten new planets the planets are orbiting stars beyond the sun.

2. Approximately fifty planets are now known of course only nine of the planets orbit our sun.

3. None of the new planets resemble Earth but astronomers still want to study the planets.

4. One planet is about the mass of Jupiter it orbits the star Epsilon Eridani.

5. Even though Epsilon Eridani is 10.5 light-years from Earth it is visible to the naked eye.

6. Scientists continue to study other planets because they hope to find a planet similar to Earth.

7. However, scientists will be surprised if they ever find a planet similar to Earth.

8. Up until six years ago, scientists could not detect planets beyond the sun because the glare from their stars was too strong.

9. New technology now enables scientists to calculate the mass and the character of the orbit of new planets but precise data is still difficult to pin down.

10. However, more direct study and optical imaging may be possible in the future for more advanced instruments on the ground and in space are being developed each year.

[Adapted from Kathy Sawyer, *Washington Post,* "10 More Planets Discovered; Extrasolar System Relatively Nearby," August 6, 2000, p. 10A]

TIP 10 **Write complex sentences with relative pronoun clauses to achieve greater sentence variety in your writing. The relative pronoun clause is a dependent clause that begins with one of the relative pronouns: *who, whose, whom, which,* and *that.* A relative pronoun clause that stands by itself is a fragment; it must be attached to an independent clause.**

Relative Pronouns

A **relative pronoun** refers to a noun that has already been stated in the independent clause. The noun that it refers to in the independent clause is called its **antecedent.** *Who, whose, whom, which,* and *that* are relative pronouns. In the following examples, the relative pronoun clauses are in bold print. An arrow points from each relative pronoun to the noun it refers to, its antecedent, in the independent clause. Notice how the relative pronoun clauses are placed as close as possible to their antecedents.

dependent clause

My English literature teacher is a person **who loves literature and enjoys writing poetry.**

dependent clause

The official **whose car was parked in an illegal zone** received a $50 parking fine.

dependent clause

My insurance agent, **whom I have known for three years,** handles both of my policies.

dependent clause

The steeple on the church, **which is lit every night,** is the subject of many photographs.

dependent clause

The food service contract **that started in January** will terminate in December.

Subjects and Verbs in Relative Pronoun Clauses

A relative pronoun clause, like all dependent clauses, has a subject and a verb. Sometimes the relative pronoun is the subject of the dependent clause; other times the relative pronoun precedes the subject of the dependent clause. In the following complex sentences, the subjects and the verbs for both the independent clause and the dependent clause are marked.

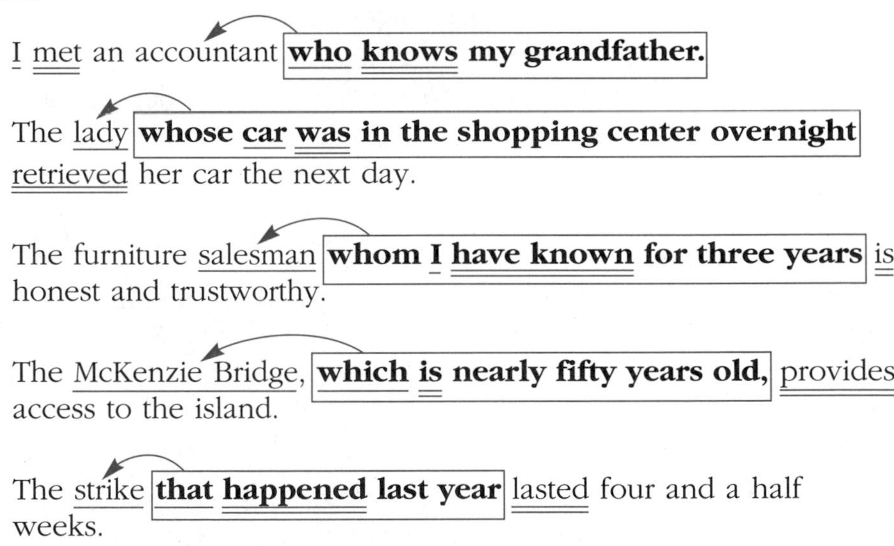

I met an accountant **who knows my grandfather.**

The lady **whose car was in the shopping center overnight** retrieved her car the next day.

The furniture salesman **whom I have known for three years** is honest and trustworthy.

The McKenzie Bridge, **which is nearly fifty years old,** provides access to the island.

The strike **that happened last year** lasted four and a half weeks.

EXERCISE 4.3 Identifying Dependent Clauses

Score: ______

Draw a box around the dependent clauses with relative pronouns in the following sentences. Underline the subjects in the dependent clauses once and the verbs twice. You do not need to underline the subjects and verbs in the independent clauses.

Example: Rudy's football story, which was true, became a box office hit.

1. She is small and delicately boned with skin that is wrinkled.

2. I know without a doubt that I am truly in the South Pacific.

3. Her right arm, which was brown with mud, hung to her side.

4. His eyes, which I could see through his glasses, became very sharp.

5. She frowned to show her displeasure with the sounds that came out of the piano.

6. I will stay late to compile the data that you requested for the meeting tomorrow morning.

7. The system has two separate programs so that users can personalize the watering cycles.

8. Beautiful gardens and rich, lush lawns will adorn the property of homeowners who use the Water Wizard.

9. This tiny screen has faded letters that no one with normal eyesight can read.

10. The engineers did not program the device in a way that a person with average intelligence can understand.

Using the Correct Relative Pronoun

1. Use *who, whose,* and *whom* to refer to people. Informally, you can use *that* to refer to people; however, in formal writing, replace the relative pronoun *that* with *who* or *whom* when the pronoun refers to people.

   who — dependent clause

   I recognized the man ~~**that**~~ **was on television last night.**

2. Use *whom* when the relative pronoun clause already has a subject.

   whom — dependent clause

   I interviewed the man ~~**who**~~ **the mayor honored at the ceremony.**

3. Use *whose* when the relative pronoun is possessive or shows ownership.

   dependent clause

   The woman **whose dog was on the commercial** treats her pet like her child.

4. Use *which* and *that* to refer to things and ideas.

   dependent clause

   This photograph, **which I took on the north shore,** is my favorite.

   dependent clause

   Several of my photographs **that won blue ribbons at the county fair** are on exhibit.

Essential and Nonessential Clauses

Essential clauses, or restrictive clauses, are essential to the meaning of the independent clause. The following guidelines can help you identify and use correct punctuation for essential and nonessential clauses.

1. Relative pronoun clauses that begin with *who, whom,* or *whose* may be essential or nonessential. When the dependent clause is essential, you do not separate the clause from the remainder of the sentence. Do not enclose essential clauses with commas. The following relative pronoun clauses are essential to the meaning of the independent clause.

   The runner **who is five feet tall** took the lead.

   [The independent clause is *the runner took the lead.* We do not know which runner took the lead without the dependent clause. The dependent clause is essential.]

   A woman **whom I used to know** is the new company's CEO.

   [The dependent clause is essential to the meaning of the sentence. Without the dependent clause we do not know which woman is the new company's CEO.]

   The man **whose father designed this building** is also an architect.

   [The dependent clause is essential to the meaning of the sentence. Without the dependent clause, we do not know which man is also an architect.]

2. Use a comma before and after a relative pronoun clause that begins with *who, whom,* or *whose* only if the information is nonessential, or nonrestrictive, to understanding the independent clause.

   specific

   The third runner, **who is five feet tall,** took the lead.

   specific

   Melissa, **whom I used to know,** is the new company's CEO.

   specific

   Roberto Chavez, **whose father designed this building,** is also an architect.

3. Relative pronoun clauses that begin with *which* are nonessential. Therefore, they are set off by commas.

   My new stereo system, **which cost three hundred dollars,** also has a turntable.

   [The independent clause *My new stereo system also has a turntable* makes sense without the relative pronoun clause. The fact the system cost three hundred dollars is not essential information to understand the independent clause.]

This inaugural ball, **which occurs every four years,** is a popular social event.

[The independent clause *This inaugural ball is a popular social event* makes sense without the relative pronoun clause. The fact that the ball occurs every four years is not essential to understand the independent clause.]

4. Relative pronoun clauses that begin with *that* are always essential. Therefore, do not set them off from the independent clause by using commas.

The bridge **that provides access to the island** is nearly fifty years old.

[The dependent clause is essential in order to understand which bridge is nearly fifty years old.]

The speech **that I presented at the state conference** lasted over an hour.

[The dependent clause is essential in order to understand which speech lasted over an hour.]

Additional Guidelines for Using Relative Pronoun Clauses

1. Place the relative pronoun clause as close as possible to the noun it refers to or replaces (its antecedent). If the relative pronoun clause is too far from its antecedent, the reader will be confused, and the meaning of your sentence will be altered.

NO

Incorrect Placement: The fans took a picture of the model **who stood in line for three hours.** [The model did not stand in line for three hours.]

YES

Correct Placement: The fans **who stood in line for three hours** took a picture of the model. [The relative pronoun clause refers to the fans, so it should be placed close to the word *fans*.]

2. The relative pronoun *that* is often implied rather than written. The pronoun can be inserted back into the sentence without altering the meaning of the sentence.

We knew **[that] he was not the perpetrator.**

3. A relative pronoun clause that is not attached to an independent clause is a **fragment.**

Fragments: **Which brought the family great joy.**

Whose insurance policy had expired.

4. The pronoun *that* may also function as an adjective or subject of a sentence. In such cases, the pronoun *that* is not used to introduce a relative pronoun clause.

   Adjective
   That job is perfect for me.
   Subject
   That was the most exciting experience in my lifetime.

5. The pronouns *who, whom, whose,* and *which* may be used to form questions.

   Who is your favorite musician?

   Whom did the students elect for their president?

   Whose name was first on the ballot?

   Which program is your favorite?

EXERCISE 4.4 Combining Sentences to Make Complex Sentences

Score: ______

Combine the two simple sentences into a complex sentence by changing one of the clauses to a dependent clause that begins with a relative pronoun. Write your answers on separate paper.

Example: The students will receive a certificate. ~~The students~~ who have a 3.5 grade point average.

The students **who have a 3.5 grade point average** will receive a certificate.

1. The house has one bay window. The bay window overlooks the canyon.
2. This logo will appear on our letterhead. Sean designed this logo.
3. Clint Eastwood stars in *Space Cowboys*. *Space Cowboys* is a movie about four retired pilots.
4. My neighbors complain about my dog at least once a week. My neighbors do not own a dog.
5. The Lion Club's car raffle takes place in September. The raffle is for a new Chrysler PT Cruiser.
6. Jake is a rodeo rider. Jake is a native of Colorado.
7. My cousin wrote this book. The book is about a Native American bounty hunter.
8. My grandmother raised five children and also two grandchildren. The grandchildren lived with her for five years.
9. Patrick Summers is a retired Navy officer. His son served in the Persian Gulf.
10. A memo had several errors. The memo went out via email.

EXERCISE 4.5 Punctuating Complex Sentences

Score: ______

In the following sentences, add the missing punctuation where necessary. Cross out commas that are incorrect. Mark **C** next to the sentences that are **correct.**

1. The stranger who stopped to help me did not give me his name.
2. I finally decided on the topic that I want to use for my writing assignment.
3. The shingles that are on the ground blew off the roof during the windstorm.
4. Your transcripts which arrived yesterday have the official college seal.
5. My brother who considers himself an honest person could not lie about the ticket.
6. The smelly, rusty garbage can which I have had for years is finally heading to the dump.
7. Because of the attendance policy several students will lose points at the end of the term.
8. The campers sang the song that they had learned at the retreat.
9. Training in martial arts is wise for women who want to increase their self-confidence.
10. When Robbie lit the candles on the table his wife smiled with appreciation.

Carefully proofread each sentence to confirm that the sentence has a complete subject and a complete verb and forms a complete thought. Correct all fragments by adding or deleting words and punctuation as needed. Correct fragments that are dependent clauses by joining them to independent clauses.

You have already learned the following four techniques for correcting fragments:

1. Add the missing subject.
2. Add the missing verb.
3. Add the missing helping verb to complete a verb phrase.
4. Remove the word or words that make the thought incomplete.

We can now add two additional techniques to use to correct fragments. Use these techniques when the fragment is a dependent clause that begins with a subordinate conjunction or a relative pronoun.

5. Correct a fragment created by a dependent clause that begins with a subordinate conjunction by joining the dependent clause to an independent clause.

Fragment:	**When parents take time to safeguard their homes.**
Correction 1:	**When parents take time to safeguard their homes,** the risk of childhood injuries decreases.
Correction 2:	The risk of childhood injuries decreases **when parents take time to safeguard their homes.**

6. Correct fragment created by a dependent clause that begins with a relative pronoun by joining the dependent clause to an independent clause. The relative pronoun clause must be placed as close as possible to the noun it refers to (its antecedent). The relative pronoun clause may be inserted between the subject and the verb of the independent clause.

Fragment:	**That overlooks the bay.**
Correction:	We toured the mansion **that overlooks the bay.**
Fragment:	**Whom Jon wants to interview.**
Correction:	The quarterback **whom Jon wants to interview** scheduled an appointment for Friday.
Fragment:	**Which involved two executives.**
Correction:	The most recent scandal, **which involved two executives,** hit this morning's newspapers and television stations.

EXERCISE 4.6 Correcting Fragments

Score: ______

Each of the following statements is a fragment. Use any of the six methods on pages 172–173 to correct the fragments. Write the corrected sentences with correct punctuation on separate paper.

1. After the fishermen reached the dock
2. When the flood level rises
3. Whom I regard as an intelligent person
4. That I should resign
5. As soon as the final report is ready
6. Because she had a lot of anger
7. Which turned out to be a wonderful experience
8. Who needs attention from other people
9. If you know the difference between right and wrong
10. Before you file your taxes

TIP 12 Proofread and edit your writing for correct use of commas. Eight comma rules can guide you with your editing.

1. Use commas between three or more nouns or verbs in a series.

   nouns

   Leather purses, wallets, and sandals attracted my attention.

   verbs

   We dashed down the aisle, called his name, and cried for help.

2. Use a comma between two or more adjectives in a series when the word *and* can replace the comma and make sense.

   adjectives [and]

   The fragrant, delicate orchids grew in clay pots.

   Notice how commas are not used between the following adjectives. The word *and* cannot be inserted between the adjectives and make sense.

   adjectives ~~and~~

   The three red balloons ascended into the blue sky.

3. Use a comma after an introductory word or phrase at the beginning of a sentence.

   Suddenly, the butcher swatted a fly.

   Without thinking, I pulled into the street without looking.

4. Use a comma between two independent clauses that are joined by a coordinating conjunction.

   independent clause / independent clause

   He was intrigued by the butcher shop**, for** he had never seen a butcher shop in the middle of a shopping center.

5. Use a comma after the conjunctive adverb in a compound sentence.

   At first, the lady was pleasant**; however,** her attitude changed.

6. Use commas before and after adverbs inside a clause when the adverbs interrupt the flow of thought.

   The meat**, however,** was not refrigerated.

7. Use a comma after a dependent clause that begins with a subordinate conjunction and appears before the independent clause in a complex sentence.

   dependent clause / independent clause

   When the lady beckoned to me, I responded with a smile.

8. Use commas before and after a relative pronoun clause that begins with *who, whom, whose,* and *which* when the clause is nonessential to the meaning of the sentence. The antecedents are already specific and clearly understood.

   specific — relative pronound clause

   Jane's lawyer**, who has an office next to mine,** charges $100 an hour for his legal services.

Grammar and Usage Tips Summary

TIP 9 Write complex sentences with subordinate conjunctions to achieve greater sentence variety in your writing. *Because, if, when, since, before, after,* and *though* are examples of subordinate conjunctions that can be used at the beginning of dependent clauses.

TIP 10 Write complex sentences with relative pronoun clauses to achieve greater sentence variety in your writing. *Who, whose, whom, which,* and *that* are the relative pronouns that begin dependent clauses. Relative pronoun clauses that are nonessential are set off with commas.

TIP 11 Carefully proofread to confirm that each group of words that poses as a sentence has a complete subject and a complete verb and forms a complete thought. Correct fragments by adding or deleting words and punctuation as needed or by joining dependent clauses to independent clauses and using correct punctuation.

TIP 12 Use the list of eight comma rules on pages 174–175 when you proofread and edit your writing.

CHAPTER 4 • Descriptive Paragraphs • Proofreading and Editing Exercises

Proofreading 1

Work with a partner or on your own. Proofread and edit the paragraph. Write the corrections or changes in the space between the lines.

Mexican Market

The central market in the middle of Juarez, Mexico, vibrates with color and activity. As I stand ten feet inside the main entrance every one of my senses becomes overwhelmed. On my left a woman with beautiful long shiny hair and sparkling eyes raises her bracelet-laden arms and motions me to step into her tiny cluttered shop. When I don't move in her direction her inviting voice shifts from friendly to sharp demanding and desperate, the sparkling eyes narrow and glare at me with an unexpected sense of hostility. Behind the shopkeeper cotton peasant blouses loose fitting sun dresses and flaring, multicolored skirts hang on the walls every inch of wall space is plastered with merchandise. Directly in front of me, a full-scale meat shop attracts customers whom want fresh meat and poultry. In this stuffy humid market full sides of beef hang from large metal hooks suspended from the wood beams of the ceiling. Each time the butcher in his white, blood-stained jacket walks by, the sides of beef sway ever so slightly. Endless links of sausages pork chops ground hamburger, and red, juicy steaks. Stacked in rows in the uncovered meat case. Occasionally, the butcher walks by and swishes his arm across the meat case to chase away the flies the flies return as soon as the butcher turns his back. To the right, a small stall displays handmade leather purses belts wallets, and sandals. As I move toward the stall the smell of newly tanned leather overpowers the other aromas of spices flowers fresh meat, and sweaty bodies. I already sense that I will spend many hours exploring and enjoying this culturally rich, vibrant, and colorful Mexican market.

Proofreading 2

Return to Writing Warm-Up 4. Proofread and edit the sentences in this writing sample. Use the proofreading and editing checklist on page 159.

Internet Enrichment

Log on to the web site for this textbook for additional exercises and links for the following topics:

Subjective and Objective Description

Central Impression

Sensory Details

Complex Sentences with Subordinate Conjunctions

Complex Sentences with Relative Pronouns

Essential and Nonessential Clauses

Fragments

Comma Rules

Go to: http://college.hmco.com. Click on "Students." Type *Paragraph Essentials* in the "Jump to Textbook Sites" box. Click "go," and then bookmark the site. Click on Chapter 4.

CHAPTER 4 • Grammar and Usage Review

Name ______________________

Date ______________________

Complex Sentences

Combine the following sentences by writing complex sentences. Write your answers on separate paper.

1. It rained yesterday. I do not need to water the lawn today.
2. There was no picture on my television. I called the cable company.
3. I filed my income tax return. I breathed a sigh of relief.
4. The books will be shipped from New York. The books will be here for the first class.
5. The boycott lasted one day. The effects on the gas station were obvious.
6. The documentary was on television last night. My uncle produced the documentary.
7. Kim knows the trails well. She is a capable mountain guide.
8. The wooden fence collapsed during the storm. The fence was built last year.

Identifying and Correcting Fragments

Write **C** if the statement is a **complete sentence.** Write **FRAG** if the statement is a **fragment.** Use any method to correct the fragment.

________ 1. My license plate fell off when I drove through the car wash.

________ 2. His dentist, who performed his root canal.

________ 3. The time management system that he has used for many years.

________ 4. Child-care expenses that most working parents must include in their budgets.

________ 5. Whom we all consider to be the best instructor on campus.

________ 6. Because I do not like to make quick decisions.

________ 7. After class, we can meet for an hour to review our notes.

________ 8. If classes are cancelled due to bad weather.

Relative Pronouns

Write a relative pronoun on the line to complete each sentence. Add punctuation as needed.

1. The hot chocolate ________ you ordered will be ready in a minute.

2. Many elderly men ________ live in the retirement home enjoy playing horseshoes.

3. The two narrow paths led to the valley floor ________ was covered with dense vegetation.

4. My math instructor ________ has taught at the college for ten years is retiring.

5. Procrastinators are people ____________ postpone the completion of necessary tasks.

CHAPTER 5

Process Paragraphs

The topic sentence introduces the subject, the controlling idea, and the word *steps* or *stages*.

The body provides specific steps in chronological order and secondary details. The body has unity, coherence, and adequate development.

The concluding sentence echoes the topic sentence and identifies the outcome.

Topic Sentence .... + controlling idea + steps/stages ....

Step 1 ....
Secondary details ....
Step 2 ....
Secondary details ....
Step 3 ....
Secondary details ....
Concluding Sentence ....

In Chapter 5 you will learn about the following:

1. Informational and directional process paragraphs
2. The structure of a process paragraph
3. The writing process for process paragraphs
4. Four additional grammar and usage tips

WRITING WARM-UP 5

Write a paragraph that explains how to do a simple task that you do as a part of your everyday life. Assume that the reader does not know how to do this task effectively or efficiently. Provide the reader with all the necessary steps to perform or duplicate this task.

The Process Paragraph

A process paragraph presents a series of well-defined steps that explain how to complete a task or how a process works. Knowing your audience is essential for writing process paragraphs. If your readers are unfamiliar with the process you are describing or the technical terms related to the process, you will need to provide more specific details and definitions than you would for readers who are familiar with the process or the terminology. Your purpose is to provide your readers with a clear explanation of the steps they could follow to do, make, or repair something or the steps involved in a process that is important or valuable for them to understand.

Informational Process Paragraphs

In an **informational process paragraph,** you provide your reader with a clear understanding as to how an operation, an event, a system, or a procedure works. Your reader is not expected to duplicate this process. For example, you may explain how lenses for eyeglasses are made, how a volcano forms, or how an initiative becomes a ballot measure, but you would not expect your reader to make a pair of eyeglasses, create a volcano, or develop an initiative to be placed on a voter's ballot. Social science and science textbooks and a variety of training materials or manuals in the workforce use informational process paragraphs extensively. Informational process paragraphs frequently are written in the third person, using the pronouns *he, she, they,* or *it.*

The following informational process paragraph explains the steps a person in Iowa must go through to become a delegate at a national convention. The paragraph provides the reader with background information about the political system of caucuses without expecting the reader to personally complete the steps to become a delegate at a national convention. Marginal notes provide brief explanations about the structure of an informational process paragraph.

Iowa's Political Process

Topic sentence

Signals a process

Secondary details offer explanations.

Citizens of Iowa who want to represent the state at the national convention must be willing to *progress through several levels* of political meetings. First, they must participate in the caucus for their precinct, or their voting area. A caucus is the lowest level of party politics; grassroots politics takes center stage at caucuses. Iowa, a state with more than 2,100 different precincts, has more than 2,100 caucuses prior to a national convention. About 180,000 people in Iowa, about 6.5 percent of the total population, participate in caucuses. Citizens at each caucus argue and debate politics, their party's platforms, and party business. A party chairperson leads the debates, and then the participants vote for their caucus's preference for their party's presidential nomination. Next, each caucus picks delegates for the county convention, which is the second level of political meetings. At the county conventions, after participants discuss the politics, candidates, and platforms, and the preference for the presidential nomination, they select their delegates for the district meetings. The *process continues* in a similar fashion for the third level of political meetings, the district meetings. Participants at the district meetings select the delegates who will attend the state convention. At the fourth level, the state convention, the representatives once again vote to show their party's preference for a presidential nomination, and they select the delegates who will represent the state of Iowa at the national convention. Delegates from Iowa who attend the national convention have logged many hours of political discussions, debates, and political experiences. They earned their positions by working their way through the four levels of political meetings.

Transition words signal each step or level of the process.

Secondary details

Concluding Sentence

[Adapted from: AP, "Iowa Caucuses Q & A," *Register Guard,* January 23, 2000, p. 3A.]

Directional Process Paragraphs

In a *directional process paragraph,* you provide your reader with specific steps and instructions to do, make, or repair something. The purpose of a directional process paragraph is to guide your reader through a series of clear, precise steps that he or she can duplicate. Following your directions will bring the reader to a result, which may be a specific product, a completed task, or some other identifiable outcome. In a directional process paragraph, you must consider your audience carefully. If you oversimplify the steps, or if you do not provide your reader with crucial details and instructions, your reader may not be able to complete the task or the process correctly.

The following directional process paragraph explains precisely how to generate more fuchsia plants by using cuttings from existing plants. The writer wants you, the reader, to be able to duplicate the process.

Growing Fuchsias

Topic sentence

To guarantee the beauty of fuchsias in the coming season, you can take fuchsia cuttings to make new plants by following these *five easy steps.*

"You" is often used in directional process paragraphs.

Preparation information

Transition words introduce each step.

Secondary details explain each step.

Concluding sentence

Before you begin the process, make sure the plants you are taking cuttings from are not in the flowering stage. Trim them back to encourage new growth. To do this, you will need a sharp knife to slice the stems without crushing the cambium layer, the layer where the new growth occurs. Water the plant well before you start taking cuttings for transplanting. For the first step, fill your containers with sterile, moist soil. Do not pack the soil; keep it light and fluffy. This prevents the tender cuttings from getting bruised or broken when you stick them in the soil. Next, count down three to four nodes from the stem tip, and then slice a little below that point. Be sure to remove the last leaves or stems on that cutting. Next, if you are using Rotone, a rooting compound, dip the cut end in the powder just enough to cover it. This is not absolutely essential, but it does promote root growth. For the fourth step, gently push the cuttings into the soil deep enough to cover the last node toward the cut end. This cutting should be pushed one to one and a half inches below the soil. Finally, water the containers with the cuttings and cover them with a cellophane wrap, such as Saran Wrap. Place the containers in a warm, bright place; the cuttings will begin to root and to grow. You can now look forward to many beautiful flowering plants in the season to come.

Kathleen Maddux
Lane Community College
Eugene, Oregon

5.1 What do you think?

Read the following process paragraph. On separate paper, answer the questions that follow the paragraph.

Piaget's Cognitive Stages

According to Jean Piaget, children progress through four stages to develop their cognitive abilities. First, infants from birth to the age of two show little understanding of their environment. Most of their behavior occurs instinctually. Gradually, they begin to learn to connect their sensory experiences to their physical environment. This first stage is called the *sensorimotor stage*. Next, children enter the *preoperational stage*. In this stage, which occurs in children ages two to seven, children begin to understand language. They begin to learn the connection between images and words and to start thinking symbolically. The third stage, the *concrete operation stage,* occurs between the ages of seven and eleven. Children's cognitive abilities develop, and they begin to reason logically about the concrete, physical world. They are able to differentiate and classify objects into various categories. Finally, in the *formal operational stage,* adolescents learn to think abstractly. They form their own concepts and understand the relationship between many existing concepts. Piaget developed this theory of cognitive development, which consists of four stages, by observing the cognitive progression experienced by a small number of children.

[Adapted from: Payne, Wenger, *Cognitive Psychology*, Houghton Mifflin, 1998, p. 353–5.]

1. Which type of process paragraph is this? Is it a directional or an informational process paragraph? Explain.
2. List the four distinct stages.
3. How do you know where in the paragraph one stage ends and the next begins? Explain.
4. What word is used frequently in the paragraph to keep the reader focused on the controlling idea?

The Structure of a Process Paragraph

A process paragraph has a topic sentence with a controlling idea, a body with supporting details, and a concluding sentence. If you are describing a process for which specific materials or tools are needed, you can tell your reader about them after the topic sentence and before you begin to explain the specific steps. You can also alert your reader to any special precautions that he or she needs to take before proceeding with your directions.

Developing the Topic Sentence

Use the following guidelines to write an effective topic sentence with a controlling idea that reveals your point of view, opinion, or attitude toward the subject of your paragraph.

1. Narrow the topic for your process paragraph so it covers a process that can be explained in one paragraph. Some processes are very complex and require several stages to complete; such topics are too large for a paragraph. For example, explaining how to build a house, how to restore a classic car, or how to design a golf course are too broad to develop well in one paragraph. You could, however, explain how to pour concrete, finish the chrome on a car, or maintain a green on a golf course.
2. State your controlling idea in the topic sentence. Tell your reader what process or procedure he or she will understand after reading your paragraph, or what he or she will learn to do, make, or repair.

3. Use the words *steps* or *stages* to signal to your reader that the paragraph will explain a process. These words "set the stage" and help the reader predict the direction your paragraph will follow.
4. Avoid weak sentence starters, such as starting your topic sentence with the words *there are* or *here are*. To make your topic sentence more effective, rearrange the sentence by reordering and adding words and by using an action verb. Avoid other kinds of weak sentence starters such as the following. Instead, get right to the point and be specific.

Weak: *There are* five steps to take cuttings to make new fuchsia plants.

Stronger: Fuchsia cuttings become new plants if you follow these five steps.

Weak: *I will tell you how to* repair a dripping faucet.

Stronger: Using four easy steps to repair a dripping faucet can save you the expense of calling a plumber.

5.2 What do you think?

Check the sentences that are effective topic sentences for a process paragraph. The subject should be narrowed sufficiently so it can be developed in one paragraph.

________ 1. Hot tubs can be cleaned easily by using the following steps.

________ 2. To wax a car properly, there are five steps you need to do.

________ 3. Genealogy is an interesting hobby.

________ 4. Here is what you need to do to raise a healthy and happy baby.

________ 5. Choosing a childcare center for your child is less stressful when you use four basic steps.

________ 6. Cleaning exterior windows need not be difficult.

________ 7. If you are caught in the rapid currents of a river, the following three steps may save your life.

________ 8. Fighting brush fires is hard work.

________ 9. My baseball coach taught me six effective steps to use to warm up before a game.

________ 10. Five things can be done to quit smoking.

Developing the Body of the Paragraph

Use the following guidelines to develop the body of your paragraph and the controlling idea stated in your topic sentence.

1. In a directional process paragraph, using the pronoun *you* is appropriate because you are giving directions or commands for the reader to follow. In *imperative sentences*, sentences that give directions or commands, the subject *you* does not need to be stated; *you* can be an implied or an understood subject.

   Stated subject: You cover the wood surface with a layer of primer.

   Implied subject: [You] Cover the wood surface with a layer of primer.

2. Plan every step carefully. Do not to leave out minor steps, for those may be the steps the reader needs the most to complete the process.
3. Provide *adequate development* by clearly naming each step and providing the reader with the necessary supporting details that explain each step. In other words, name or identify the step, and then follow it with another sentence or two to provide secondary details, such as cautions, words of encouragement, definitions, or extra clarification. Secondary details can also alert readers to common mistakes that frequently occur during that step so they can avoid making those mistakes. If you cannot think of any secondary details for a step, perhaps the "step" would work better as a secondary detail of the previous step.
4. Develop *coherence* by presenting details in chronological order and by using transition words.

TRANSITION WORDS FOR PROCESS PARAGRAPHS					
as long as	in the meantime	after	as	next	third
as soon as	the first step	afterward	before	once	until
at the same time	the following step	also	first	second	when
		another	finally	then	while

Use a comma after transition words that begin a sentence; they are introductory words.

First, sand the surface with a fine grade sandpaper.

Next, apply a thin coat of shellac.

Finally, buff the surface with a soft cloth.

5. Develop *coherence* by repeating key phrases from the topic sentence.

   The first *stage* in *Piaget's theory* of child development . . .

   In the second *stage* of *his theory* . . .

   The final *stage* of *Piaget's theory* . . .

6. Develop *unity*. Check carefully that every sentence develops or supports the topic sentence. Because there often are many secondary details in a process paragraph, you will want to maintain a focus on the main idea and not wander off course.
7. Define technical terms or any terms that may be unfamiliar to the reader. Select an appropriate level of wording for and secondary details.
8. Avoid "recipe or cookbook language" that is often shortened, missing words, and grammatically incorrect.

   Recipe language: Wash brushes.

   Correct: Wash the brushes.

5.3 What do you think?

Working with a partner or on your own, read the following paragraph. On separate paper, answer the questions that follow the paragraph.

Picture Frames

What do you do when you notice a bare spot on your wall? You can fill the bare spot by creating a fabric picture frame in five easy steps. To begin, find a sturdy piece of material with a print, a design, or a quote that you like. T-shirts make great possibilities. Next, purchase a picture frame complete with a cardboard backing and a glass face. You can often pick up a used picture frame at a secondhand store. If the frame has a picture in it, be sure the picture can be removed so you can replace it with your finished product. An 8" x 10" frame is a good, standard size; an 11" x 14" frame also works well, but it can be a little more difficult to handle. The third step is to take a pair of sharp scissors and trim the fabric so it is 1/4" wider than the cardboard backing of your picture frame. Now, starting with the sides, stretch the fabric so it is taut around the edges. Use a stapler to secure it to the cardboard. Repeat this step for the top and the bottom, beginning with the corners. Fifth, press the glass frame and the covered cardboard into the frame. Most frames have built-in clips to hold the cardboard in place. Most frames also have a hook on the side or the top for hanging. The finished product is a fabric picture that can dress up any wall in your home. These fabric pictures are a fun and inexpensive craft; they also make exceptionally special gifts.

Mindy Hollingsworth
Lane Community College
Eugene, Oregon

1. Which sentence is the topic sentence?
2. In the draft, the writer used the following topic sentence:

   I could teach you how to make a picture frame from fabric.

   Why is the revised topic sentence more effective than the draft version? Explain.
3. Briefly list the individual steps used in this process paragraph.
4. Does each step have an adequate number of secondary details? Explain.
5. List the transition words used in this paragraph and explain why transition words are important in a process paragraph.
6. Does the paragraph use good sentence variety? Explain.
7. Are the steps clear enough for you to duplicate? Explain.

5.4 What do you think?

Read the following paragraph. On separate paper, answer the questions that follow the paragraph.

Yahoo

Yahoo began as an idea, grew into a hobby, and later turned into full-time positions. In 1994, two Ph.D. candidates in electrical engineering at Stanford University, Filo and Yang, started Yahoo as a way to keep track of their personal interests on the Internet. In 1995, Yahoo became a commercial company. The goal of Yahoo was to create a great service that many people could use. The first office of Yahoo in 1995 was in Mountain View, California, a few miles south of the Stanford campus. Visitors could not open the front door without hitting a desk. Now the new suburban office complex near San Jose, California, is much larger. The Yahoo site is visited by 80 million people a month, and the number will likely increase by tens of millions in the near future. Yahoo's stock recently rose to a stunning $30 billion. The owners, Filo and Yang, are worth $3 billion. The *New York Times* and the *Washington Post* combined are worth less than Yahoo. This success is not bad for a company that is only five years old.

Natalia Loubskaia
Bellevue Community College
Bellevue, Washington

1. Is this an informational process paragraph or a directional process paragraph? What process does it show? Explain.
2. Does the topic sentence state the controlling idea of the paragraph? Explain.

3. Does the writer use transition words effectively to introduce each stage of the process? Explain.
4. List the individual steps or stages in the development of Yahoo.
5. Does the paragraph have unity? Explain.

Developing the Concluding Sentence

Use the following guidelines to bring your paragraph to an end.

1. Echo, summarize, or reinforce the topic sentence and the controlling idea.
2. In a directional process paragraph, the concluding sentence may summarize what the reader will accomplish by following the prescribed steps.
3. In an informational process paragraph, the concluding sentence may echo or reinforce the controlling idea from the topic sentence.

5.5 What do you think?

The following topic sentences and concluding sentences appeared in previous paragraphs. Read the sentences carefully. Do you think the concluding sentence for each paragraph is effective? Write your answers on separate paper.

1. Iowa's Political Process, pages 180-181:

   Topic Sentence: Citizens of Iowa who want to represent the state at the national convention must be willing to progress through several levels of political meetings.

   Concluding Sentence: They earned their positions by working their way through the four levels of political meetings.

2. Growing Fuchsias, pages 181-182:

   Topic Sentence: To guarantee the beauty of fuchsias in the coming season, you can take fuchsia cuttings to make new plants by following these five easy steps.

   Concluding Sentence: You can now look forward to many beautiful flowering plants in the season to come.

3. Piaget's Cognitive Stages, pages 182-183:

   Topic Sentence: According to Jean Piaget, children progress through four stages to develop their cognitive abilities.

   Concluding Sentence: Piaget developed this theory of cognitive development, which consists of four stages, by observing the cognitive progression experienced by a small number of children.

4. Picture Frames, page 186:

   Topic Sentence: You can fill the bare spot by creating a fabric picture frame in five easy steps.

   Concluding Sentence: These fabric pictures are a fun and inexpensive craft; they also make exceptionally special gifts.

The Writing Process for Process Paragraphs

Step 1: Generate ideas.

You have learned to brainstorm and create clusters to generate ideas. **Freewriting** is another prewriting method that generates ideas. For the process of freewriting, select a specific length of time, such as five minutes. Instead of writing lists of ideas, the goal is to write in a continuous stream of words, phrases, or sentences. Write down every idea that pops into your head. The sentences do not necessarily need to be connected or closely related to each other. During freewriting, you will often find yourself skipping from one topic to another. One idea triggers an association to another idea, and you quickly move along another thought pattern. If you stall or get stuck, simply repeat the last word several times until a new thought enters your mind. Strive to keep your pen moving the entire time. Refer back to the freewriting example about the term *apathy* in Chapter 1 (page 9).

To generate ideas for a directional process paragraph, use the topic *I know how to.* Begin writing sentences that name and briefly tell about the things you know how to do, make, or repair. You can use concrete examples, such as how to repair a toaster or hang wallpaper, or you can use abstract processes that involve human transitions, changes, or self-improvement. Abstract processes, for example, could tell how to reduce stress or improve test scores. Following is an example of freewriting after about one minute.

> I know how to make my own flies for fly-fishing. I could tell about the different flies and the different knots used. I could tell how to break brush and make a trail in the woods. That could include some of the things I remember from Boy Scouts. I could tell how to get street smart real fast. There are several steps I could teach someone about being safe on streets. I could explain how to burglar-proof a home. I know how to make a home childproof. I could tell the steps to make the home safe for toddlers. I could explain how to teach kids to do their own laundry. I don't know if I could explain how to teach a husband to keep a neat bedroom. Haha. I could give steps to follow to be a good friend or a good partner in a specific situation, like when my husband watches his football and basketball games. I could teach the steps to making a free throw shot at the line. I could . . .

Now it is your turn to generate some ideas and be amazed at the number of items that come up during the prewriting process of freewriting. Let the ideas flow. Remember, you are not writing a complete paragraph here, so do not stay with one idea too long. Write a few sentences or comments about one idea and then move on to other possibilities. On separate paper, freewrite about things you could teach someone else to do.

Step 2: Get a focus.

Look back at the ideas you generated in your freewriting. If there is an idea in your freewriting that you would like to consider for a process paragraph, examine the topic carefully. Consider answers to the following questions:

1. Is the topic narrow enough to be developed in one paragraph? If not, can you narrow it to a manageable size?
2. Is the process one that will interest your reader? Will the reader learn something from your paragraph? If the process is an everyday process that most people know how to do, your paragraph will have little value or significance. Select a different topic.
3. Can you identify clear steps that need to be done in chronological order in order to achieve the outcome or final product?
4. How much does your reader know about your topic? Do you need to give minute details and explain technical terms, or can you safely assume that your reader knows the basics?

If your first attempt at freewriting did not produce a range of topics, the following topics may interest you. If you see a suggestion in the following chart that you would like to use, answer the four preceding questions for the topic.

POSSIBLE TOPICS FOR A DIRECTIONAL PROCESS PARAGRAPH			
How to:	replace a car battery	give a newborn a bath	change oil in a car
	replace brakes	repair a hole in a wall	paint a sweatshirt
	choose a Christmas tree	get access to your credit rating	apply makeup
	repair a scratch on a car	critique a movie	plan a budget
	study for a test	quit smoking	register for a class
	chat online	make greeting cards	saddle a horse
	make candles	clean a gun	gut a deer
	clean fish	win at paintball	stop hiccups
	plan family meals	soothe hurt feelings	stop a child's temper tantrum

Step 3: Gather and organize information.

After you select your topic, narrow it, and consider your reader's knowledge or familiarity with your subject, the next step is to gather and organize the information you will use in your process paragraph. **Listing** is a prewriting organizational technique that works well for Step 3 of the writing process for a process paragraph.

Listing the Steps

Begin by making a chronological list of the steps involved in the process. You can also show secondary details under each step. Use these guidelines to carefully examine your list of steps:

1. Be sure that each item in the list is an individual step, not a secondary detail for one of the other steps.
2. Look to see whether you can combine several small steps into one larger step, thus reducing the number of individual steps in the paragraph.
3. Jot down significant supporting details that you will want to use to explain each step. You can later add additional details when you write the draft for the paragraph.

Steps for Cleaning a Hot Tub

Topic: cleaning a hot tub

Steps:

1. Drain the tub.
   - -Takes three hours
   - -Bucket out water.
2. Wipe down the sides and bottom.
3. Polish.
   - -Seals the tub and adds shine
   - -Apply the polish (dry paste).
   - -Use elbow grease.
   - -Let it dry.
4. Clean the filter.
   - -Hose it off.
   - -Replace it if dirty.
5. Fill the tub.
   - -Add the chemicals.

With this list, the writer knows there will be five steps. The writer can use this information to write an effective topic sentence.

Writing the Topic Sentence

After you focus on your topic and make the list of steps, which may include some of the secondary details, you are ready to use this information to write a strong topic sentence. The topic sentence should state the controlling idea, inform the reader what the result will be after following the steps, and, preferably, use the word *steps* or *stages*. Stating the number of steps in the topic sentence helps focus the reader's attention on the individual steps in the process. Write several versions of your topic sentence and consider which option is strongest and most effective. Since your topic sentence controls the information in the paragraph and must capture your reader's interest, plan to write, rewrite, and revise several sentences before selecting a topic sentence. The following examples show the options drafted by the writer before his strong topic sentence emerged.

Options for a Topic Sentence

1. There are several steps involved in cleaning a hot tub.

   [No. This begins with a weak sentence starter: *There are*.]

2. Because of all the germs and grime that build up in a hot tub, you need to know how to clean and sanitize your hot tub.

   [No. This is too long and wordy.]

3. Hot tubs are a lot of work.

   [No. This does not signal that a process paragraph follows.]

4. I can tell you from experience how to clean a hot tub.

   [No. The announcement, *I can tell you how*, is not effective.]

5. You might hate it, but you need to clean your hot tub.

   [No. This is too negative.]

6. Hot tubs can be easily cleaned by following five steps.

   [Yes. The process is stated and the number of steps is clear.]

Step 4: Write the rough draft.

Using your list of steps as a "roadmap," write the rough draft. The following checklist will guide you through the process:

1. After you state the topic sentence and before you begin to discuss the steps, provide the reader with a list of supplies, materials, tools, or equipment that will be needed to successfully complete the process.
2. Give careful consideration to your readers (your audience) and their level of familiarity with your topic. Select the appropriate level and simplicity or complexity of details to match their general level of knowledge with your topic.
3. Use transition words at the beginning of each step. Transition words signal the reader that the direction has shifted to a new step in the process.
4. Strive for *unity*. Include only information that directly supports or develops the topic sentence and the individual steps. Do not get sidetracked with irrelevant information.
5. Achieve *coherence* by listing the steps in chronological order, repeating key words from the topic sentence, such as the word *step*, and using transition words.
6. Provide *adequate development* by including every step in the process and by giving meaningful secondary details for each step.

5.6 What do you think?

Read the following draft about cleaning hot tubs. On separate paper, answer the questions that follow the paragraph.

Cleaning Hot Tubs

Hot tubs can be easily cleaned by following five steps. Before you begin, gather old towels, the polish for your hot tub, a hose, and your hot tub chemicals. Begin by draining your hot tub. Pull the plug on the bottom of the hot tub to let the water run out either on the ground or through a hose. Allow approximately three hours for the hot tub to drain. Very few hot tubs completely drain themselves empty, so you will need to climb inside the hot tub to finish this step. Use a large cup or a bucket to bail out the remaining water. Your hot tub must be completely empty. The second step involves wiping down the inside and the outer rim of the hot tub. Use old towels to wipe down or scrub off any scum or residue that has built up on the walls. Once you have completely wiped the hot tub you are ready for the next step: polishing. Polishing your hot tub with a wax polish that is specifically designed for hot tubs is essential, for the polish seals the hot tub surface and puts a shine back on the walls. Most polishes for hot tubs come in the form of a paste. Use an old cloth to spread the polish evenly on all the plastic surfaces both inside and outside of the hot tub. Let the polish dry for thirty minutes; a misty film on the surface of your hot tub appears when the polish is dry. Climb in the hot tub with several old towels. With a circular motion, start wiping away the dried paste. Apply pressure and a lot of elbow grease. The shine will return to your hot tub. The fourth step involves cleaning the filter. Unscrew the filter and rinse it off with a hose. If the grime and dirt do not wash off the filter, you need to replace the filter. Finally, you are ready to fill your hot tub with water. Add the appropriate chemicals. Check that the water is chemically balanced before you enter your clean hot tub. This five-step process should be followed every six months. If you use your hot tub frequently and use a lot of chemicals, you will need to clean it more often. Though this five-step process takes time, a clean, shiny, smooth-surfaced hot tub with clear, clean water is your reward.

1. Following the topic sentence, does the writer inform the reader about all the necessary supplies required to clean a hot tub? Explain.

2. Is the level of details appropriate? Could you clean a hot tub by following these directions? Explain.
3. List the transition words used in this process paragraph.
4. Does the paragraph have unity? Explain.
5. How does the writer achieve coherence? Explain.
6. Does the writer develop each step adequately with secondary details? Explain.

Step 5: Revise, revise, revise.

Revising is your opportunity to refine and improve your paragraph. The goal of writing a rough draft is to get your ideas on paper. The goal of the revision step of the writing process is to examine, modify, and revise the rough draft. Seldom are rough drafts in a good enough form to be the final revision. The following questions can guide you through the revision process:

1. Is the topic sufficiently narrowed? If not, narrow the topic to give it a sharper focus.
2. Is the topic sentence clear and effective? If not, write several new topic sentences and then select the best one.
3. How many steps are in the paragraph? Can you clearly identify the beginning of each step? Do you use transition words effectively? Select ways to improve the body of the paragraph.
4. Does each step have sufficient secondary details? If not, add the necessary secondary details.
5. Does the paragraph have unity? If not, delete the unnecessary and unrelated sentences.
6. Does the paragraph have coherence? Are the steps organized in a logical order?
7. Do you use formal language in the paragraph? If not, replace slang or informal language with formal language. Replace contractions with the two words the contractions represent.
8. Is the concluding sentence effective? Does it echo the topic sentence?

5.7 What do you think?

Working with a partner or on your own, read the following paragraph that provides you with valuable information and tips for changing a tire. On separate paper, revise the paragraph. Use the revision checklist on page 194 provided to guide your revision.

Changing a Tire

The following instructions will guide your through the process of changing a tire. This can be a good thing to know, especially if you're in the middle of nowhere without a cell phone to call the auto club. The first thing you want to do is locate your owner's manual and review the section on changing a tire. Here's where you hope and pray your spare tire is full of air. Position the jack in the spot specified by your manual. Insert the handle in the jack and pump the jack, just enough so it starts to raise the car. The next thing you want to do is loosen all the lug nuts. After all the nuts have been broken loose, continue to raise the car until it is sufficiently off the ground. Remove all the nuts, and remove the tire. Place the new tire on the car and replace the nuts. After all the lug nuts are on, tighten them just enough so the wheel does not spin. Before you lower the car, make sure the tire is firmly seated against the hub. You can now begin lowering the car to its original position. Once the jack is removed, you can now start by tightening all the lug nuts in a crisscross fashion to make sure they set against the rim properly. Place your jack, the handle, and the flat tire in your trunk, and you are ready to roll. I would suggest a little preventive maintenance though. Every couple of months, check your spare tire to make sure it is full of air. Nothing is worse than having a flat tire and finding out your spare tire is as flat as the tire you want to change.

Arthur Leimetter
Devry College
Addison, Illinois

Step 6: Proofread and edit.

Proofreading involves careful analysis of different aspects of each sentence. The Grammar and Usage Tips in each chapter provide you with specific aspects of sentences that you can analyze during proofreading. In addition to proofreading individual sentences, proofreading can include one final look at the relationship between sentences and the various options for combining sentences effectively. The items on each proofreading checklist will increase as we add more grammar and writing tips. For now, use the following proofreading and editing checklist:

1. Does every group of words punctuated as a sentence have a complete subject and a complete verb and form a complete thought so it can stand on its own and make sense?
2. For sentence variety, do some sentences have compound subjects or compound verbs? Is there a variety of simple, compound, and complex sentences?
3. Do you use correct punctuation between the clauses in compound and complex sentences?
4. Have you corrected all fragments, run-on sentences, and comma splice errors?
5. Do you use commas correctly throughout the paragraph?
6. Have you checked the spelling of all words?
7. Does each sentence begin with a capital letter and end with proper punctuation?

5.8 What do you think?

Not all process paragraphs express a serious tone. You can use lightheartedness and humor in a process paragraph. **Irony** is one method that you can use to convey a serious process through a humorous tone. A writer who uses irony cleverly selects words and ideas that are exactly the opposite of their literal or true meaning. Read the following paragraph that conveys an idea through irony. Complete the directions that follow the paragraph.

How to Lose Friends

You can become proficient at losing friends by following these four basic steps. First overbook yourself with many different schedules and responsibilities so you don't have time to spend with friends. When they call to invite you to get together with them for lunch dinner a movie or a sporting event make it clear to them that you have other priorities and that you simply do not have time for them. Second avoid returning their calls. If you call them back each time they call they will get the idea that you want to build a strong friendship and that you care about them. Never give the impression that you care about them or about what's happening in their lives. They need to know that their problems and concerns are not your problems and concerns. The third step is a little harder. Whenever you have the opportunity to talk about your friends behind their back don't hold back. If you are privileged to have some personal information about your friends. Share it with other people. Remember, nothing is really sacred when it comes to personal information confidential feelings or gossip. The most important point in this step is to be careful not to praise your friends, talk about their positive traits, or stick up for them if someone else says negative things about them. The final step involves your own character. Strive to be as untrustworthy as possible. You will lose your friends more quickly. If they are given ample opportunity to distrust your actions and your words. Your friends will vanish quickly if you're labeled a liar and if you have proven worthy of the label. These four steps, when used properly, will rid you of your friends and leave you alone isolated happy, and self-reliant.

Locate and correct the following errors that were identified during the proofreading step:

1. Two commas missing after introductory words
2. Seven commas missing between words in a series
3. Three commas missing after dependent clauses
4. Two fragments
5. Four contractions that should each be written as two separate words

---

Step 7: Prepare the final version of your process paragraph.

Follow your instructor's directions for preparing the final version of your paragraph. As always, save all your prewriting materials, rough draft, and revisions. You may be asked to turn them in with the final version of your work.

WRITING ASSIGNMENT

Write a directional process paragraph to teach the reader to do, make, or repair an item. Use steps and secondary details that make it possible for the reader to duplicate the process.

Complete each of the following steps for writing a directional process paragraph. Unless your instructor indicates a different approach, use the Planning Sheet on page 199 for each step of the writing process.

Step 1: Generate ideas.
Select a topic for your directional process paragraph. You may select one of the ideas you generated through freewriting or one of the ideas listed on page 190. If you need additional ideas, consider one of the following "how to" ideas.

plan a surprise party
enjoy a trip to a dentist
chip to the green (golf)
approach a difficult person
assemble an object
reduce sibling rivalry
scan photographs on a computer
develop trust
winterize a home
study more efficiently
stop procrastinating
plan a camping trip
hotwire a car
ask for a raise
weed without pesticides
handle jealousy
learn to skateboard
understand a teenager
prepare for a storm
organize a study area
open a locked car door
organize a productive meeting
help children with homework
patent an invention
end a relationship amicably
detail a car
create friendships
choose a nursing home
install a car radio
be an effective discussion leader

Step 2: Get a focus.
Narrow your topic, consider your audience, and be certain that you understand the steps involved in the process you will describe. Complete Step 2 on the Planning Sheet.

Step 3: Gather and organize information.
On separate paper, list the individual steps for your process paragraph. You may include secondary details. Examine the list carefully and reorganize the information if necessary. Draft a topic sentence. Complete Step 3 on the Planning Sheet.

Step 4: Write the rough draft.
Use your topic sentence and your list of steps to write a draft paragraph. Refer to the checklist on page 192 to guide you with this step. Answer the questions for Step 4 on the Planning Sheet.

Step 5: Revise, revise, revise.
Make at least one revision of your paragraph. Use the revision checklist on page 194 to guide you with the revision process. Save each of your revisions. Share your revised draft with a partner and ask your partner to complete the feedback questions on the Planning Sheet.

Step 6: Proofread and edit.
Use the proofreading and editing checklist on page 196. Make corrections on your paper. Write the date you completed step 6 on your Planning Sheet. Save your edited paragraph.

Step 7: Prepare the final version of your process paragraph.

PROCESS PARAGRAPH PLANNING SHEET

Name ______________________________

Step 1: Write the topic for your paragraph: ______________________________

Step 2: Did you need to narrow your topic? Explain. ______________________________

____

____

How does your level of details reflect your audience's level of familiarity with your subject?

____

____

Step 3: On separate paper, list the steps for your paragraph chronologically. Organize or reorder the steps if necessary. Include key secondary details that you will want to use for the individual steps.

Write several possible topic sentences. Star the one you prefer to use.

1. ______________________________

2. ______________________________

3. ______________________________

4. ______________________________

Step 4: When did you complete your rough draft? ______________________________

Step 5: Revise, revise, revise. Save all your revisions. Show your revised draft to a partner. Ask your partner to answer the following questions. Use your partner's comments for further revisions of your paragraph.

PARTNER FEEDBACK FORM

1. Is the topic sentence effective? Explain. ______________________

____

2. Does the writer provide any necessary introductory information, such as a list of tools, materials, or supplies, before the steps begin? ______________________

3. Is it easy to identify the beginning of each new step? Explain. ______________________

____

4. Does the writer use transition words effectively? Explain. ______________________

____

5. Does the paragraph have unity? Explain. ______________________

____

6. Does the paragraph have sufficient secondary details for each step? Explain. ______________________

____

7. Does the paragraph have adequate development? Are any steps or directions missing? Explain.

____

8. How does the writer develop coherence in this paragraph? ______________________

____

9. Is the concluding sentence effective? Explain. ______________________

____

10. Did you notice any word, sentence, or punctuation errors that the writer needs to edit during the proofreading process? __________ If yes, use a pencil to make notes in the margins of your partner's paper, or personally alert your partner to the errors.

Partner's name ______________________

Step 6: Proofread and edit.
Write the date you completed this step. ______________________

Step 7: Prepare the final version of your process paragraph.

Grammar and Usage Tips

The four new grammar and usage tips in this chapter focus on verb phrases and verb tenses. After you complete the exercises, carefully check your work with the answer keys in Appendix A and record your number of errors for each exercise. Review the tip and examine the correct answer. In the margins of each exercise, jot down questions that you would like to ask your instructor regarding the grammar and usage points covered. Before the new tips are introduced, review the following information about simple verb tenses and verb phrases.

Simple Verb Tenses

Simple verb tenses show action that occurs, occurred, or will occur in a specific time period.

Simple Present Tense

1. The simple present tense tells about actions that occur now, in this time period, or actions that are habitual or repeated on a regular basis.
2. The simple present tense is formed by one word, not by a verb phrase.
3. Simple present tense verbs change their form to show number and person. *Number* is determined by the subject of the sentence. *Person* refers to whether the subject of the sentence is the speaker (I, we), the one spoken to (you), or the one spoken about (he, she, it, or they). A *singular subject* requires a singular verb form, which has an *-s* or an *-es* suffix in third-person present tense. A *plural subject* requires a plural verb form in third-person present tense. This plural verb, as you will notice in the following chart, does not have a suffix.

SIMPLE PRESENT TENSE VERBS		
FIRST PERSON	SECOND PERSON	THIRD PERSON
Singular: I walk. I watch.	Singular: You walk. You watch.	Singular: He walk**s**. She walk**s**. Sally walk**s**. Ramos walk**s**. The dog walk**s**. A horse walk**s**. He watch**es**. She watch**es**. The dog watch**es**. A horse watch**es**.
Plural: We walk. We watch.	Plural: You walk. You watch.	Plural: They walk. People walk. Dogs walk. Horses walk. They watch. People watch. Dogs watch. Horses watch.

4. Simple present tense verbs often make generalizations and state facts.

Simple Past Tense

1. The simple past tense for regular verbs uses the main verb form with an *-ed* suffix.

   Simple Past Tense of Regular Verbs: planned, walked, responded, carried, smiled, nodded

2. The simple past tense for irregular verbs is not made with an *-ed* suffix; instead, a new form of the word is used or no change at all is made with the main verb. (See Appendix B for a list of simple past tenses of irregular verbs.)

   Simple Past Tense of Irregular Verbs: shot, cut, spun, ran, told, wrote, caught, drove

3. The simple past tense uses a one-word verb, not a verb phrase.

   Simple Past Tense: The paramedic **carried** her from the car to the ambulance.

   Not Simple Past Tense: The woman's car **had struck** a utility pole.

4. Simple past tense verbs are frequently used in narrative writing.

   I **entered** the tunnel and **held** my breath. The stench **was** overwhelming.

Simple Future Tense

1. The simple future appears as a verb phrase. The helping verb *will* is added to the main verb form.
2. Singular and plural subjects use the same helping verb for simple future tense.

Singular Subjects	**Plural Subjects**
I will walk three miles a day.	We will watch the performance on television.
You will know the answer soon.	You will receive your contracts on Friday.
She will announce her decision.	They will elect their officers at the next meeting.

Verb Phrases

Verb phrases are two or more verbs used together to express the action of a clause or a sentence. A verb phrase consists of one or more helping verbs and the main form of the verb, which may have an *-ed* suffix or an *-ing* suffix. The following chart shows the four categories of helping verbs. Note that each category of helping verbs attaches to a specific form of the main verb.

KINDS OF HELPING VERBS			
FORMS OF THE VERB *TO BE*[1]	FORMS OF THE VERB *TO DO*[2]	FORMS OF THE VERB *TO HAVE*[3]	OTHER HELPING VERBS
Use these helping verbs to form a **progressive verb.** Attach helping verbs from the verb *to be* to a **present participle.** A present participle is a verb with an *-ing* suffix. (See Chapter 2, page 82.)	Use these helping verbs to emphasize an action or to form a question. Attach helping verbs from the verb *to do* to a base form of the verb without any suffixes.	Use these helping verbs to form **perfect tenses.** Attach helping verbs from the verb *to have* to a **past participle.** A past participle for a regular verb has an *-ed* suffix. A past participle for an irregular verb has a different form or remains the same as the base verb without any suffix. (See Chapter 2, page 82.)	Use these helping verbs to form verb phrases that show degrees of certainty, obligation, suggestion, or necessity. Attach these helping verbs to the base verb without any suffixes.
am is are was were be been	do does did	has have had	can will shall could should would may might must
Examples: I am talking too loudly. They were thinking about you.	Examples: They do care about this. Does he work for you?	Examples: She has taken the test. I had driven home.	Examples: We can register today. She must allow sufficient time to study.

[1]When these verbs are not used in a verb phrase, they function as linking verbs.
[2]When these words are not used in a verb phrase, they function as action verbs.
[3]When these words are not used in a verb phrase, they function as action verbs.

Each of the following sentences has a verb phrase. Note that adverbs such as *not, never, always, just,* and *often* may appear between the helping verb and the base form of the verb.

> The trees **were swaying** in the gentle breeze.
>
> Professor James **does** not **articulate** his ideas clearly during his lectures.
>
> We **have** always **been** friends.
>
> I **can** never **recite** the entire poem.
>
> Members of the class **would** often **choose** to give reports for extra credit.
>
> They **should allocate** more money to the project.
>
> She **must have lost** her car keys in the parking lot.

Avoid shifting back and forth between present and past tenses in a paragraph unless you have a reason for shifting the tenses. Stay in the past tense to tell about events that happened in the past; stay in the present tense to state current facts, generalizations, and information that are habitual or occur on a regular basis.

Shifting verb tenses within a paragraph can confuse and convey inaccurate information to your reader. For example, shifting from past tense to present tense in a narrative weakens the paragraph, breaks the unity, and disrupts the coherence of the paragraph. Notice the shift in verb tenses in the following excerpt from a narrative:

> I **stood** (past) up to the challenge, but my heart **pounds** (present) and my stomach **churns** (present). A little bell **rings** (present) when I **opened** (past) the big wooden door and **walked** (past) into the musty-smelling store.

Since narratives are usually in past tense, the verbs in the excerpt can all be expressed in the simple past tense. The consistency in the verb tense expresses the ideas more clearly and logically.

> I **stood up** (past) to the challenge, but my heart **pounded** (past) and my stomach **churned** (past). A little bell **rang** (past) when I **opened** (past) the big wooden door and **walked** (past) into the musty-smelling store.

In descriptive paragraphs, each sentence that describes what the reader is observing at that given moment should be in present tense. Inserting past tense verbs can confuse the reader and break the unity and coherence of the paragraph. Notice the shift in the verb tenses in the following excerpt from a descriptive paragraph:

> The photograph **shows** (present) hundreds of Holocaust victims in crowded living quarters. The victims **peer** (present) at the camera with hollow, sunken eyes. Cheek bones **protruded** (past) from the sides of their faces. The pictures **served** (past) as a daily reminder of the atrocities that mankind **is** (present) capable of inflicting on other human beings.

To correct the shift in verb tenses for this descriptive excerpt, all the verbs are written in present tense.

> The photograph **shows** (present) hundreds of Holocaust victims in crowded living quarters. The victims **peer** (present) at the camera with hollow, sunken eyes. Cheek bones **protrude** (present) from the sides of their faces. The pictures **serve** (present) as a daily reminder of the atrocities that mankind **is** (present) capable of inflicting on other human beings.

Grammar and Usage Tip 13 does not say that you can never shift verb tenses in a paragraph. Sometimes the shift is necessary for accuracy. The following examples show correct shifts in verb tenses.

Correct: My son **attended** (past) Stanford University, which **is** (present) in Palo Alto, California.
[The present tense verb **is** must be used in this sentence for accuracy. Replacing **is** with the past tense **was** would indicate that Stanford University is no longer in Palo Alto.]

Correct: We all **knew** (past) that Washington, D.C., **is** (present) not a state.
[The present tense verb **is** must be used for accuracy. Replacing **is** with **was** would indicate that at one time Washington, D.C., was not a state, but that now it is a state.]

Correct: I **know** (present) that Royce **lived** (past) in Tucson, Arizona.
[The past tense verb **lived** indicates that Royce no longer lives in Tucson. Replacing **lived** with **lives** would indicate that Royce still lives in Tucson.]

Some sentences in an introductory portion of a paragraph may reflect on the past or project into the future, but as soon as the body of the paragraph with the controlling idea begins, the verb tense remains consistent. In the following excerpt, background information appears in past tense.

When the description begins, the verb correctly shifts to present tense and remains in present tense throughout the remaining description.

Past tense correct:	When Chip first **returned** from overseas duty, his young children **did** not **recognize** him. They **did** not **welcome** his hugs and kisses, nor **did** they **want** to climb up onto his lap. They **cried** each time he approached them.
Keep the description of what you see at the time in present tense.	Thirty days **does make** a difference. Now Chip **gazes** upon his children as they **curl** up on his lap, snuggling securely against his chest and in the warmth of his arms. He **smiles** gently, knowing that he **is** home, and he **is** also safe and secure.

EXERCISE 5.1 Finding Incorrect Shifts in Verb Tenses

Score: ______

In each of the following groups of sentences, circle the incorrect shifts in verb tenses. Write the correct verb in the margin. You will need to decide whether the group of sentences should be written in past, present, or future tense.

1. A thousand hot air balloons participate in Albuquerque's Balloon Fiesta every October. Each morning before 5:30, balloon enthusiasts and pilots assemble at the fairgrounds. The wicker or aluminum baskets of the balloons then drag along the ground until the hot air took over, and the balloons joined all the other balloons in the air.

2. Many tourists enjoy a ride on the world's longest tramway. The tramway soars to the top of Sandia Ridge. The Ridge will offer geological explanations of the surrounding valley and its popularity as the site of the Balloon Fiesta. The Albuquerque Box is a unique wind pattern that exists in the valley. Simultaneous breezes blew in different directions at different altitudes, which enabled pilots to steer their balloons in and out of different altitudes. In addition, the surrounding mountains protect balloon ascents and descents from overzealous winds.

3. In the evening, hundreds of inflated balloons return to the fairgrounds for special races. The night sky filled with a bright, flickering glow of three hundred to five hundred balloons. Sometimes one balloon accidentally bumped another balloon; balloonists call this "kissing." Usually, however, the balloons that kiss do not cause any harm. These special races were a spectacular sight that is unparalleled.

[Adapted from Jay Heinrichs, "Rise and Shine," *VIA-AAA Magazine*, October, 2000, pp. 25–27.]

Use the progressive form of verbs to express continuous action or activity that occurs uninterrupted through a given period of time. Progressive verb phrases consist of a helping verb from the verb *to be* (*am, is, are, was, were, be,* and *been*) and the present participle. The present participle is the base form of the verb with an *-ing* suffix. The helping verb indicates the time period (past, present, or future) and the number (singular or plural).

The following chart shows the progressive forms of verbs in the simple present, past, and future tenses.

PROGRESSIVE FORMS OF SIMPLE TENSE VERBS

HELPING VERB	+	BASE VERB + *-ING*	
am	+	driving	Present Progressive
is	+	driving	
are	+	driving	
was	+	driving	Past Progressive
were	+	driving	
will be	+	driving	Future Progressive

I **am waiting** for the meeting to adjourn.

At least one council member **is planning** to challenge the findings of the report.

The city planners **are presenting** the report to the mayor.

The union **was negotiating** for a new contract.

Members **were asking** for better benefit packages.

I **will be taking** notes for a newspaper article.

Tense and Number

Helping verbs in verb phrases indicate the tense and the number of the verb. Simple progressive verbs show continuous actions in the past, in the present, or in the future. The number of the verb, which is determined by the subject, can be singular or plural. The subject may be first person, second person, or third person.

Progressive Forms of Simple Tense Verbs			
	PAST PROGRESSIVE	PRESENT PROGRESSIVE	FUTURE PROGRESSIVE
First person singular:	I *was calling* for more details.	I *am calling* for more details.	I *will be calling* for more details.
First person plural:	We *were asking* questions.	We *are asking* questions.	We *will be asking* questions.
Second person singular and plural:	You *were walking* alone.	You *are walking* alone.	You *will be walking* alone.
Third person singular:	He *was looking* for a job.	He *is looking* for a job.	He *will be looking* for a job.
Third Person Plural:	They *were taking* orders.	They *are taking* orders.	They *will be taking* orders.

Avoiding Progressive Form Errors

1. Do not use the regular form of a verb in situations where the progressive form is needed.

Incorrect: She cannot drive you to the mall right now. She studies (present) for her midterm.

[The action of studying is an ongoing activity that occurs at this present time. Therefore, the action needs to be stated in the progressive form.]

Correct: She cannot drive you to the mall right now. She is studying (present progressive) for her midterm.

Notice the difference in the ideas expressed by the simple present and the present progressive verbs in the following sentences. The present tense gives the impression that the situation is permanent; the progressive form gives the impression that what is happening is only temporary and will soon change.

Simple Present: The chef cooks lasagna and linguini.

Present Progressive: The chef is cooking lasagna and linguini.

Simple Present: I work in Scottsdale.

Present Progressive: I am working in Scottsdale.

Simple Present: My mother tells her friends everything.

Present Progressive: My mother is telling her friends everything.

2. Do not use different verb forms or tenses in a series of verbs. In other words, there should be **parallelism** among the verbs in the clause or the sentence.

Verbs are not parallel: The voters are listening, ponder, and prepared to make their choices at the polls.

Verbs are parallel: The voters are listening, pondering, and preparing to make their choices at the polls.

In a series of progressive verb phrases, the helping verb may be implied rather than repeated. The same helping verb that is used in the first verb phrase is understood to be a part of the other verb phrases in the series. So, in the previous example, three verb phrases are embedded in the sentence: **are listening, are pondering,** and **are preparing.**

The water **is flowing, accumulating,** and **flooding** the streets.

[The water **is flowing, is accumulating,** and **is flooding** the streets.]

The inspector **was peering** under the sinks, **looking** at the wiring, and **examining** the outlets.

[The inspector **was peering** under the sinks, **was looking** at the wiring, and **was examining** the outlets.]

3. Avoid subject-verb agreement errors in third person past progressive and third person present progressive verbs. Use *is* (present) and *was* (past) for singular subjects. Use *are* (present) and *were* (past) for plural subjects.

singular
She *is applying* for the job.

singular
She *was applying* for the job.

plural
They *are buying* a house.

plural
They *were buying* a house.

4. Do not treat all words that end with an *-ing* suffix as a verb. When verb forms that end in *-ing* appear without a helping verb, they are often working as nouns (called **gerunds**) or are present participles working as adjectives (called **verbals**). Participles and gerunds cannot express the action of a sentence. Notice in the following examples how the *-ing* form of the verb is not the verb for the sentence; instead, the present participle functions as an adjective or noun.

adjective
The **swimming** coach encouraged each student to establish a warm-up routine.

adjective
The **annoying** buzzer continued for several minutes.

noun **Running** in a marathon requires months of hard noun **training** and dedication.

noun **Caring** for elderly parents is difficult for many families.

EXERCISE 5.2 Identifying Progressive Verbs

Score: ______

In the following sentences, underline the subjects once and the complete verbs twice.

Example: The siren was sounding and announcing the beginning of the parade.

1. The marketing director is distributing the marketing plans for three new products.
2. My daughters are playing on two different soccer teams and enjoying this new sport.
3. The highway crews are sanding and salting the icy overpasses.
4. Whether you are planning to drive or carpool, you will find hazardous conditions today.
5. The computers are running on backup batteries until the electricity comes on.
6. The computer lab assistants were documenting the problems when the department head announced the decision to buy new hardware and software.
7. Paying college tuition gets harder and harder; many students are working part-time jobs to pay their bills.
8. I will be paying two times more rent, but I will have two additional roommates.
9. Ramos was studying for his physics test, so he could not attend the concert.
10. Earning solid grades in his major is his primary goal; he is reaching his goal so far this term.

Progressive Forms of Perfect Tense Verbs

In Grammar and Usage Tip 14, you learned that the progressive form of simple present, past, and future tense verbs is created by using a form of *to be* with the present participle of the main verb. In the next Grammar and Usage Tip, you will learn about another verb tense, the *perfect tense*. **Perfect tense verbs** use helping verbs from the verb *to have* (*have, has,* and *had*). The perfect tense verbs can also appear as progressive verbs; an *-ing* suffix is also used for progressive verbs in the perfect verb tense. Simply be aware that progressive verbs can appear with helping verbs from the verb *to have*.

PROGRESSIVE FORMS OF PERFECT TENSE VERBS			
HELPING VERB	+	BASE VERB + *-ING*	
has been	+	walking	Present Perfect Progressive
have been	+	walking	
had been	+	walking	Past Perfect Progressive
will have been	+	walking	Future Perfect Progressive

I *have been seeing* the same dentist since I was a child.

His hygienist *has been working* for him throughout his career.

He *had been planning* to retire next year but changed his mind.

As of next month, he *will have been practicing* for thirty-five years.

They *have been threatening* to strike.

Management *has been refusing* to reopen the discussion.

Mediators *had been trying* to reach a compromise.

As of next month, union members *will have been working* without a contract for one year.

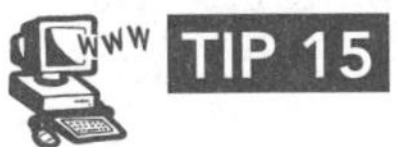

Use perfect tense verbs to express actions that are perfected or completed within a specific time period. Perfect tense verbs are expressed in verb phrases that consist of a helping verb from the verb *to have* and the past participle of the main verb.

In perfect tense verbs, a helping verb from the verb *to have* expresses the time period (past, present, or future).

The **present perfect tense** expresses action that . . .

1. started in the past and continues in the present:

   The initiative **has received** a lot of media attention.

2. began and ended in a nonspecific time in the past:

   The backers of the initiative **have** finally **collected** enough signatures.

The **past perfect tense** expresses action that began and ended in the past before another past action occurred:

> The backers of the initiative **had collected** enough signatures before the mandatory Friday deadline arrived.
>
> Supporters of the initiative **had campaigned** extensively for the measure before the voters went to the polls.

The **future perfect tense** expresses action that will start and end in the future:

> The backers of the initiative **will have collected** enough signatures by next Friday.

PERFECT TENSE VERBS

HELPING VERB	+	PAST PARTICIPLE	
(has, have, had)		(*-ed* suffix for regular verbs; other forms for irregular verbs)	
has	+	earned	Present perfect singular
has	+	driven	
have	+	requested	Present perfect plural
have	+	seen	
had	+	discovered	Past perfect singular or plural
had	+	cut	
will have	+	known	Future perfect singular or plural

Past Participles

Past participles function as verbs in sentences when they are joined with forms of the helping verb *to have*. The past participle for regular verbs is the same as the simple past tense: the *-ed* suffix is attached to the main (the base) verb:

Regular verbs, present perfect tense:	Student government **has achieved** its goals for the year.
	Students **have participated** in many social causes.
Regular verbs, past perfect tense:	The announcer **had interrupted** the speaker.
	Many contestants **had wanted** to win the prize.
Regular verbs, future perfect tense:	I **will have earned** my degree by then.
	The group **will have practiced** before the event.

For irregular verbs, a new form of the verb without an *-ed* suffix is used. For a complete list of past participles, see Appendix B.

Irregular verbs, present perfect tense:	I **have taken** almost every required course. The teacher **has written** comments on every paper.
Irregular verbs, past perfect tense:	Three students **had given** the correct answers. I **had** already **spent** my tuition money.
Irregular verbs, future perfect tense:	With this sale, the realtor **will have sold** ten homes. Bob **will have made** the honor roll five times.

Notice in the following chart that the past participle of irregular verbs is often different from the simple past tense form. Again, refer to Appendix B for a list of past participles of irregular verbs.

FORMS OF IRREGULAR VERBS

MAIN VERB	SIMPLE PAST TENSE	PAST PARTICIPLE
to arise	arose	arisen
to become	became	become
to begin	began	begun
to break	broke	broken
to choose	chose	chosen
to do	did	done
to drink	drank	drunk
to drive	drove	driven

Avoiding Perfect Tense Verb Errors

1. Do not use the simple past tense when a past perfect or a present perfect tense is called for. The differences in the verb tenses are subtle, but understanding these differences can help you select the most appropriate verb form and show the time sequence between different events or actions.

   My brother **served** in the Army for eight years.
   [The action has already taken place. The verb is in the simple past tense.]

   My brother **has served** in the Army for eight years.
   [This verb in the present perfect tense indicates that the action began in the past and continues in the present time.]

My brother **had served** in the Army for eight years before he became a security guard.
[This verb in the past perfect tense indicates that the action started and ended in the past. The action took place before some additional action occurred in the past.]

In the following example, note how the sequence of events or actions is not clear when each of the verbs is in simple past tense.

We **discussed** buying the property ever since we **saw** the "for sale" sign.
[Which action occurred first in the sentence? Did the writer discuss buying the property first, or did the writer see the "for sale" sign first? Which action is completed? The relationship between these verbs is expressed more precisely with the following revision.]

We **have discussed** buying the property ever since we **saw** the "for sale" sign.
[This choice of verbs conveys the ideas that we started discussing the property in the past, after we saw the sign, and that we continue to discuss the possibility in the present.]

2. Avoid subject-verb agreement errors in third person in the present perfect tense. Use a singular helping verb with a singular subject. Use a plural helping verb with a plural subject.

singular
The pilot *has notified* the control tower about the heavy rain.

plural
The pilots *have notified* the control tower about the heavy rain.

3. Do not treat every word that ends with an *-ed* suffix as a verb. Like present participles, past participles can work as adjectives when they appear without a helping verb from the verb *to have*. Participles that function as adjectives cannot at the same time work as verbs and express the action of the sentence. Notice in the following examples how the past participle is not the verb for the sentence; the past participle functions instead as an adjective.

adjective
The program addresses the problems that many **troubled** youths encounter on the streets.

adjective
The **determined** accountant worked on the file until he found the error.

EXERCISE 5.3 Using Past Participles

Score: ______

Circle the correct verb form to complete the following perfect tense verb phrases.

1. We had (forgot, forgotten) to renew the permit.
2. The wild geese have (flew, flown) more than nine hundred miles.

3. The news had (come, came) as a total shock.

4. His public confession has (broke, broken) the vow of silence.

5. The tenants had (gave, given) a thirty-day notice to the owners.

6. All of the students have (went, gone) home for the holiday.

7. The frightened boys had (hidden, hid) under the front porch.

8. The elders have (spoke, spoken) before the tribal council.

9. Dozens of church bells had (rung, rang) to announce the peace treaty.

10. During the night, someone had (stole, stolen) the signs.

EXERCISE 5.4 Using Past Participles and Present Participles

Score: ______

Complete the verb phrases in the following sentences by adding the present participle or the past participle to make a logical sentence. Remember that present participles use helping verbs from the verb *to be*. Past participles use helping verbs from the verb *to have*. Use the main verbs shown in the left margin.

Examples: leave — The security patrol had *left* the campus earlier. [Use the past participle.]

call — The stranded motorist was *calling* for help. [Use the present participle.]

consider 1. My roommate had ________ the offer but then declined.

work 2. He was currently ________ a swing shift job.

find 3. He had ________ a better job with better hours.

have 4. Many employers are ________ problems with absenteeism.

arrive 5. The early morning crew was ________ a half hour late every day.

take 6. Some employees had ________ excessively long coffee breaks.

offer 7. My boss had ________ us new incentives.

hope 8. She was ________ to get a greater commitment from us.

speak 9. I had ________ to him about my work environment.

write 10. They have ________ a new set of guidelines for all employees.

EXERCISE 5.5 Proofreading for Perfect Tense Verb Errors

Score: ______

Each of the following sentences can be improved or corrected by using a past perfect or present perfect verb tense. Add the appropriate helping verb—*has, have,* or *had*—to one of the verbs in the following sentences. Make any other changes that are needed to correct the sentences.

1. The co-pilot took control of the plane after the pilot suffered a heart attack.
2. We had financial problems ever since we opened all these credit card accounts.
3. Carla lived in California for three years before she moved here to Texas.
4. The peace agreements existed for several months and, hopefully, will continue to be honored.
5. The airlines cancelled every morning flight, so travelers slept on the benches and the floors.
6. When I saw my dog in pain, I realized that he encountered a porcupine.
7. Mr. Benson gave the directions five times before the majority of the class finally understood.
8. Luther recorded two new albums this year and may record one more before December.
9. Before an accident disabled me, I worked ten-hour shifts at the local bakery.
10. We argued with Janet for four hours before we finally realized we could not alter her decision.

TIP 16 **To avoid fragments, check that each clause has a complete subject and a complete verb. A complete verb may be a simple verb (one verb) or a verb phrase (a helping verb and the base form of the verb). Participles without helping verbs are adjectives or gerunds and therefore cannot function as the verbs in the sentence.**

Incorrect use of participles results in fragment errors. Learning to identify and correct these errors will improve your ability to proofread and edit your own writing. Remember that every independent and dependent clause must have a complete subject and a complete verb and form a complete thought.

1. A present participle (a verb form that ends with an *-ing* suffix) by itself without a helping verb cannot function as the verb of a clause or a sentence. When a present participle without a helping verb poses as the verb of the sentence, the result is a fragment.

   Fragment: The construction workers **quitting** their jobs for safety reasons.

   You can easily correct this type of fragment by using one of two methods.

   Method 1: Use the progressive form by adding a helping verb from the verb *to be* that shows the correct tense, person, and number.

   Correction: The construction workers **are quitting** their jobs for safety reasons.

   The construction workers **were quitting** their jobs for safety reasons.

   The construction workers **will be quitting** their jobs for safety reasons.

   Method 2: Remove the *-ing* suffix. Use a simple or perfect tense verb.

   Correction: The construction workers **quit** their jobs for safety reasons.

   The construction workers **will quit** their jobs for safety reasons.

   The construction workers **have quit** their jobs for safety reasons.

2. A past participle by itself without a helping verb can also create a fragment. However, remember that past participles of regular verbs are the same as the simple past tense form, so a fragment created by a past participle of a regular verb may be more difficult to detect. Fragments caused by past participles of irregular verbs are easier to detect in sentences. When these participles appear in a sentence without a helping verb, they cannot be the verb of the sentence. If the sentence or the clause has no other verbs, the result is a fragment.

   Fragment: The men **spoken** about their involvement in the incident.

   Two methods can be used to correct this type of fragment.

   Method 1: Use the perfect tense form by adding the missing helping verb from the verb *to have* that expresses the person, the number, and the tense.

   Correction: The men **have spoken** about their involvement in the incident.

Correction: The men **had spoken** about their involvement in the incident.

Method 2: Change the verb to a simple past tense.

Correction: The men **spoke** about their involvement in the incident.

3. If the fragment begins with a participle, use one of the three methods to correct the error.

   Method 1: Add a helping verb to create a complete verb phrase.

   Fragment: **Taking** responsibility for the children in her care.

   Correction: The young mother **is taking** responsibility for the children in her care.

   Correction: The young mother **was taking** responsibility for the children in her care.

   Method 2: Change the participle to a simple verb tense.

   Fragment: **Taking** responsibility for the children in her care.

   Correction: The young mother **took** responsibility for the children in her care.

   Correction: The young mother **takes** responsibility for the children in her care.

   Method 3: Use the participle as a gerund. Add a complete verb.

   Fragment: **Taking** responsibility for the children in her care.

   Correction: **Taking** responsibility for the children in her care **requires** long hours and hard work.

EXERCISE 5.6 Correcting Fragments

Score: ______

Use any method to correct the following fragments. Remember that every independent and dependent clause must have a complete subject and a complete verb and form a complete thought.

1. Drivers on the freeway swerving to miss the garbage can in the middle of the road.

2. I got this computer mouse pad free because the store giving it away with every twenty-dollar purchase.

3. The man choosing to end his contract with the company, for he could no longer support the company's goals.

4. Wanting to expand the operation and move into three new states before the end of the year.

5. Determined to get to the bottom of the problem that was bothering him.

6. Family values were the topic of the debate; however, candidates wandering off the topic and talking about economic and medical topics.

7. Every student in our study group contributing study aids and study notes for specific chapters of the textbook, but I still like to make my own for every chapter.

8. Many financial planners getting vital information about investments from the Internet.

9. Preston hoping to prevent bankruptcy, so he scheduled an appointment with a loan officer to discuss his financial situation.

10. Charging up the steps and shoving people aside.

Grammar and Usage Tips Summary

TIP 13 Avoid shifting back and forth between present and past tenses in a paragraph unless you have a reason for shifting tenses.

TIP 14 Use progressive verbs to express continuous action or activity that occurs uninterrupted through a given period of time. Progressive verb phrases consist of a helping verb that is a form of the verb *to be* (*am, is, are, was, were, be,* or *been*) and the present participle. The present participle is the base form of the verb with an *-ing* suffix.

TIP 15 Use perfect tense verbs to express actions that are completed within a specific time period. Perfect tense verbs are expressed in verb phrases that consist of a helping verb that is a form of the verb *to have* (*has, have, had*) and the *past participle* of the base verb.

TIP 16 To avoid fragments, check that each clause has a complete subject and a complete verb. A complete verb may be a simple verb (one verb) or a verb phrase (a helping verb and the correct base form of the verb). Participles and gerunds cannot function as verbs in a sentence.

CHAPTER 5 • Process Paragraphs • Proofreading and Editing Exercises

Proofreading 1

With a partner or on your own, proofread and edit the following paragraphs. Carefully check the sentence structure, punctuation, and spelling. Write your corrections in the space between the lines. In many cases, you can correct errors in more than one way.

Save a Life

Learning the six basic steps of CPR may save the life of a person who is having cardiac arrest. First check to see if the person is responsive. Talk to the person, if you get no response, quickly call 911, return to the person's side, and start step two. For step two, find out if the victim is breathing. To do this, position the person flat on his or her back. Kneel by the side of the person, place one of your hands under the person's chin. The other hand on the person's forehead. Tilt the person's head back and lift the chin. The person's teeth should almost be touching. Put your ear close to the person's mouth listen for breathing, at the same time, watch the person's chest for signs of breathing. Move to the third step, if the person is not breathing normally. In step three, give the person two breaths. To do this, pinch the person's nose and cover his or her mouth with your mouth. Puff two full breathes into the person. You should be able to see the person's chest rise. When you give each breath. The fourth step is to check the person's pulse. Place your fingertips on the person's neck; for men, this would be near the Adam's apple. Slide your fingers into the small groove, that is next to the windpipe. Feel for the pulse. Move to step five if you feel no pulse or if you are uncertain that there is a pulse. In step five, position yourself close to the body. Place your hands in the center of the person's chest. Place one hand on top of the other hand. You are ready for step six. Using the heels of your flat hands, push down firmly on the person's chest and begin counting. Push firmly fifteen times. Continue to give two breaths and the fifteen chest pushes, until help arrives. Knowing these six steps of CPR prepares you to respond in an emergencey and possibly safe a person's life.

Proofreading 2

Proofread your Writing Warm-Up 5. Use the checklist on page 196 to guide you through the proofreading and editing process.

Internet Enrichment

Log onto the web site for this textbook for additional exercises and links for the following topics:

Process Paragraphs
Transitional Words
Shifting Verb Tenses
Progressive Verbs
Perfect Tense Verbs
Fragments

Go to: http://college.hmco.com. Click on "Students." Type *Paragraph Essentials* in the "Jump to Textbook Sites" box. Click "go," and then bookmark the site. Click on Chapter 5.

CHAPTER 5 • Grammar and Usage Review

Name ______________________

Date ______________________

Using Present and Past Participles

Complete each of the following verb phrases by using the past or the present participle for the base verb that appears next to each sentence.

strike 1. The lighting had __________ in three different locations on the golf course.

spin 2. Toni and Natasha have __________ yarn from angora sheep many times.

drain 3. The maintenance crews were ____________ all the sprinkler systems.

dread 4. Alex was ____________ the conversation he had to have with his father.

drive 5. I am ____________ fifty miles a week to and from school.

choose 6. Many customers have ____________ not to purchase extended warranties.

buy 7. Few of the students had ____________ the supplemental insurance.

stick 8. We are ____________ campaign posters all over the campus.

fit 9. The orthodontist had ____________ Jeremiah with a new type of braces.

run 10. Both dealerships have ____________ extensive advertisements on television.

Subjects and Verbs

Underline the subjects once and the complete verbs twice in the following sentences.

1. I was not looking forward to skinning the chicken.
2. My uncle, a traveling car salesman, has worked in every state except Hawaii and Alaska.
3. Purchasing a phone card was an option, but I decided to call collect.
4. Insulting a referee will be grounds for a penalty and a fine.
5. Many of the musicians had never received recognition for their work.

Fragments

On separate paper, use any method to correct the following fragments.

1. Caring for his elderly parents.
2. The computer printout taken from the computer lab.
3. The ball thrown across the line of scrimmage.
4. Dented by the hail during an unexpected storm.
5. Dancing to the music for hours at the graduation party.
6. The advertisements featuring the new vehicle that would be available this month.

CHAPTER 6

Comparison and Contrast Paragraphs

The topic sentence introduces two subjects and states how they are similar or different.

The body of the paragraph compares or contrasts subject A and subject B through a point-by-point or block method. Both subjects have subtopics with secondary details.

The concluding sentence echoes the topic sentence.

Topic Sentence = Subject A + Subject B + comparison or contrast signal word ....

Unity + Coherence + Adequate Development (subtopics + secondary details)

$A_1B_1A_2B_2A_3B_3$ $A_1A_2A_3B_1B_2B_3$

Concluding Sentence..

In Chapter 6 you will learn about the following:

1. Comparison and contrast paragraphs
2. The structure of comparison and contrast paragraphs
3. The writing process for comparison and contrast paragraphs
4. Four additional grammar and usage tips

WRITING WARM-UP 6

Write a paragraph that tells about the differences between two places you have lived. You may write about two different cities or towns, two different houses or apartments, or perhaps your childhood home and your current home. If you have resided in the same house all your life, tell about the differences in the house (or a specific room, such as your bedroom) from your early childhood years to the current year.

The Comparison or Contrast Paragraph

The purpose of a comparison or contrast paragraph is to explain or prove how two people, places, objects, events, or situations are similar or different. A **comparison** paragraph discusses the similarities between two subjects. A **contrast** paragraph discusses the differences between two subjects. A contrast paragraph may also discuss two different perspectives, points of views, or opinions about a given subject. To stay within the scope of a paragraph, your purpose should be limited to comparing or contrasting two subjects, but not trying to compare *and* contrast within a single paragraph.

Comparison and contrast paragraphs are **expository paragraphs.** When you write expository paragraphs, your purpose is to explain, discuss, instruct, or provide your reader with meaningful information about a specific topic. Writing about two subjects without making a significant point does not provide your reader with useful or meaningful information and does not fulfill the expectation of an expository paragraph. Your reader should not react to a comparison or contrast paragraph by saying, "So what? Who cares about this?" Instead, after reading one of your comparison or contrast paragraphs, your reader should clearly understand a significant idea about how the two subjects are alike or different. Your reader should also be able to identify the individual supporting details that develop the purpose of the paragraph and prove your main and controlling idea.

The following paragraph is an example of a contrast paragraph. Marginal notes provide brief explanations about the structure of a contrast paragraph.

Traditional Schools Versus Charter Schools

Topic Sentence (main and controlling idea)

A_1 = size and structure

A_2 = decisionmakers

A_3 = parents' power

The differences between traditional public schools and charter schools have led to the rapid popularity of charter schools. A_1 Traditional public schools frequently belong to large school districts. They have multiple layers of administrators, a multitude of faculty, and a wide variety of support staff personnel. (secondary detail) A_2 Most decision-making is top-down and centralized in the district offices. Traditional public schools are run by school boards, which tell teachers how to teach, what to teach, what hiring policies to use, and how to spend their budgets. (secondary detail) A_3 In traditional schools, parents have limited power. In most cases, they must send their children to the school assigned to their neighborhood. (secondary detail)

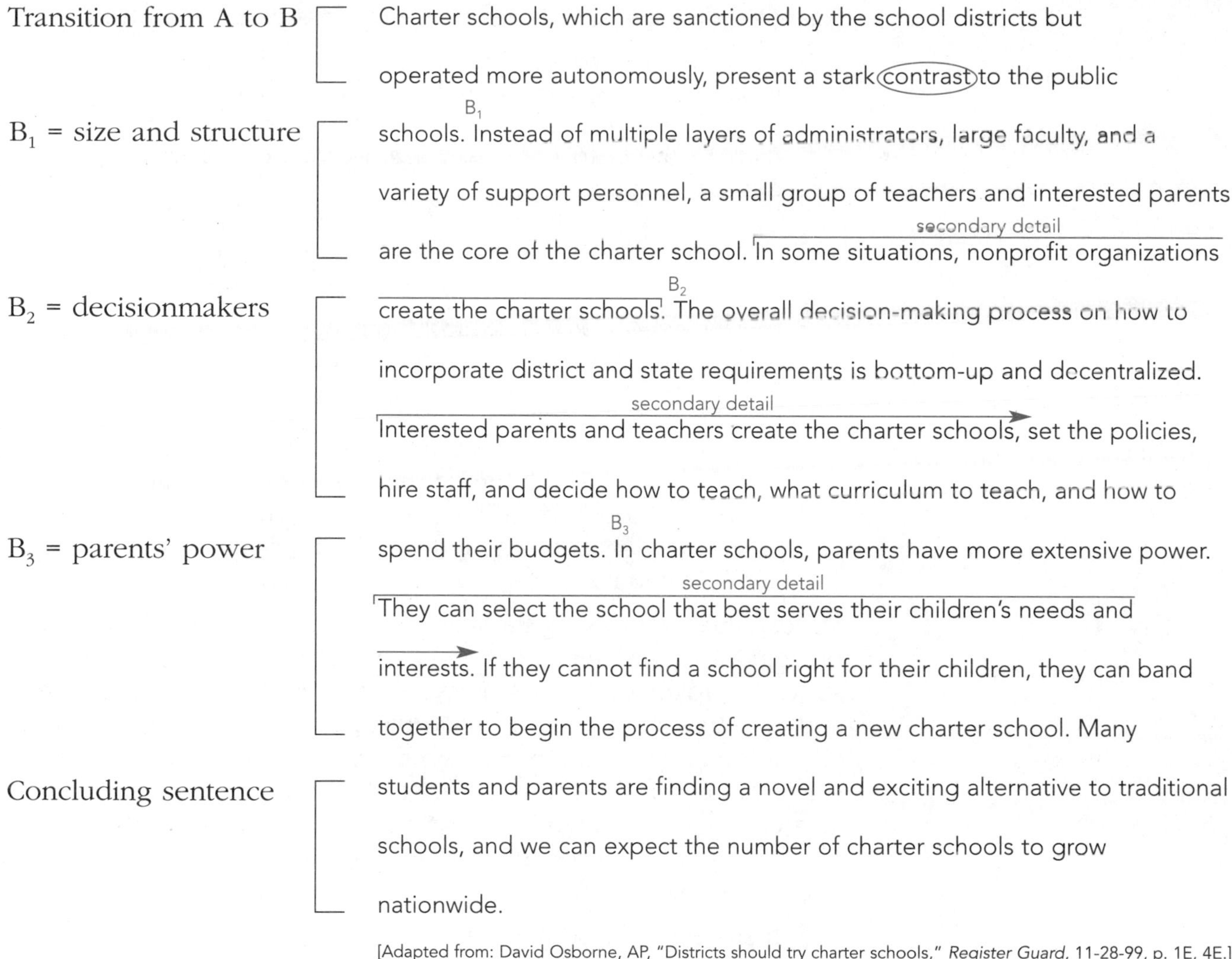

Charter schools, which are sanctioned by the school districts but operated more autonomously, present a stark contrast to the public schools. Instead of multiple layers of administrators, large faculty, and a variety of support personnel, a small group of teachers and interested parents are the core of the charter school. In some situations, nonprofit organizations create the charter schools. The overall decision-making process on how to incorporate district and state requirements is bottom-up and decentralized. Interested parents and teachers create the charter schools, set the policies, hire staff, and decide how to teach, what curriculum to teach, and how to spend their budgets. In charter schools, parents have more extensive power. They can select the school that best serves their children's needs and interests. If they cannot find a school right for their children, they can band together to begin the process of creating a new charter school. Many students and parents are finding a novel and exciting alternative to traditional schools, and we can expect the number of charter schools to grow nationwide.

[Adapted from: David Osborne, AP, "Districts should try charter schools," *Register Guard,* 11-28-99, p. 1E, 4E.]

The Structure of a Comparison or Contrast Paragraph

When you write a comparison or contrast paragraph, continue to use the basic structure of a paragraph: a topic sentence with the controlling idea, a body with the supporting details, and a concluding sentence.

Developing the Topic Sentence

Use the following guidelines to write an effective topic sentence with a controlling idea that reveals your point of view, opinion, or attitude toward the subject of your paragraph.

1. **Select a topic that will interest and inform your readers.** You may need to research the topic to locate specific and accurate supporting details to use in your paragraph.

2. **Narrow the topic by identifying the class of information.**
   - For example, choosing *vehicles* as your topic is too broad. You can narrow *vehicles* to a more specific class of vehicles, such as *sport-utility vehicles,* which you could narrow further to *Ford sport-utility vehicles.* Within this topic, two specific subjects to compare or contrast could be, for example, the *Ford Explorer* and the *Ford Expedition.*
   - Similarly, you could narrow the broad topic of *furniture* to *living room furniture,* and then two subjects, such as *Early American and French provincial.*
3. **Narrow the two subjects.**
   - Subjects that are too broad are difficult to adequately develop. Instead of informing your reader, paragraphs with broad topics often include nothing more than vague or meaningless supporting details and insignificant generalizations.

   For example, contrasting the United States with Canada is too broad. One or two sentences about the different political structures, followed by one or two sentences about social services and general economics of the two countries provide your reader with too little information. However, narrowing the subjects to significant differences between the two countries in one specific area or category of information, such as Canada's socialized medicine and America's HMOs, will result in a more meaningful, informative paragraph.

   - If subjects are too narrow, you may struggle to find a sufficient number of meaningful supportive details to develop into a paragraph.

   For example, if Subject A is one insurance company's policy regarding office visits to a doctor, and Subject B is a different insurance company's policy regarding office visits to a doctor, you will lack a variety of subtopics after you state each company's policies. When subjects are too narrow, the solution is to broaden them so you can use a wider range of subtopics to develop the paragraph.
4. **Select subjects from the same class of information.**
   - In other words, "do not mix apples and oranges." Comparing or contrasting two people, places, objects, events, or situations from different classes is often meaningless. Why, for example, would anyone want or need to know how a cat is different from a bird, or a

bowl is similar to a vase? What consumer would be interested in the differences between a used van and a new Cadillac? Comparing or contrasting paragraphs should make a meaningful point and inform the reader with facts, concepts, or opinions that have some significance or value.

- There is one exception: You may want to use an **analogy,** a comparison between two unlike things, or two subjects that do not belong to the same class of information.

For example, in "Divorce and a Battlefield," on page 60 of Chapter 2, divorce and a battlefield are compared even though they do not belong to the same class of information. Analogies are more difficult to write, but you can use them to make a significant point by linking the point to two subjects from different classes. In the following list, you could develop analogies that make a meaningful point or statement by comparing these two subjects:

- A best friend and a dog
- Dieting and war
- A specific person and a specific animal (an uncle and a weasel; a bureaucrat and a turtle)
- A political arena and a sitcom

5. **State the purpose of the paragraph in the topic sentence.** Your reader should know whether you will compare or contrast the two subjects. Use words such as *likenesses, similarities,* or *alike* to signal that the purpose of the paragraph is to compare the two subjects. Use words such as *differences, differ,* or *unlike* to signal that the purpose of the paragraph is to contrast the two subjects.

Subject A: Coach Barnes; Subject B: Coach Willingham

Coach Barnes and Coach Willingham use **similar** coaching methods to train and develop student athletes.

Subject A: Teenage; Subject B: senior citizen drivers

Teenage and senior citizen drivers encounter **similar** problems learning to drive a car for the first time.

Subject A: drive in rural areas; Subject B: drive on the Los Angeles freeways

Beginning drivers need **different** sets of skills to drive in rural areas and to drive on the Los Angeles freeways.

Subject A: Obtaining a fishing license; Subject B: obtaining an elk hunting license

Obtaining a fishing license and obtaining an elk hunting license in Oregon are very **different** processes.

6.1 What do you think?

Check the following sentences that you find to be effective topic sentences for a comparison or a contrast paragraph.

_________ 1. If you know American football but want to learn to play British rugby, you will need to learn many new skills and rules because these two sports have very little in common.

_________ 2. The basic rules of American football differ from the basic rules of soccer.

_________ 3. Though the professional careers of John Elway and Steve Young have some similarities, their careers ended quite differently.

_________ 4. Most professional wrestlers in the ring today are phonies.

_________ 5. Two surprisingly successful television programs from the year 2000, *Who Wants to Be a Millionaire* and *Survivor,* used similar marketing strategies to attract viewers.

_________ 6. American viewers are more critical of television programming than European viewers.

_________ 7. Many cities in the United States are quite similar to cities in northern Europe.

_________ 8. The flight from Cleveland was the only flight I have been on that required an emergency landing.

_________ 9. The different formats of *The Star Tribune* and *The Pioneer Press* attract different readers of daily newspapers.

_________ 10. Mountain bikes and racing bikes differ in four significant ways.

Developing the Body of the Paragraph

Use the following guidelines to develop the body of your paragraph and the controlling idea stated in your topic sentence.

1. Provide your readers with **subtopics,** or categories of details, to show how Subject A and Subject B are similar or different. The subtopics prove or develop the controlling idea of the topic sentence. In the paragraph "Traditional Schools Versus Charter Schools" on pages 224–225, the subtopics are as follows:

    1. Size and structure
    2. Decisionmakers
    3. Parents' power

2. Develop Subject A and Subject B equally. What you discuss about Subject A, you must also discuss about Subject B. For example, if you discuss the size of Subject A, you must also discuss the size of Subject B. If information about a subtopic is given for Subject A but not for Subject B, your paragraph will lack unity and coherence.

3. Create *unity* by selecting only subtopics that prove and develop, or relate closely to, your topic sentence. Also, if you are writing a comparison paragraph, do not digress into points about differences. If you are writing a contrast paragraph, do not digress into points about similarities. To digress breaks the unity of the paragraph and its purpose.

4. Create *coherence* by using the following three methods.

   - Establish in your topic sentence what Subject A and Subject B are and use the terms you have established in this order throughout your paragraph. For example, in the topic sentence for "Traditional Schools Versus Charter Schools," the term *traditional schools* was mentioned first, so it functions as Subject A throughout the paragraph. *Charter schools* functions as Subject B. The body of the paragraph begins by discussing Subject A.
   - Use one of two common organizational patterns for your subtopics and the secondary details in your paragraph: the **point-by-point method** or the **block method.** (See the next section for an explanation of these methods.)
   - Use **transition words** to connect ideas within subtopics and to transition from Subject A to Subject B. The following transition words frequently appear in comparison and contrast paragraphs:

COMPARISON TRANSITION WORDS				
again	also	and	as	as well as
both	further	furthermore	in addition	like
likewise	moreover	next	similarly	too

CONTRAST TRANSITION WORDS				
although	but	conversely	despite	
even so	however	nevertheless	on the contrary	
on the other hand		though	unlike	yet

5. Provide *adequate development* to prove or explain your topic sentence clearly and accurately to your reader. Carefully select subtopics that clearly demonstrate key similarities or differences between the two subjects. Then, expand each subtopic by giving the reader additional information, called **secondary details,** about the subtopic. Adequate development of a topic occurs when both the subtopics and the secondary details explain, support, and develop the controlling idea of the topic sentence. Though you may use more than three subtopics, three well-selected subtopics usually develop the topic sentence adequately.

The Point-by-Point Method

The point-by-point method discusses one subtopic at a time. The writer discusses the first subtopic for Subject A, followed by the same subtopic for Subject B, then the second subtopic for Subject A, and the corresponding subtopic for Subject B, and so on. For example, an outline for a comparison or contrast paragraph about two singers could look like this:

I. Topic Sentence
- A. Subtopic 1: Style of music
  - 1. Subject A: Style of music of Singer #1
  - 2. Subject B: Style of music of Singer #2
- B. Subtopic 2: Greatest hits
  - 1. Subject A: Greatest hits of Singer #1
  - 2. Subject B: Greatest hits of Singer #2
- C. Subtopic 3: Audience Appeal
  - 1. Subject A: Audience appeal of Singer #1
  - 2. Subject B: Audience appeal of Singer #2

The point-by-point method is most effective for paragraphs in which:

1. You want to emphasize the individual points about each subject.
2. You have numerous or complex supporting details that you want to identify clearly for your reader.

The following graphic presentation shows the point-by-point method.

Point-by-Point Method

	Topic sentence ....
Body	**Subtopic A_1** ....
	Secondary details for A_1 ....
	Subtopic B_1 ....
	Secondary details for B_1 ....
	Subtopic A_2 ....
	Secondary details for A_2 ....
	Subtopic B_2 ....
	Secondary details for B_2 ....
	Subtopic A_3 ....
	Secondary details for A_3 ....
	Subtopic B_3 ....
	Secondary details for B_3 ....
	Concluding sentence ....

The Block Method

The block method gives all the subtopics and secondary details about Subject A first. Then, after a transition word or phrase such as *similarly* or *on the other hand,* you present the same subtopics for Subject B in the same order they appeared for Subject A. You add secondary details to each subtopic. For example, the outline for a comparison or contrast paragraph about two different singers would look like this:

I. Topic Sentence

- A. Subject A: Singer #1
  1. Subtopic 1: Style of Music of Singer #1
  2. Subtopic 2: Greatest Hits of Singer #1
  3. Subtopic 3: Audience Appeal of Singer #1
- B. Subject B: Singer #2
  1. Subtopic 1: Style of Music of Singer #2
  2. Subtopic 2: Greatest Hits of Singer #2
  3. Subtopic 3: Audience Appeal of Singer #2

The block method is most effective for paragraphs in which:

1. You want to develop a strong image or impression of Subject A in your reader's mind before introducing Subject B.
2. You have fewer, less complex details.

The following graphic presentation shows the block method:

Block Method

Topic sentence ....

Body

Subtopic A_1 ....
Secondary details for A_1 ....
Subtopic A_2 ....
Secondary details for A_2 ....
Subtopic A_3 ....
Secondary details for A_3 ....
Transition sentence. ....
Subtopic B_1 ....
Secondary details for B_1 ....
Subtopic B_2 ....
Secondary details for B_2 ....
Subtopic B_3 ....
Secondary details for B_3 ....

Concluding sentence ....

6.2 What do you think?

Developing a comparison or a contrast paragraph by using both organizational methods provides you with an opportunity to critique and select the method that works better to convey the information and achieve the purpose of your paragraph. The following contrast paragraph is written by using first the point-by-point method and then the block method. On separate paper, answer the questions that follow the paragraph.

Point-by-Point Method: American Dollars

Fortunately for the U.S. Mint, the differences between the Susan B. Anthony dollar and the Sacagawea dollar are great. From 1979 to 1981, the U.S. Mint produced 857 million Susan B. Anthony silver dollars. When the stockpile of silver dollars was depleted, the U.S. Mint decided not to mint any more of this unpopular dollar. The U.S. Mint first produced the "golden" Sacagawea dollar in January, 2000. The U.S. Mint predicts that it will mint more than one billion golden dollars. Within the first month of its distribution, production doubled to five million a day to keep up with the demand for this popular dollar. The two coins are different in other ways as well. The Susan B. Anthony silver dollar depicts the nineteenth-century suffragette. Her profile is stern and unfriendly. The Sacagawea dollar depicts Sacagawea, a Shoshone Indian teenager who helped guide the Lewis and Clark expedition. Sacagawea carries a child on her back and conveys a friendly and proud image. The Susan B. Anthony silver dollar is the size and color of a quarter. Though the edges are different from those of a quarter, the coin is frequently mistaken for a quarter. The Sacagawea golden dollar cannot be confused with a quarter, mainly because of its distinctive color. Though both coins have the same value, the differences between the coins indicate that the Sacagawea dollar will triumph over the Susan B. Anthony dollar for both popularity and longevity.

Block Method: American Dollars

Fortunately for the U.S. Mint, the differences between the Susan B. Anthony dollar and the Sacagawea dollar are great. From 1979 to 1981, the U.S. Mint produced 857 million Susan B. Anthony silver dollars. When the stockpile of silver dollars was depleted, the U.S. Mint decided not to mint any more of this unpopular dollar. The Susan B. Anthony silver dollar depicts the nineteenth-century suffragette. Her profile is stern and unfriendly. The Susan B. Anthony silver dollar is the size and color of a quarter. Though the edges are different from those of a quarter, the coin is frequently mistaken for a quarter. The U.S. Mint, on the other hand, produced the first "golden" Sacagawea dollar in January, 2000. The U.S. Mint predicts that it will mint more than one billion golden dollars. Within the first month of its distribution, production doubled to five million a day to keep up with the demand for this popular dollar. The Sacagawea dollar depicts Sacagawea, a Shoshone Indian teenager who helped guide the Lewis and Clark expedition. Sacagawea carries a child on her back and conveys a friendly and proud image. Unlike the Susan B. Anthony dollar, the Sacagawea golden dollar cannot be confused with a quarter, mainly because of its distinctive color. Though both coins have the same value, the differences between the coins indicate that the Sacagawea dollar will triumph over the Susan B. Anthony dollar for both popularity and longevity.

[Adapted from: Libby Quaid, AP, "Feds distribute Sacagawea coins," *Register Guard,* 2-2-00, p. 1D, 2D.]

1. Do you prefer the point-by-point method or the block method? Why?
2. Create an outline for the point-by-point method that shows the subtopics. Use the outline format that is shown on page 230.
3. List transition words, phrases, or sentences that appear in the point-by-point method.

4. List transition words that appear in the block method.
5. How is coherence developed in the block method?
6. Do both paragraphs have unity? Explain.
7. Do both paragraphs have adequate development? Explain.

Developing the Concluding Sentence

Use the following guidelines to bring your paragraph to an end.

1. Reinforce or echo the controlling idea of the topic sentence to bring closure to the paragraph. Do not use the exact wording of the topic sentence; however, show the purpose (to compare or contrast) and the main idea in the concluding sentence.
2. Include an additional comment about the relationship between the subjects or the significance of the information when such a comment seems appropriate. In the following example, the words in italic show the extra comment.

   Many students and parents are finding a novel and exciting alternative to traditional schools, *and we can expect the number of charter schools to grow nationwide.*

6.3 What do you think?

Read each of topic sentences that follow. Then read the concluding sentences. Decide whether the concluding sentence is effective for a paragraph with that topic sentence. Explain your answer on separate paper.

1. Topic sentence: Deciding between attending a community college or a four-year university is difficult because both forms of higher education have many common characteristics.

   Concluding sentence: Because both universities and community colleges are similar in so many ways, the decision to attend one or the other may best be made by looking at the differences rather than the similarities of the two forms of higher education.

2. Topic sentence: Though many Elvis impersonators try to keep the spirit of Elvis alive, the differences between them and Elvis are too great for a true Elvis fan to ignore.

   Concluding sentence: Even though they make sincere attempts to keep the spirit of Elvis alive, the impersonators will never be able to capture the audiences, project the charisma, or produce the vocal qualities of Elvis.

3.	Topic sentence:	Fortunately for the U.S. Mint, the differences between the Susan B. Anthony dollar and the Sacagawea dollar are great.
	Concluding sentence:	Though both coins have the same value, the differences between the coins indicate that the Sacagawea dollar will triumph over the Susan B. Anthony dollar for both popularity and longevity.
4.	Topic Sentence:	For geologists, living in the Alaskan tundra is not much different from living in Iceland.
	Concluding Sentence:	Geologists have found that life in the Alaskan tundra and Iceland are equally difficult and challenging.

The Writing Process for Comparison and Contrast Paragraphs

Step 1: Generate ideas.

Comparison and contrast paragraphs consist of two subjects that usually belong to the same class of information, such as singers, books, games, players, television shows, trucks, authors, tribes, or languages. The easiest way to begin the process of generating ideas is to **brainstorm** a list of classes of people, places, things, events, or situations. Consider the following as starting points for brainstorming.

1. personal experiences that convey significant meaning that would interest the reader:

family experiences	family traditions	family feuds
different cultures	ethnic backgrounds	methods of child-raising
job experiences	job benefits	employers
work environments	work responsibilities	kinds of employees

2. specific content from a course you are taking this term:

health:	kinds of food supplements, first aid techniques, vitamins
computer:	software programs, kinds of viruses, different drives
psychology:	theories of psychology, memory systems, phobias
literature:	American authors, recurring themes, poets

Brainstorm eight different classes of information that could become topics for comparison or contrast paragraphs:

____________________ ____________________

____________________ ____________________

____________________ ____________________

____________________ ____________________

Step 2: Get a focus.

After identifying classes of information that could be compared or contrasted, your next task is to narrow your topic and identify two specific subjects to write about. Also, you must decide whether the two specific subjects lend themselves better to comparison or contrast. Do they have more things in common for a comparison, or do they have more differences and thus lend themselves better to contrast? Because comparison and contrast paragraphs emphasize expository writing, select subjects that you can make a significant point about and discuss in a meaningful and informative way. Avoid subjects that result in the reader saying, "So what? Who cares?" The controlling idea in your topic sentence needs to make an important point about the two subjects, a significant point that will unify your subtopics.

You can get a focus by completing the phrase "two ________."

For example you can focus the following classes of information by naming two subjects for the class:

writers	athletes	movie stars	singers	employers
philosophers	historical figures	teachers	leaders	politicians
restaurants	movie theaters	schools	islands	volcanoes
holidays	pieces of art	books	sitcoms	kinds of music

Identifying the Two Subjects

For the following classes of information, write two possible subjects that you could use for a comparison or a contrast paragraph. The first one is done for you as an example.

Class	**Subject A**	**Subject B**
styles of cooking	Korean	Chinese
planets	________	________
methods to control weeds	________	________
tribes	________	________
presidents	________	________
writers	________	________
athletes	________	________
team sports	________	________
political parties	________	________
Internet providers	________	________

Deciding to Compare or Contrast

Frequently, after thinking about the two subjects you want to use in a paragraph, the decision to compare or contrast the two subjects becomes apparent. When you are unsure which direction to take with two subjects, make a list of all the ways they are alike and all the ways they are different. Use these lists to make the decision to write a comparison or a contrast paragraph. For example, assume you know about two languages, Portuguese and Spanish. After compiling the following lists, more similarities than differences suggest that you plan to formulate a topic sentence for a comparison paragraph and select subtopics that show similarities.

Similarities

1. phonetically regular
2. masculine and feminine forms
3. formal and informal verb tenses
4. formal and informal titles/pronouns
5. diacritical marks on words
6. based on Latin
7. Romance language
8. same word order in sentences

Differences

1. roll the letter *r* in Spanish
2. *b* and *v* can sound the same in Spanish
3. Portuguese speakers can understand Spanish but not vice versa
4. Different question marks

Step 3: Gather and organize information.

After you identify the two subjects and make the decision to compare or contrast them, the next step is to gather information to show the possible subtopics or primary details you could use to discuss both subjects.

Create a Grid of Details

A **grid** works well to organize this information. A grid is an organizational diagram that consists of rows and columns. The first column identifies subtopics, the middle column is Subject A, and the last column is Subject B. For each subtopic, add details about Subject A and Subject B.

Two Singers		
SUBTOPICS	SUBJECT A	SUBJECT B
Kind of music		
Biggest hits		
Audience appeal		

Any time you list a subtopic but cannot add secondary details that support or develop the subtopic for both Subject A and Subject B, that subtopic is not suitable for your paragraph. Listing possible subtopics on the grid is another form of brainstorming. After you have exhausted the possibilities for subtopics, answer these questions:

1. Could I combine some of the subtopics?
2. Which subtopics are the most significant or express the greatest similarities or differences between the subjects?
3. Which subtopics can I ignore?

Write the Topic Sentence

After you select the subtopics, write several possible topic sentences. The topic sentences should do the following:

1. State your purpose (compare or contrast).
2. Name Subject A and Subject B.
3. Make a significant main point about the topic that the supporting details will prove.
4. Capture the reader's interest.

Develop an Outline

Select a possible topic sentence. Write the topic sentence on the first line of an **outline.** Then complete two basic outlines to show the point-by-point and the block methods of organization. List the subtopics in a logical order. You may jot down secondary details after each subtopic if you would like, or you may simply add the secondary details when you write the rough draft. Use the following outlines to organize the subtopics.

Point-by-Point

I. Topic sentence:
  A. Subtopic 1:
    1. Subject A
    2. Subject B
  B. Subtopic 2:
    1. Subject A
    2. Subject B
  C. Subtopic 3:
    1. Subject A
    2. Subject B

Block

I. Topic sentence:
  A. Subject A
    1. Subtopic 1
    2. Subtopic 2
    3. Subtopic 3
  B. Subject B
    1. Subtopic 1
    2. Subtopic 2
    3. Subtopic 3

6.4 What do you think?

The following grid shows details for two relationship gurus: John Gray, Ph.D., the author of *Men Are from Mars, Women Are from Venus*, and John Gottman, Ph.D., the author of *Why Marriages Succeed*. The left column shows the subtopics. The middle and the right columns show secondary details about Subject A and Subject B for each of the subtopics. Read the chart carefully. On separate paper, answer the questions that follow the chart.

CONTRAST		
SUBTOPICS	SUBJECT A: JOHN GRAY	SUBJECT B: JOHN GOTTMAN
best-selling book	*Men Are from Mars, Women Are from Venus* (more than six million copies)	*Why Marriages Succeed* (55,000 copies)
number of journal articles	none	109
number of couples studied	none	760
cardinal rule of relationships	"Men and women are different."	"What people think they do in relationships and what they actually do are two different things."
what makes marriages work	"Heeding gender stereotypes"	"Making mental maps of each other's world"
what makes marriages fail	"Gender differences in communication styles"	"Heeding gender stereotypes; reactions to stress"
relationship heroes	"Men who escape to their caves"	"Men who put the toilet seat down"
key gender differences	"Women talk too much about feelings"	"Men's and women's bodies respond differently when negative emotions become intense"
men's biggest mistake	"Trying to solve her problems"	"Failing to take a deep breath during conflict"
women's biggest mistake	"Giving advice"	"Stating complaints as criticism"

[Source: Hara Estroff Marano, "Gottman and Gray: The Two Johns," *Psychology Today*, Nov/Dec. 1997, p. 28.]

1. Which subtopics are the most significant or express the greatest similarities or differences between the subjects?
2. Which subtopics could you combine?
3. Which subtopics could you ignore?
4. Based on the information on the grid would you compare or contrast the two relationship gurus? Explain your answer.
5. Write two or more possible topic sentences for a comparison or a contrast paragraph about John Gray and John Gottman.

Step 4: Write the rough draft.

Begin with either a point-by-point or a block outline. Use the outline as your guide to write your rough draft. After you state a subtopic for one of the subjects, add secondary details to expand the subtopic. Secondary details help clarify or explain the subtopics. They give your reader additional information so the points or the impression you wish to convey are clear and understandable.

Use the following checklist when you write your rough draft:

1. Double space so you have room to revise.
2. Use transition words to connect subtopics and secondary details—to move back and forth from Subject A to Subject B in the point-by-point method or to make a smooth transition from Subject A to Subject B in the block method.
3. Decide if the point-by-point or the block method is more effective. If you know how to use a computer, copy the first paragraph. Then use the cut and paste features to convert the paragraph from point-by-point to block, or the reverse.

Step 5: Revise, revise, revise.

If your instructor asks you to write both the point-by-point and the block paragraphs, select the paragraph that you believe conveys the comparison or the contrast more effectively. Focus your revision work on the paragraph of your choice. As with all paragraphs, you may need to revise several times. Use the following checklist to guide your revision:

1. Examine the structure of the paragraph. Is there an effective topic sentence? Does the body of the paragraph follow your outline? Does the concluding sentence echo the topic sentence in its purpose, subjects, and main point or impression?
2. Check that you use point-by-point or block organization consistently throughout the paragraph. Do you develop each subtopic equally for both subjects? In other words, do you discuss for Subject A exactly what you discuss for Subject B?
3. Identify the transitional words. Do you use transition words effectively so ideas flow together smoothly and logically? Do the transition words show the desired relationship between ideas?
4. Examine the paragraph for *unity*. Does every sentence belong in the paragraph, and does every sentence directly or indirectly support the topic sentence? Do all the sentences support the purpose of the paragraph, which is to compare or contrast the two subjects?
5. Examine the paragraph for *coherence*. Are the subtopics and secondary details in the same order for Subject A and Subject B?
6. Evaluate the paragraph for *adequate development*. Do you expand the subtopics for each subject with effective secondary details? Do you need more secondary details to clarify or explain the subtopics? Are any of the secondary details unnecessary?

6.5 What do you think?

Work with a partner or on your own. Read the paragraph carefully. On separate paper, answer the questions that follow the paragraph.

Historical Periods

[1]The Classical Period of music, art, and literature differed greatly from the subsequent Romantic Period. [2]During the Classical Period, music, art, and literature emphasized formal rules, patterns, and structure. [3]Greek and Latin traditions influenced the arts during this period. [4]Complexity and a heavy feeling or pressure cloaked all forms of art. [5]Artists, musicians, and writers restrained emotions. [6]They honored and respected traditional standards; they suppressed or refrained from using creativity and originality. [7]During the onset of the Romantic Period, however, musicians, artists, and writers sought to escape the formal, stiff, stifling rules of formality, set patterns, and inflexible structures. [8]New forms of expression emphasized a light, joyful, and frivolous side of human nature. [9]Society as a whole placed a high value on creativity, experimentation, and originality. [10]Individuals received validation; individual expression of emotions, passions, and the human soul became valued. [11]Romantic art often depicted amoral love with an abundance of cupids and thinly clad nymphs. [12]During this cultural revolution at the end of the eighteenth century, two opposing periods with extremely different values collided.

1. Is this paragraph organized around the point-by-point or the block method?
2. Does the topic sentence state the purpose (to compare or contrast), identify Subject A and Subject B, state a significant point, and capture your interest? Explain.
3. Which two sentences break the unity? Do you think it would be better to delete the sentences or expand the paragraph by developing a new subtopic? Explain.
4. Create a grid to show the subtopics of the paragraph.
5. Rewrite the paragraph using the point-by-point method. Then be prepared to discuss which organizational pattern you prefer for this paragraph.

6.6 What do you think?

Work with a partner or on your own to discuss the structure, the balance, and the adequate development of the following draft for a contrast paragraph. On separate paper, answer the questions that follow the paragraph.

Not Like My Mother

My mother is very opposite from me. [A1]I am not superstitious. In fact, I think I am a rational person. I feel that something larger than myself is trying to control my way. [B1]On the other hand, my mother is so superstitious. She pays attention to dates, the Japanese dates, that come from an old Japanese calendar. *Taian* is a good day to do or to start something. So, people have weddings, move to new places, or start new things on *Taian*. *Butsumetsu* is a bad day to start something new. On a *Bustumetsu* day, my mother does not wear her new clothes or her new shoes. She waits until the next *Taian* comes. [A2]I do not pay much attention to superstitions, but I feel peaceful when I hear my mother's superstitions. They are one of the ways I know she cares so much about me. I know she is trying to keep me away from bad luck. [B2]My mother, on the other hand, follows the superstitions that her mother taught her. She says the same things that my grandmother said. She does not cut her nails at night because that will bring bad luck. She does not point at a snake because when you see a snake, it will also bring bad luck. My mother prays in the morning and at night to thank her parents. Her parents have already passed away, but she still believes that they are protecting her. [A4]I live in the United States. [B4]My mother lives in Japan. Even though I am different from my mother and do not believe in my mother's superstitions, I will probably pass them on to my children some day as a way to keep our family's love and support in their minds.

Hiromi Hasegawa
Bellevue Community College
Bellevue, Washington

1. In the topic sentence, who is Subject A? ________ Who is Subject B? ________ Does the author use the order of Subject A and Subject B that is established in the topic sentence throughout the paragraph? Explain.
2. Does the author develop Subject A and Subject B equally? In other words, does the author discuss the same subtopics for Subject A and Subject B? If not, identify the subtopics that do not show balance or equal development.

3. Does the paragraph have unity? Explain. (See page 229.)
4. Does the paragraph have adequate development? (See page 230.) Explain.
5. Complete a grid or an outline for this paragraph.

Step 6: Proofread and edit.

After you revise your paragraph at least one time, you are ready to proofread and edit. As you acquire more grammar and usage skills, proofreading should expand to include these new grammar skills. Use the following checklist to proofread current paragraphs that you are developing:

1. Does every sentence have a complete subject and a complete verb and form a complete thought so it can stand on its own?
2. Is there sentence variety in the paragraph? Do you use compound subjects or compound verbs? Does the paragraph have a variety of simple, compound, and complex sentences?
3. Do you use the correct punctuation between words in a series, between two independent clauses (compound sentences), and between dependent and independent clauses (complex sentences)?
4. Are all fragments, comma splice errors and run-on sentence errors corrected?
5. Are all words spelled correctly?
6. Do you avoid shifting back and forth between past and present verb tenses?
7. Do you use logical verb tenses throughout the paragraph to show the accurate tense in which the action of the sentence occurred?
8. Are participles used correctly? If the participles show the action of the sentence, do you state them as verb phrases with helping verbs?

Step 7: Prepare the final version of your comparison or contrast paragraph.

Follow your instructor's directions for preparing the final version of your paragraph. As always, save all your prewriting materials, your rough draft, and your revisions. You may be asked to turn them in with the final version of your work.

WRITING ASSIGNMENT

Write a comparison or a contrast paragraph about a topic that makes a significant point and interests you and your readers.

Complete each of the following steps for writing a comparison or a contrast paragraph. Unless your instructor indicates a different approach, use the Comparison or Contrast Paragraph Planning Sheet on page 245 for each step of the writing process.

Step 1: Generate ideas.
Select a class of information for your comparison or contrast paragraph. You may use the classes of information from your brainstorming lists on page 235, you may add to your brainstorming list, or you may select a class of information from the following possibilities. Complete Step 1 on the Planning Sheet.

political points of view	airplanes	historical battles	mountains
teachers	endangered species	local landmarks	languages
heating systems	classic cars	catastrophes	family structures
diets	fads	lifestyles	laws
potting soils	kinds of insurance	personalities	medical treatments

Step 2: Get a focus.
Narrow your topic and select two subjects, Subject A and Subject B, that belong to the same class of information. Decide whether you will compare or contrast the two subjects. Complete Step 2 on the Planning Sheet.

Step 3: Gather and organize information.
On separate paper, create a planning grid, a point-by-point outline, and a block outline. Experiment with several topic sentences before you select the most effective topic sentence for your paragraph. See Step 3 on the Planning Sheet for details.

Step 4: Write the rough draft.
Use your outline to write a draft that follows the point-by-point method. Then write a draft that follows the block method. Decide which of the two is more effective. Use the checklist on page 240 for draft-writing suggestions. Complete Step 4 on the Planning Sheet.

Step 5: Revise, revise, revise.
Use the revision checklist on page 240 to guide you through the revision process. Revise as many times as needed to achieve your desired effect. Save your revisions. Share your revised draft with a partner and ask your partner to complete the feedback questions on the Planning Sheet.

Step 6: Proofread and edit.
Use the checklist on page 243 as a guide to proofread and edit your paragraph. Complete Step 6 on the Planning Sheet.

Step 7: Prepare the final version of your paragraph.

COMPARISON OR CONTRAST PARAGRAPH PLANNING SHEET

Name ______________________________

Step 1: Write the class of information you will use: ______________________________

Step 2: Write the two subjects you will use: ______________________________

Step 3: On separate paper, design a planning grid that shows possible subtopics to discuss for Subject A and Subject B. Star the subtopics you decide to use. Fill in the spaces on the grid with key words to show the ideas you will discuss. Then, create a point-by-point outline and a block outline.

Planning Grid

SUBTOPICS	SUBJECT A	SUBJECT B

Point-by-Point

I. Topic sentence: ________
- A. Subtopic 1: ________
  1. Subject A:
  2. Subject B:
- B. Subtopic 2: ________
  1. Subject A:
  2. Subject B:
- C. Subtopic 3: ________
  1. Subject A:
  2. Subject B:

Block

I. Topic sentence: ________
- A. Subject A ________
  1. Subtopic 1
  2. Subtopic 2
  3. Subtopic 3
- B. Subject B ________
  1. Subtopic 1
  2. Subtopic 2
  3. Subtopic 3

Write several possible topic sentences. Star the one you prefer to use.

1. ______________________________
2. ______________________________
3. ______________________________
4. ______________________________

Step 4: When did you finish writing the rough draft? ______________________________

Step 5: Save all your revisions. Show your revised draft to a partner. Ask your partner to answer the following questions. When the feedback is returned to you, use your partner's comments for further revisions of your paragraph.

PARTNER FEEDBACK FORM

1. Is the topic sentence effective? Why or why not? ______

2. Does the writer use the point-by-point or block method? ______

3. Does the paragraph follow the prewriting outline? ______

4. Does the concluding sentence reflect the content of the topic sentence? Explain: ______

______

______

5. Explain your answers for the following questions.

   Are the subtopics clear? ______

   Are the subtopics for Subject A and Subject B developed equally? ______

   Are transition words used effectively? ______

6. Does the paragraph have unity? Explain: ______

______

7. Does the paragraph have coherence? Explain: ______

______

8. Does the paragraph have adequate development? Does the writer use sufficient subtopics? Does the writer provide sufficient secondary details for each subtopic? Explain:

______

9. Provide your partner with suggestions for proofreading and editing:

10. What did you like about this paragraph?

Partner's name ______

Step 6: Write the date that you finished your proofreading and editing: ______

Step 7: Prepare the final version of your comparison or contrast paragraph.

Grammar and Usage Tips

A complete sentence has a subject and a complete verb and forms a complete thought that can stand on its own. However, sentences become richer, more descriptive, and more detailed through the use of other sentence elements. The four grammar and usage tips in this chapter focus on expanding sentences by adding more descriptive details to nouns and pronouns. After you complete the following exercises, carefully check your work with the answer keys in Appendix A and record your number of errors for each exercise. Review the tip and examine the correct answer. In the margins of each exercise, jot down questions that you would like to ask your instructor regarding the points covered in the exercises.

TIP 17 **Use appositives to add descriptive details to nouns or pronouns in sentences. Appositives are nouns, noun phrases, or noun clauses that rename or give more specific information about a preceding noun or pronoun. Place appositives directly after the noun or pronoun that they rename. Set appositives off with commas when the information is nonessential; do not set appositives off with commas when the information is essential to the meaning or the clarity of the sentence.**

In the following sentences, the **appositives** rename the preceding noun. The arrows point from the appositive to the noun or pronoun that it refers to or renames.

> The Shoshone Indian teenager **Sacagawea** guided the Lewis and Clark expedition.

> The two explorers **Lewis and Clark** established trading posts in the Northwest.

Notice in each of the preceding sentences that the sentence would not be fully understood without the appositives. The appositives are essential to the meaning of the sentences. To show their importance, they are not set off by commas.

> The golden dollar depicts Sacagawea, **a Shoshone Indian teenager,** with a child on her back.

> Susan B. Anthony, **a nineteenth-century suffragette,** appears on the most recent silver dollar.

> The Sacagawea dollar, **the golden dollar,** was instantly in high demand.

Notice in each of the preceding sentences that the appositives are set off by commas to show that they are nonessential to the meaning of the sentences. Appositives that rename proper nouns (nouns that are capitalized) are always nonessential and are set off by commas. Information that is set off by commas is a "sentence extra." The appositive adds details and information, but the sentence is clear without the appositive.

Creating Appositives

1. Add appositives to sentences when one or more of the nouns or pronouns seem vague or lack sufficient detail to express the idea you wish to convey to the reader. Notice how appositives enhance the following sentences.

Without an Appositive:	Salem does not have a major airport.
With an Appositive:	Salem, **the capital of Oregon,** does not have a major airport.
Without an Appositive:	The ships frequently dock in Coos Bay.
With an Appositive:	The ships frequently dock in Coos Bay, **a port on the Oregon coast.**
Without an Appositive:	The ship sank in the sand and eventually split into two pieces in the Oregon coastal waters.
With an Appositive:	The ship **The New Carissa** sank in the sand and eventually split into two pieces in the Oregon coastal waters.

2. For more concise wording and greater clarity of expression, look for ways to combine sentences by converting information from one of the sentences into an appositive. When one noun is repeated in two separate sentences, this is a signal that an appositive may be possible.

Two Sentences:	The *freighter* could not be towed out of the sand. The *freighter* was a Panamanian cargo ship.
Combined with an Appositive:	The freighter, **a Panamanian cargo ship,** could not be towed out of the sand.
Two Sentences:	Seventy thousand gallons of *fuel oil* spilled into the ocean. *Fuel oil* is a life-threatening substance for birds, shellfish, and wildlife.
Combined with an Appositive:	Seventy thousand gallons of fuel oil, **a life-threatening substance for birds, shellfish, and wildlife,** spilled into the ocean.

Two Sentences: *Captain James Spitzer* headed the U.S. Coast Guard's clean-up efforts.

Captain Spitzer was the federal on-scene coordinator.

Combined with an Appositive: Captain James Spitzer, **the federal on-scene coordinator,** headed the U.S. Coast Guard's clean-up efforts.

You can combine more than two sentences into one sentence by using appositives. When a noun is repeated in two or more sentences, explore the possibility of creating an appositive.

Three Sentences: *Professor Woo* retired to *Las Vegas.*

Las Vegas is the city of glamorous casinos and endless entertainment.

Professor Woo is the author of our textbook.

Combined with Appositives: Professor Woo, **the author of our textbook,** retired to Las Vegas, **the city of glamorous casinos and endless entertainment.**

3. Use appositives to define unfamiliar terms.

   Cooking tomatoes releases lycopene, **the nutrient that makes tomatoes red.**

   Alpha-linolenic acid, **one of the omega-3 fatty acids,** may prevent heart disease.

EXERCISE 6.1 Identifying Appositives

Score: ______

Circle the appositives in the following sentences.

1. Lance rode across the country on his bike, a 1995 Harley Davidson.
2. My mother-in-law, a woman of Hawaiian heritage, captivated listeners with her Hawaiian legends.
3. Marissa's friend Anna Marie appeared on the talk show with the host Rosie O'Donnell.
4. Chinatown, a famous tourist spot in San Francisco, hosts annual celebrations for the Chinese New Year.
5. Neanderthals, a primitive hominid, appeared in Europe about 100,000 years ago.
6. My English literature assignment, a thousand-word essay, forced me to examine the characters and the plot of the story carefully.
7. My counselor, an experienced therapist, taught me how to visualize and relax.

8. Robert Redbird's latest painting, a portrait of a strong Native American woman, is a limited edition.

9. My favorite aunt, a freelance photographer, leads an exciting, energetic life.

10. An increasing number of Americans practice yoga, a system of physical and mental exercise.

EXERCISE 6.2 Combining Sentences by Using Appositives

Score: ______

Combine the following sentences into one sentence by converting information into appositives. Place each appositive directly after the noun that it renames. Write your answers on separate paper.

Example: Alligators reside in the Everglades of Florida.

Alligators are amphibious reptiles.

Alligators, **amphibious reptiles,** reside in the Everglades of Florida.

1. Minneapolis is the home of the Vikings, the Timberwolves, and the Twins.

   Many large corporate headquarters are located in Minneapolis.

2. Denver is the hub for United Airlines.

   United Airlines is one of America's largest airlines.

   Denver is the capital of Colorado.

3. The company conducts drug screening on all its employees.

   The company is a chain of retail stores.

4. My car stalled in the middle of a busy intersection.

   My car is an old, beat-up Plymouth.

5. An antique clock caught my eye.

   The antique clock was a relic from the Civil War years.

Use participial phrases to describe nouns or pronouns. Participial phrases begin with a present participle (*-ing* form of the verb) or a past participle. Participial phrases often, but not always, refer to the subject of the sentence. Place participial phrases directly before or after the noun or the pronoun that they describe. The participles in this case are working as adjectives. They are not part of a verb phrase and are not the verb of the sentence.

In Chapter 5, you learned that present participles are words that end with *-ing,* and that past participles are words that end in *-ed* or another form for irregular verbs. Participial phrases begin with a present or a past participle. They provide another method for adding details to sentences by describing nouns, which often are the sentence's subject. Notice in the following examples that the participles do not have helping verbs and, thus, are not a part of verb phrases. Instead, participles function as adjectives. The arrows point to the noun that the participial phrase describes.

> Mona, **wanting to please her boss,** volunteered to work overtime.

The subject in this sentence, Mona, is already clearly defined. Therefore, the participial phrase is a nonessential element; it is not needed to define or clarify the noun. Use a comma to set off a participial phrase with nonessential information. In this case, the participial phrase describes the subject.

> Three of the electricians **involved in the labor dispute** filed a formal complaint.

> The man **standing near the site of the accident** explained the sequence of events.

The nouns *electricians* and *man* are not clearly defined. The participial phrase is essential in order to define or clarify the subject. Do not use commas to set off participial phrases with essential information.

> **Wanting a new challenge,** Pat selected computer science as her major.

> **Disappointed by voter turnout,** the school board launched a publicity campaign.

Participial phrases that begin sentences are introductory information and are always followed by a comma. When a participial phrase begins a sentence, it must modify the subject. If it does not modify the subject, the result is an error known as a dangling participle. See Tip 19.

Creating Participial Phrases

1. When a specific noun or pronoun appears in two or more sentences, examine the sentences to determine whether you could form a participial phrase. To make a participial phrase, convert one of the verbs to a present or a past participle. Add appropriate words from the sentence to the participle to create a participial phrase. Place the participial phrase next to the noun it describes.

Two Sentences:	**I** wanted to help in some way.
	I held the man's hand until the paramedics arrived.
One Sentence with a Participial Phrase:	participle phrase **Wanting to help in some way,** I held the man's hand until the paramedics arrived.
Three Sentences:	The **man** appeared disoriented.
	He cried out for help.
	He grasped my hand firmly.
One Sentence with a Participial Phrase:	participial phrase The man, **appearing disoriented and crying out for help,** grasped my hand firmly.

2. Try placing a participial phrase before or after the noun it describes to see which sounds better.

   participial phrase

   I, **wanting to help in some way,** held the man's hand until the paramedics arrived.

   participial phrase

   Wanting to help in some way, I held the man's hand until the paramedics arrived.

   participial phrase

   Appearing disoriented and crying out for help, the man grasped my hand firmly.

   participial phrase

   The man, **appearing disoriented and crying out for help,** grasped my hand firmly.

3. Shorten a complex sentence with a relative pronoun clause by removing the relative pronoun (the subject) and converting the base or main form of the verb into a present or a past participle.

Complex Sentence:	relative pronoun clause Six college students, **who hoped to save money,** decided to share an apartment.
Sentence with a Participial Phrase:	participial phrase Six college students, **hoping to save money,** decided to share an apartment.
	participial phrase **Hoping to save money,** six college students decided to share an apartment.

EXERCISE 6.3 Identifying Participial Phrases Score: ______

Circle the participial phrases in the following sentences.

1. Yung Soona, tired of studying for her nursing exam, went for a long bike ride.

2. Trying to understand my feelings, I started to write in my journal.

3. Believing in traditional Japanese superstitions, my mother consulted the Japanese calendar.

4. Trying to keep me away from bad luck, she shares her superstitions with me.

5. Elected to the highest office in the nation, John F. Kennedy stated his goals for the nation.

6. Running from the warehouse, Oswald tried to escape the authorities.

7. Emphasizing formal rules, patterns, and structure, the Classical musicians did not put great value on originality in their compositions.

8. Romantic artists, depicting different aspects of human nature, emphasized human emotions.

9. Known as the "warm event," El Nino reversed weather patterns and created havoc in many parts of the country.

10. El Nina, spreading colder water across the Pacific, caused heavier rainfall and snow packs.

EXERCISE 6.4 Identifying Appositives and Participial Phrases

Score: ________

Circle the appositives and participial phrases in the following sentences.

1. Dr. John Gray, a former monk, earned his psychology degree through correspondence courses.

2. Gray, believing in gender stereotypes, emphasizes the different communication styles of men and women.

3. His famous book *Men Are from Mars, Women Are from Venus* has sold more than six million copies.

4. John Gray, the contemporary psychologist, created a commercial empire with audio- and videotapes, seminars, CD-ROMs, and a franchise of counseling centers.

5. Another popular relationship guru in the United States, Dr. John Gottman, received his degree from the University of Illinois.

6. A prolific writer, John Gottman has published many articles in scholarly journals.

7. Dr. Gottman, a professor of psychology at the University of Washington, observes the behavior of people in relationships.

8. Couples wanting to strengthen their relationships can increase their levels of understanding by making mental maps of each other's world.

9. Riane Eisler, a cultural historian and relationship expert, believes that cultural values determine attitudinal differences.

10. Equalizing the balance between men and women, Eisler's proposed form of social change would promote stronger and healthier partnerships.

EXERCISE 6.5 Creating Participial Phrases

Score: ______

On the following blanks, write a participial phrase to complete the sentence. The participial phrase must begin with a present or a past participle and relate to the noun that appears in bold print.

Example: *Wanting to be hired for the job,* the **applicant** prepared a detailed cover letter and resume.

1. ______________________________, the **woman** hired a new babysitter for after-school childcare.

2. ______________________________, the **soldiers** followed all the instructions.

3. **Mario,** ______________________________, scheduled an appointment with a tutor.

4. The **clothes** ______________________________ were stolen during the night.

5. ______________________________, **Rachel** did not respond.

6. ______________________________, the **night patrol** reported the unusual situation.

7. ______________________________, the **customers** asked to talk with the manager.

8. ______________________________, the **band** was banned from future football games.

9. ______________________________, the **teachers** instructed everyone to leave the building.

10. ______________________________, the **reporter** arrived for the interview early.

TIP 19 **The error known as a dangling participle occurs when a participial phrase is not placed next to the noun or the pronoun it describes. With this error, the participial phrase does not clearly describe what it was intended to describe.**

Dangling participles distort the intended meaning of the sentence and often result in comical or illogical sentences. In the following examples, the dangling participles appear in bold print. The arrows and the word *no* show that the participial phrase does not describe the noun.

no

Dangling participle: **Barking all night,** the neighbors filed a complaint about the dog.

[The dangling participle suggests that the neighbors barked all night.]

no

Dangling participle: **Sailing on the catamaran,** the dolphins surfaced near us.

[The dangling participle suggests that the dolphins were sailing on the catamaran.]

Errors with dangling participles can be corrected by changing either the participial phrase or the noun or pronoun placed closest to the participial phrase. The arrows and the word *yes* show that the participial phrase describes the noun.

yes

Correct: **Barking all night,** the dogs annoyed the neighbors.

yes

Correct: **Annoyed by the barking dogs,** the neighbors filed a complaint.

yes

Correct: **Sailing on the catamaran,** we saw dolphins surfacing near us.

yes

Correct: **Swimming near the catamaran,** the dolphins surfaced near us.

EXERCISE 6.6 Identifying Dangling Participles

Score: ______

Read the following sentences carefully. Some sentences are correct and some contain dangling participles. Use any method to correct the sentences with dangling participles. Put a **C** next to correct sentences.

1. Wishing to stay anonymous, the cash donation was left in a sealed envelope.

2. Waiting for the morning train, I reviewed my notes and recited my flash cards.

3. Damaged extensively by the water, Eduardo threw his magazine in the garbage.
4. Surprised by the announcement of the merger, stocks sold rapidly.
5. Hearing a loud explosion, chaos erupted in the streets.
6. Knowing her children were safe, Kim called her relatives with the news.
7. Motivated by the loud fans, the team rallied to win the game.
8. Swollen by the record-setting rainfall, the river passed its flood stage.
9. Not wanting to respond to the rumors, the senator ignored the reporters' questions.
10. Worried about heavy holiday traffic, the parking lot of the arena was half empty before the event ended.

TIP 20 **Avoid fragments caused by participial phrases posing as complete sentences. Participial phrases must be attached to complete clauses to avoid fragments.**

The following participial phrases lack a complete subject and complete verb and do not form a complete thought that can stand on its own as a sentence. Each participial phrase is a fragment.

Demanding to see the officer in charge.

Shattered on the marble floor.

Correct fragments created by participial phrases in the following ways.

1. Attach the participial phrase to a complete sentence. Place the participial phrase next to or close to the noun it describes.

   Demanding to see the officer in charge, the irrate citizen pounded on the front desk.

   Shattered on the marble floor, the crystal vase could not be repaired.

2. Add a subject and change the verb to a verb phrase or a simple tense verb to form a complete sentence.

   She was demanding to see the officer in charge.

   She demanding to see the officer in charge.

   The crystal vase had shattered on the marble floor.

   The crystal vase shattered on the marble floor.

EXERCISE 6.7 Correcting Fragments Score: ______

Use any method to correct the following fragments caused by participial phrases. Write complete sentences on separate paper.

1. Listening to the pitter-patter of rain on the roof.
2. Starving after the long hike.
3. Destroyed by the flames.
4. Hanging from the telephone wire.
5. Beaten and defeated.
6. Sneezing, coughing, and wheezing.
7. Wanting to attend school next term.
8. Concerned about the consequences.
9. Dancing and singing on stage for the first time.
10. Living in the utmost poverty.

Grammar and Usage Tips Summary

TIP 17 Use appositives to add descriptive details to nouns or pronouns in sentences. Place the appositives directly after the nouns or pronouns they rename. Use a comma before and after appositives with essential information; do not use commas for appositives with nonessential information.

TIP 18 Use participial phrases to describe nouns or pronouns. Place participial phrases, which begin with present participles or past participles, directly before or after the noun or the pronoun they rename.

TIP 19 Avoid errors with dangling participles by placing participial phrases next to or close to the noun or the pronoun they describe.

TIP 20 Avoid fragments caused by participial phrases posing as complete sentences. Participial phrases must be attached to complete clauses to avoid fragments.

CHAPTER 6 • Comparison and Contrast Paragraphs • Proofreading and Editing Exercises

With a partner or on your own, proofread and edit the following paragraphs. Read the directions at the beginning of each proofreading exercise.

Proofreading 1

Each sentence or group of words is numbered. Proofread for fragments and dangling participles. On the lines below the paragraph, indicate whether the group of words is a complete sentence without errors (S), a sentence with a dangling participle (DP), or a fragment (F).

Shifting Demographics

[1]The composition of the population in California forty years ago differs greatly from the state's population today. [2]In fact, the difference is so great that California is now the largest state in the Union in which the racial majority is not Caucasian. [3]In 1960, more than 80% of Californians from Anglo-European ancestry. [4]Immigrating from Great Britain or Canada, English was the most common language spoken by foreign-born Californians. [5]English, the dominant language, was the only language seen on billboards, signs, and storefronts in Los Angeles. [6]Shifting over the last forty years, California no longer has a racial or an ethnic majority. [7]The current population now represents more diversified ancestries. [8]Many immigrants now residing in California come from Latin America, Iran, Korea, and other Asian countries. [9]In fact, the largest Korean population outside of Korea and the largest concentration of Iranians in the Western world in the Los Angeles area. [10]There no longer is a most common language among foreign-born Californians. [11]Appearing in many languages other than English, billboards, signs, and storefront advertisements in Los Angeles reflect the city's demographics. [12]The differences shown between the composition of California's population today and in 1960 exemplify the growing diversification of the American population.

[Adapted from: Todd Purdum, "California soon to be without racial majority," *Register Guard*, July 4, 2000, p. A1, A11.]

S = correct sentence **DP = dangling participle** **F = fragment**

1. ________	5. ________	9. ________
2. ________	6. ________	10. ________
3. ________	7. ________	11. ________
4. ________	8. ________	12. ________

Proofreading 2

Proofread and edit the following paragraph. Correct any errors by writing the corrections in the space between the lines. Refer to the proofreading checklist on page 243.

Diabetes

Though both Type I diabetes and Type II diabetes are metabolic disorders that affect the way the body uses food, they are more dissimilar than similar. Type I diabetes the insulin-dependent diabetes affects 5% to 10% of the 16 million Americans; who have diabetes. Type I diabetes surfaces during childhood or young adulthood for that reason it is called *juvenile onset diabetes.* With Type I diabetes, the immune system attacks the pancreas and destroys its ability to make insulin as a result diabetics need to track the food they eat their activity levels, and their blood sugar levels. Several times during the day. They must inject themselves with insulin to keep the body's sugar levels in balance. Type II diabetes has different characteristics. Type II diabetes, the non–insulin-dependent diabetes, affects 90%–95% of Americans who are diagnosed with diabetes. Type II diabetes usually surfaces after the age of forty it is called *adult onset diabetes.* With this form of diabetes, the pancreas produces insulin, but the body and its tissues, especially its muscles, do not use the insulin effectively. Type II diabetes is linked to inactivity, weight gain, and obesity 80% of people with Type II diabetes are overweight. Type II diabetics can reduce or eliminate the health threats related to diabetes by lifestyle changes more exercise better nutritional habits and possibly medication. Even though Type I diabetes and Type II diabetes differ considerably in their time of onset. Effects on the body, and forms of treatment. Both are autoimmune disorders that must be diagnosed and treated; in order to avoid serious, life-threatening health problems.

[Source: Janet Filips, "Diabetes fair: Time is of the essence," *Register Guard*, January 28, 2000, p. 6A, 6B.]

Proofreading 3

Proofread and edit your Writing Warm-Up 6.

Internet Enrichment

Log on to the web site for this textbook for additional exercises and links for the following topics:

Comparison and Contrast Paragraphs
Point-by-point method
Block method
Appositives
Participial Phrases
Dangling Participles
Avoiding Fragments with Participial Phrases

Go to: http://college.hmco.com. Click on "Students." Type *Paragraph Essentials* in the "Jump to Textbook Sites" box. Click "go," and then bookmark the site. Click on Chapter 6.

CHAPTER 6 • Grammar and Usage Review Name ______________________
Date ______________________

Appositives

Combine the following sentences by converting information from one of the sentences to an **appositive**.

1. Mr. Sanchez helped me plan my class schedule. Mr. Sanchez is my advisor.

____

____

2. The campaign manager predicted a win. She is always an optimistic person.

____

____

3. Fatigue has several health consequences. Fatigue is a common stress indicator.

____

____

4. Carlos has a promising future. He is an amateur athlete.

____

____

5. Sam's Place accepts reservations. Sam's Place has the best barbecue ribs in town.

____

____

Participial Phrases

Each of the following sentences has a participial phrase. On the line, use the following codes to indicate how the participial phrase is working in the sentence. If the participial phrase creates a dangling participle or a fragment, use any method to correct the error.

COR = correct sentence DP = dangling participle F= fragment

_______ 1. Immigrating from Poland, my parents left many personal belongings behind.

_______ 2. Wanting to adopt a child, the adoption board explained the process to the couple.

_______ 3. The supervisor walking directly toward the new employees with a broad smile.

_______ 4. Located on the north side of town, near the old church and the river.

_______ 5. Pretending not to hear his father, the young boy continued to bounce the ball.

_______ 6. The assistant, wanting to impress her new boss, reorganized all the file cabinets.

_______ 7. The leaves blowing all over the yard and into the street.

_______ 8. Hiding her embarrassment, the movie made the young girl quite uncomfortable.

CHAPTER 7

Exemplification and Classification Paragraphs

The topic sentence introduces your topic and the controlling idea for the paragraph.

The body consists of three or more subtopics, each with secondary details. The body has unity, coherence, and adequate development.

The concluding sentence echoes the topic sentence or makes a concluding statement of fact or opinion.

Topic Sentence with a controlling idea ....

Subtopic 1: ....
Secondary details...
Subtopic 2: ....
Secondary details...
Subtopic 3: ....
Secondary details...

Concluding Sentence..

In Chapter 7 you will learn about the following:

1. Exemplification and classification paragraphs
2. Four additional grammar and usage tips

WRITING WARM-UP 7

Begin your writing sample by making a general statement about something you can develop by using a series of examples. Use one of the following topics, or write your own.

More than one teacher has made an impact on my life.
I teach my children some traditions that my parents taught me.
Different kinds of nontraditional students now enroll in college.
Several sports require team effort.

Follow your statement with three different examples that develop the main idea.

Exemplification and Classification Paragraphs

Exemplification paragraphs develop one controlling idea through three or more examples. Classification paragraphs develop one controlling idea by explaining the individual stages, categories, types, or parts of a whole. Exemplification and classification paragraphs have slightly different purposes, but they are paired together in this chapter because they use the same paragraph structure. The structure consists of a topic sentence with a controlling idea, the body of the paragraph divided into separate parts or **subtopics,** each with **secondary details,** and a concluding sentence.

Exemplification Paragraph	Classification Paragraph
Topic sentence........................	Topic sentence........................
Example 1	Part 1 ....
....	....
Example 2	Part 2 ....
....	....
Example 3	Part 3 ....
....	....
Concluding sentence	Concluding sentence ....

Both exemplification and classification paragraphs are **expository paragraphs.** They inform the reader about a specific topic. As you select topics, therefore, you will want to focus on information that will be significant or valuable to your readers. Sometimes you can draw on personal experiences to select your topic; other times you will want to abstract information from textbooks, lectures, the Internet, or the library. Both exemplification and classification paragraphs use three (or more) subtopics with secondary details to develop the topic sentence.

The Exemplification Paragraph

In an exemplification paragraph, the topic sentence with a controlling idea makes a statement of fact, opinion, or judgment about a specific topic. The body of the paragraph provides the reader with examples to develop or support the controlling idea. The concluding sentence relates back to the topic sentence. The following exemplification paragraph shows how three examples develop the controlling idea. The bold print shows transition words, phrases, or sentences that move the reader from one example to another. Notes in the margin provide additional explanations.

Broken Promises

Topic sentence
Example 1: the mayor
Secondary details
Example 2: city council members
Secondary details
Example 3: governor
Secondary details
Concluding sentence

Many elected officials do not keep their campaign promises. **For example,** our last mayor promised that he would keep communications open for his constituents. He promised to write a weekly column in the newspaper to keep the public informed about local issues. He also promised to schedule open office hours twice a week. During his entire term, he wrote one column. Several groups tried futilely to schedule appointments with him to discuss issues dear to them. Our city council provides us with **another example** of broken promises. Last June, three of the five current city council members swore that they would not approve airport expansion plans. Despite their promises, new runways and larger maintenance facilities are currently under construction. **Broken promises are not made only by local officials.** Our governor promised his constituents three years ago that crime reduction and increased funding for education would be his top priorities. The crime rate in the state has risen 16 percent in the last three years. Schools are in a worse shape than they were before he took office. Teachers have lost their jobs due to budget crises. Classroom sizes have increased. Valuable programs that benefit students have been cut. Broken campaign promises seem to occur throughout all levels of government.

A **hierarchy** is an organizational plan that you read from the top down. The topic appears on the top line; the subtopics, in this case the examples, appear on the next lower level. The following hierarchy clearly shows the three examples used in "Broken Promises."

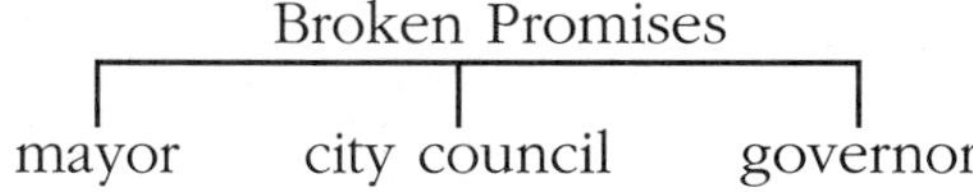

The Classification Paragraph

In a classification paragraph, the topic sentence names a subject that can be divided into several categories or **subtopics.** The body of the paragraph provides secondary details that explain or discuss each of the subtopics. The concluding sentence relates back to the topic sentence. The following classification paragraph shows the individual subtopics of the subject as a whole. The bold print indicates the beginning of each new subtopic. In this paragraph, the subtopics are types of controlling behaviors.

Control Freaks

Topic sentence	Psychologist and author John Oldham identifies four styles of controlling behavior that affect the ways people interact.
Subtopic 1	**One style of controlling behavior** is the *conscientious style.*
Secondary details—definition	This type of controller exhibits a heightened level of worry or concern about how things are done. According to this type of controller, there is only one way to do things correctly; fortunately, he or she knows that way.
Subtopic 2	**A second type of controlling behavior** is the *self-confident style.*
Secondary details—definition	A controller with this style is absorbed in self-importance. Rather than worrying about the correct or most efficient ways of working or interacting, this style of controller expects everyone to do things the way the controller suggests, recommends, or demands.
Subtopic 3	**A third type of controlling behavior** is the *vigilant style.*
Secondary details—definition	A controller with this style feels compelled to control so as not to be taken advantage of or demeaned. This controller lacks confidence, has low self esteem, and has an obsessive fear and distrust of anyone who demonstrates control.
Subtopic 4	**The last controlling style,** an *aggressive style,*
Secondary details—definition	shows control through force, aggression, domination, and sometimes exploitive ways. This controller has problems compromising or working as a team player.
Concluding sentence	These four types of controlling behaviors surface in the workplace, in the classroom, in social situations, and within family units on a regular basis.

[Adapted from Peterson, Karen S., "In Charge . . . Out of Control," *USA Today*, July 31, 2000, p. 60.]

The following hierarchy clearly shows the four examples or subtopics used in "Control Freaks."

Control Freaks

conscientious | self-confident | vigilant | aggressive

The Structure of Exemplification and Classification Paragraphs

When you write an exemplification paragraph, your purpose is to support, explain, or prove a statement with a controlling idea through specific examples. When you write a classification paragraph, your purpose is to show the stages, categories, types, or parts that exist within a whole entity. In the process of developing any type of paragraph, you can use different organizational patterns to organize the details. For example, in the "Control Freaks" paragraph (page 266), the secondary details that appear after the subtopics use a definition pattern. In many paragraphs, you will use narrations, descriptions, comparisons, contrasts, examples, definitions, and classifications to support, explain, or prove the main idea stated in your topic sentence.

Developing the Topic Sentence

Use the following guidelines to write an effective topic sentence with a controlling idea that reveals your point of view, opinion, or attitude toward the subject of your paragraph.

1. Narrow your subject. For example, statements about all cultures or every kind of car are far too broad to address in the scope of a paragraph. The following examples show the narrowing process from subjects that are too broad to those that are manageable and focused:

   All cultures
   Native American cultures
   Native American cultures in the Southwest United States
   Native American cultures in New Mexico
   Cars
   American-made cars
   American-made economy cars
   This year's American-made economy cars

2. Narrowing also occurs by selecting only one specific aspect to discuss about your subject. This specific aspect is called a **denominator.** For example, in a topic sentence about this year's American-made cars, the denominator could be the prices of these cars or the performance ratings of these cars, but not both. The denominator is a part of the controlling idea of the sentence.

   Only three of this year's American-made economy cars have earned *high performance ratings from independent consumer research groups*. [denominator]

3. Include a controlling idea that conveys your point of view, opinion, or attitude toward the subject. This controlling idea should express a significant, meaningful point and capture your reader's attention.

   Native American cultures in New Mexico *embrace many traditional tribal values*. [controlling idea]

   The positive influence [controlling idea] of Native American cultures in New Mexico is apparent in many ways.

4. State the subject and use a signal word, which is often a plural noun, to help your reader predict the subtopics you will include in the paragraph. Signal words, such as *types, kinds, stages,* or *categories,* frequently appear in the topic sentence of classification and exemplification paragraphs. In the two previous examples, the plural words *values* and *ways* serve as signal words. Readers can predict that the writer will provide examples or categories of information about *tribal values* or *ways* the Native American culture has positively influenced society in New Mexico.

7.1 What do you think?

Working with a partner or on your own, read each of the following topic sentences carefully. Circle the words that help you predict the subtopics that will appear in the body of the paragraph.

Example: The air quality in the state will steadily improve because of **three crucial environmental laws** that voters approved in the last election.

[You, the reader, can predict that the paragraph will discuss each of the three laws.]

1. By watching the behavior of coaches during a game, parents can easily identify three kinds of coaches.
2. Marla Santos deserves the Teacher of the Year Award for several reasons.
3. Piaget's theory of child development covers distinct stages of growth.
4. Family counselors use four different approaches to strengthen communication skills in families.
5. As a bartender, I can readily recognize the different kinds of drinkers.
6. Three kinds of freeway drivers jeopardize the safety of all other drivers and passengers on the roadways of America.
7. Through his many victories, Tiger Woods has earned the title of the world's greatest golfer.
8. Concerned about the loss of culture and native languages, several Native American tribes are implementing a new program to revive their cultural heritage.
9. Four types of plants flourish in the arid climates of the Southwest.
10. Current late night talk shows can be divided into three distinct categories.

Developing the Body of an Exemplification Paragraph

Use the following guidelines to develop your exemplification paragraph and the controlling idea stated in your topic sentence:

1. Select the most effective examples from those you generated in the prewriting process. Use only examples that support the controlling idea in the topic sentence. You will often find that some of the examples generated in the prewriting process are too weak or insignificant to use effectively to develop the controlling idea.
2. Use three to five examples, or subtopics, in the body of an exemplification paragraph to develop, clarify, illustrate, explain, or prove the controlling idea. If you use only one or two subtopics, your paragraph will likely be underdeveloped. If you use more than five subtopics, your paragraph may read like a long list of unorganized ideas.
3. Consider combining two or more examples into one subtopic if the examples are closely related and you want to include each of them in the paragraph but want to avoid too many separate subtopics. The paragraph "Changing Misperceptions" on page 272 combines two examples for the fourth subtopic.

   example 1 example 2

   Other sites, such as Navajos.com and oyate.org, strive to distinguish Native American materials from the phony, stereotyping materials that pose as Indian work.

4. Achieve *adequate development* by selecting the most powerful examples that develop the controlling idea and then expanding or developing each example with secondary details. Examples do not need to be equally developed. In an **extended example,** one example may have more secondary details than the other examples.

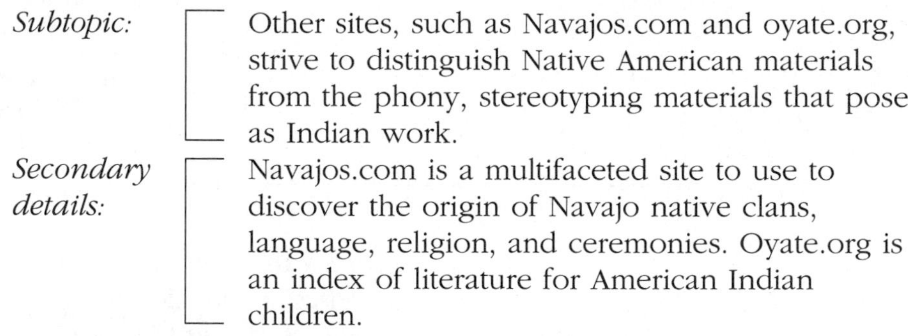

Subtopic:	Other sites, such as Navajos.com and oyate.org, strive to distinguish Native American materials from the phony, stereotyping materials that pose as Indian work.
Secondary details:	Navajos.com is a multifaceted site to use to discover the origin of Navajo native clans, language, religion, and ceremonies. Oyate.org is an index of literature for American Indian children.

5. Achieve *unity* in the paragraph by using examples and secondary details that support the controlling idea in the topic sentence. Do not wander from the controlling idea. Delete sentences that do not fit within the boundaries set by the controlling idea.

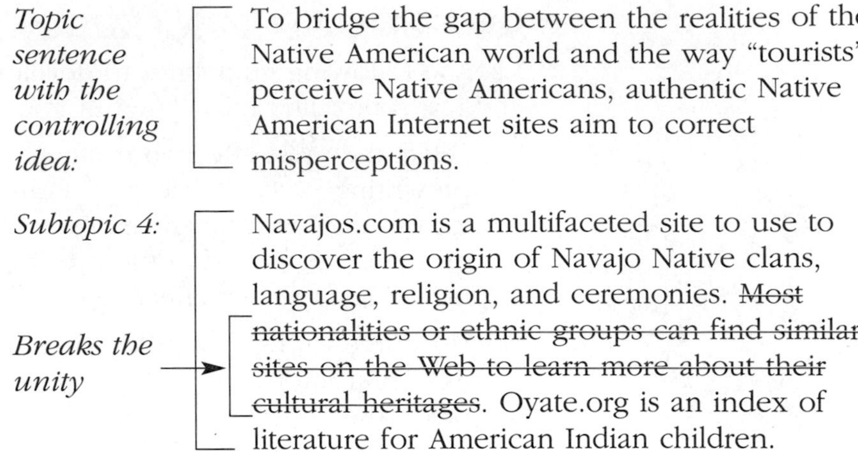

Topic sentence with the controlling idea: To bridge the gap between the realities of the Native American world and the way "tourists" perceive Native Americans, authentic Native American Internet sites aim to correct misperceptions.

Subtopic 4: Navajos.com is a multifaceted site to use to discover the origin of Navajo Native clans, language, religion, and ceremonies. ~~Most nationalities or ethnic groups can find similar sites on the Web to learn more about their cultural heritages~~. Oyate.org is an index of literature for American Indian children.

Breaks the unity →

6. Achieve *coherence* and help your reader follow your thoughts by using one or more of the following techniques:
   a. Enumerate or use number words to signal the first example, the second example, another example, or one final example.
   b. Restate a key word or phrase from the topic sentence each time you introduce a new example. This technique keeps the reader focused on the main point of the paragraph.
   c. Use transition words to connect ideas smoothly and logically.

COMMON TRANSITION WORDS FOR EXEMPLIFICATION	
Addition or continuation of an idea	accordingly, again, also, another, besides, furthermore, in addition, moreover, likewise, in the same way, similarly, in other words
Ordinals and signals for examples	the first example, the second example, another example, a final example, an illustration of this, for example, for instance, in fact
Other relationships	certainly, definitely, indeed, though, although, thus, therefore, consequently, hence, next, then, so, finally

   d. Choose a meaningful organization for the examples to achieve coherence. Organize the examples emphatically (according to importance or the size of the concept), spatially, or chronologically. Experiment to determine which order is most effective for your paragraph.

ORGANIZATIONAL PATTERNS FOR EXAMPLES	
Emphatically by order of importance	☼ Organize examples from the most important to the least important, or in the reverse order. ☼ Placing the most important example first focuses the reader's attention immediately on the controlling idea. ☼ Placing the most important example last leaves a strong, final image or understanding in the reader's mind.
Emphatically by size or complexity	☼ Organize examples from the broadest to the most specific. ☼ Placing the broadest, the most general, or the most complex example first sets the framework to move to more specific, less complex examples. ☼ This general-to-specific organizational pattern can also be reversed by beginning with the most specific example and proceeding to the broadest or most complex example.
Spatially	☼ Organize the examples according to their position in space. ☼ The first example may be the one that is the most distant; the final example would be the closest. ☼ Spatial order may also go from top to bottom, from left to right, and so on. ☼ Spatial organization helps your reader visualize the details clearly.
Chronologically	☼ Organize the examples according to their occurrence in time. ☼ Begin with the example that occurred furthest in the past and end with the example that occurred most recently, or vice versa.

7.2 What do you think?

The following exemplification paragraph is an adaptation from an article written by Academy Award–winning singer and songwriter Buffy Sainte-Marie, founder of the Nihewan Foundation and the Cradleboard Teaching Project, an educational project that reaches out to both Indian and non-Indian children. Work with a partner or on your own to answer the questions that follow the paragraph. Write your answers on separate paper.

Changing Misperceptions

[1]To bridge the gap between the realities of the Native American world and the way "tourists" perceive Native Americans, authentic Native American Internet sites aim to correct misperceptions. [2]One shining example is the First Nations web site, www.schoolnet.ca/aboriginal, which is based in Canada, where the term *first nations* is preferred over *Indian* or *Native American.* [3]This web site is a hub full of resources to learn about Native American languages, tribal nations, Native American people's literature, cultural centers, stories and legends, and herbal lore. [4]Links to various sites provide audio of words or phrases from the Ojibwa, Cree, and eight other endangered languages. [5]A second web site, an award-winning hub of Native American resources, is hanksville.phast.umass.edu. This web site is the work of Karen Strom at the University of Massachusetts. [6]A personal photo journal approach carries the Web user through the lands of the Lakota, Cheyenne, Navajo, and Mayans. [7]This site provides information about Red Cloud, Sitting Bull, and other great leaders. [8]Another site with a large library of resources is Paula Giese's Native American Indian web site (indy4.fdl.cc.mn.us/~isk). [9]Beyond the playful, flashy front doors are more than three hundred pages to browse. [10]The site includes historic maps, indigenous-language resources, lists of Indian books and authors, and articles on Native American products, art, and astronomy. [11]In other words, this is a cornucopia of miscellaneous wonders. [12]Other sites, such as Navajos.com and oyate.org, strive to distinguish Native American materials from the phony, stereotyping materials that pose as Indian work. [13]Navajos.com is a multifaceted site to use to discover the origin of Navajo native clans, language, religion, and ceremonies. [14]Oyate.org is an index of literature for American Indian children. [15]The numerous authentic Native American web sites surfacing on the World Wide Web serve a valuable purpose in teaching all people the realities of the Native American world.

[Adapted from Buffy Sainte-Marie, "Native American Culture," *Yahoo! Internet Life*, July, 1999, pp. 120–122.]

1. Use the superscript numbers at the beginning of each sentence. Which sentences introduce new examples or subtopics?
2. Is there adequate development in the paragraph? Are there sufficient secondary details for each example or subtopic? Explain.
3. Are examples equally developed? In other words, are they all about the same length and do they all contain the same amount and degree of detail? Explain.
4. List the words in the paragraph that work as transition words to shift the reader's attention from one example to the next.

7.3 What do you think?

Work with a partner or on your own to answer the questions that follow this paragraph about soccer. Write your answers on separate paper.

Soccer

Soccer is not popular in the United States. First, not many Americans like watching or playing soccer. There are a lot of soccer games played every day in countries around the world, but the networks in the United States seldom broadcast them on television. I've been in the United States for two years and am never able to find any soccer games on television from Spain, Italy, or England. The U.S. networks only broadcast games with American soccer teams or important soccer games like the World Cup. Second, there are not many soccer fields in America. Most of the soccer fields in the U.S. are actually football fields. I still remember how confused I was when I was watching a soccer match on a football field. The lines were messed up, and I did not know which lines were for soccer and which lines were for football. One final example of how soccer is not popular in America is the fact that most soccer players who play in U.S. leagues are Hispanic. American teenagers prefer to play basketball and football. For that reason, not many American teenagers want to be professional soccer players. There are many great sports in the United States, but soccer is not one of them.

Thanh Than
Bellevue Community College
Bellevue, Washington

1. How many examples does the writer use?
2. Does the writer expand each example with secondary details? Do all of the secondary details relate back to and support the controlling idea in the topic sentence?
3. In the prewriting materials, the writer possibly had other examples but then eliminated them. What other examples might have been on the list?
4. Soccer is increasing in popularity with younger children. Why do you think the writer does not mention this in the paragraph?
5. What technique or techniques did the writer use to help you follow the ideas and identify each of the separate examples?
6. What order of the examples does the writer use to develop coherence?

7.4 What do you think?

Work with a partner or on your own to answer the questions that follow this paragraph. Write your answers on separate paper.

My Worst Holiday

Thanksgiving is my worst holiday for several reasons. First of all, my strange yet lovable grandmother always has Thanksgiving at her house. Her house is the size of a Crackerjack box that literally holds ten people; however, my relatives probably populate the entire town of Mt. Airy. Picture my family and me, elbow to elbow, crammed into this tiny little house, trying to get organized for this grand turkey feast. Suddenly, my ninety-eight-pound grandfather throws another log into the fire-roaring inferno, a wood stove, which is staged in the living room full of hot-blooded, cherry-red-faced siblings who are sweating to death. This event displays part of his charm because my grandfather knows we are uncomfortable. The kitchen is another reason this holiday is so unlikable. The kitchen has illuminated characteristics and smells from that of the seventies. The yellow and brown flowered wallpaper, with matching pea-green stove and refrigerator, is congruent with the dining room table that displays the fixings of a holiday meal that is sure to be bland. The glazed turkey is dry and crisp, the mashed potatoes run gooey, and the sauerkraut, dressing, and cranberry sauce never quite taste right. After the wretched meal, I go to the fresh, cool cellar to get away from the madness that stirs upstairs. A final reason I dislike this holiday is that I have to deal with the annual routines. I have to listen to relentless questions that my aunts and uncles ask. "Do you have a boyfriend?" or "What are you doing with your life?" At the end of the evening, we all sing "Happy Birthday" to my aunt and uncle since we must, of course, group all birthdays and holidays together. With the gift-wrapping crushed and thrown to the floor, we then take family pictures: first, the grandbabies, then the brothers and sisters, and finally the mothers and fathers. At the end of a long, tumultuous day, we kiss and say good-bye. I find myself praying for the next Thanksgiving holiday to be better.

Katy Tabler
Carroll Community College
Westminster, Maryland

1. How many primary reasons does the writer use in this paragraph? Does she clearly state each new reason? Explain.
2. Does the writer use transition words between the different reasons and between secondary details effectively? Explain.

3. Does the paragraph have adequate development? Does the writer provide secondary details for each reason? Explain.
4. Does the paragraph have unity? Do all details support the controlling idea in the topic sentence? Explain.
5. Does the paragraph have coherence? How does the writer organize the details? Explain.
6. List descriptive words from the paragraph that create a strong image in your mind.

Developing the Body of a Classification Paragraph

Use the following guidelines to develop the body of your classification paragraph and the controlling idea stated in your topic sentence.

1. Identify the number of subtopics (kinds, parts, types, stages, or categories) in a classification paragraph by identifying the number of parts to a whole entity (the subject). Generally speaking, a subject with more than five parts may best be developed through more than one paragraph; thus, as a general guideline, strive to select subjects that have three to five subtopics or categories.
2. Check that each category (or subtopic) is distinctly different from the other categories. No overlapping can exist among the categories. In the following lists, a person could belong to more than one of the groups; therefore, the categories are not distinctly different and should not be used for a classification paragraph.

Types of Parents	**Kinds of Friends**
authoritative	lifelong, loyal friends
permissive	short-term, casual friends
nurturing	supportive, nurturing friends
young	deceitful, phony friends
middle-aged	false friends with ulterior motives

3. Select secondary details that highlight specific characteristics of each category. You do not need to directly state the comparisons or the contrasts between the different categories; however, your readers should be able to make their own comparisons or contrasts between each of the categories.
4. Avoid using stereotypes about different groups of people. To label a specific group of people as all behaving, thinking, or valuing something in the same way shows insensitivity and, often, disrespect and discrimination. As an informal test for stereotyping, ask yourself if you read your paragraph to a person who belongs to the group you are discussing, would the person take offense and argue that not all people are the way you have portrayed them? If you would be uncomfortable reading your paragraph to a person from the group you describe, you are likely stereotyping. Rethink your stance; find a new way to make your point, or discard your point and select another subtopic.

5. Achieve *adequate development* by discussing each of the subtopics with clear, vivid, significant secondary details. Eliminate weak details or details that stray from the controlling idea. For example, if your topic sentence and controlling idea are about three parts of the standard paragraph structure, to have adequate development, you must discuss each of the three parts (topic sentence, body, and concluding sentence). Failure to discuss one or two of the parts of a standard paragraph structure would result in lack of adequate development. Likewise, failure to include sufficient details for one or more of the parts of a paragraph would result in a lack of adequate development.
6. Achieve *coherence* by using the same techniques discussed for exemplification paragraphs:
   a. Enumerate or use number words to signal each part or subtopic.
   b. Restate a key word or phrase from the topic sentence each time you introduce a new subtopic. For example, an introductory phrase such as *the second type of personality* helps your reader follow your thinking process.
   c. Use transition words to connect ideas smoothly and logically.

COMMON TRANSITION WORDS FOR CLASSIFICATION	
Addition or continuation of an idea	accordingly, again, also, another, besides, furthermore, in addition, moreover, likewise, in the same way, similarly, in other words
Ordinals and signals for examples	the first part, the second type of, another stage, a final category of
Other relationships	certainly, definitely, indeed, though, although, thus, therefore, consequently, hence, next, then, so, finally

   d. Choose a meaningful organization for the categories or subtopics. Subtopics may be organized chronologically, spatially, or emphatically. (See page 271.) In some cases, subtopics may be introduced alphabetically. Experiment to determine which order is most effective for your paragraph.

7.5 What do you think?

Work with a partner or on your own to answer the questions that follow this paragraph about conflict management styles in the work force. Write your answers on separate paper.

Conflict Management Styles

According to Kenneth Thomas, managers can use five styles of management for conflict resolution. The first is the *competitive style,* which involves a tendency to dominate, to win at the expense of the other party, and to engage in win-lose power struggles. This style of management does not result in conflict resolutions that satisfy both parties. The second style, the *accommodative style,* favors appeasement. It attempts to satisfy the other person's concerns first and self-sacrifices in order to maintain a functioning relationship. The *sharing style* of conflict management, the third style, is halfway between domination and appeasement. Sharers prefer moderate but incomplete satisfaction for both parties through compromise. In a compromise, each party accepts and gives up a portion of what is desired. The fourth style, the *collaborative style,* uses a "win-win" approach and reflects the desire to resolve conflict by fully satisfying the desires of both parties. Both parties gain something of value without damaging or harming the welfare of the other side. This is the favored style of conflict resolution because the outcome leads to increased productivity and satisfaction. The last style of conflict resolution, the *avoidance style,* combines a lack of cooperation and a lack of assertiveness. A manager with this style is indifferent to the concerns of the parties involved, withdraws from the conflict, and relies on fate to eventually solve the problem. Though managers may tend to use one style of conflict resolution more consistently, most managers typically combine elements of several of the styles or use specific styles for specific kinds of conflicts.

[Adapted from: DuBrin, *Leadership,* Houghton Mifflin, 1998, pp. 323–324.]

1. How many categories or subtopics appear in "Conflict Management Styles?" What techniques helped you identify each of the subtopics? Explain.
2. Is there an overlap in the categories or is each category distinctly different from the others? Explain.
3. What kinds of secondary details does the writer use to develop each subtopic?
4. Does the writer include enough secondary details for each subtopic so the paragraph has adequate development? Explain.
5. In your mind, can you compare or contrast the different styles of conflict management? For example, can you state the differences between the competitive style and the accommodative style or the avoidance style and the collaborative style? Explain.
6. What is the order or sequence of the styles? Would you suggest an alternative approach to ordering or sequencing the styles? Explain.
7. Draw a hierarchy that shows the topic and the subtopics for this paragraph.

7.6 What do you think?

In the following paragraph, the writer applied textbook information from "Conflict Management" to personal experiences. As you read this paragraph, notice that the paragraph is wordy and needs revision and editing work. Work with a partner or on your own to answer the questions that follow this paragraph. Write your answers on separate paper.

Bosses Are Not All Alike

Through my years of work experiences, I can identify five different kinds of bosses based on the ways they deal with conflict. When I worked as a grocery store stocker, I was often frustrated by my boss, Sam, who never addressed problems directly. For example, one of the stockers took excessive breaks and didn't pull her share of the weight. When we brought this to Sam's attention, he simply told us to work it out and then closed his eyes to the situation. I sure don't know where he learned his management skills. When I worked at the car wash, Karen, the manager, resolved problems in a completely different way. She simply told us if we did not like something and did not do it her way, we were fired. She was good on her word. When I complained about inconsistencies in work hours, she fired me right then and there. I was glad to get out of there. Sharon, the manager of a restaurant where I worked as a waiter, always wanted to accommodate everyone. She always softened up and gave in every time an employee or a customer complained. Her idea of a perfect situation was to keep everyone happy. She reminded me a lot of my mother. As a result, the squeaky wheels got the most grease. In many situations, the people who complained the most or the loudest got preferential treatment. There was no consistency in terms of how she treated people or what work conditions she granted. Since I am not a whiner or a complainer, I had less desirable work conditions and finally quit. José, a manager at another restaurant where I worked, was much more understanding of our complaints or conflicts. Several of us attended school and worked at the restaurant on a part-time basis. Many students found working part-time was a necessity. We had problems with José because he would make out the work schedule without considering our school schedules. He wanted the right to assign work hours based on the restaurant's slow and peak hours. We were not able to get consistent schedules one week to another; however, he eventually considered our hours of availability when he assigned the weekly schedules. We still did not know from week to week how many hours we would work, but we at least knew the work hours would not interfere with our school schedules. I currently work part-time as an office clerk in a tax accountant's office. Ula, my current boss, uses the style of conflict management that I prefer. I feel comfortable knowing that problems will be resolved fairly. Ula is interested in employee satisfaction; she values loyal and responsible employees. We had one problem with paper flow in the office. Things just weren't working out, and we couldn't respond to Ula's requests for information because of the disorganization. Instead of everyone getting into a blaming mode for the chaos, Ula scheduled an organizational meeting. The result was a win-win situation; she revamped the paper flow process so we could all be more productive. If I were a manager, I would fire Sam, Karen, and Sharon. They are ineffective and lack adequate management skills. José has potential to be a better manager; maybe he could take lessons from Ula. Needless to say, I believe the conflict management style of a boss affects the working atmosphere of any business.

1. Do you get a clear picture of each of the different types of managers? Do any overlap? Explain.
2. In "Conflict Management Styles," the writer uses textbook terminology to label each type of manager. In "Bosses Are Not All Alike," the writer does not use textbook labels. Would the paragraph be more effective with textbook labels for each type of manager? Explain.
3. Cross out the sentences that wander off the course of discussion and break the unity of the paragraph.
4. The order of details in "Bosses Are Not All Alike" is different from the order used in "Conflict Management Styles." What order does the writer use in this paragraph? Do you prefer the order used in "Conflict Management Styles" or "Bosses Are Not All Alike?" Explain.
5. This paragraph is long and wordy. Revise the paragraph by deleting sentences and combining or shortening other sentences.

Developing the Concluding Sentence in Exemplification and Classification Paragraphs

Use the following guidelines to bring your paragraph to an end.

1. Write a concluding sentence that is closely related to the topic sentence. Though the concluding sentence does not always need to echo or restate the topic sentence, the concluding sentence must work in partnership with the topic sentence.
2. Use one of three different approaches to write the concluding sentence:
   a. Echo or restate the topic sentence in slightly different words.

      Topic Sentence: Soccer is not popular in the United States.

      Concluding Sentence: There are many great sports in the United States, but soccer is not one of them.

   b. Draw a logical conclusion based on the information in the paragraph.

      Topic Sentence: Psychologist and author John Oldham identifies four styles of controlling behavior.

      Concluding Sentence: The four types of controlling behaviors surface in the workplace, in the classroom, and in social situations on a regular basis.

   c. Pose a thought-provoking question or comment that encourages the reader to judge, evaluate, or apply the information to his or her personal life.

      Topic Sentence: By watching the behavior of coaches during a game, parents can easily identify three different kinds of coaches.

      Concluding Sentence: If your children were involved in a sports program, which type of coach would be the best for your children?

7.7 What do you think?

Read the following paragraph about a student's grandfather. Work with a partner or on your own to answer the questions that follow the paragraph. Write your answers on separate paper.

Generosity

My grandfather's generosity has no bounds when it comes to assisting others in the community. Grandfather Joe spends every day of the week sharing his time with others in the community. For example, since his retirement as a schoolteacher sixteen years ago, he has made a commitment to tutor middle school and elementary students in the subjects of math, reading, and writing. The time spent with these students three times a week is very rewarding to him. In addition to his generosity with students, his unlimited generosity with church involvement extends to the community. He takes communion to the elderly in nursing homes, to patients in hospitals, and to a few inmates. He is generous in other ways as well. During the summer, he volunteers at the community flea market twice a month. He assists with cleaning, sorting, and pricing items that will be sold at the flea market. Since he knows that most of the profits will go toward helping the poor in the community, he values the time spent on this event and shares his enthusiastic attitude. Because his love and generosity know no bounds, Grandfather Joe believes that his time and energy will be fruitful and well rewarded in the near future.

Norma Scovell
Lane Community College
Eugene, Oregon

1. Is this an exemplification or a classification paragraph?
2. How many subtopics does the writer include in this paragraph? Where does each subtopic begin?
3. Does the concluding sentence echo the topic sentence, draw a logical conclusion based on the information in the paragraph, or pose a thought-provoking question or comment for the reader to ponder?

The Writing Process for Exemplification and Classification Paragraphs

Step 1: Generate ideas.

Brainstorming and media searching are two effective methods for generating ideas for exemplification and classification paragraphs.

Brainstorming

For an exemplification paragraph, select a subject that you feel strongly about, feel a commitment toward, or have factual information about to share with the reader. The content may be related to textbook topics, current events, or your personal life or experiences. Select a subject that you can develop, explain, or prove through examples. What issues or subjects stir strong feelings in you? Add to the following list:

Family dynamics	Parenting	Siblings	Childcare benefits
Roles of women	Roles of men	Adoption rights	Grandparents
Unions	Labor laws	Equal pay	Affirmative action
____________	____________	____________	____________
____________	____________	____________	____________
____________	____________	____________	____________
____________	____________	____________	____________

For a classification paragraph, brainstorming may also be used to produce lists of possible subjects that consist of individual parts, categories, or types. Add possible topics to the following lists.

Kinds/Types of		**Parts of a/an**	
cars	boats	computer	speech
friends	employers	orchid	deciduous tree
neighbors	teachers	vacuum cleaner	human eye
____________	____________	____________	____________
____________	____________	____________	____________
____________	____________	____________	____________
____________	____________	____________	____________

Media Searching

Spend thirty minutes at home or in the library looking through newspapers, magazines, and your textbooks for topics that could be developed into an exemplification or a classification paragraph. List possible topics for either type of paragraph:

__________________________ __________________________

__________________________ __________________________

__________________________ __________________________

__________________________ __________________________

__________________________ __________________________

Step 2: Get a focus.

Narrow the topic or the subject so it is more specific and focused. The following examples demonstrate the narrowing process for an exemplification or a classification paragraph. (Also see page 267.)

Family dynamics
  step family dynamics
    dynamics between stepmothers and stepchildren
      dynamics between stepmothers and stepdaughters

Pesticides
  dangers of pesticides
    dangers of garden pesticides
      dangers of garden pesticides to pets

Discipline
  kinds of discipline
    kinds of discipline for children
      kinds of discipline for toddlers

Select one of the topics listed on your brainstorming lists in Step 1 (page 282). In the space below, show possible ways to narrow the topic.

____

____

____

____

Step 3: Gather and organize information.

Gathering and organizing information involves two steps: creating a hierarchy and writing an effective topic sentence with a controlling idea.

Creating a Hierarchy

Hierarchies work well to show the subtopics of exemplification and classification paragraphs. To make a hierarchy, place the narrowed topic on the top line. As shown in the following examples of hierarchies, branch down from the top line to show the separate subtopics. For an exemplification paragraph, each subtopic is an example that will be developed with secondary details. For a classification paragraph, each subtopic is a specific category or part of the whole subject that will be developed with secondary details.

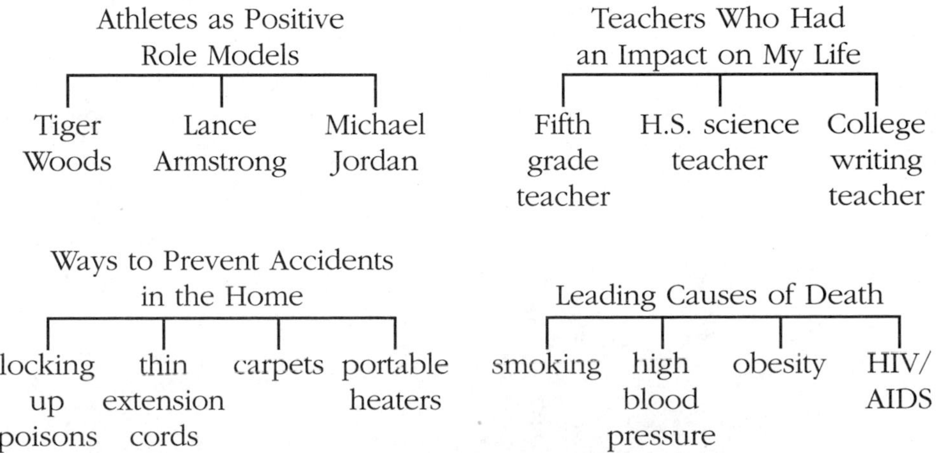

Writing a Topic Sentence

Experiment with several possible topic sentences with controlling ideas until a strong topic sentence emerges. Remember, your topic sentence must clearly identify your narrowed subject and express a controlling idea about your subject. See pages 267–268 for the guidelines to use to write a topic sentence for an exemplification or classification paragraph.

7.8 What do you think?

The following topic sentences are possibilities for the four previous hierarchies. For each set of options, place a check next to the topic sentence you think is the most effective topic sentence with a controlling idea.

1. Athletes

   ________ Though the media highlights athletes who are in trouble, many athletes serve as positive role models.

   ________ Attention needs to be focused on professional athletes who are positive role models for children.

   ________ Children need positive role models; some athletes fulfill this need.

   ________ Many athletes serve as positive role models for children.

2. Teachers

   ________ Not all of my teachers went unnoticed.

   ________ Three teachers truly had an impact on my life.

   ________ My life has been influenced by three teachers.

   ________ At different times during my life, I have had teachers who affected the course of my life.

3. Accidents

   ________ Through careful planning and attention, many accidents in the home can be prevented.

   ________ Many accidents in the home are avoidable.

   ________ Poison, cords, carpets, and heaters cause accidents in the home.

   ________ Accidents in the home are going to happen, but they don't have to happen to you.

4. Causes of Death
   ________ Four of the leading causes of death result from human decisions.
   ________ Personal habits often contribute to four leading causes of deaths.
   ________ Doctors recognize four causes of death.
   ________ Though cancer is one leading cause of death, four other causes of death exist.

Step 4: Write the rough draft.

Use the information you have gathered and organized to write a rough draft. Use the hierarchy as your guide. Begin your paragraph with your topic sentence that has your controlling idea. Then, decide the order to present the subtopics. Add supporting details for each of the subtopics in your hierarchy. As with all previous paragraphs, the goal for the rough draft is to get your ideas on paper. Revision work then follows.

Step 5: Revise, revise, revise.

By now you are familiar with the notion that revisions occur in several stages. During this process, you will want to examine the structure of the paragraph. Answers to the following questions can guide you through the revision process.

1. Is there a strong topic sentence that clearly states the controlling idea?
2. Does the body of the paragraph follow the structure designed for that type of paragraph?
3. Does the body have unity, coherence, and adequate development?
4. Does the concluding sentence reflect the controlling idea that is stated in the topic sentence?
5. Are the secondary details effective and sufficient?
6. Are signal words and transition words used effectively?
7. Does the paragraph have good sentence variety and word choices?

7.9 What do you think?

Read the following paragraph about Chinese good luck foods. Work with a partner or on your own to discuss possible revisions for this paragraph. On separate paper, answer the questions that follow the paragraph.

Chinese Good Luck Foods

When I was in China, my favorite part of the Chinese New Year was the New Year's Eve feast my grandmother prepared, because the food was not only colorful and delicious, but each of the dishes had a good luck meaning. I loved the sweet, spicy, orange-sauce–covered, roasted chicken with its dry, crispy skin and green onions glued to the surface with the sauce. This chicken dish represents good fortune and prosperity. I loved to think about my long life when I ate the ten-inch ling, uncut. These light brown noodles were stirfried with green string beans, finely shredded carrots, and white, crispy bean sprouts. I loved to hear my grandmother say the name of the carp fish in Cantonese, *Li Yu, Li Yu,* when she placed the whole steamed fish on the table. The fish was coated smoothly with hot peanut oil and soy sauce and was garnished with finely chopped spring onions, fresh ginger, and garlic. The name of this fish is the same sound as the word in Chinese that means profit and abundance. I loved the taste as well as the symbolism. At the end of the meal, I loved to sip a cup of delicate, aromatic, green tea to calm my taste buds and refresh me for the midnight excitement. The feast represents a new year for me.

Yick Chan
Bellevue Community College
Bellevue, Washington

1. What do you like about the topic sentence?
2. Write two other possible topic sentences for this paragraph.
3. Write a different concluding sentence for this paragraph.
4. How many different dishes does the writer discuss? Do the secondary details for each of the subtopics support the topic sentence and the controlling idea? Explain.
5. What secondary details, if any, would you want to add to this paragraph? Explain.
6. Does the paragraph have unity? Explain.
7. What order does the writer use to present the subtopics? Explain.
8. How does the writer achieve coherence in this paragraph? Explain.
9. Does this paragraph capture your interest? Why or why not?

Step 6: Proofread and edit.

You have already learned many proofreading and editing techniques. The following proofreading checklist includes the grammar and usage tips from Chapter 6.

1. Does every sentence have a complete subject, and a complete verb and form a complete thought so it can stand on its own?
2. Is there sentence variety in the paragraph? Are compound subjects or compound verbs used? Does the paragraph have a variety of simple, compound, and complex sentences?
3. Does the paragraph have correct punctuation between words in a series, between two independent clauses (compound sentences), and between dependent and independent clauses (complex sentences)?
4. Have all fragments, comma splice errors, and run-on sentence errors been corrected?
5. Do you use correct spelling?
6. Do you avoid shifting back and forth between past and present verb tenses?
7. Do you use logical verb tenses throughout the paragraph to show the accurate tense in which the action of the sentence occurred?
8. Do you use participles correctly? Do past and present participles that are intended to be the verbs for the clause have helping verbs?
9. Do you use appositives and participial phrases effectively and correctly? Do they appear next to the noun or the pronoun they modify?
10. Do you avoid using dangling participles? Do all the participial phrases at the beginning of sentences refer to the closest noun, the subject of the sentence?

Step 7: Prepare the final version of your exemplification or classification paragraph.

Follow your instructor's directions for preparing the final version of your paragraph. As always, save all your prewriting materials, your rough draft, and your revisions. You may be asked to turn them in with the final version of your work.

WRITING ASSIGNMENT

Write an exemplification or a classification paragraph that has three to five subtopics that can be developed through the use of secondary details.

Complete each of the following steps for writing an exemplification or a classification paragraph. Unless your teacher assigns a different approach, use the Planning Sheet on page 289 for each step of the writing process.

Step 1: Generate ideas.
Select a topic from the topics generated on page 282 or add new ideas to the list. Write your topic on the Planning Sheet. If you need additional ideas, consider one of the following:

Exemplification		Classification	
police profiling	air pollution	unusual names	types of sports fans
poisons	stereotyping	forms of discipline	forms of discrimination
hunting	Neighborhood Watch	ranks in the military	styles of athletic shoes
school support	deceptive advertising	parts of a heart	parts of a human eye
voter responsibility	teenage pregnancies	kinds of taxes	types of jealousy

Step 2: Get a focus.
Narrow the topic so it is specific and manageable and can be adequately developed in one paragraph. Complete Step 2 on the Planning Sheet.

Step 3: Gather and organize information.
Create a hierarchy by writing the narrowed topic on the top line. Branch down from the top line to show the subtopics you will use in your paragraph. Experiment with several topic sentences with the controlling idea until a strong topic sentence emerges. Complete the directions for Step 3 on the Planning Sheet.

Step 4: Write a rough draft.
Use your hierarchy as a guide. Write the rough draft. On the Planning Sheet, indicate when you finished the rough draft.

Step 5: Revise, revise, revise.
Use the checklist on page 285 to guide you through the revision process. Save each of your revisions. Share your revised draft with a partner and ask your partner to complete the feedback questions on the Planning Sheet.

Step 6: Proofread and edit.
Use the proofreading and editing checklist on page 287 to guide you through this process. You may also work with a partner or a tutor during this step. On the Planning Sheet, write the date that you finished proofreading and editing.

Step 7: Prepare the final version of your paragraph.

EXEMPLIFICATION/CLASSIFICATION PARAGRAPH PLANNING SHEET

Name ______________________

Step 1: Write the topic you will use for your paragraph: ______________________

Step 2: Show the narrowing process you used to reduce the topic for your paragraph:

____

____

____

Step 3: Create a hierarchy to show your narrowed topic and your subtopics.

Topic:

Subtopics:

Will this paragraph be an exemplification or a classification paragraph?

____

Write several possible topic sentences with a controlling idea for your paragraph:

Option 1. ______________________

Option 2. ______________________

Option 3. ______________________

Option 4. ______________________

Star the topic sentence that you prefer.

Step 4: When did you complete the rough draft? ______________________

Step 5: Ask a partner to read your paragraph and respond to the following questions.

PARTNER FEEDBACK FORM

1. Is the topic sentence effective for the type of paragraph? Why or why not? ____________

____

2. Are the subtopics easy to identify? Explain. ____________________

____

3. Comment on the quantity and the quality of secondary details for each of the subtopics. (Ignore the extra lines if the paragraph does not have five subtopics). Do the details effectively provide the reader with meaningful information? Are they sufficient?

   Subtopic 1: ____________________

   Subtopic 2: ____________________

   Subtopic 3: ____________________

   Subtopic 4: ____________________

   Subtopic 5: ____________________

4. Does the paragraph have coherence? How does the writer develop coherence? Explain.

____

____

____

5. Are there any sentences that break the unity of the paragraph? Does each subtopic support or develop the topic sentence? Does each secondary detail support the subtopic? Explain.

____

____

____

6. Provide your partner with suggestions for proofreading and editing:

Partner's name ____________________

Step 6: Write the date that you finished your proofreading and editing: ____________

Step 7: Prepare the final version of your exemplification or classification paragraph.

Grammar and Usage Tips

The four grammar and usage tips in this chapter focus on kinds of agreement that occur between two elements in the sentence. After you complete the exercises for these four grammar and usage tips, carefully check your work with the answer keys in Appendix A and record your number of errors for each exercise. Review the tip and examine the correct answer. In the margins of each exercise, jot down any questions that you would like to ask your instructor regarding the grammar and usage points covered in the exercises.

TIP 21 Select the correct form of verbs so the verbs agree in number with the subject (a noun or a pronoun). Use the singular form of verbs with singular subjects; use the plural form of verbs with plural subjects. Errors with subject-verb agreement occur most frequently in sentences that have third-person present tense or in sentences that contain a helping verb in a verb phrase.

Singular and Plural Subjects in Third Person

The term **first person** refers to the speaker (I). The term **second person** refers to the person or people the speaker is addressing (you). The term **third person** refers to everyone and everything that is not the speaker or the people being addressed. Following are important points about the number of nouns and pronouns in third person.

1. Singular noun subjects do not have an *-s* or an *-es* suffix. The term *singular* means *one.*

box	book	report	student	belief	promise

2. Some singular nouns end in the letter *s;* however, the *s* is not a suffix but a part of the original nouns, that is, the nouns do not exist by removing the *s.* These nouns are singular even though they look plural because of the *s:*

athletics	economics	physics	ethics	analysis
sports	crisis	radius	oasis	parenthesis
gymnastics	mumps	summons	measles	checkers

3. **Collective nouns** are words that represent a group. When the group acts as one fixed unit, not as individuals separately, a collective noun works as a singular noun.

audience	band	board	bunch	cast	choir
chorus	class	crew	committee	company	council
couple	crowd	family	flock	government	group
herd	jury	league	panel	public	squad
society	staff	team	tribe	troop	union

4. Plural nouns usually end with an *-s* or an *-es* suffix. The term *plural* means *any number greater than one.* Adding plural suffixes to nouns sometimes results in spelling changes of the word.

boxes	matches	dishes	books	reports	students
beliefs	promises	worries	parties	knives	wolves

5. Some nouns are plural nouns even though they do not end with the typical *-s* or *-es* suffix.

antennae	children	dice	feet	geese	media
men	mice	oxen	phenomena	teeth	women

6. Third-person pronouns also have number. Following are the singular and plural subject pronouns in third person:

Singular	**Plural**
he, she, it	they

7. **Indefinite pronouns** are pronouns that replace names of people, places, things, or ideas that are indefinite or not clearly defined. Some indefinite pronouns are always singular; other indefinite pronouns are always plural. (See the following chart.) Remember when you are working with identifying subjects and verbs in sentences, you begin by identifying the prepositional phrases. Usually you can disregard or ignore the prepositional phrases because the subject of the sentence is never inside a prepositional phrase. (You can review subjects of sentences in Chapter 2, page 71.)

singular subject ↓ singular verb ↓

Singular: Anyone (~~with any common sense~~) refrains from buying Rolex watches from Slick.

Plural subject ↓ Plural verb ↓

Plural: Many (~~of the young voters~~) want to vote for tuition reductions.

SINGULAR AND PLURAL INDEFINITE PRONOUNS	
ALWAYS SINGULAR	ALWAYS PLURAL
anyone, anybody, another, anything, each, either, neither, nothing, everyone, everybody, everything, no one, nobody, one, someone, somebody, something	both, few, many, others, several

8. Six indefinite pronouns can be singular or plural depending on the noun they replace. These indefinite pronouns refer to a noun that is *inside the closest prepositional phrase.* Use the context of the sentence and the information inside the prepositional phrase to determine whether the pronoun is functioning as a singular or a plural pronoun.

INDEFINITE PRONOUNS THAT CAN BE SINGULAR OR PLURAL
all, any, none, most, more, some

Singular: **All** (of the ice) is in the bucket.

Plural: **All** (of the teachers) use the software to record students' grades.

Singular: **Any** (of your fabric) is appropriate for this project.

Plural: **Any** (of your suggestions) are better than none at all.

Singular: **None** (of your wisdom) works in this situation.

Plural: **None** (of the soccer players) are going to the state tournament.

Singular: **Most** (of the ice cream) has melted.

Plural: **Most** (of the programs) require a two-year commitment.

Singular: **More** (of the money) is necessary this year for education.

Plural: **More** (of the activists) are planning to attend this next rally.

Singular: **Some** (of my debt) is from my college years.

Plural: **Some** (of the leaders) advocate peaceful solutions and compromises.

EXERCISE 7.1 Identifying Subjects

Score: ______

As a review, mark the prepositional phrases with parentheses in the following sentences. Then underline the subject or subjects of the sentence with one line. Remember that each clause has a subject, so mark the subjects in both the dependent and the independent clauses. Above each subject, write **S** if the subject is singular and **P** if the subject is plural.

Example: When the computer system (S) crashes, a complete analysis (S) (of the problem) usually takes several days.

1. Many elected officials do not keep the promises that they make during election campaigns.

2. During his entire term, he wrote one column; needless to say, everyone was very surprised.

3. Nothing that I do is quite right in the opinion of my father.

4. Controllers often want to feel that they are powerful and superior.

5. Men and women share many common interests.

6. Some of the writers use excessive stereotyping, which reduces their credibility.

7. Migrating geese fly over the lake and land near the cabin on a daily basis.

8. The committee meets twice a month to discuss employee performance.

9. The summons to appear in court at the end of the month arrived yesterday.

10. Athletics at our school encourages excellent performance on the court or fields as well as in the classrooms.

Singular and Plural Verbs in Third Person

Errors with subject-verb agreement often occur in sentences with a third-person subject and a simple present-tense verb.

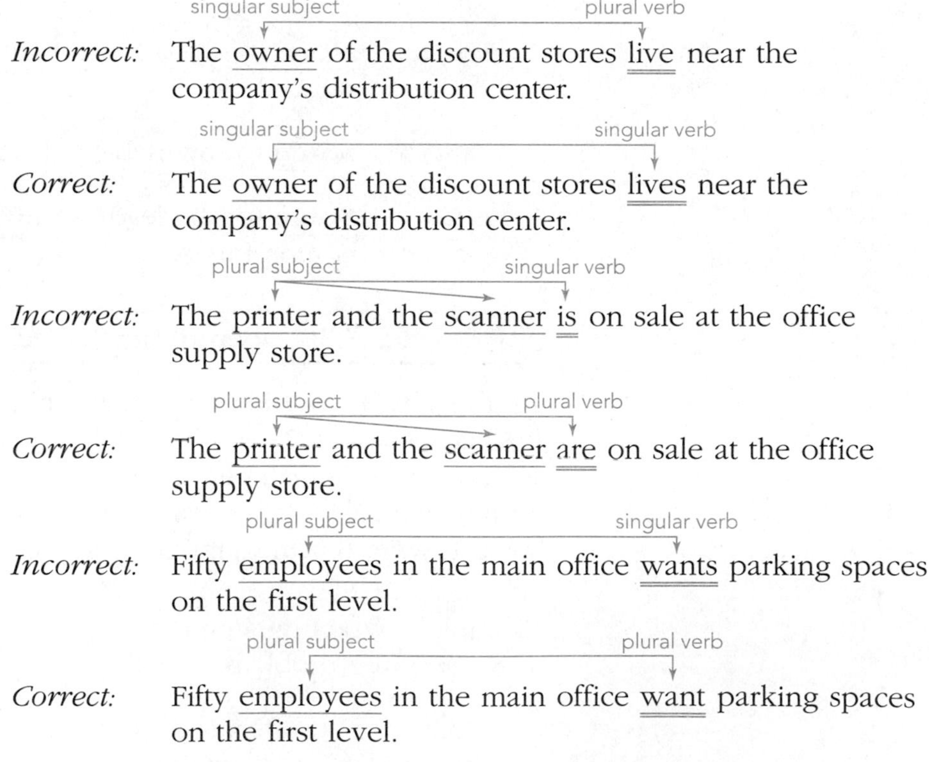

To avoid problems with subject and verb agreement of this nature, use the following guidelines:

1. Remember that subjects and verbs show number. Do not think of the terms *singular* and *plural* as referring only to noun subjects. Both subjects and verbs can be singular or plural.

2. Sentences that are in third person, present tense should have either an *-s* on the noun subject or an *-s* on the verb. (Exceptions to this general rule are discussed in point 3 below.)

no *-s* on the singular subject — *-s* on the singular verb

Singular subject and singular verb: The catalog from Sears shows several kinds of lawn mowers.

-s on the plural subject — *no -s* on the plural verb

Plural subject and plural verb: Catalogs from my university show a wide range of career options and degree programs for undergraduates.

3. As discussed on page 291, some singular nouns end in *-s* but must be treated as singular:

singular noun ends in *-s* — *-s* on the singular verb

Singular subject and verb: Gymnastics involves coordination, concentration, and flexibility.

Also, some plural nouns do not end in *-s* but must be treated as plural.

plural noun does not end in *-s* — plural verb does not end in *-s*

Plural subject and verb: The men collect their pension checks every month.

4. Verbs forms from the verbs *to be, to do,* and *to have* show number in both present tense and past tense, as well as in verb phrases. The following chart shows the present and past tense singular and plural verb forms for the verbs *to be, to do,* and *to have.*

THIRD-PERSON VERB FORMS		
	THIRD-PERSON SINGULAR	THIRD-PERSON PLURAL
Present Tense	is, has, does	are, have, do
Past Tense	was, had, did	were, had, did

singular subject — singular present-tense verb

The printer **is** on sale at Office Max.

plural subject — plural present-tense verb

The printers **are** on sale at Office Depot.

singular subject — singular present-tense verb

The store **has** a wide selection of fax machines.

plural subject — plural present-tense verb

The stores **have** a wide selection of fax machines.

The following examples show the same pattern of singular subjects with singular present-tense verbs and plural subjects with plural present-tense verbs.

The clerk **does** her job efficiently.	The clerks **do** their jobs efficiently.
The salesperson **is** friendly.	The salespeople **are** friendly.
The customer **has** the final word.	The customers **have** the final word.

When you use a verb phrase, the helping verb indicates the tense and the number of the verb.

singular subject / singular helping verb in the verb phrase	plural subject / plural helping verb in the verb phrase
The technician **has learned** this system.	The technicians **have learned** this system.
The company **does employ** teenagers.	The companies **do employ** teenagers.
The teacher **is recording** our grades.	The teachers **are recording** our grades.

EXERCISE 7.2 Making Subjects and Verbs Agree Score: ______

Identify and underline the subjects in the following sentences. Then circle the correct form of the verb to match the subject number (singular or plural). Remember to mark subjects in both independent and dependent clauses.

Example: A multifaceted site, which (provide, provides) Internet users with authentic Indian folklore, (is, are) popular with students in my ethnic studies course.

1. Links to various sites on the Internet (include, includes) sites with audio and animation.

2. Another award-winning hub of Native American resources (utilize, utilizes) a photo journal approach so that visitors to the site (receive, receives) vivid images of authentic daily life of indigenous people.

3. In other words, a cornucopia of miscellaneous wonders (await, awaits) visitors to her web site.

4. The yellow and brown flowered wallpaper, with matching pea green stove and refrigerator, (is, are) congruent with the dining room table.

5. Managers with this style of management (tend, tends) to be generous or self-sacrificing in order to maintain a relationship that (function, functions).

6. A manager who (use, uses) this style of conflict resolution (is, are) genuinely concerned about reaching a settlement that (meet, meets) the needs of both parties and (do, does) not damage or harm the welfare of the other side.

7. Defensive linemen (consist, consists) of defensive tackles and defensive ends.

8. The middle linebacker (has, have) an outside linebacker to his left and to his right.

9. This roasted chicken dish with a sweet, spicy orange sauce (represent, represents) good fortune and prosperity.

10. The name of this fish (has, have) the same sound as the word in Chinese that (mean, means) profit and abundance.

EXERCISE 7.3 Proofreading for Subject-Verb Agreement

Score: ______

Proofread and edit the following sentences for subject-verb agreement errors. Correct any errors by writing the correct verb form above the errors. Write C next to sentences that are correct.

1. Everyone in intramural sports pay for personal lockers and uniforms.
2. A few of the students prefer to shower when they get home.
3. None of the games this season is scheduled as a night game.
4. One of my friends attend every home game and most of the away games.
5. Many of the students at my school do not attend sporting events on campus.
6. Some want to join a team, but they hesitate to commit to the practices and the games.
7. Ticket prices for each game varies; of course, the best seats in the stadium are always more expensive.
8. Anything that the coaches request get done immediately.
9. Aerobics provide a way to exercise, burn calories, and firm up muscles.
10. Many health threats for adults decrease through daily exercise and an active lifestyle.

TIP 22 **Subjects and verbs must agree when a sentence has compound subjects (two or more subjects). Use plural verbs when the conjunction *and* joins the compound subjects. When the conjunctions *or, neither/nor,* or *either/or* join the compound subjects, the subject closest to the verb determines whether the verb is singular or plural.**

Compound Subjects Joined by *and*

When the conjunction *and* joins two or more subjects, the subject is plural and uses a plural verb. In third-person present tense, the plural verb does not have an *-s* or *-es* suffix. The linking verbs or the helping verbs in any verb tense also express the plural form when the conjunction *and* joins the compound subjects.

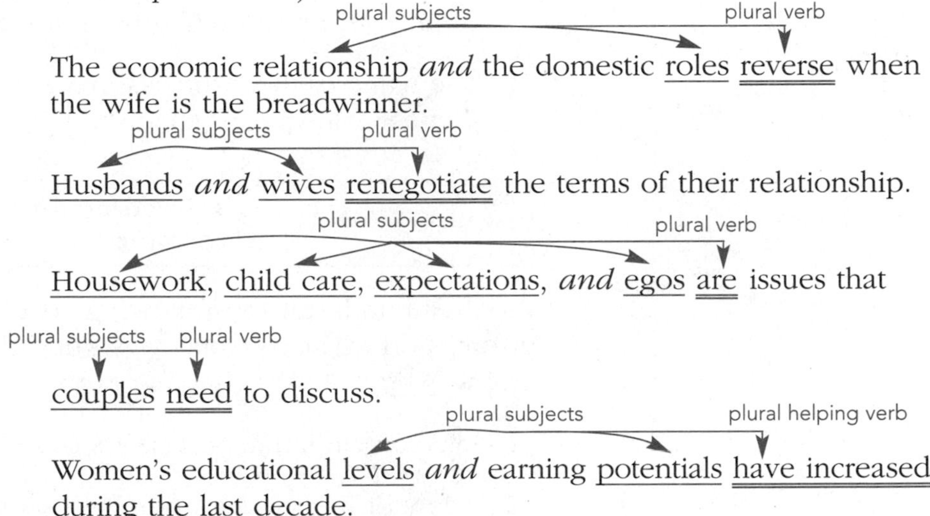

Compound Subjects Joined by *or*

Subject and verb agreement requires careful attention when the conjunction *or* joins compound subjects. This conjunction conveys the idea that one or the other of the subjects receives the action of the sentence, but not both. The verb agrees in number with the subject that is closer or closest to the verb.

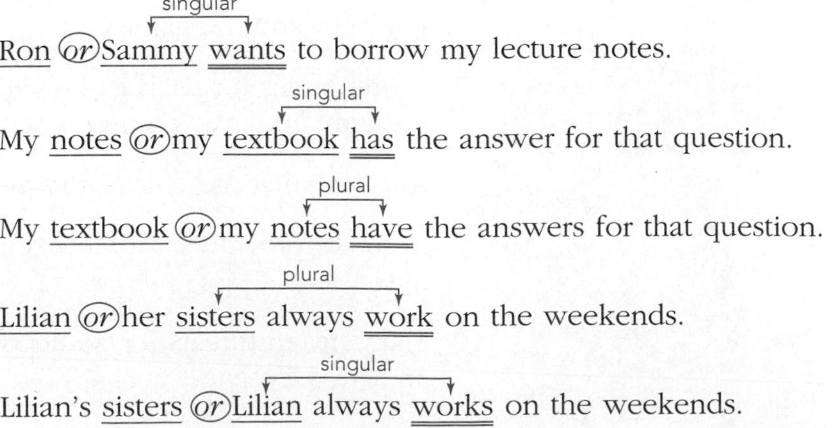

Compound Subjects Joined by *either/or* or *neither/nor*

The conjunctions *either/or* and *neither/nor* follow the same rules that you use for the conjunction *or*. The combination of *either/or* expresses that only one of the subjects receives the action of the verb. The combination *neither/nor* expresses that neither subject receives the action of the sentence. In both combinations, the verb agrees in number (singular or plural) with the subject that is closer to the verb.

plural

Either Rachel *or* her dance partners make mistakes during every performance.

singular

Either Rachel's dance partners *or* she makes mistakes during every performance.

plural

Either eggs *or* egg substitutes are necessary for this recipe.

plural

Neither Mary *nor* her parents want to move to Nebraska.

plural

Neither the administration *nor* the teachers want to see a strike.

singular

Neither the teachers *nor* the administration wants to see a strike.

EXERCISE 7.4 **Subject-Verb Agreement** Score: ______

Circle the correct verb in the following sentences.

1. Either of the web sites (explain, explains) the origins of the Aborigines.
2. Neither (consider, considers) himself to be an expert.
3. Jamaal and Norma (has, have) two young children.
4. Neither the rent nor the utility bills (is, are) due until next week.
5. Neither insults nor rumors (bother, bothers) my thick-skinned boss.
6. The cost of airline tickets and the travel schedule (make, makes) the trip impossible.
7. Each of the consultants and all of the members on the advisory board (recommend, recommends) approval of the construction budget.
8. Many of the counselors in the child center (has, have) psychology degrees.
9. Every client in the clinic (expect, expects) immediate attention.
10. Neither the menus nor the decor (has, have) changed in the last ten years.

TIP 23 **Pronouns must agree in number and in gender with the nouns they rename. The nouns they rename are called *antecedents.* When the antecedent is singular, the pronoun must be singular. When the antecedent is plural, the pronoun must be plural. Pronouns in third-person singular must be the same gender as the antecedent.**

Antecedents are the nouns that pronouns replace. The antecedent appears first in the sentence or paragraph; the pronoun appears later in the sentence or the paragraph.

antecedent pronoun

Antonio collects antique coins; **he** has more than fifty rare coins.

antecedent antecedent pronoun pronoun

Giorgio has a very doting mother. **She** does everything for **him,**

pronoun

including **his** laundry.

Pronoun-antecedent agreement occurs when the writer selected the correct number and gender of the pronoun so the pronoun and the antecedent agree. The following chart shows singular and plural pronouns. Notice that some pronouns are specifically masculine or feminine.

PRONOUNS						
SINGULAR PRONOUNS				PLURAL PRONOUNS		
I	me	my	mine	we	us	our
myself	you	your	yours	ours	ourselves	you
yourself	he*	him*	his*	your	yours	yourselves
himself*	she*	her*	hers*	they	them	their
herself*	it	its	itself	theirs	themselves	

*Pronouns that show gender, masculine or feminine

The following examples show pronoun-antecedent agreement with subject, object, and possessive pronouns. The antecedents and the pronouns appear in bold print. Notice that the number and, when appropriate, the gender (masculine or feminine) of the antecedent and the pronoun agree.

Subject Pronouns: I, you, he, she, it, we, they

antecedent pronoun

El Nino occurs every five to seven years; **it** lasts for twelve to eighteen months.

antecedents

Terrell, Jerry, and **Brian** have known each other for

pronoun

years; **they** treat each other like brothers.

Object Pronouns: *me, you, him, her, it, us, them*

antecedents / pronoun

> My **husband** and **I** are so appreciative. The Foundation helped **us** build a new home.

antecedents / pronoun

> **Carla Gonzales** and **Tony Mesquita** helped me out of a difficult situation. I respect **them** so much.

Possessive Pronouns: *my, mine, your, yours, his, her, hers, its, our, ours, their, theirs*

antecedent / pronoun

> The **Reeves** live next door to me; for that reason, I know **their** daily routines quite well.

antecedent / pronoun

> **Joaquim** longs for the opportunity to help **his** grandparents during this difficult time.

antecedent / pronoun

> The **contestant** in the beauty contest dropped **her** crown.

antecedent / pronoun

> The **students** in the women's dorm all signed **their** names on the huge poster.

When the gender of the antecedent is unknown, selecting the correct pronoun can be confusing. For example, in the following sentence, unless the writer knows the gender of the wrestler, selecting the correct pronoun is difficult because male and female wrestlers now get into the ring.

> The **wrestler** wears ___(his, her)___ silly costume and make-up into the ring.

Use the following guidelines when the gender of the antecedent is unknown.

1. When the gender is unknown, use the phrase *his or her* rather than use only one of the pronouns (masculine or feminine). At times, this sounds awkward, but it is correct.

> The *wrestler* wears **his or her** silly costume and make-up into the ring.
>
> A daily *commuter* often leaves **his or her** newspaper on the train.
>
> A young *child* without parental guidance can easily lose **his or her** way in the world.
>
> A new *employee* needs to buy a lock for **his or her** personal storage bin.

2. With some writing, you can avoid the awkwardness of the pronouns *his and her* by making the antecedent plural. In some cases, you will need to change the verb so it agrees with the plural subject.

   The *wrestlers* wear **their** silly costumes and make-up into the ring.

   Daily *commuters* often leave **their** newspapers on the train.

   Young *children* without parental guidance can easily lose **their** way in the world.

   New *employees* need to buy locks for **their** personal storage bin.

EXERCISE 7.5 Using Pronouns for Pronoun-Antecedent Agreement

Score: ______

In each of the following sentences, write the missing pronoun.

1. A high school senior's decision about where ________ wants to attend college is difficult.
2. Students can select ________ instructors and class times.
3. The university expects ________ students to follow the honor code.
4. Students sometimes struggle with learning how to balance ________ academic and social lives.
5. The main campus and the satellite campuses post ________ schedules on ________ web pages.
6. Tuition is less expensive at the community college; ________ is often one-third of the tuition at the university.
7. The Financial Aid Office assists students with ________ application forms; ________ main concern is that students fill the forms out correctly the first time.
8. Many students feel a strong sense of loyalty to ________ school and ________ faculty.
9. To run for a position in the student government, a student must complete a questionnaire and submit ________ formal transcript.
10. The student newspaper lost ________ editor, so members of the editorial staff are trying to find a new editor to work with ________ on ________ upcoming issues.

Pronouns must agree in number with antecedents that are indefinite pronouns. Indefinite pronouns do not express gender, so use the combination *he or she* for singular indefinite pronouns. Use plural pronouns to form pronoun-antecedent agreement with plural indefinite pronouns.

Page 292 introduced you to singular and plural indefinite pronouns. The following chart summarizes the singular indefinite pronouns, the plural indefinite pronouns, and the indefinite pronouns that can be singular or plural depending on the nouns they replace.

INDEFINITE PRONOUNS		
ALWAYS SINGULAR	ALWAYS PLURAL	SINGULAR OR PLURAL*
anyone, anybody, another, anything, each, either, neither, nothing, everyone, everybody, everything, no one, nobody, one, someone, somebody, something	both, few, many, others, several	all, any, none, most, more, some

*Look for clues inside prepositional phrases.

An indefinite pronoun can work as an antecedent. A pronoun that renames an indefinite pronoun must agree with the number expressed by the indefinite pronoun. Notice the pronoun-antecedent errors and the method of correction in the following examples. Remember that indefinite pronouns must also agree in number with the verbs; therefore, sometimes you can use the verb as a clue to determine whether an indefinite pronoun is singular or plural.

singular — **his or her**

Anyone can express **their** opinion at the forum.
[*Anyone* is singular. The verb in this sentence does not provide a clue. The *his or her* combination agrees with the singular antecedent, *anyone.*]

singular — **its**

Voting measures need to be studied carefully; *each* has **their** own pros and cons.
[The antecedent is *each,* which is a singular indefinite pronoun. The verb *has,* which is singular, provides a clue. The pronoun *its* is singular to match the antecedent.]

singular

Each (of the voting machines) has a serial number printed on **its**
their side.
[The antecedent *each,* is singular. The verb *has* provides a clue. The pronoun *its,* which is singular, agrees with the antecedent.]

plural ... their

None (of the local businesses) want to have **its** name on the initiative.
[The antecedent *none,* can be singular or plural. *None* in this case refers to *businesses,* which is plural. The verb *want* is plural and provides a clue. The correct plural pronoun is *their.*]

Members (of the NAACP) encourage citizens to register to vote; *many* volunteer **his or her** time to the cause.
[The antecedent *many* is always plural. The plural pronoun is *their.*]

Many *citizens* do vote on a regular basis; *some* never vote even when **he or she** have registered to vote.
[The antecedent *some* can be singular or plural, depending on the noun it replaces. In this sentence, *some* refers to *citizens,* which is plural. The plural pronoun *they* must be used to agree with its antecedent. The plural verbs *do, vote,* and *have* provide a clue.]

EXERCISE 7.6 Pronoun Agreement with Indefinite Pronoun Antecedents

Score: ______

Circle the correct pronoun to agree with the antecedent. All the antecedents are indefinite pronouns.

1. *Each* of the golfers wants to see (their, his or her) name on the leader board.
2. *Everyone* wants to see (their, his or her) favorite golfer after the tournament ends.
3. Fans gather around players and show their appreciation; some even want to get (their, his or her) picture taken with a professional golfer.
4. *Many* wait for hours to see (their, his or her) favorite player at the eighteenth hole.
5. *Others* head to (their, his or her) cars as quickly as possible to avoid traffic jams.
6. *Several* of the caddies are also becoming well known; fans ask (them, him or her) for autographs.
7. *Most* of the fans at golf tournaments select one place on the course as (their, his or her) spot for the entire tournament.

8. *Anybody* can learn to enjoy golf if (they, he or she) takes the time to learn about the game.

9. My parents love to watch golf, but *neither* has (their, his or her) own set of clubs.

10. Many of my cousins are learning to play golf, but *few* have (their, his or her) own clubs and golf shoes.

EXERCISE 7.7 Either and Neither

Score: ______

In the following sentences, write **Conj.** when the word *either* or *neither* works as a **conjunction.** Write **IP** when the word works as an **indefinite pronoun** in the subject position. Write **A** when the word works as an **adjective.**

conjunction

___conj___ Either the *Honda* or the *Mazda* is a good choice for a new car.

indefinite pronoun

___IP___ *Either* is a good choice for a new car.

adjective

___A___ Either *car* is a good choice for you.

______ 1. Neither my sister nor I know how to change a flat tire.

______ 2. Neither mechanic is willing to give an estimate over the phone.

______ 3. Either car is going to be expensive to insure.

______ 4. Neither of us wants a high premium.

______ 5. Either you or I need to have the car inspected by an independent garage.

______ 6. I would love to own a BMW or a Mercedez, but neither is an option for me.

______ 7. Neither vehicle is in my price range.

______ 8. Either my father or my brother will cosign on my car loan.

______ 9. Either bank offers a good interest rate on new car loans.

______ 10. Neither has a rate lower than 7 percent.

Grammar and Usage Tips Summary

TIP 21 Select the correct form of verbs so the verbs agree in number with the subject (a noun or a pronoun). Use the singular form of verbs with singular subjects; use the plural form of verbs with plural subjects. Carefully check for subject and verb agreement in sentences that are in third person, present tense.

TIP 22 Subjects and verbs must agree when a sentence has compound subjects. Use plural verbs when the conjunction *and* joins the compound subjects. When the conjunctions *or, neither/nor,* or *either/or* join the compound subjects, the subject closest to the verb determines whether the verb is singular or plural.

TIP 23 Pronouns must agree in number and in gender with their antecedents, the nouns they rename. When the antecedent is singular, the pronoun must be singular. When the antecedent is plural, the pronoun must be plural. Pronouns in third-person singular must be the same gender as the antecedent.

TIP 24 Pronouns must agree in number with antecedents that are indefinite pronouns. Indefinite pronouns do not express gender, so use the combination *he or she* for singular indefinite pronouns. Use plural indefinite pronouns to form pronoun-antecedent agreement with plural indefinite pronouns.

CHAPTER 7 • Exemplification and Classification Paragraphs • Proofreading and Editing Exercises

Working with a partner or on your own, proofread and edit the following paragraphs. Read the directions for each exercise.

Proofreading 1

Proofread and edit the following classification paragraph for punctuation errors. Replace the incorrect punctuation with correct punctuation. Correct any run-on sentences or comma splices. Add any missing punctuation or capital letters.

Quitters

Though I have never been a smoker, I am easily amused by watching four different kinds of quitters. The first kind of quitter I call the *wannabes.* They always say that they want to quit but they never show a single sign of effort for their cause. They say they'll quit next week next month at the beginning of the year, or when they reach a certain birthday it never happens they continue to puff away their money through their cigarettes. The second kind of quitter I call the *supporters.* They make an earnest effort to quit. Instead of spending money on cigarettes. They spend their money on patches and nicotine gum to stop their cravings. With the right kind of support from products family, and friends. They gainfully earn the title of quitter after several months of battle. The third kind of quitter I call the *sneakers.* They do not use any products to help them quit they use will power determination, or a health threat to motivate them to quit. They almost reach the point of no desire; and then the urge sweeps over them. They buy a fresh pack and sneak outside, possibly behind a garage or shed, to grab a few puffs. They actually believe a little mouthwash gum and a hearty spray of cologne or perfume will mask their regression. They are always so close to earning the label of quitter. The last kind of quitter I call the *cold turkeys.* They simply do it they smoke the last cigarette, crumple up the last empty pack, and they stop. They fill their mouths with suckers, gum, and hard candy. They put their mind, and their urges elsewhere, and simply move on into their lives as quitters. I know some cold turkeys, and they are truly the quitters. If you are a smoker, are you also a quitter?

Proofreading 2

Proofread the following classification paragraph for errors. Look carefully for errors in subject and verb agreement and pronoun-antecedent agreement. Write your corrections above the errors.

Three Levels of Listening

The process of listening occurs on three levels. In the first level of listening, *basic listening,* the listener reacts to sounds and pay attention to words in order to comprehend and interpret the message. The listener blocks out other noises, distractions, thoughts, or feelings. Listeners on this level strives to understand the language and the speaker's point of view. In the next level of listening, *critical listening,* listeners analyze and evaluate the message and then responds appropriately with constructive feedback to the speaker. This feedback may be in the form of visual clues, such as smiles, frowns, puzzled looks, or nods. Feedback may also be verbal in the form of a question or comment. In the third level of listening, *constructive listening,* listeners seek to identify his or her personal value in the message. The listener sifts through the message for special applications for their life. He or she seeks to extend the meaning of the speaker's words and then personalizes the message internally. These listeners listen with their ears, their minds, and their hearts. They may later enter into a dialogue with the speaker by asking questions or entering into a discussion to learn more about the topic. As listeners become more skilled in the process of listening, they are able to move through the first two levels to reach the most complex level and become master listeners.

[Adapted from Osborn. *Public Speaking,* Houghton Mifflin, 1997, pp. 69–70.]

Proofreading 3

Proofread and edit your Writing Warm-Up 7. Use all the grammar and usage skills you have learned throughout this textbook.

Internet Enrichment

Log onto the web site for this textbook for additional exercises and links for the following topics:

Exemplification Paragraphs
Classification Paragraphs
Subject and Verb Agreement
Indefinite Pronouns
Pronoun-Antecedent Agreement

Go to: http://college.hmco.com. Click on "Students." Type *Paragraph Essentials* in the "Jump to Textbook Sites" box. Click "go," and then bookmark the site. Click on Chapter 7.

CHAPTER 7 • Grammar and Usage Review

Name ______________________________

Date ______________________________

Agreement

Circle the word or words in each sentence to show agreement between the subject and the verb or the antecedent and the pronoun.

1. The reference books on the first shelf (provide, provides) students with useful information.
2. The league (require, requires) (their, its) players to agree to conduct standards.
3. The media (cover, covers) current events and (provide, provides) (its, their) audience with stories.
4. Everyone on the roster (receive, receives) an award with (his or her, their) name imprinted in gold letters.
5. None of the forms (has, have) a place for the administrator to sign (his or her, their) name.

Proofreading

Read the following paragraph carefully. Use any method to correct errors. Write the corrections above the errors.

Breadwinner Wives

Breadwinner wives renovate the traditional partnership roles in marriage. More than one in three working wives in America brings home larger paychecks than her husband's. This role reversal in marriages create imbalance in the marriage and cause some uncomfortable gender role shifts, or more precisely, gender role jolts. For example, many husbands must learn to deal with their male egos. When his wife starts bringing home more bacon, or in some cases, the whole pig, many husbands feel threatened. They have to learn that their self-worth and their contributions to the marriage encompass more than just a paycheck. They also must accept the fact that he no longer holds the financial power in the relationship. The gender roles in marriage also force renovations in the areas of household responsibilities and childcare. Women who bring home juicy pieces of bacon often trades time at home with time at the office. Their jobs demand more attention and increasingly more hours. The husbands in these marriages assume greater household responsibilities and childcare responsibilities. They do the laundry, the grocery shopping, the cleaning, and some become "soccer dads" by attending all of his children's extracurricular activities. In addition to the domestic shifts, the social side of the marriage shift. Many domestic husbands find that his male friends have problems accepting the role reversal. Domestic husbands face ridicule and finds himself excluded more and more from his circle of friends. The breadwinner wives have less time to be involved with school, community, or volunteer activities. Her circle of friends and close relationships dwindle, for most of their spare time is spent with their husbands and their children. As increasing numbers of women obtain higher levels of education, more and more ambitious, talented women will be tipping the marriage scales when their paychecks grow and surpass those of their mates.

[Adapted from: Amy Goldstein, "Breadwinner wives tip marriage scales," *Register Guard*, February 29, 2000, p. 1D, 2D.]

CHAPTER 8

Definition Paragraphs

The topic sentence introduces a term that will be defined.

The body provides an expanded definition. A variety of methods may be used to define the term.

The concluding sentence echoes the topic sentence or summarizes the paragraph.

Topic Sentence with term to be defined............

Expanded definition

Unity + Coherence + Adequate Development

Concluding Sentence...

In Chapter 8 you will learn about the following:

1. The definition paragraph
2. The structure of a definition paragraph
3. The writing process for definition paragraphs
4. Four additional grammar and usage tips

WRITING WARM-UP 8

Think of a word or an expression that you know your readers may not be familiar with or may not clearly understand. Write a paragraph that explains this word. This word may be any one of the following:

1. A term (vocabulary word) from one of your courses or a technical word from a job-related experience.
2. A concept such as *ambiguity, apathy, ingenuity, spontaneity,* or *philanthropy.*
3. An idiom (a nonliteral expression) or a slang expression.

The Definition Paragraph

A definition paragraph is a form of expository writing that provides your reader with an expanded definition of a term. The term refers to a concrete object, a concept, an unusual or unfamiliar word, an idiom, or an expression. When you write a definition paragraph, you dedicate the entire paragraph to explaining the term so the reader can grasp its meaning. Your reader should be able to form a clear image or understanding of the term or expression, which may include how it works, how it is used, or why it is significant.

As you know, a paragraph is a group of sentences that focuses on one specific main or controlling idea. To develop a definition paragraph, you must provide more than a one-sentence, limited definition. To develop the body of the paragraph, you will need to select additional details to expand the basic definition and express your interpretation of the meaning of the word. You have considerable latitude or choices of methods to use to develop an expanded definition. You can use a combination of any of the following methods: a formal dictionary definition, an informal definition written in your own words, synonyms (words with similar meanings), antonyms (words with opposite meanings), a statement that tells what the term is *not,* word history (etymology), quotations, or detailed explanations. This chapter discusses each of these methods.

In addition to the above methods, you can develop your definition paragraph by using sentences that show narration (short anecdotes), comparison, contrast, process, classification, cause and effect, or exemplification (examples).

Frequently, we hear a familiar term, but we do not have a clear or detailed understanding of its meaning. A well-written definition paragraph provides us with specific information so we are able to define the term accurately. For example, you have probably heard the term *optimist.* What does this term mean to you? Write an informal definition of an *optimist:* ______________________________

____

After reading the following paragraph, you will be asked again to define the term *optimist.* Read the paragraph and the marginal notes carefully.

OPTIMISTS

The topic sentence uses contrast to introduce the term optimist.

The body of the paragraph continues by contrasting optimists and pessimists.

Instead of turning setbacks into personal hardships or disasters, optimists see setbacks as valuable lessons and opportunities for personal growth. Optimists are the opposite of pessimists, people who tend to focus on the negative aspects of their lives and tend to see their accomplishments as minimal, insignificant, or nonexistent. According to Martin Seligman, a psychology professor who has done more than

A quotation from a leading psychologist expands understanding of the term *optimist.*

An informal definition explains several behavior patterns of optimists.

An extended example shows how an optimist reacted to being stood up at the altar.

The concluding sentence ends with a formal dictionary definition.

thirty years of research in the area of optimism and positive psychology, "Optimistic people tend to distance themselves from and minimize the causes of their misfortune, instead taking credit for the good things that happen to them. Pessimists, on the other hand, blame themselves for their misfortune and ascribe good events to chance." Optimists focus their attention and their energy on seeing life from a positive perspective. They learn to nurture their own strengths and goodness and believe that things happen for reasons that are in their best interest. As an example, my cousin Betsy was stood up at the altar. After the initial shock wore off, rather than drown in sorrow or be consumed by the pity that her family and friends doused her with on a regular basis, she proclaimed that for some reason the wedding was not in her best interest. Someone or something different was meant for her; she became grateful that her fiancee found the nerve to not show up. Betsy may be known by some as a positive thinker, a person wearing rose-colored glasses, a Pollyanna, or a free spirit. To me, she exemplifies the American Heritage Dictionary's definition of an optimist: "One who habitually or in a particular case expects a favorable outcome."

[Adapted from: Patricia Wen, "To be happy, look on the bright side," *Register Guard*, March 15, 2000.]

After reading the definition paragraph "Optimists," your understanding of the term *optimist* has most likely broadened, enabling you to write a more accurate definition. Using your own words, define an *optimist:*

____

____

Many paragraphs in your college textbooks are definition paragraphs designed to explain unfamiliar or complex terms. Take time to analyze the methods used in textbook paragraphs to develop definitions. You will notice that many definition paragraphs in your textbooks do not have concluding sentences because the paragraphs are not designed to stand alone. They are part of a larger piece of writing that consists of multiple paragraphs.

The Structure of a Definition Paragraph

When you write a definition paragraph, your purpose is to provide your reader with the specific details that clearly explain an unfamiliar term or your special interpretation of a term. A definition paragraph accomplishes this purpose by using the standard three-part paragraph: topic sentence, body, and concluding sentence. Within these three parts, however, you will see that you have many options to use in writing an effective definition paragraph.

Developing the Topic Sentence

Use the following guidelines to write an effective topic sentence with a controlling idea for your definition paragraph.

1. Narrow the topic for your definition paragraph to one specific word or phrase to define. A topic that is too broad or a topic that includes more than one term to define will confuse your reader and will create difficulties for you to develop into an expanded definition.
2. Include the term or the expression in the topic sentence so your reader immediately knows what term you intend to define. Your topic sentence is your controlling idea for the paragraph; the details will support or expand the term you identify in your topic sentence.
3. Use a signal word in the topic sentence to let your reader know that a definition paragraph follows. These signal words can also be used within the body of the paragraph to show that definitions follow.

DEFINITION SIGNAL WORDS				
defined as	is	is called	means	is known as
is referred to as	which is	which means		

4. Define any other words used in the topic sentence (or in any sentence in the body of the paragraph as well) that may be unfamiliar to your reader. Notice in the following example that a reader may not clearly understand the topic sentence if he or she does not understand the word *humerus*.

Unfamiliar word within the definition:	A **rotator cuff** (is) a small group of four muscles that hold a person's humerus into the ball-and-socket joint in the shoulder. [definition: small group of four muscles that hold a person's humerus into the ball-and-socket joint in the shoulder]
Unfamiliar word also defined within the definition:	A **rotator cuff** is a small group of four muscles that hold a person's humerus (upper arm bone) into the ball-and-socket joint in the shoulder. [definition: upper arm bone → humerus]

5. Do not use the words *is where* or *is when* in your definition sentence. [*Where* refers to location, and *when* refers to time; actual definitions seldom refer to a place or a time.]

A rotator cuff ~~is where~~ is a small group of muscles that connect your upper arm bone to your shoulder socket.

Epicondylitis ~~is when a person has~~ is a painful condition known as tennis elbow.

6. Do not use a **circular definition** in the topic sentence or in the body of the paragraph. A circular definition forms a circle: the term is used to define itself. A circular definition does not inform, explain, or clarify the definition of a term.

   Incorrect: A **starter** on a car *starts the car.*

   Incorrect: An **enzyme formula** is a *formula that has enzymes.*

   Incorrect: A **topic sentence** is a *sentence with a topic.*

Methods to Use to Develop Your Topic Sentence

You can use a variety of methods effectively to develop a topic sentence for your definition paragraph. Experiment with several possible topic sentences before you begin writing your draft. You may use the following methods to develop a topic sentence in a definition paragraph.

1. Give a **formal definition** of the word or the phrase by using a definition from a dictionary or a textbook. When you use the exact dictionary or textbook definition, place quotation marks around the definition and cite the source.

   According to the American Heritage Dictionary, a **tendon** is "a bond of tough, inelastic fibrous tissue that connects a muscle with its bony attachment."

   A sentence with a formal definition structure usually has three distinct parts:

   a. The term or expression.

   b. Reference to the larger category (or class) to which the term belongs

   c. Distinguishing characteristics that differentiate the term from other terms in the same category. For example, there are many kinds of strained muscle conditions, but the distinguishing characteristics of the following condition differentiate it from muscle strains in other parts of the body:

   term

   Epicondylitis as defined by CBS Health Watch, is "a strained muscle condition characterized by pain that originates in the outer portion of elbow and works its way down the forearm."

   category — distinguishing characteristics

2. Give an **informal definition** of the term or the phrase. An informal definition defines the term in your own words.

   Informal: **Epicondylitis** is the medical term for tennis elbow.

3. Include **synonyms** for the term you intend to define in your paragraph. Synonyms are words with similar meaning. A thesaurus, a special dictionary of synonyms, is an excellent reference for locating synonyms. Synonyms may be a part of the main clause in

the sentence, or they may be placed inside commas as an appositive. (See point 5.)

synonyms

A **cunning** person is sly, crafty, and clever.

synonyms

A **serene** setting is calm, quiet, peaceful, and tranquil.

synonyms

A **tongue lashing,** a harsh scolding or reprimand, is sometimes used as a form of discipline.

4. State what the word or the phrase is *not.* (This is called **negation.**) These statements negate or explain the opposite meaning of the term or the phrase you are defining.

   Occasionally feeling sad or lonely is *not* the same as **clinical depression.**

   A **renegade** does *not* stay loyal or committed to his or her party, movement, or cause.

   An **ogre** is *not* a kind, gentle person.

5. Combine two methods of defining the term by using a *dependent clause* (see Chapter 4, page 163), an *appositive* (see Chapter 6, page 247), or a *participial phrase* (see Chapter 6, page 250). For example, you can define the term and include one additional piece of information about the term, such as its significance, word history, or additional detail. Use commas, dashes, or parentheses to separate the definition from additional information in the remainder of the sentence.

   dependent clause — informal definition

   Malamutes, which are named after an Eskimo tribe, are strong dogs that are often used to pull sleds across the tundra.

   the definition stated as an appositive — a second definition

   A **scab**—a nonunion worker—is a person who crosses a picket line to work during a strike.

   the definition stated as a participial phrase — additional detail

   The word **sage,** meaning a very wise person, comes from a Latin verb that means *to know.*

   the definition stated as an appositive — an additional detail

   Apnea (a sleep disorder that occurs when a person temporarily stops breathing) occurs most frequently in men.

6. Pose a question that captures the reader's interest or curiosity. With this option for a topic sentence, introduce the term, but do not provide a definition until the following sentences in the body of the paragraph.

   If you had a large sum of money, would you invest during a **bull market?**

8.1 What do you think?

Check the topic sentences that would work well to introduce a definition paragraph. They should clearly identify the specific term to be defined, provide a specific controlling idea, and capture the reader's interest.

________ 1. A **face-off** in hockey occurs at the start or resumption of play when the referee drops the puck between two opposing players.

________ 2. A **puritan** is not a liberal, permissive person.

________ 3. Have you ever had a stroke of good fortune that was nothing more than a **fluke?**

________ 4. **Fluoridation** of the city water supply has recently been under attack.

________ 5. A **tongue-and-groove joint** is a joint in which a projection on one board fits into the groove in another.

________ 6. A **prodigy** is a child genius.

________ 7. Ramos is a member of a **mariachi** band.

________ 8. You could go to the masquerade party **incognito.**

________ 9. A **mantra** is a chant of a hymn or a phrase.

________ 10. The expression **to gain ground** does not refer to acquiring ground or land.

Developing the Body of the Paragraph

Use the following guidelines to develop the body of your paragraph and the controlling idea stated in your topic sentence.

1. Use a combination of supporting details to expand the basic definition of a term or a phrase and to create a clear image and understanding of the word or the phrase in your reader's mind.
2. Achieve *unity* by including only details that support the topic sentence and that develop the definition that you wish to explain to the reader.
3. Create *coherence* by arranging the details in a logical sequence so ideas flow smoothly. Experiment with the order of your sentences until you find a sequence that works effectively. Use transition words as needed.

DEFINITION PARAGRAPH TRANSITION WORDS				
also	another meaning	another definition	in addition	similarly

4. Provide adequate development by selecting and including a sufficient number of specific details to explain or define the term clearly. Too few details or details that are too general or too vague will result in an underdeveloped paragraph. In addition to a **formal** and an **informal definition** (see page 315), you can use the following kinds of details to expand the basic definition in the body of the paragraph.

a. **Synonyms** (see page 316 for examples) should be selected carefully. Do not use synonyms that are more unfamiliar or more complex than the term you are defining; you will confuse your reader and weaken the impact of your paragraph. Be certain that you clearly understand the meaning of the synonyms before you use them in your writing. In the following examples, if *persnickety* and *obloquy* are unfamiliar terms to your reader, the use of these words does not help the reader understand the definition of *perfectionist* or *infamy*.

unfamiliar term
A **perfectionist** is fussy and *persnickety*.

unfamiliar term
Infamy is a noun that means *obloquy*.

b. **Antonyms** are words with opposite meanings. Antonyms can often be included in prepositional phrases with the preposition *unlike*.

antonym
Optimists, unlike pessimists, look for the positive value in their hardships.

c. **Statements that tell what the term is *not*** may also be used in the body of the paragraph (see page 316 for examples). Conjunctions such as *but, however, on the other hand*, and *in contrast* are often part of this kind of statement.

d. **Word history**, or etymology, sometimes adds interest to a definition paragraph and clarifies the meaning of the word by showing the reader the history or the origin of the word.

informal definition
The term **mania,** which refers to a violent or obsessive disorder,
word history
comes from a Greek word that means madness.

definition
Philanthropy, the desire to help others through financial gifts,
word history
comes from the Greek word *philein,* to love, and *anthropos,* which means man.

e. **Quotations** from experts in the field, historical figures, or well-known public speakers can add credibility and relevancy to your definition paragraph. When you use quotations, remember to place quotation marks around the exact words of the speaker and cite the source of the quotation.

> Mihaly Csikszentmihalyi, Ph.D., defines *flow* as "a source of mental energy in that it focuses attention and motivates action." He also says that flow is "the sense of effortless action they [people] feel in moments that stand out as the best in their lives. Athletes refer to it as 'being in the zone,' religious mystics as being in 'ecstasy,' and artists and musicians as 'aesthetic rapture.'"
>
> [Source: Mihaly Csikszentmihalyi, Ph.D., "Finding Flow," *Psychology Today*, July/August, 1997, pp. 46, 71.]

To provide adequate development in your definition paragraph, use a variety of supporting details. Experiment with different kinds and combinations of supporting details. In the following definition paragraph, notice how the first draft of the paragraph lacks adequate development. The details are vague, nonspecific, and insufficient. A reader unfamiliar with the term *peerage* does not have a clear image of its meaning by reading the draft version of this paragraph.

PEERAGES

Peerages are used in Great Britain. People who are granted peerages become a part of Great Britain's nobility. One kind of peerage is given only to men; a different kind of peerage can be granted to both men and women. Not everyone is eligible or considered for nobility. People without nobility are called commoners.

In the revision, the writer adds more specific details and uses classification to explain Great Britain's two kinds of peerage. After reading the revision, a reader unfamiliar with the term *peerage* has a much clearer image and understanding of this form of British nobility.

PEERAGES

The king or the queen of Great Britain on the recommendation of the prime minister grants two kinds of **peerages,** which are titles of nobility. *Hereditary peerages* are titles of nobility that are passed on through family bloodlines from the *peer,* the person with the title of nobility, to the oldest son or to the closest male heir. The titles of nobility used for hereditary peerage are, beginning with the highest order, *duke, marquis, earl,* and *viscount.* A few ancient peerages allow the titles of nobility to be passed to daughters, in which case *duchess, marchioness, countess,* and *viscountess* are the titles of nobility. *Life peerage* is the second kind of peerage. Life peerages, created annually by the king or queen, honor people of distinction. Unlike hereditary peerages, life peerages cannot be passed on to heirs, but the title of nobility remains for the person's lifetime. Life peerages awarded to men receive the title *Baron,* and women receive the title *Baroness.* Granting the titles of nobility through hereditary and life peerages is a British tradition that continues to this day.

[Adapted from: *The New York Public Library Desk Reference,* Simon & Schuster, 1989, p. 330.]

8.2 What do you think?

Working with a partner or on your own, carefully read the paragraph and answer the questions that follow the paragraph. Write your answers on separate paper.

Fear

Fear is the feeling that haunts the human race. No one, from the strongest man to the weakest child, is safe or immune from fear. Fear captures everyone and spares no one. There's something for everyone on the Wheel of Fear: fear of life, fear of death, fear of deadlines, and fear of work. Many of us, especially the young, boast of being fearless. However, we also boast of being liars. For me, my fear is my imagination. When I was a sweet little girl with golden curls and uncontrollable fits of giggles, fear terrified me. I'd sit in this big chair when I was completely alone and my imagination would take over. I would sit there telling myself not to get scared. Then I'd hear the monster. I'd hear it and I knew it was waiting for me. I just knew that it was hiding right behind me, just waiting for me to look. I'd be so terrified that I couldn't move. I was convinced that if I ran for the door, the monster would catch me as soon as I left my chair. I could hear it breathing, and I could feel its breath against the back of my neck. I knew. I just knew that the horrible monster was going to rip me up into little pieces and eat the pieces one at a time. The fear become even worse in my little tiny head because I could "see" all those things. For years, I thought that I'd finally overcome the fears created by my own imagination. I can walk all night on a deserted city street or an old dirt road without ever becoming alarmed or feeling fear. However, as soon as I sit down and am left completely alone with my thoughts and my imagination, the demons appear and fill me with fear. They like to remind me that although I may run the show for the next sixty or so years, my eternity is theirs. The childhood images of monsters and the fear they created in me still haunt me. As a grown woman, the vividness of my own imagination still has the power to create fear and terror in me. I now realize that the scariest thing in my life is, in fact, myself.

Kristin Zapf-Kent
Eastern Arizona College
Thatcher, Arizona

1. Is the topic sentence a formal or an informal definition? Explain.
2. What examples does the writer give for different kinds of fear?
3. What anecdote (narration) does the writer use to expand the definition of fear?
4. Do you think this anecdote is effective? Why or why not?
5. Does the author's choice of details provide you with a clear definition and visual image of the term *fear*? Explain.
6. If you were to write your own definition paragraph for *fear,* how would you define the term?

8.3 What do you think?

Working with a partner or on your own, carefully read the paragraph and answer the questions that follow the paragraph. Write your answers on separate paper.

Fibromyalgia

Fibromyalgia, defined by Medscape as "a chronic disorder characterized by widespread muscular pain, fatigue, and tenderness in one or more tender points on the body," afflicts more than 3.7 million Americans. Victims of fibromyalgia have pain on both sides of their body, both above and below the waist, and have tenderness in at least one point, such as the neck, elbow, chest, hip, or knee. The pain occurs at the point in the body where muscles attach to the bones or the ligaments and then radiates from that point of origin. Unlike the condition of arthritis, the joints themselves are not affected, deformed, or deteriorated. Related symptoms may include sleep disorders, morning stiffness, anxiety, digestive problems, weakness, tension, migraine headaches, and numbness of the feet or the hands. Doctors do not fully understand the cause of this disorder, but it may be the result of an injury to the central nervous system, or it may be triggered by some type of virus. Physicians now more readily recognize fibromyalgia, which is also called fibrositis or fibromyositis. Researchers are striving to learn more about this disease and find a cure. Breakthroughs in methods of treatment are beginning to provide some relief from pain for the victims of fibromyalgia.

[Adapted from: *http://www.CBSHealthWatch.com*. 2000.]

1. What methods does the writer use to develop the topic sentence for this paragraph? (See pages 315–317.)
2. Does the paragraph have unity? Explain.
3. List the different kinds of details the writer uses to expand the definition of fibromyalgia.
4. Does the paragraph have adequate development? Explain.
5. Does this paragraph have coherence? Explain.
6. Does the paragraph achieve its purpose? Does it inform you and clarify the definition of fibromyalgia for you? Explain.

Developing the Concluding Sentence

Use the following guidelines to bring your paragraph to a close.

1. Restate or echo the topic sentence, or summarize the information in the paragraph in a meaningful way. The concluding sentence signals to your reader that you are finished developing the paragraph.
2. Examine your topic sentence and the concluding sentence. You should have a strong sense that the two sentences are closely related and reflect the same controlling idea that is in the topic sentence. Notice how the following topic sentences and concluding sentences reflect the same controlling idea.

Topic Sentence: Instead of turning setbacks into personal hardships or disasters, optimists see setbacks as valuable lessons and opportunities for personal growth.

Concluding Sentence: To me, she exemplifies the American Heritage Dictionary's definition of an optimist: "One who habitually or in a particular case expects a favorable outcome."

Topic Sentence: The king or the queen of Great Britain on the recommendation of the prime minister grants two kinds of peerages, which are titles of nobility.

Concluding Sentence: Granting the titles of nobility through hereditary and life peerages is a British tradition that continues to this day.

8.4 What do you think?

Working with a partner or on your own, read the following definition paragraph. Answer the questions that follow the paragraph. Write your answers on separate paper.

The Greenhouse Effect

The **greenhouse effect** is the warming of the earth and its lower atmosphere through a process that traps infrared radiation and prevents heat from escaping into space. A layer of atmospheric gases, called greenhouse gases, allows solar radiation to reach the earth and warm it. The earth absorbs some of the solar radiation in the form of heat. The radiation that the earth does not absorb radiates upward into the atmosphere. Much of this heat, however, cannot escape into space because the greenhouse gases (carbon dioxide, methane, nitrous oxide, and ozone) block or trap them. This trapped heat radiates back to the earth to warm the lower atmosphere and the earth's surface. The greenhouse effect is vital for life on the planet to exist. Without the greenhouse effect, the planet would be too cold to support life. In summary, the greenhouse effect provides an insulation that warms the earth's surface and makes life on earth possible.

[Adapted from: "Greenhouse Effect," Microsoft@Encarta@Online Encyclopedia 2000, *http://encarta.msn.com*, 1997–2000.]

1. What is the formal definition of the greenhouse effect? Where does the writer state this formal definition?
2. In addition to the greenhouse effect, the writer defines other terms in the body of the paragraph. List the other unfamiliar words that the writer defines and briefly tell what methods the writer uses to define the words.
3. Does the paragraph have unity? Explain.
4. How does the writer develop coherence in this paragraph?
5. Does the paragraph have adequate development? Explain.
6. Reread the paragraph. Draw a basic diagram that shows how the greenhouse effect works.
7. Without looking back at the paragraph, in one or two sentences, write your own definition of the term *greenhouse effect*.

8.5 What do you think?

Working with a partner or on your own, read the following definition paragraph. Answer the questions that follow the paragraph. Write your answers on separate paper.

Moochers

Moochers are people who obtain things by begging or imposing on others. Moochers do not pay or barter for the items they desire. Three kinds of moochers are common. The *empty-pocket moochers,* for a variety of reasons, lack financial resources to buy their own items. At times they have money, but they do not manage it wisely. Without any signs of embarrassment or wrongdoing, they ask their friends for cigarettes, cups of coffee, spare change, or rides to and from various locations around town. They time their visits so they arrive at their friends' homes just in time for lunch or dinner. These moochers seldom reciprocate the good deeds or services. The *street moochers* spend time on the streets asking strangers for money to buy food, cigarettes, a cup of coffee, or work. However, when people offer them work, they tend to decline. They feed on the goodwill and compassion of others. The *money-in-their-pocket moochers* are capable of purchasing their own items, but they habitually ask their family members, friends, and neighbors for free items instead of spending their own money. These moochers borrow cups of sugar, eggs, sticks of butter, gas for lawn mowers, stamps, or home office supplies without ever offering or intending to repay or reimburse others for their generosity. These moochers show little understanding of boundaries or social appropriateness. They just keep asking and just keep getting. Until family members, friends, and neighbors learn to say "No," moochers will continue to be rewarded and their mooching habits will continue to bring them positive results.

1. Is the topic sentence effective? Explain your answer.
2. What methods does the writer use to define the term *moocher?*
3. Does the paragraph have adequate development? Explain.
4. How does the writer develop coherence in this paragraph? What order does the writer use for the details? Is the order effective? Explain.
5. Is the concluding sentence effective for this paragraph? Explain.

The Writing Process for Definition Paragraphs

Step 1: Generate ideas.

Brainstorming works well to generate ideas for terms or expressions to define in your definition paragraph. Following are six categories that you can use to generate possible words or expressions to define. Enlarge the following chart on your own paper. Take two minutes per category to list as many terms or expressions that may be unfamiliar to your reader, or terms or expressions that you would like to interpret in an unusual way. Each category begins with an example.

WORDS THAT NAME FEELINGS OR EMOTIONS		TECHNICAL WORDS OR COURSE-SPECIFIC TERMS FROM ONE OF YOUR CLASSES		EXPRESSIONS OR IDIOMS (EXPRESSIONS THAT DO NOT HAVE LITERAL MEANINGS)	
fear	____________	CPR	____________	Out on a limb	____________
____________	____________	____________	____________	____________	____________
____________	____________	____________	____________	____________	____________
____________	____________	____________	____________	____________	____________

WORDS THAT END IN *-ISM*		WORDS THAT END IN *-IST*		WORDS THAT END IN *-HOOD*	
patriotism	____________	pessimist	____________	parenthood	____________
____________	____________	____________	____________	____________	____________
____________	____________	____________	____________	____________	____________
____________	____________	____________	____________	____________	____________

Another method you can use to generate ideas involves a dictionary. Open your dictionary and skim several pages. Identify possible words that are unusual or unfamiliar to your reader. Add the words to the brainstorming lists that you developed on separate paper.

Dictionary words	____________	____________	____________	____________	____________
	____________	____________	____________	____________	____________
	____________	____________	____________	____________	____________

Step 2: Get a focus.

Getting a focus for a definition paragraph involves selecting the term (a word or a phrase) to define. Use the following questions to help you select a term to use for your definition paragraph.

1. What is your purpose for writing a definition paragraph? Would the reader learn something valuable or useful? Would the reader see the word from a new perspective or interpretation? Would the reader be entertained or amused?
2. Are there enough different kinds of details you can use to expand the definition?
3. How familiar are you with the term? Do you need to do some research for additional details?

In addition to selecting the term to define, think about the category and the characteristics that distinguish the term from other words that belong to the same category. Use the following questions to help you focus your ideas before you begin Step 3.

1. Does the term belong to a larger category? For example, **agoraphobia** belongs to a larger category: abnormal fears.
2. What are some distinguishing characteristics that differentiate this term from other terms in the category? For example, **agoraphobia** refers to a fear of open spaces. Other kinds of phobias refer to fears of other situations or objects.

Step 3: Gather and organize information.

Gathering and organizing information involves three tasks: gather possible details to use, create an outline or a list of the details you intend to use, and write an effective topic sentence.

Gathering Different Kinds of Details

Begin gathering possible details that you can use to expand the basic definition of the word or expression you intend to define. Reference materials, such as a dictionary, a thesaurus, your textbooks, an encyclopedia, and the Internet are valuable resources to use to locate additional information to expand your definition. The following list shows the different kinds of details you can use in your paragraph. For the term you plan to define, jot down information for as many of the different kinds of details as possible. You will then have many options to consider for your paragraph.

Word or expression you plan to define: ____________

1. A formal dictionary definition
2. An informal definition expressed in your own words
3. Synonyms
4. Antonyms
5. A statement that tells what the term is *not*

6. Word history (found in dictionary)
7. Quotation
8. Short anecdote
9. Comparison to ____________
10. Contrast to ____________
11. Process (steps or stages)
12. Classification (categories)
13. Cause-effect
14. Exemplification (examples)

Creating a Basic Outline or a List of Details

After you gather as many different kinds of details as possible, select the ones that provide the reader with the clearest understanding of the term. Rewrite the information in a **basic outline** or a **list** that flows logically and smoothly. Experiment with the order of the details to achieve the best effect. Remember, as with all paragraphs, you may end up revising several times. One of your revisions may involve reordering the details. You can use the following three methods to organize your details.

1. *Formal to informal:* For example, begin with a formal definition, word history, or synonyms. Follow the formal information with other kinds of informal details.
2. *Informal to formal:* For example, begin with an informal definition, a statement that tells what the word is *not,* a quotation, or an anecdote. End the paragraph with a formal definition, synonyms, or word history.
3. *One form of discourse:* For example, begin with a comparison, contrast, process, classification, cause-effect, or exemplification. Expand the definition by using any of the other kinds of details at appropriate places throughout the paragraph.

Notice the order of the details in the following organizational lists for three previous paragraphs. In "Optimists," the writer could experiment with reordering the details. In "The Greenhouse Effect," the steps that explain the greenhouse effect must appear in chronological order; the writer has the option, however, of placing the last detail in the beginning of the paragraph. In "Moochers," the writer could experiment with rearranging the order of the categories because they do not need to appear in a fixed order.

"Optimists" (pages 312–313)

1. Characteristic—informal definition
2. Opposite of pessimists
3. Quotation
4. Behaviors and attitudes

5. Anecdote—Betsy
6. Formal definition

"The Greenhouse Effect" (Uses process) (page 323)

1. Formal definition
2. Solar radiation reaches earth
3. Earth absorbs some heat
4. Some heat radiates up
5. Greenhouse gases trap heat
6. Heat radiates back
7. Significance

(Items 2–6: Steps in the process)

"Moochers," (Uses classification) (page 324)

1. Empty-pocket moochers—have no money
   - Informal definition
   - Examples
2. Street moochers—sometimes have money
   - Informal definition
   - Examples
3. Money-in-their-pocket moocher—have money
   - Informal definition
   - Examples

Writing a Topic Sentence

Use the suggestions on pages 314–315 for writing effective topic sentences. You have many options, so write several possible topic sentences. Revise until an effective topic sentence emerges.

Step 4: Write the rough draft.

Begin the paragraph with the topic sentence. Then use your list of details from Step 3 to develop the paragraph. When appropriate, use transition words to connect ideas and use sentence-combining techniques to add sentence variety that includes simple, compound, and complex sentences. Double space when you write your draft so you have room to revise, proofread, and edit. End with a concluding sentence that echoes the topic sentence or refers to the controlling idea (the term being defined) in the topic sentence.

Step 5: Revise, revise, revise.

Select a specific aspect of the paragraph to analyze and evaluate. You can use the following checklist to guide the revision process.

1. Is there an effective topic sentence? Does the body of the paragraph follow the informal outline or list of details from Step 3? Does the paragraph have an effective concluding sentence?
2. Does your paragraph have adequate development? Do you have enough different details to expand the definition? Do you think the reader will have a clear understanding of the term after reading your paragraph? If not, how can you strengthen your paragraph?
3. Does your paragraph have unity? Do all the details support the controlling idea and develop the definition? Does the paragraph stay focused on the term and its definition?
4. Does your paragraph have coherence? Do the details flow smoothly and logically? Should one or more sentences be reordered? Would the ideas flow together more smoothly with the addition of transition words?
5. Is the concluding sentence closely related to the topic sentence? Does it echo the topic sentence or refer to the controlling idea that you expressed in the topic sentence?

8.6 What do you think?

Working with a partner or on your own, read the following paragraph and answer the questions that follow. Write your answers on separate paper.

Over the Hill

Ronnie's friends, all wearing black, gathered to recognize that Ronnie was *over the hill*. Ronnie did not do anything as taxing as hike up a hill and descend down the back side; no, Ronnie simply had his fiftieth birthday. The term *over the hill* implies many things. First, it implies that the half-century mark is the halfway point in a person's life; it assumes that the person will live to be one hundred years old. Second, it implies that a person reaches his or her pinnacle or peak at the age of fifty. After fifty, life goes downhill along with health, fulfilling activities, career performance, happiness, and lifestyle in general. Because many people have proven that life does not go downhill after the age of fifty, a person's fiftieth birthday can be a joyful, memory-building time filled with humor, teasing, and celebration. Finally, the term *over the hill* implies that the best things in life have already happened. Many people over the age of fifty dispute this notion as they find immense joy in the later years of their lives. They finally have more time to travel, pursue hobbies, and get involved in community service. They are able to spoil their grandchildren and watch them grow. They are able to sleep whenever they feel tired, stay up late if they want, or sleep in any day of the week. During Ronnie's *over the hill* party, he announced that the view on the other side of the mountain is spectacular.

1. Does the paragraph use the standard paragraph structure with a topic sentence, a body with supporting details, and a concluding sentence? Explain.
2. Does the paragraph have adequate development? What kinds of details does the writer use to expand the definition? Explain.
3. Does the paragraph have unity? Do all the details support the controlling idea and develop the definition? Explain.
4. Does the paragraph have coherence? Do the details flow smoothly and logically? Should one or more sentences be reordered? Would the ideas flow together more smoothly with the addition of transition words? Explain.
5. Is the concluding sentence closely related to the topic sentence? Does it echo the topic sentence or refer to the controlling idea that is expressed in the topic sentence?

8.7 What do you think?

Working with a partner or on your own, read the following paragraph and answer the questions that follow. Write your answers on separate paper.

S & P 500

The **S & P 500** is an index of the stock market. It groups the biggest 500 companies in all markets: the New York Stock Exchange, NASDAQ, and the American Stock Exchange. The S & P 500 is given a symbol, SPT. Anyone can buy the index at the price of the market. The S & P is a good measure of the stability of the stock market. In a good year, the S & P may be up 20%. Every year the S & P picks the new and profitable companies. The first Internet companies of the S & P were Ebay and Yahoo.

Michael Morcos
Bellevue Community College
Bellevue, Washington

1. Does the paragraph use the standard paragraph structure with a topic sentence, a body with supporting details, and a concluding sentence? Explain.
2. Does the paragraph have adequate development? Does the paragraph have enough different details to expand the definition? Explain.
3. Does the paragraph have unity? Do all the details support the controlling idea and develop the definition? Explain.
4. Does the paragraph have coherence? Do the details flow smoothly and logically? Should one or more sentences be reordered? Would the ideas flow more smoothly with the addition of transition words? Explain.

5. Does the paragraph have an effective concluding sentence? If yes, explain why it is effective. If no, write a concluding sentence for the paragraph.
6. In your own words, what is the S & P 500?

Step 6: Proofread and edit.

Use the Grammar and Usage Tips from the previous chapters to proofread and edit your paragraph. Correct any mechanical or sentence errors in your definition paragraph. Use the following checklist to guide your proofreading and editing work.

1. Does every sentence have a subject and a complete verb and form a complete thought so it can stand on its own?
2. Is there sentence variety in the paragraph? Do you use compound subjects or compound verbs? Does the paragraph have a variety of simple, compound, and complex sentences?
3. Do you use the correct punctuation between words in a series, between two independent clauses (compound sentences), and between dependent and independent clauses (complex sentences)? Do you use the correct punctuation for appositives and participial phrases?
4. Have you corrected any fragments, comma splice errors, and run-on sentence errors?
5. Do you use correct spelling?
6. Do you use participles correctly? Do past and present participles that are intended to be the verb for the clause have helping verbs?
7. Have you corrected any dangling participles? Do all the participial phrases at the beginning of sentences refer to the closest noun, the subject of the sentence?
8. Do you use appositives and participial phrases effectively and correctly? Do they appear next to the noun or the pronoun they modify?
9. Do the subjects and the verbs in every sentence agree?
10. Do pronouns and antecedents agree in number and gender?

Step 7: Prepare the final version of your definition paragraph.

Follow your instructor's directions for preparing the final version of your paragraph. As always, save all your prewriting materials, your rough draft, and your revisions. You may be asked to turn them in with the final version of your work.

WRITING ASSIGNMENT

Select a term to define. Write an expanded definition of the term. Include an appropriate number of details to explain the term to your reader.

Complete each of the following steps for writing a definition paragraph. Unless your instructor assigns a different approach, use the Definition Paragraph Planning Sheet on page 333 for each step of the writing process. Save all your prewriting and draft materials.

Step 1: Generate ideas.
Select a term or expression to define from your brainstorming list. You may add to your brainstorming list, or you may use one of the following terms or expressions to define:

independence	emancipation	tolerance	patience	virtues
excellence	persistence	intelligence	wit	common sense
confidant	snitch	con artist	mentor	jealousy
perfectionist	activist	anarchist	capitalism	spoonerism
oxymoron	nurturing parent	genuine friend	white lie	hot merchandise

Step 2: Get a focus.
Think about the term in a formal sense. What larger category does the term belong to? What are some distinguishing characteristics? Write your answers on the Planning Sheet.

Step 3: Gather and organize information.
On separate paper, jot down possible ideas to use for each of the different kinds of details shown on pages 326–327. On the Planning Sheet, make an outline or a list to show the order of the details you intend to use in the paragraph. Write several possible topic sentences on the Planning Sheet. Star the one you prefer.

Step 4: Write a rough draft.
On the Planning Sheet, indicate when you completed the rough draft.

Step 5: Revise, revise, revise.
Use the revision checklist on page 329 to guide you through the revision process. Revise at least once. Save your revisions. Share your revised draft with a partner and ask your partner to complete the feedback questions on the Planning Sheet.

Step 6: Proofread and edit.
Use the checklist on page 331 to guide you through the proofreading and editing process.

Step 7: Prepare the final version of your paragraph.

DEFINITION PARAGRAPH PLANNING SHEET

Name ______________________

Step 1: Write your brainstorming lists for terms to define on separate paper.

Step 2: Write the term you will define in your paragraph: ______________________

What larger category does this term belong to? ______________________

What are some distinguishing characteristics that make this term different from other terms in the same category? ______________________

____

Step 3: On separate paper, jot down possible details to use for each of the kinds of details shown on pages 326–327. Select the most effective details to use. In the space below, write a list or an outline that shows the order of the specific details you intend to use in the body of your definition paragraph.

Write several possible topic sentences. Star the most effective topic sentence for your definition paragraph.

1. ______________________
2. ______________________
3. ______________________
4. ______________________

Step 4: When did you complete the rough draft? ______________________

Step 5: Ask a partner to read your paragraph and respond to the following questions.

PARTNER FEEDBACK FORM

1. Did you get a clear understanding of the term that the writer defines in this paragraph?

   Explain. ____

   ____

2. Does the paragraph have adequate development? Are the choice of details effective?

   Explain. ____

   ____

   ____

   ____

3. Does the paragraph have unity? Explain. ______________________________

   ____

   ____

4. Does the paragraph have coherence? How does the writer achieve coherence in the paragraph? Explain. ______________________________

   ____

   ____

5. How could the writer strengthen this paragraph? ______________________________

   ____

6. What, if any, mechanical or sentence errors do you notice that the writer needs to edit? Be specific.

7. What did you like about this paragraph?

Partner's name ______________________________

Step 6: Write the date that you finished proofreading and editing: ______________________

Step 7: Prepare the final version of your definition paragraph.

Grammar and Usage Tips

An effective style of writing is developed through **diction,** the careful choice and use of words that are appropriate for your audience. This chapter discusses four aspects of diction: denotation and connotation, levels of diction, cliches, and euphemisms. After you complete the exercises for these four grammar and usage tips, carefully check your work with the answer keys in Appendix A and record your number of errors for each exercise. Review the tip and examine the correct answer. In the margins of each exercise, jot down any questions you would like to ask your instructor regarding the grammar and usage points covered in the exercises.

TIP 25 **Attend to the denotation and connotation of words so that you clearly convey the images, definitions, and meanings you intend to convey. *Denotation* is the explicit meaning of a word as it is defined in a dictionary. *Connotation* is the meaning that goes beyond the literal dictionary definition. Connotations often suggest or imply a positive or negative meaning of the word; dictionaries often give connotations after the definition. To make the best choice of words, use a dictionary to explore and fully understand the connotations of words.**

Denotation, an explicit dictionary or textbook definition, provides a formal definition for a word or an expression. Denotation is especially important when you are explaining a technical term or a key word that may be unfamiliar to your reader or when you are defining a textbook term on a test. When you use the exact words from a dictionary or a textbook to define a term, place quotation marks around the words to indicate that the definition is quoted from a specific source. In the following example, an explicit dictionary definition (denotation) appears in bold print.

> According to *Webster's New World Compact Desk Dictionary,* the *greenhouse effect* is **"the warming of the earth and its lower atmosphere, caused by trapped solar radiation."**
>
> She exemplifies *The American Heritage Dictionary*'s definition of an *optimist:* **"One who habitually or in a particular case expects a favorable outcome."**
>
> *Fibromyalgia,* defined by Medscape as **"a chronic disorder characterized by widespread muscular pain, fatigue, and tenderness in one or more tender points on the body,"** afflicts more than 4 million Americans.

Connotation refers to the ideas or associations connected to the word (apart from the word's literal meaning). In a comprehensive dictionary, connotations for some words appear after the formal definitions in a section labeled *synonyms.* In the following example from the New Collegiate Edition of *The American Heritage Dictionary,* the connotation for the word *comfortable,* as well as the connotations for its synonyms, helps you select the most appropriate word for the context of your sentence.

> **com•fort•a•ble** (kŭm′fər•tə•bəl, kŭmf′tə•bəl) *adj.* **1.** Providing physical comfort: *a comfortable chair.* **2.** Free from stress or anxiety; at ease: *not comfortable about the interview.* **3.** Producing feelings of ease or security: *a comfortable person; a comfortable evening at home.* **4.** Sufficient to provide financial security: *comfortable earnings.*—**com′fort•a•ble•ness** *n.* —**com′fort•a•bly** *adv.*
>
> ***Synonyms*** *comfortable, cozy, snug, restful* These adjectives mean affording ease of mind or body. *Comfortable* implies the absence of sources of pain or distress: *wears comfortable clothes.* The word may also suggest peace of mind: *felt comfortable with the decision. Cozy* suggests homey and reassuring ease: *sat in a cozy nook near the fire.* Snug brings to mind the image of a warm, secure, compact shelter: *children snug in their beds. Restful* suggests a quiet conducive to tranquillity: *spent a restful hour reading.*

In the following example, each of the words means **not beautiful,** yet each word has varying connotations and evokes different reactions from the reader.

The beautician is **unattractive.**	The beautician is **ugly.**
The beautician is **homely.**	The beautician is **plain.**

Each of the following words refers to a person's body weight, yet reactions to each word differ because of connotation.

That person is **slender.**	That person is **thin.**
That person is **lean.**	That person is **skinny.**
That person is **scrawny.**	That person is **anorexic.**

Use a dictionary when you are uncertain about the denotation and the connotation of a word, especially when you are using synonyms. Select words that are consistent with the overall tone of your writing.

EXERCISE 8.1 Quoting Definitions

Score: ______

Use a dictionary to quote definitions for the following terms. In your definition, cite the source and place quotation marks around the exact dictionary words. Write your answers on separate paper.

1. irony	2. gourmet	3. preposterous	4. alliteration	5. cumulus
6. blockade	7. clairvoyance	8. simulcast	9. emigrate	10. volt

EXERCISE 8.2 Using Connotation Correctly

Score: ______

Working with a partner or on your own, read each sentence carefully to get a sense of the desired tone (the attitude or emotion) of the sentence. Three words (synonyms) appear at the end of the sentence. Circle the word that is the best word choice for the context of the sentence.

1. In an act of desperation, my roommate ________ me to lend him $100 so he could make his car payment. (asked, begged, ordered)
2. At my last job, I worked diligently to produce high-quality work. However, my employer was so ________ that nothing ever seemed to be up to his standards or expectations. (fastidious, prudish, oversensitive)
3. An angry ________ gathered outside the hotel where the World Trade Organization held its meeting. (group, crowd, mob)
4. The young actress was ________ when she appeared on stage to receive her Oscar for her performance in the box-office hit. (glad, exuberant, jolly)
5. I could hardly catch my breath when I learned that a distant uncle had left me $100,000 in his will. I was ________ because I had never even met this relative. (surprised, amused, flabbergasted)
6. My husband's family was ________ , but they refused to seek public assistance. All the children learned to be self-sufficient and supportive of each other. (disadvantaged, needy, deprived)
7. President Wallen's decision to resign is a/an ________ loss for the University, for he brought prestige and excellence to the entire university system. (big, vast, immense)
8. I worked in that candidate's campaign office. I ________ her commitment to the community and to her personal principles; I wish I could create that much passion in my own life. (idolize, admire, like)
9. The car salesmen tried to convince me that the ________ was rare and that it would not remain on the lot for much longer. (car, jalopy, vehicle)
10. My grandpa Amos is an expert storyteller; however, he ________ a story to such a degree that we never know what to believe. When he tells about my first prom date, I wonder if he was on someone else's front porch that night. (embellishes, expands, improves)

TIP 26 **Use formal language in most college expository writing. Avoid using informal language, also known as *colloquial* language. Informal language includes word choices that have a casual and conversational tone and slang. Dictionaries label words as informal (or colloquial), slang, or vulgar (obscene). Words that do not have a label in a dictionary are formal words. Refer to a dictionary if you are uncertain of the status of a particular word.**

In selecting the proper tone in your writing, consider the following factors:

1. *The vocabulary level of your readers.* Formal words that are outside of your readers' level of understanding will lead to confusion and misinterpretation and will sound unnatural. Select words that express your ideas but do not overwhelm your readers.
2. *The need at times to use words that may be unfamiliar to your readers.* At times, you may find that you need to use technical terms or unfamiliar words to express a specific idea. In such cases, define the unfamiliar word so your readers can fully understand the ideas you are conveying.
3. *The level of diction or the level of formality that is expected in your writing.* If you are writing a formal report, paper, or essay, you will want to use formal English and avoid using colloquialisms, slang, or obscene or offensive wording. If your writing is informal, such as writing in a journal or writing a personal letter, informal language is acceptable.
4. *The tone that you intend to convey.* The topics for some writing assignments may lend themselves to informal writing. If you are recounting an event, such as in a narrative, in which an informal tone seems more appropriate, informal language is acceptable. For most college expository writing, however, you should use the formal tone.

Levels of Language

The English language is fluid; it changes, grows, and expands. Some words that once were considered vulgar are now considered slang. While most slang words become outdated, some slang words over time may be reclassified as informal (also called colloquial). Through continued use and acceptance, some colloquial words may eventually be classified as formal.

In your first draft of a paper, slang or colloquial language may appear as a reflection of your informal, conversational way of speaking. As you revise your written work, watch for informal words and slang; replace them with more formal alternatives. By using formal language, your writing will be more polished, effective, and appropriate for college-level writing. In the following examples, formal language replaces slang expressions.

Informal	**Formal**	**Sentence Revision**
really get into	enjoy and appreciate	enjoy and appreciate I ~~really get into~~ soft jazz and light rock music.
hang out	spend time together	spend time together We often ~~hang out~~ on Friday nights.

In the following examples, formal language replaces informal language and slang words.

INFORMAL	FORMAL	INFORMAL	FORMAL
folks	parents or relatives	kids	children
lots of	many	nice	considerate
cute	attractive	junk bond	speculative bond
real sharp	extremely sharp	pretty clever	quite clever

EXERCISE 8.3 Shifting from Informal to Formal Language

Score: ________

Above each slang expression (in italics), substitute a formal equivalent that would be appropriate in a college paper.

Example: Cornelius was ~~all jazzed up~~ excited about the opportunity to audition for the role.

1. I get *ticked off* when she starts acting *as dumb as a doorknob.*
2. I *crashed* on the couch to take a short *snooze.*
3. Shelley has *a bunch of* problems that she needs to *get a handle on* before they *get the best of her.*
4. You look *kind of cute* in those *duds.*
5. The movie was *the bomb.* I would like to *cruise by* Hollywood Videos and rent it again.
6. My partner gets *uptight* whenever I want to *chill* with my friends from school.
7. I think it is *cool* that you want to meet him, but I think it will *mess up* your relationship with Maurice.

8. The contestant was *stumped by* the question; only a *nerd* would know that answer.
9. I was *really bushed* after I *worked my tail off* all day on the farm.
10. You are *awfully stupid* to believe that *baloney.*

Contractions

Contractions, another type of informal writing, are a shortened form of two words. An apostrophe indicates the place where a letter or letters have been omitted when the two words were combined. In formal writing, avoid using contractions. Instead, use the two individual words that the contraction represents. The following list shows contractions and the words they represent.

FORMAL INFORMAL	FORMAL INFORMAL	FORMAL INFORMAL	FORMAL INFORMAL
I am = I'm	I had = I'd	I would = I'd	was not = wasn't
it is = it's	you had = you'd	you would = you'd	were not = weren't
he is = he's	he had = he'd	he would = he'd	has not = hasn't
she is = she's	she had = she'd	she would = she'd	have not = haven't
you are = you're	it had = it'd	it would = it'd	had not = hadn't
we are = we're	we had = we'd	we would = we'd	does not = doesn't
they are = they're	they had = they'd	they would = they'd	do not = don't
it has = it's	I will = I'll	let us = let's	did not = didn't
he has = he's	you will = you'll	what is = what's	should not = shouldn't
she has = she's	it will = it'll	who is = who's	would not = wouldn't
I have = I've	she will = she'll	where is = where's	could not = couldn't
you have = you've	he will = he'll	there is = there's	cannot = can't
we have = we've	they will = they'll	is not = isn't	will not = won't
they have = they've		are not = aren't	

TIP 27 Avoid using cliches in your formal writing. Cliches are overused expressions that have lost their effectiveness. Use fresh and more effective expressions in your writing rather than relying on tired cliches.

The English language is full of cliches. The following list shows only a few of the many common cliches that may have been effective in the past, but today evoke little emotional response from readers.

take a bull by the horns	break a leg	over the hill
as sharp as a tack	as wise as an owl	born with a silver spoon
a crying shame	green with envy	as fat as a pig
cry your eyes out	under the weather	sad but true
workhorse	too little, too late	short but sweet
sick and tired of it	drop in the bucket	dumber than a doorknob

between a rock and a hard place	poorer than sin	filthy rich
cooking up a storm	kindled my fire	last but not least
as angry as a bear	older but wiser	missed the boat
joined at the hip	as strong as an ox	as quick as a flash of light

EXERCISE 8.4 Replacing Cliches with Formal Language

Score: ______

Select any ten cliches from the preceding list. Write a sentence that uses the cliche. Replace the cliche with words or an expression that is formal language. Using the following format, write your sentences on separate paper.

Cliche: joined at the hip

Revised sentence: My daughter and her best friend Carlita ~~are joined at the hip~~. spend endless hours together.

TIP 28 **Use euphemisms sparingly. The American Heritage Dictionary defines *euphemism* as a "mild, indirect, or vague term that is substituted for a harsh, blunt, or offensive one." In other words, euphemisms attempt to soften a message and make it less offensive or disturbing. Limited use of euphemisms is acceptable if you want to protect the reader from blunt statements of a disturbing nature, but in general, it is better to use direct, straightforward language in college writing.**

If you have ever had a loved one die, you most likely heard euphemisms when people consoled you. Instead of saying that they were sorry to hear that your loved one died, they would say that they were sorry to hear that he or she *passed away, moved on to another world, made his or her transition,* or *departed this world.* The intent behind these euphemisms is to express sensitivity, kindness, and empathy. Other times people use euphemisms to mislead or falsely represent a status or a situation. The following list shows some common euphemisms and their more direct wording.

EUPHEMISM	=	DIRECT WORDING
senior citizens, people in their golden years	=	the elderly
disadvantaged	=	poor
adult entertainment	=	pornography
left unattended	=	abandoned

(Continue on page 342)

EUPHEMISM	=	DIRECT WORDING
pre-owned, recycled	=	used/second-hand
inner city	=	slums/ghetto
released due to restructuring, given notice	=	fired
gave their lives for	=	killed (as in war)
strategic withdrawal	=	retreat, defeat
would benefit from exercise	=	overweight
did less than satisfactory work	=	failed
under-motivated	=	lazy
modular home	=	pre-fabricated home
customer service charge	=	fee
corporal punishment	=	spanking

EXERCISE 8.5 **Rewording Euphemisms**

Score: ______

Write a more direct, straightforward word for the following euphemisms.

1. sanitation engineer
   ____
2. put to sleep
   ____
3. less than honest person
   ____
4. hair color enhancer
   ____
5. person who does not work up to his or her potential
   ____
6. marriage dissolution
   ____
7. inappropriately borrowed
   ____
8. outside of your means
   ____
9. not inexpensive
   ____
10. did less than acceptable work
    ____

Grammar and Usage Tips Summary

TIP 25 Be aware of the denotation and connotation of words you use to convey images, expand definitions, and express your ideas. Denotation is the formal dictionary or textbook definition. Connotation refers to the association or subtle emotions connected to a word beyond its literal meaning.

TIP 26 Use formal language in most expository writing. Avoid informal language and a conversational tone. Avoid using slang, contractions, and obscenities.

TIP 27 Avoid using cliches, which are expressions that have been overused and have lost their effectiveness. Instead, use fresh and more effective expressions in your writing.

TIP 28 Use euphemisms sparingly.

CHAPTER 8 • Definition Paragraphs • Proofreading and Editing Exercises

Proofreading 1

Proofread the following definition paragraph. Strengthen the paragraph through more effective word choices for the words shown in italics. Substitute formal language for informal language.

Criticism

Criticism, as defined by *The American Heritage Dictionary,* is "the act of criticizing; esp. adversely." Criticism may be directed toward a person's actions, behaviors, decisions, or work. Though the receiver of criticism often interprets the comment as negative, the intent behind the criticism may be to help the person improve or change. For example, I criticize my son because he is the *biggest slob on the face of the earth.* His room looks like *a hurricane hit.* Dirty and clean clothes cover his bedroom floor. His *junk* is everywhere in the house. *It's totally unreal* and *it's driving me nuts.* After he *grabs* something to eat, he leaves food scraps and *gook* all over the kitchen counter. He stacks his dirty dishes in the sink without ever thinking a little water to rinse them might *not hurt.* Through my criticism, I want him to *get it* that taking personal pride in his belonging and showing a *good* sense of responsibility for his actions will benefit him *in the long run.* I want him to *get down to earth* and *grow up.* Another example of criticism with a positive intent comes from my writing instructor. He always writes *bunches* of comments all over my paper. His comments are a form of criticism designed to instruct me on ways to improve the quality of my work. I *kind of* feel *a little bent out of shape* with some of his comments, but overall, I try to learn from his comments. Criticism, in the long run, is a roadmap to meet the ideals that some other *guy* has established. Responding to critical comments can lead to actions, behaviors, decisions, and work that meet higher standards and are worthy of praise and recognition.

Proofreading 2

Reread your Writing Warm-Up 8 and one other Writing Warm-Up that you have already completed. Highlight any informal or slang words or expressions. Use a dictionary or thesaurus to locate formal words or expressions that you can substitute for the informal language. Write your revisions above the words or expressions that you highlighted in the paragraph.

Internet Enrichment

Log on to the web site for this textbook for additional exercises and links for the following topics:

Definition Paragraphs
Synonyms
Antonyms
Word History/Etymology
Denotation and Connotation
Cliches
Euphemisms

Go to: http://college.hmco.com. Click on "Students." Type *Paragraph Essentials* in the "Jump to Textbook Sites" box. Click "go," and then bookmark the site.

CHAPTER 8 • Grammar and Usage Review

Name ______________________________

Date ______________________________

Word Choice

Use a dictionary or a thesaurus to substitute a more effective choice of words for the words in italics.

1. Shannon is *pretty* creative; her sculptures reflect her talent.

2. The reception was *real nice*, but it was not *cheap*.

3. The Financial Aid papers were *sort of hard* to understand.

4. Your presentation was *good*; you convinced me to change my point of view.

5. Your landscaped yard is *real pretty*.

Formal Language

Cross out words or expressions that are informal language, slang, cliches, or euphemisms. Substitute formal language for each of these words or expressions. Write your new choice of words in the space above the sentence.

1. My brother-in-law prefers to sponge off everyone instead of getting a job and making his own way.

2. I think the guy in the news got a bum rap from the top brass.

3. I want to jazz up this room with new furniture, but money doesn't grow on trees.

4. This new boom box is nifty.

5. Jacquie wants to score a position in the company that is a notch higher.

6. Muhammed is the spitting image of his father.

7. You can stay at my pad until you land a job.

8. You're a chicken if you don't try to make the team.

Contractions

Replace informal language with formal language by writing the original two words above the contractions in the following sentences.

1. There's something for everyone on the Wheel of Fear.
2. I'd be so terrified that I couldn't move.
3. It's a muscular disorder that afflicts adults.
4. They're continuing to research the cause of this disorder.
5. Don't use cliches in formal writing.
6. There won't be ample space to make corrections.
7. I've wasted too much time on this project.
8. You'd be promoted to the position of marketing manager.
9. They'd train you and pay your travel expenses.
10. You should've notified your advisor before you dropped your classes.

Connotations

Circle the word that is most appropriate for the context of each sentence.

1. My parents purchased a cozy ________ (dwelling, bungalow, shack) on a river bank for their weekend retreats.
2. Ruth is not happy that her husband has become a ________ (workaholic, hard worker, working man).
3. The neighborhood children are afraid of old Mr. Blackwell because of his ________ (unusual, eccentric, quaint) behavior.
4. The two professors frequently ________ (talk, chatter, converse) about current research studies.
5. The sales associates resented the way Michael boasted about his sales record and ________ (showed, exhibited, flaunted) his "Salesman of the Year Award."
6. The board of directors ordered the vice-president to ________ (yield, forgo, relinquish) her duties as the budget director.

CHAPTER 9

Cause-Effect Paragraphs

The topic sentence introduces the cause-effect relationship and establishes the controlling idea.

The body provides supporting details to explain the cause-effect relationship.

The concluding sentence echoes the topic sentence or summarizes the paragraph.

Topic Sentence with a controlling idea ....

cause → effect
→ effect

Unity + Coherence + Adequate Development

Concluding Sentence..

In Chapter 9 you will learn about the following:

1. The cause-effect paragraph and its structure
2. The writing process for cause-effect paragraphs
3. The final two grammar and usage tips

WRITING WARM-UP 9

Write about a recent situation in your life that shows one event that occurred *because of* a previous event. Use the word *because* in your opening sentence. For example:

I was late getting home *because* the main thoroughfares were flooded.

My girl friend was annoyed with me *because* I forgot an important event.

I received a bonus *because* my sales doubled last month.

The Cause-Effect Paragraph

A cause-effect paragraph examines or analyzes a relationship between actions or events. The paragraph explains why or how an action or event causes one or more other actions or events to occur. The first action (the **cause**), creates, changes, or influences a second action and produces a specific outcome (the **effect**). For example, imagine you are driving through a woody area and a deer suddenly jumps out in front of you, causing you to swerve and hit a tree. The deer jumping onto the road was the *cause* of the accident; the accident was the *effect*.

Understanding and writing about cause-effect relationships require analytical thought processes and critical thinking skills. When writing cause-effect paragraphs, it is essential that you distinguish which action occurs first as the cause and which action follows as the effect. At the sentence level, sometimes you will state the cause first, but other times you will lead with the effect.

When [the wind suddenly shifted]cause (first action), the [hot air balloon left our field of vision]effect (outcome).

[Frequent absences]cause (first action) led to the [installation of a time clock]effect (outcome).

[Marina's self-confidence has soared]effect (outcome) since she [became a member of the debate team]cause (first action).

[Fifty passengers aboard the cruise ship were taken to the hospital]effect (outcome) [after experiencing nausea and dizziness]cause (first action).

A cause-effect paragraph can include more than one cause or more than one effect. Given the boundaries and length limitations of a paragraph, however, it is best not to include too much information by discussing multiple causes and multiple effects. The following topic sentences and diagrams, appropriate for treatment in a paragraph, show either multiple causes or multiple effects.

[Excessive gambling]one cause creates [numerous problems in people's lives]multiple effects (outcomes).

gambling →
- loss of income
- denial and excuses
- inability to pay bills
- relationship problems

[I am able to make significant changes in my life]multiple effects (outcomes) because [I received a full scholarship]one cause.

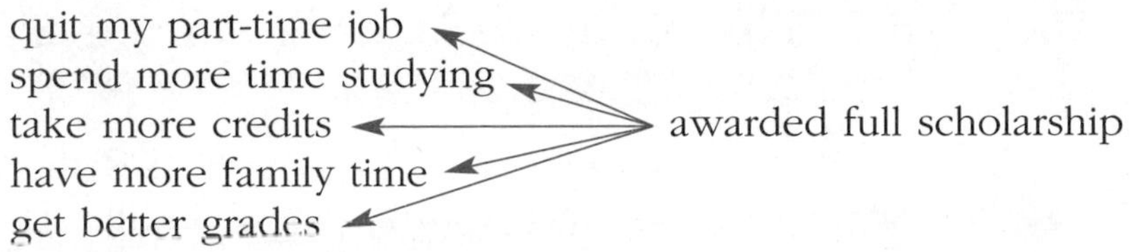

quit my part-time job
spend more time studying
take more credits ← awarded full scholarship
have more family time
get better grades

You may choose to write your cause-effect paragraph in first person (using I) or in third person. The first person is useful when you are writing a cause-effect paragraph about a situation you know from direct experience. The third person is useful to discuss a relationship between actions or events that happened to someone else or that happened outside of your own life. Social science and science books commonly use third-person cause-effect paragraphs. Read and examine the following cause-effect paragraph, the notes in the margin, and the diagram that follows the paragraph.

Older Brains

Topic sentence with a controlling idea

The first cause is explained.

The second cause is explained.

There is no concluding sentence because this is part of a longer piece of writing.

The human brain in late adulthood is [effect: smaller and slower in its functioning] than the brain in early adulthood because [causes: of two changes] that occur in the brain. The [cause # 1: death of neurons], which do not regenerate, is thought to be one cause. Neurons die at an increasing rate over age 60. The proportion of neurons that die varies across different parts of the brain. In the visual area, the death rate is about 50 percent. In the motor areas, the death rate varies from 20 to 50 percent. In the memory and reasoning areas, the death rate is less than 20 percent. [cause # 2: The production of certain neurotransmitters] also declines with age. Dendritic connections (connections made from the dendrites of one cell to portions of other cells), however, continue to form throughout the lifespan.

[Adapted from: David Payne, Michael Wenger, *Cognitive Psychology*, Houghton Mifflin 1998, p. 359.]

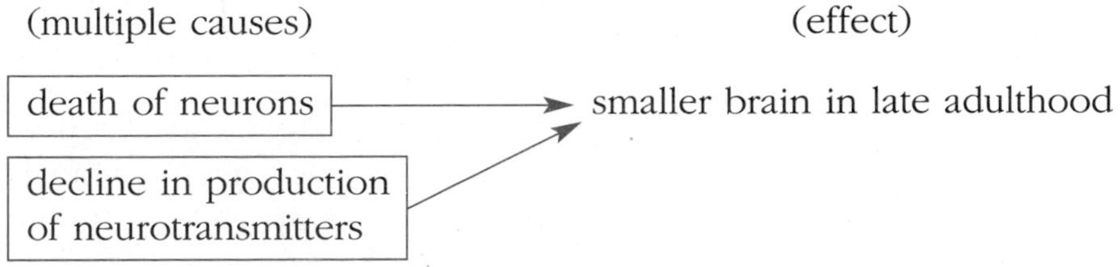

(multiple causes)		(effect)
death of neurons	→	smaller brain in late adulthood
decline in production of neurotransmitters	→	

The Structure of a Cause-Effect Paragraph

A cause-effect paragraph uses the standard three-part structure: topic sentence with a controlling idea, body with supporting details, and a concluding sentence. In a longer piece of writing, a transition sentence that links the paragraph to the next paragraph may replace a concluding sentence. The cause-effect paragraphs that you will write in this chapter should be able to stand alone, so you will use a concluding sentence. As with all paragraphs, when you write a cause-effect paragraph, you must focus on the three key elements of a paragraph: *unity*, *coherence*, and *adequate development*.

Developing the Topic Sentence

Use the following guidelines to write an effective topic sentence with a controlling idea that reveals your point of view, opinion, or attitude toward the subject of your paragraph.

1. Select a cause-effect relationship to write about that has interest, depth, or widespread significance to your audience. A reader does not necessarily want or need to know why you woke up one hour late or the reasons you chose to order a pizza. In other words, strive to write a cause-effect paragraph that is expository, teaches your reader important information, makes an interesting point, or shows your reader the significance of a specific action.
2. Do not try to include too much information in your topic sentence. Instead, generalize in a way that sets up the more specific points that will follow in the body of the paragraph. A topic sentence with too many clauses or too many details will not capture your reader's attention.

   Too long: Public concern about the content of rap music has increased because reports show that more hours are spent listening to music, teenagers do model what they perceive as being cool, and the music desensitizes teenagers to conditions that others know are wrong, amoral, or unethical.

   More appropriate: Public concern about the content of rap music has increased after the release of several studies on teenage behavior.

3. Use a **cause-effect signal word** in the topic sentence. The following words signal to your reader that a discussion of a cause-effect relationship will follow the topic sentence.

SIGNAL WORDS FOR CAUSE-EFFECT			
as a result of	affects	because	brings about
causes	creates	consequence of	effects
leads to	makes	outcomes	produces
reasons	results	why	

4. State the cause-effect relationship in your topic sentence. If you are going to present multiple causes or multiple effects, use a plural word, such as *causes, reasons, effects, consequences,* or *outcomes,* rather than a list of all the causes or all the effects in the topic sentence.

   Rapid global warming [cause] will result in serious consequences for our planet [effects].

   Several health conditions [effects] are associated with chewing tobacco [cause].

   Many employers resist the unionization of their work force [effect] because of the costs for additional employee benefits and the loss of their decision-making power [causes].

9.1 What do you think?

Check the topic sentences that you think could function as effective topic sentences for a cause-effect paragraph.

_______ 1. I had an injury in 1998.

_______ 2. Failure to abide by safety standards on the job can lead to work-related accidents.

_______ 3. My teenager volunteers in community projects for several reasons.

_______ 4. The massive recall of tires created many problems for dealerships.

_______ 5. Lying to your best friend causes many problems.

_______ 6. Several work conditions at the plant led to the strike.

_______ 7. Poor urban planning resulted in a lack of essential infrastructures.

_______ 8. Destruction of the rain forests accelerates global warming.

_______ 9. The river beds were bone dry.

_______ 10. Use of antibiotics should be limited.

Developing the Body of the Paragraph

Use the following guidelines to develop the body of your paragraph and the controlling idea stated in your topic sentence.

1. Identify the specific causes and effects in your cause-effect relationship. The cause is the first action. The effect is the consequence or the outcome of the first action. The following diagrams show several options for a cause-effect paragraph. Notice that there may be multiple causes or multiple effects and that the order of the cause and the effect in a sentence may vary.

2. Identify two, three, or four of the most significant causes or effects when there are multiple causes or multiple effects. Exclude causes or effects that are less significant.

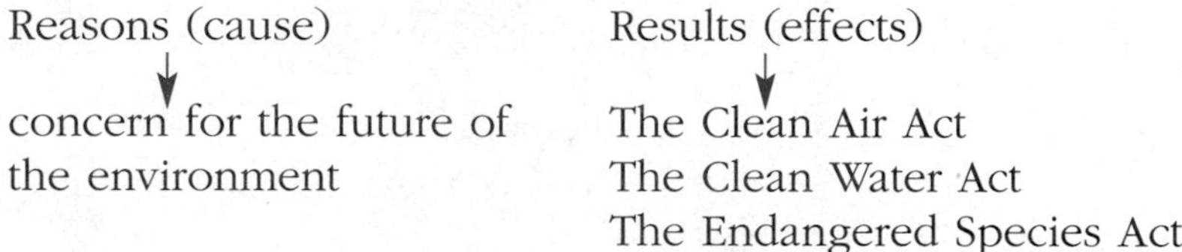

3. Achieve *unity* by limiting the supporting details to those that explain or support the topic sentence and the controlling idea. Exclude details that sidetrack from the topic sentence. Maintain a focus on the primary causes and effects throughout the paragraph.
4. Achieve *coherence* by using the following methods.
   a. Organize the details chronologically or emphatically (by order of importance). Use the organizational pattern that provides your reader with the most logical sequence of actions or events. You may want to experiment with different sequences of details to find the sequence that is the most effective and powerful to present your ideas to the reader.

      Use **chronological order** when you begin the paragraph with the first action (the cause) and then proceed to explain the effects in the order the effects occur. (See "Autumn Leaves" on page 355 for an example.) In some instances, one effect causes another effect, which produces a chain of effects in chronological order. You can also use reverse chronological order; that is, you can begin the paragraph with the most recent effect and move through time to the most distant action, the first action (the cause).

      Use **emphatic order**, or order of importance, when you want to organize the effects in the order of most important to least important or least significant. The reverse order may also be used: organize the details from the least important to the most important or the most significant. (See "My Baldness" on page 354 for an example.)

b. Use **transition words** to connect details logically and smoothly. Transition words can connect ideas within a sentence as well as connect one sentence to the next.

TRANSITION WORDS FOR CAUSE-EFFECT PARAGRAPHS				
also	as	as a result of	affects	because
brings about	causes	consequence of	consequently	hence
in order that	effects	leads to	makes	now that
outcomes	produces	reasons	results	since
so that	then	therefore	thus	why

Connect ideas within one sentence: The Air Quality Act *resulted in* a reduction of smog levels and emissions of lead and sulfur dioxide.

Connect sentences: The United States passed the Clean Water Act in 1970. *As a result* of this act, the Great Lakes are much cleaner than they had been before 1970.

c. Repeat key words from the topic sentence, especially when the paragraph has multiple causes or multiple effects. Phrases such as the following keep your reader's focus on the points you wish to express:

A second cause . . . Another cause . . .

A second effect . . . Another effect . . .

5. Include *adequate development* by providing specific details that clearly show or explain the cause-effect relationship between the actions or events. If you use multiple causes or multiple effects in the paragraph, you do not need to develop each one equally. Explain each cause or each effect to the degree you feel is necessary to provide your reader with sufficient information to understand the cause-effect relationship.
6. Use a variety of details and forms of discourse, such as process, definition, and exemplification (examples) to explain the cause-effect relationship.
7. Avoid covering too much in one paragraph. A paragraph can cover multiple causes that lead to one outcome, or multiple effects that occur because of one cause. Avoid discussing multiple causes and

multiple effects in one paragraph; a topic with multiple causes and multiple effects is more appropriate for an essay rather than a paragraph.

Too much information for a paragraph

9.2 What do you think?

Working with a partner or on your own, read the following paragraph and then answer the questions that follow. Write your answers on separate paper.

My Baldness

At the age of thirty, I was getting a bald head, and I wanted to know why this was happening to me. My doctor told me that sometimes baldness is the result of taking certain medications for conditions such as cancer, circulatory disorders, ulcers, or arthritis. Baldness may also occur following a crash diet or a prolonged illness, hypothyroidism, or ringworm. None of these conditions pertain to me. I also learned that half of all men have significant hair loss before the age of fifty. Their hair tends to fall out in the front and on the top of the head. Of course, some try to deny they are losing hair by growing the side hair long and pulling it up over the bald spot and gluing it in place with gels and hair sprays. However, I am twenty years shy of the age when many men start getting bald. My doctor then informed me that I have a genetic condition called *androgenetic alopecia,* which sounds a bit intimidating. In layman's terms, this condition is called *male pattern baldness.* Differences in the way the scalp cells metabolize male hormones cause the baldness. This hereditary condition runs in my family. For me, my baldness comes from my genes. Perhaps I will deal with my male baldness by shaving my head and pretending the baldness is by choice.

[Adapted from: *http://www.cbshealthwatch/library/hairloss*]

1. What word in the topic sentence provides you with a clue that a cause-effect paragraph follows?
2. In this cause-effect paragraph, is the emphasis on the cause or the effects of baldness? Explain.
3. This paragraph explains multiple causes of baldness. However the writer explains in detail only one cause, the one that is most significant to him. Which cause does he explain in detail?
4. How does the writer achieve coherence in this paragraph? Explain.

5. Is there adequate development in this cause-effect paragraph? Explain.
6. Is there unity in the paragraph? Does every sentence support the topic sentence? Explain.
7. Draw a diagram of the cause-effect relationship that is shown in the paragraph.

9.3 What do you think?

Working with a partner or on your own, read the following paragraph and then answer the questions that follow. Write your answers on separate paper.

Autumn Leaves

The decrease of chlorophyll, the green pigment in leaves, causes the vivid colors in autumn leaves. When chlorophyll is present, leaves absorb light efficiently. When deciduous trees sense a decrease in daily sunlight, water in the soil, and warm temperatures, they decrease their production of chlorophyll in order to conserve energy for the winter months. Within a few weeks, the true inner colors of the leaves—the red, yellow, gold, and orange colors—replace the green color in the leaves. After several weeks, the production of chlorophyll shuts off completely. The leaves then drop from the trees and return to the earth. The vivid colors that adorn the countryside will not appear until the cycle repeats itself the following autumn.

[Adapted from: Brian Doyle, "Legends of the Fall," *VIA-AAA*, Sept/Oct. 2000, pp. 35–9, 47.]

1. How many causes and how many effects are in this paragraph?
2. Some paragraphs include a chain or series of cause-effect relationships. With this in mind, draw a diagram that shows the cause-effect relationship or relationships in this paragraph.
3. What other forms of discourse (process, narration, definition, classification, or exemplification) does the writer use in this paragraph to explain the cause-effect relationship? Explain.
4. List transition words or cause-effect signal words that the writer uses throughout this paragraph.
5. Are the topic sentence and the concluding sentence effective? Explain.

Developing the Concluding Sentence

Use the following guidelines to bring your paragraph to an end.

1. Echo the topic sentence or reinforce the cause-effect relationship and the controlling idea stated in the topic sentence.

2. Compare the concluding sentence and the topic sentence to confirm that the two sentences are closely related and that you did not wander off course in the body of the paragraph. If the two sentences are not closely related, your paragraph will lack unity.

9.4 What do you think?

Working with a partner or on your own, read the following topic sentences and concluding sentences. Explain whether the concluding sentence echoes or reinforces the topic sentence. Write your answers on separate paper.

1. *Topic sentence:* Several factors lead to the higher level of academic performance in college athletes.

   Concluding sentence: Thus, eligibility requirements, academic support services, and graduation expectations lead to greater academic success for many athletes.

2. *Topic sentence:* Homelessness for many people is the result of one specific situation that altered the course of their lives.

   Concluding sentence: Homelessness is one of America's most serious problems and must be addressed through legislation.

3. *Topic sentence:* Annually the NAACP runs a campaign to increase voter registration because individual votes can affect outcomes at the polls.

   Concluding sentence: The ballot measure passed by a margin of one vote.

4. *Topic sentence:* Everyone in the community feels the effects of electricity brownouts.

   Concluding sentence: To avoid brownouts, we as a society must learn to conserve our natural resources more effectively and consistently.

5. *Topic sentence:* Commercial airtime during the Super Bowl is the most expensive airtime of the year because of the large, captive audience tuned in for the NFL championship game.

   Concluding sentence: Advertisers, obviously, believe the multimillion-dollar commercials eventually pay off with improved product image and increased sales.

The Writing Process for Cause-Effect Paragraphs

Step 1: Generate ideas.

The **clustering** technique is an excellent way to generate ideas for possible topics. The beginnings of several clusters designed to generate topics for cause-effect paragraphs appear below. Spend two minutes on each cluster. Write as many topics as possible for each cluster. You may add additional lines to each cluster. Write any ideas that pop into your mind that you could possibly develop into an interesting and effective cause-effect paragraph.

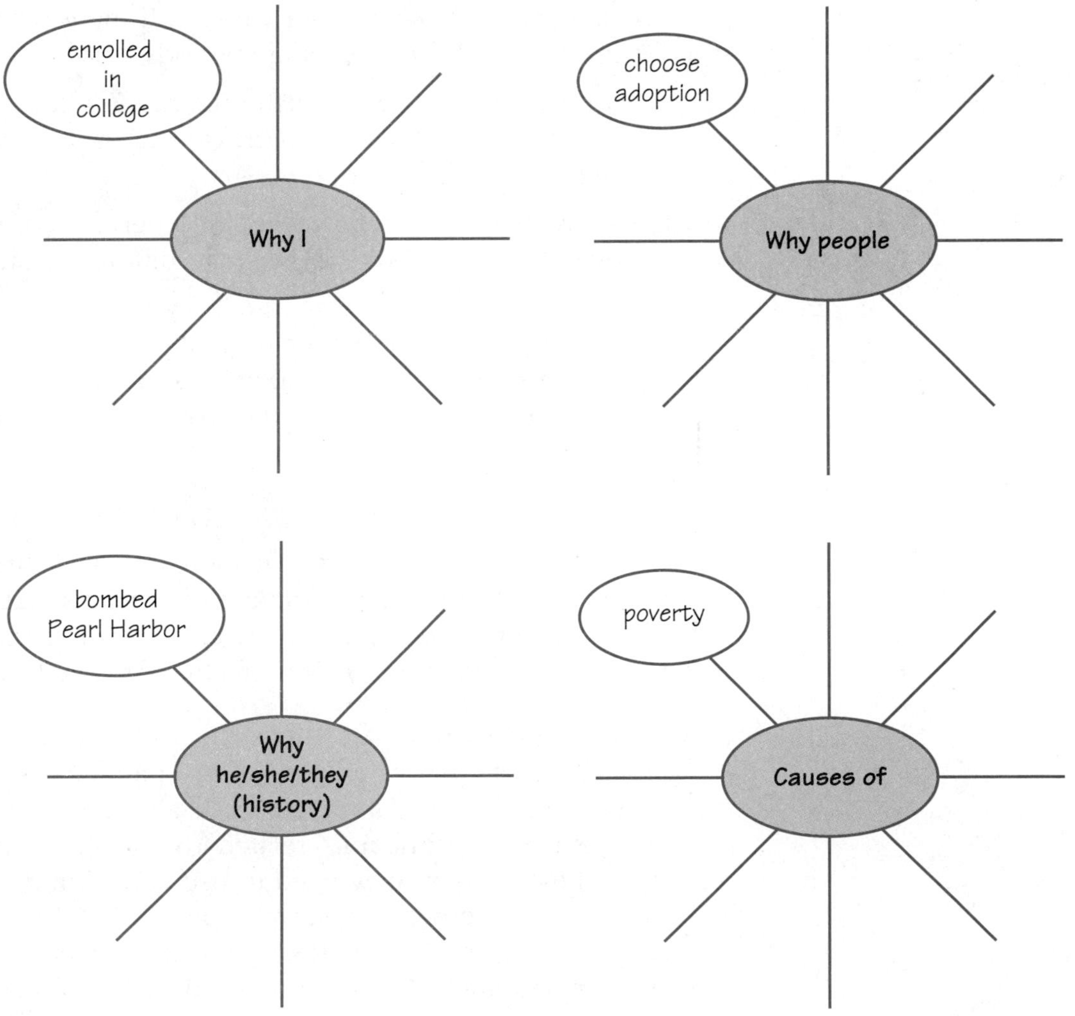

(Continue on page 358)

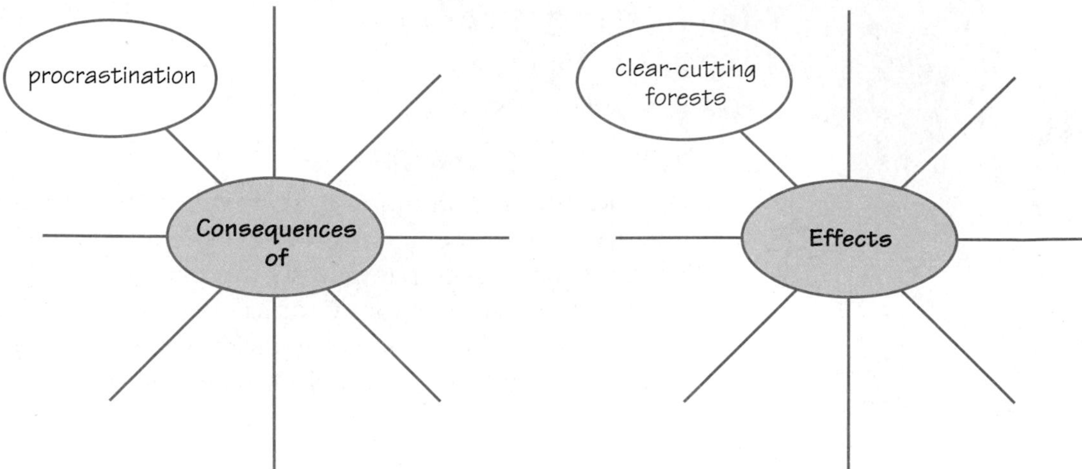

Step 2: Get a focus.

Select a topic from one of your clusters. If the topic is too broad, narrow it by using one of the following methods:

1. Narrow the topic to a specific setting. For example, consequences of procrastination can be narrowed to procrastination *in school, at work,* or *around your home.*
2. Narrow the topic to a specific time period. For example, causes of poverty *in the 1800s* will be quite different from causes of poverty *in the year 2002.*
3. Narrow the topic to a specific group of people. For example, why *teenagers* choose to use adoption services is more specific than why *any woman at any age* chooses to use adoption services.

Step 3: Gather and organize information.

Gathering and organizing information involves three tasks: identifying pertinent details, drawing a diagram of the cause-effect relationship, and drafting an effective topic sentence. Thoughtful planning for each of these tasks will lead to a more effective cause-effect paragraph.

Identifying Pertinent Details

Cause-effect paragraphs are expository paragraphs, so they should provide your reader with informative details. For many cause-effect paragraphs, such as paragraphs related to social, political, economical, or historical events, you may need to use your library resources, your textbook, or the Internet to research specific details to explain the cause-effect relationship. Take notes on the information you locate and read. In your notes, include the sources where you found the information. If you photocopy the information to keep in your files, note the sources from which you are photocopying so that you can give proper credit to the source. (See Chapter 1, pages 24–25.)

Diagramming the Cause-Effect Relationship

In your cause-effect paragraph, you may have one cause and one effect, or you may have multiple causes or multiple effects. Use a basic diagram to show the cause-effect relationship clearly. For example, the following diagram shows a cause-effect paragraph on *Why many people choose to attend college,* a topic with multiple causes and one effect.

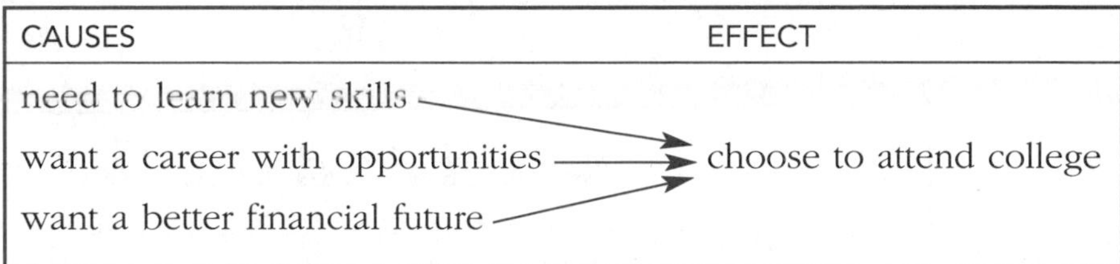

If the details in your diagram are not in a logical sequence, either number the details in the order that you will present them in the paragraph, or redraw the diagram to show the logical order of the details for your paragraph. Remember, you have two options for developing coherence so the details flow together smoothly and logically: chronological or emphatic order.

Writing the Topic Sentence

Use the information you have gathered and organized to write a topic sentence. See pages 350–351 for suggestions on writing topic sentences. Revise your possible topic sentences as necessary until you have an effective topic sentence with a controlling idea. Remember, an effective topic sentence for a cause-effect paragraph uses a signal word, such as *causes, affects, because, creates, leads to, produces, reasons,* or *results,* and alerts your reader to the cause-effect relationship you intend to discuss in the paragraph.

Step 4: Write the rough draft.

Use the information from Steps 1–3 to write a rough draft. Remember that the goal of a rough draft is to get your ideas on paper. You can then analyze, revise, and strengthen your ideas.

Step 5: Revise, revise, revise.

Revision work often occurs in several steps. Use the following checklist to guide you through the revision process.

1. Is the topic sentence effective? Is the subject sufficiently narrowed, or is it too broad for the scope of a paragraph? Does the sentence have a controlling idea? Does it use a word to signal that a cause-effect paragraph follows?
2. Does the body of the paragraph clearly show the cause(s) and the effect(s)? Is the cause-effect relationship clear?

3. Is there adequate development? Do you include only the most important causes or effects in the paragraph? Are there enough details to explain the relationship clearly to your reader?
4. Does the paragraph have unity? Do all the sentences relate to the topic sentence and the controlling idea?
5. How do you achieve coherence? Is the order of the details effective? Do you use transition words effectively?
6. Is the concluding sentence closely related to the topic sentence?

Step 6: Proofread and edit.

Use the same proofreading techniques that you used in Chapter 8 (page 331), but add the following items to the list:

1. Examine the diction in your paragraph. Do you use an effective choice of words throughout the paragraph? Do you use effective synonyms? Do you avoid using slang, contractions, and euphemisms?
2. Do you use formal language throughout the paragraph? Do you need to replace some informal language with formal language?

After you proofread for sentence structure and mechanical errors, share your paragraph with a writing partner, a tutor, or your instructor in order to get feedback on the paragraph. Finally, provide a partner with a revised version of your paragraph; ask him or her to complete the Partner Feedback Form on the Cause-Effect Paragraph Planning Sheet on page 363.

Step 7: Prepare the final version of your cause-effect paragraph.

Follow your instructor's guidelines for writing the final version of your paragraph.

9.5 What do you think?

Working with a partner or on your own, read the following paragraph and answer the questions that follow. Write your answers on separate paper.

Eruption of Mount St. Helens

[1]The effects of the May 18, 1980 eruption of Mount St. Helens in the state of Washington are well documented. [2]The most apparent effect is the mountain itself. [3]Prior to the eruption, the summit of Mount St. Helens had an altitude of 9,677 feet, making it the fifth highest peak in the state of Washington. [4]The eruption blew the peak off the mountain and left behind a

horseshoe-shaped crater that opened to the north. [5]The blast reduced the highest part of the crater rim on the southwestern side to an altitude of 8,365 feet. [6]The force of the eruption removed about 1,300 feet or 3.4 billion cubic yards of earth and rock. [7]Five hundred forty tons of ash covering more than 22,000 square miles of land resulted from the eruption. [8]People with respiratory problems had greater problems breathing; the quality of air and the air pollution were grave effects of the eruption. [9]Within one day, the ash cloud spread to the central United States. [10]Within three days, fine volcanic ash had drifted to the northeastern United States. [11]Within two weeks, some of the ash drifted around the entire globe. [12]Drifts of ash lined roadsides in many places that normally experience drifts of snow. [13]The filters of many cars clogged up with the heavy ash fallout; the ash fallout destroyed many vehicles and pieces of machinery. [14]The blast stripped the mountain sides of their vegetation. [15]The blast stripped bark, leaves, and pine needles off the trees; the trees, which had been uprooted and thrown through the air, lay on the barren hillsides. [16]The force of the eruption destroyed or buried animals and plants in ash, dirt, or mudflows. [17]While the effects of Mount St. Helens were most apparent at the site of the volcano, the effects stretched around the globe.

[Adapted from: Tilling, *The Eruption of Mount St. Helens*: USGS General Interest Publication, 1990.]

1. Refer to the numbers at the beginning of each sentence. Write the numbers of the sentences that are out of sequence and break the logical flow (the coherence) of the paragraph.
2. Should the sentences that break the flow of the paragraph be placed earlier in the paragraph, placed later in the paragraph, or deleted completely? Explain.
3. Except for the misplaced sentences, is chronological or emphatic order used to organize the details? Explain.
4. Write an alternative topic sentence for this paragraph.
5. Does the paragraph have adequate development? Explain.
6. Is the concluding sentence effective? Explain.

WRITING ASSIGNMENT

Write a cause-effect paragraph with one cause and one effect, or multiple causes or multiple effects (but not both).

Complete each of the following steps for writing a cause-effect paragraph. Unless your teacher assigns a different approach, use the Cause-Effect Paragraph Planning Sheet on page 363 for each step of the writing process. Save all your prewriting and draft materials.

Step 1: Generate ideas.
Use an idea from one of your clusters or generate additional ideas. Consider using one of the following ideas if you prefer.

Why people:	Why:	Causes of:	Effects/Consequences of:
cheat on taxes	a law changed	freeway accidents	cheating
tell lies	an event happened	forest fires	driving uninsured
drop out of school	volcanoes erupt	water shortages	credit card misuse
have low self-esteem	hurricanes form	droughts	radiation
get married	a team succeeds	high meat prices	stress
become sports fans	life with a teenager is difficult	cavities	young parenthood
		unemployment rates	good preschool programs

Step 2: Get a focus.
Select a topic for your cause-effect paragraph and narrow it if necessary. Write the topic on the Planning Sheet.

Step 3: Gather and organize information.
Gather details; research your topic if necessary. Save any photocopied pages and your notes on your topic and the resources you used. On Step 3 of the Planning Sheet, draw a diagram to show the cause-effect relationship between the actions or events in your paragraph. Then write several possible topic sentences before selecting the best sentence to use.

Step 4: Write a rough draft.
On the Planning Sheet, indicate when you finished the rough draft.

Step 5: Revise, revise, revise.
Use the revision guidelines on pages 359–360 to strengthen your paragraph. Ask a partner to read your revised paragraph and complete the Partner Feedback Form on the Planning Sheet.

Step 6: Proofread and edit.
Proofread each sentence and edit any errors. Examine each sentence carefully. Your work should be error-free. On the Planning Sheet, write the date you completed the proofreading and editing step.

Step 7: Prepare the final version of your paragraph.

CAUSE-EFFECT PARAGRAPH PLANNING SHEET

Name ______________________________

Step 1: Complete the cluster to generate ideas. You may be asked to turn in your clusters.

Step 2: Write your narrowed topic: ______________________________

Step 3: If you use the library, your textbook, or the Internet to gather details, save your notes, including information about sources you used, and save all photocopied pages.

Draw a diagram to show the cause-effect relationship in your paragraph:

Write several possible topic sentences. Star the sentence you plan to use.

1. ______________________________

2. ______________________________

3. ______________________________

4. ______________________________

Step 4: When did you complete the rough draft? ______________________________

Step 5: Revise your paragraph one or more times. Work with a partner. Ask your partner to read your revised paragraph and answer the following questions.

PARTNER FEEDBACK FORM

1. Does the topic sentence clearly identify the topic and provide a signal word to indicate that a cause-effect paragraph follows? Explain. ______

______

______

2. Does the body of the paragraph follow the cause-effect diagram? Explain. ______

______

______

3. Is there adequate development of the cause-effect relationship in the body of the paragraph? Explain. ______

______

______

4. How does the writer achieve coherence in the paragraph? ______

______

______

Does the coherence need to be strengthened in any way? Explain. ______

______

______

5. Does the paragraph have unity? Explain. ______

______

6. List any sentence or mechanical errors that need the writer's attention during the proof reading and editing process. ______

______

7. What did you like about this paragraph? ______

______

Partner's name ______

Step 6: Write the date that you finished proofreading and editing: ______

Step 7: Prepare the final version of your cause-effect paragraph.

Grammar and Usage Tips

The Grammar and Usage Tips in this chapter cover two important keys to strong writing and a clear, readable style: parallelism and avoiding wordiness. As you write and revise, keep these tips in mind and edit your writing as necessary. After you complete the exercises for these two grammar and usage tips, carefully check your work with the answer keys in Appendix A and record your number of errors for each exercise. Review the tip and examine the correct answer. In the margins of each exercise, jot down any questions you would like to ask your instructor regarding the grammar and usage points covered in the exercises.

Parallelism involves a repetitive pattern of words that are the same part of speech or words, phrases, clauses, or sentences that use the same grammatical structure. For example, when you write items in a series you should use the same grammatical form or part of speech for each item in the series: nouns should be parallel to nouns, verbs should be parallel to verbs, infinitives should be parallel to infinitives, adjectives should be parallel to adjectives, and so on. Similarly, when you write sentences with paired items that are joined by a coordinating conjunction *(and, but, for, nor, or, so, yet)* or a correlative conjunction *(either/or, neither/nor, not only/but also)*, the two items joined by the conjunction should be in the same grammatical form (parallel). Parallelism enhances the smoothness, correctness, and coherence of your writing.

Coordinating conjunctions link two or more words, phrases, or clauses that are of equal rank or importance. Each of the following coordinating conjunctions can link words, phrases, and clauses in parallel structures:

COORDINATING CONJUNCTIONS*						
and	but	for	nor	or	so	yet

*Mnemonic for the coordinating conjunctions: fan boys.

The coordinating conjunction *and* is frequently used in parallel structures, but you may use the other coordinating conjunctions. To learn more about parallel structures with coordinating conjunctions, read the following information and carefully examine the parallelism in the sentences. Italics show the parallel words, phrases, and clauses.

Parallel Structures: Words

When words appear in a series, each word should be from the same part of speech. In the first example, all the words in the series are nouns. You will notice in the remaining examples that words in a series may also be adjectives, verbs, or adverbs. When the words in a series are verbs, each verb should be in the same verb form and tense.

nouns

Sandra grows *orchids, dahlias,* **and** *roses.*

adjectives

Your accounting method is *accurate, logical,* **and** *detailed.*

adjectives

The part-time actor was *old, penniless,* **and** *discouraged.*

verbs

The basketball players *run, lift weights,* **and** *visualize.*

verbs

Mr. Yamamoto *signed, sealed,* **and** *delivered* the documents to his attorney.

adverbs

The young children responded *enthusiastically* **and** *honestly.*

Parallel Structures: Phrases

Parallel structures can be used with infinitives, prepositional phrases, verb phrases, and noun phrases. In the following examples, notice how parallel structures occur with infinitives (verb forms that begin with *to*) and prepositional phrases. When you use verb phrases in parallel structures, the verb tense and verb form must be the same for each of the verb phrases. In the last two examples, noun phrases that begin with gerunds show parallelism. (Gerunds are nouns that end with an *-ing* suffix.)

infinitives

All my life my parents worked hard *to budget* their money **and** *to save* for my college fund.

infinitives

My parents wanted *to help* me with college expenses **but** not *to pay* for everything.

verb phrases

The tornadoes *were destroying* crops, *causing* property damage, **and** *taking* lives.

gerunds

Eating out every night **and** *buying* unnecessary gadgets will put a dent in a person's pocketbook.

gerunds

Attending classes, *doing* homework assignments, **and** *studying* for tests are keys to college success.

Parallel Structures: Clauses

Independent clauses and dependent clauses can be linked by a coordinating conjunction and arranged in parallel structures. In the first example below, parallel structure appears in a compound sentence that has two independent clauses. The second and third sentences show parallel structure for complex sentences with dependent clauses that begin with relative pronouns. The final complex sentence shows parallel structure for two dependent clauses that begin with the subordinate conjunction *because*. (See Chapter 3, page 122 to review compound sentence structures and Chapter 4, page 163 to review complex sentence structures.)

independent clauses

During a drought, *the forests dry out,* **and** *the crops wither.*

dependent clauses

I realized *that I had made some poor decisions* **but** *that I had learned some valuable lessons.*

dependent clauses

My grandfather was a man *who cared about others* **and** *who dedicated his life to social issues.*

dependent clauses

She was an effective spokesperson *because she was articulate* **and** *because she was charismatic.*

Correlative conjunctions are conjunctions that appear as a pair of words and link a pair of items in parallel structure. The following chart shows correlative conjunctions.

CORRELATIVE CONJUNCTIONS (PAIRS)		
either . . . or	neither . . . nor	not only . . . but also
both . . . and	if . . . then	whether . . . or

As you will notice in the following examples, the grammatical structure that follows the first part of the conjunction must also follow the second part of the conjunction.

prepositional phrases

Sandy wishes to work **either** *in the field of juvenile corrections* **or** *in the field of school counseling.*

nouns

Both *the college placement test* **and** *the SAT scores* predicted her ability to succeed in the honors college program.

nouns

Neither *the computer programmers* **nor** *the software developers* had a solution.

clauses

If *you stay up all night,* **then** *you will be tired tomorrow.*

infinitives

I wish **not only** *to follow* **but also** *to lead.*

nouns

I wonder **whether** *the herbal remedies* **or** *the prescribed medication* will clear up her acne.

Avoid **faulty parallelism,** which occurs when you link sentence elements that do not have the same grammatical form or structure. In a sentence with faulty parallelism, the items joined together may not be the same part of speech, or the items joined together may not use the same sentence structure. When faulty parallelism occurs, the sentence sounds fragmented, and the ideas do not flow together smoothly. In the following sentences, faulty parallelism can be corrected by changing one or more of the words to create a parallel structure and by deleting unnecessary words.

Faulty Parallelism: My English teacher has *a great sense of humor* (noun) **and** is *knowledgeable* (adjective).

Correct: My English teacher has *a great sense of humor* (noun) **and** *a wealth of knowledge* (noun).

Faulty Parallelism: *Taking classes* (participial phrase) **and** *I work part-time,* (independent clause) I have little time for a social life.

Correct: *Taking classes* (participial phrase) **and** *working part-time,* (participial phrase) I have little time for a social life.

Faulty Parallelism: I knew that my keys were *in one* (prepositional phrase) *of my jackets,* (prepositional phrase) *in my car,* (prepositional phrase) **or** *fallen under my couch* (past participle).

Correct: I knew that my keys were *in one* (prepositional phrase) *of my jackets,* (prepositional phrase) *in my car,* (prepositional phrase) **or** *under my couch* (prepositional phrase).

Sometimes faulty parallelism can be corrected in more than one way. In the following example, three methods are used to achieve parallelism. The sentence elements on each side of the conjunction are modified so they are parallel.

Faulty Parallelism: My brother did not enter the Army because *he was not interested in military life* **or** *wanting to leave his girlfriend.*

Correct: My brother did not enter the Army *because he was not interested in military life* **and** *because he did not want to leave his girlfriend.*

Correct: My brother did not enter the Army because *he was not interested in military life,* **and** *he did not want to leave his girlfriend.*

Correct: My brother did not enter the Army because he was not interested *in military life* **or** *in leaving his girlfriend.*

EXERCISE 9.1 Identifying Parallelism

Score: ______

Underline the words, phrases, or clauses in the following sentences that are parallel elements.

Example: Neither the <u>teachers</u> nor the <u>administrators</u> support the ballot measure.

1. My hobbies include skiing, inline skating, and swimming.
2. His response was not only direct but also honest.
3. The movie received poor reviews, not only from the critics, but also from the public.
4. The reduction of violence and the improvement of test scores are the two most crucial challenges facing our nation's schools.
5. The tourists wanted to see the ancient ruins, visit the museums, and shop at the local markets.
6. Both the toddlers and the kindergarteners waved at the cameras.
7. The interviewer was rude, insensitive, and disrespectful.
8. In my last position, I managed the front office, ordered supplies, and coordinated the work orders.
9. Neither rain nor snow affects postal delivery services.
10. During the Olympics, players traveled from all over the world, participated in their specific events, and left Olympic Village with fond memories.

EXERCISE 9.2 Identifying Faulty Parallelism

Score: ______

Correct the sentences that contain faulty parallelism. Place a **C** next to sentences in which elements are parallel.

1. My professor told us that his role is to guide us through the curriculum, instill a sense of enthusiasm for the content, and the evaluation of our work.
2. Her main virtues are that she is loyal and dependable.
3. Before I begin my paragraph, I need to generate ideas and narrowing the topic is important.
4. The young artist exhibited his work in New York but did not exhibit his work in Miami.

5. The chairman of the board, the chief executive officers, and the managers signed the document.
6. Preschool children and even older children in adolescent years need a stable life.
7. To earn credit in that class, I had to write three papers, take three tests, and give an oral presentation.
8. The wind tossed garbage cans in the air, blew over fences, and the electricity was knocked out.
9. I told my wife that I would either mow the lawn this morning or mow it after the game.
10. I do not understand why you want to move out of the state or planning to change your major.

Avoid wordiness. Explore different ways to express an idea; eliminate unnecessary words. Ideas are clearer and more effective when you express them in a direct way. Repetitious wording reduces the impact your words have on the reader.

Wordy writing is clogged with unnecessary words that slow down the reading process and result in reader disinterest. In the following sentences, more words are used than are needed to convey the meaning. The unnecessary words have been crossed out; in some cases, shorter words or phrases have been substituted. When you write, examine each sentence carefully; delete unnecessary words or reword the sentence to be more concise.

> The shortage occurred ~~due to the fact that~~ *because* the distributor filed for bankruptcy.
>
> ~~A large number of~~ *Many* individuals file for bankruptcy every ~~single~~ year.
>
> The car was red ~~in color~~ and ~~in my own opinion~~ an older model ~~car~~.
>
> ~~During the time that~~ *While* I was in physical therapy, I had to reduce my work hours.
>
> ~~In the very near future~~ *Soon* we will try to purchase an inexpensive home ~~for our dwelling~~.

EXERCISE 9.3 Eliminating Wordiness

Score: ______

Cross out the words in the following sentences that result in wordiness.

1. When the wind suddenly, unexpectedly, quickly shifted, the hot air balloon drifted off course.
2. Ever since I became a vegan and decided not to eat meat or dairy products, my cholesterol level has improved.
3. Fast, rapid global warming will have dire, serious consequences for our planet.
4. I was injured and hurt during a routine inspection of the wiring in the attic upstairs.
5. Poor urban planning resulted in the lack of essential, necessary infrastructures.
6. To the best of my knowledge, I think the woman should be charged with fraud.
7. Lying in the form of being dishonest to your best friend causes many problems.
8. At the age of thirty years old, I was getting bald because I was losing hair.
9. My doctor told me that I have a genetic condition that I inherited.
10. The decrease of chlorophyll in the fall causes the vivid, bright colors in the autumn leaves.

Sentence Combining

Through effective sentence combining, you can also eliminate wordiness and express your ideas clearly and efficiently. As shown in the following examples, you can use many techniques to combine ideas and achieve sentence variety. Look for opportunities to use these approaches as you write and revise.

Combine phrases (prepositional phrases, infinitives, verb phrases):

Separate sentences:	By increasing exercise, people can lose weight.
	By decreasing calories, people can lose weight.
Combined:	*By increasing exercise and decreasing calories,* people can lose weight.

Separate sentences: We wanted to look at the new schedule.

We wanted to read the course descriptions.

We wanted to choose our classes early.

Combined: We wanted to *look at the new schedule, read the course descriptions, and choose our classes early.*

Separate sentences: The security guard was looking inside my car.

He was asking me questions.

He was writing down my license plate.

Combined: The security guard *was looking inside my car, asking me questions, and writing down my license plate.*

Combine Clauses:

Separate sentences: The effects of the May 18, 1980 eruption of Mount St. Helens are well documented.

Mount St. Helens is in the state of Washington.

Combined into a simple sentence: The effects of the May 18, 1980 eruption of Mount St. Helens in the state of Washington are well documented.

Separate sentences: People with respiratory problems had greater problems breathing.

The quality of the air was a grave effect of the eruption.

The air pollution was a grave effect of the eruption.

Combined into a compound sentence: People with respiratory problems had greater problems breathing; the quality of the air and the air pollution were grave effects of the eruption.

Separate sentences: The eruption blew the peak off the mountain.

The eruption left behind a horseshoe-shaped crater.

The crater opened to the north.

Combined into a complex sentence:	The eruption blew the peak off the mountain and left behind a horseshoe-shaped crater that opened to the north.
Separate sentences:	The blast stripped the bark off the trees.
	The blast stripped the leaves off the trees.
	The blast stripped the pine needles off the trees.
	The trees lay on the barren hillsides.
	The trees had been uprooted.
	The trees had been thrown through the air.
Combined into a compound-complex sentence:	The blast stripped the bark, leaves, and pine needles off the trees; the trees, which had been uprooted and thrown through the air, lay on the barren hillsides.

Grammar and Usage Tips Summary

TIP 29 Check for parallelism when you are writing words in a series or using a structure like *either/or* or *neither/nor.* Make sure all coordinate elements match each other in grammatical structure. Words, phrases, and clauses joined by coordinating conjunctions or correlative conjunctions often require parallel structures. Avoid faulty parallelism.

TIP 30 Avoid wordiness. Explore ways to express your ideas without unnecessary words. Eliminate redundant words, replace longer phrases with single words, and combine sentences into simple, compound, complex, and compound-complex sentences.

CHAPTER 9 • Cause-Effect Paragraphs • Proofreading and Editing Exercise

Work with a partner. Read each other's Writing Warm-Up 9 and then together discuss answers to the following questions for each of your paragraphs.

1. Focus on the first five sentences in your paragraph and your partner's paragraph. Analyze each sentence:

   a. Is it a simple, compound, complex, or compound-complex sentence?

   b. Are there any compound subjects or compound verbs?

   c. Are there any appositives or participial phrases?

2. Look for sentences throughout the writing that the writer could combine.

   a. Which sentences could the writer combine?

   b. Would ideas be clearer and would the writer avoid wordiness by combining sentences?

   c. Does the paragraph need greater sentence variety? Explain.

After you have answered the above questions, revise Writing Warm-Up 9 and write a final version. Strive for greater sentence variety and clarity. Be creative!

Internet Enrichment

Log on to the web site for this textbook for additional exercises and links for the following topics:

Cause-Effect Paragraphs

Parallelism

Wordiness

Sentence Combining

Go to: http://college.hmco.com. Click on "Students." Type *Paragraph Essentials* in the "Jump to Textbook Sites" box. Click "go," and then bookmark the site. Click on Chapter 9.

CHAPTER 9 • Grammar and Usage Review

Name ______________________________

Date ______________________________

Parallelism

Read the following paragraph carefully. Underline or highlight the parallel elements that are linked by the conjunctions in bold print.

> "In the end, it took the U.S. Supreme Court **and** its vast store of institutional prestige to end our 36-day national electoral nightmare. When people like Katherine Harris, the Florida legislature, **and** the House majority whip Tom DeLay talked about ending the recounts **and** declaring Bush the winner, they were widely attacked as mere political partisans. But when five Supreme Court Justices did very much the same thing, Al Gore started drafting his concession speech."
>
> [Source: Adam Cohen, *Time*, Volume 156, No. 26, December 25, 2000, p. 76.]

Writing With Parallelism

Complete each sentence below by adding words, phrases, or clauses that show the use of parrallelism.

1. The course syllabus states that we must attend classes, ____.

2. Many drivers on the freeway drive too fast, ____.

3. The benefit package includes ____.

4. The apartment that we rented is ____.

Avoiding Wordiness

Avoid wordiness by combining the following sentences into one sentence.

1. Law professors attacked the ruling as antidemocratic.

   They also attacked the ruling as politically motivated.

   Some of the court's own members also attacked the ruling for the same reasons.

Combined sentence: ______________________________

____

____

2. The Supreme Court's ruling in Bush v. Gore will be taught in law schools for many years.

   This same Supreme Court's ruling will also be taught in high school civics classes.

   Bush v. Gore will be analyzed in many government courses in higher education.

Combined sentence: ______________________________

____

____

3. The Democrats wanted to develop a uniform standard for counting votes.

   The Democrats wanted to continue counting Florida votes up to December 18.

   They wanted to assure voters that every vote for the presidency counted.

Combined sentence: ______________________________

____

____

[Adapted from: Adam Cohen, *Time*, Volume 156, No. 26, December 25, 2000, p. 76, 77.]

CHAPTER 10

Summary Paragraphs

The topic sentence includes the author's full name, the name of the article inside quotation marks, and the thesis of the article to be summarized.

The body of the paragraph introduces each new main idea with the author's last name and a present-tense verb. The body of the paragraph consists of main ideas and key details expressed in your own words.

The concluding sentence summarizes the thesis of the article.

Topic Sentence ....

Author's last name + present-tense verb + main idea with key supporting details

Author's last name + present-tense verb + main idea with key supporting details

Author's last name + present-tense verb + main idea with key supporting details

Concluding Sentence..

In Chapter 10 you will learn about the following:

1. The summary paragraph
2. Writing informal and formal summaries
3. The structure of a summary paragraph
4. The writing process for summary paragraphs

WRITING WARM-UP 10

Read the following article "The Great Spin Machine." Write a paragraph that summarizes the thesis (the author's overall main idea) and the main points. Use your own words to write the summary.

Spin is sometimes seen as a euphemism for lying, but as Michael Kinsley shows in the following article, spin is an indifference to the truth. Politicians, lawyers, journalists, and marketing experts all use *spin* to distort the reality and to promote themselves, their clients, or their products. The spin machine geared up and ran at full power during the year 2000.

THE GREAT SPIN MACHINE

You wouldn't have thought it possible early this year that spin could play an even larger role in American life than it already did. Straight-talking politicians (John McCain) were all the rage, and trendoids assured us that in the larger culture as well, sincerity was in while irony was out. But 2000 turned out to be a milestone year for the Great American Spin Machine. It was no surprise that spin was more copious than ever during the election campaign; it is more copious than ever in every election campaign. What made 2000 a special year for spin was the postelection recount crisis.

Spin is sometimes dismissed as a simple euphemism for lying. But it's actually something more insidious: indifference to the truth. Spinning means describing a reality that suits your purposes. Whether it resembles the reality we all share is an issue that doesn't even arise.

A small example of the distinction between spinning and lying occurred when Dick Cheney had his latest heart attack. George W. Bush told reporters, "Secretary Cheney is healthy. He did not have a heart attack." That would have been a lie if Bush had known otherwise. But his campaign aides said he hadn't been told, which is easy to believe. So it wasn't a lie. It was just spin. Journalists would have leaped on evidence that Bush knew about Cheney's heart attack, but they didn't care that he spoke without knowing anything one way or another. They hate the liar but love the spin.

The belief that politicians are liars is so widely cherished that it is almost part of America's civic religion, along with that stuff about being created equal. But outright whoppers by politicians are fairly rare.

Americans are right to feel that our political culture is infused with dishonesty. We are obsessed with fibbing about facts because this is less elusive than the real problem, which is intellectual dishonesty. This means saying things you don't really believe. It means starting with the conclusion you wish to reach and coming up with an argument. It means being untroubled by inconsistency between what you said yesterday and what you say tomorrow, or between standards you apply to your side or the other guy's. It means, in short, spin.

The Florida recount was five weeks of spin overload. The sheer volume of the stuff (in the sense of both quantity and noise level) was impressive enough. Consider as well how effortlessly the spin machine handled all the hairpin turns. Every amazing development and reversal in the drama was converted within minutes into two or three talking points for each side to repeat without mercy.

Lawyers are, in a way, the fathers of spin. They call it "vigorous representation of my client." The central distinction of spin—between knowingly lying and ignorantly or disingenuously misleading—is a positive ethical obligation of the legal profession. Lawyers are forbidden to do the former and required to do the latter as best they can. This includes what's known as "arguing in the alternative"—the practice, infuriating to lay people, of saying, "My client never stole the money, Your Honor, and anyway, he gave it all to charity."

Lawyers are free, of course, to take any side of a given case and are not restricted in what they say on behalf of today's client by what they may have said on behalf of yesterday's. In recent years, these necessary lawyerly hypocrisies have leached out of the courtroom as lawyers have taken on broader roles and big legal cases have become multifront battlefields. The most important battlefield is often the courthouse steps.

Journalists—truth seekers and cynics that we are—have no tolerance for spin. Right? Well, not exactly. The truth is that journalism has bought into the spin culture. Getting spun is flattering, like being seduced, or like being admitted to the club. And if politicians didn't spin, reporters and pundits would have nothing to interpret and act knowing about.

Every presidential election year, thousands of journalists fly to strange cities to sit in the overflow room and watch on TV the presidential debates they could be watching on TV at home. They do it mainly in order to be in another large room after the debate, where spinners for the candidates recite lines written before the debate about how their clients won the debate. The ritual is so well known and so completely accepted that CNN recently started a nightly program called *The Spin Room.* Twenty-first century pols and pundits don't mind appearing on a show based on the official premise that whatever they say will be calculated and insincere.

The year 2000 was also a good one for spin in the private sector, where it goes by the name of marketing. For intellectual-integrity buffs, marketing has an advantage over political spin: you can often design the product around the sales message. In other words, reality can come to you. You don't face the Hobson's choice of either following reality wherever it leads (which can put you off-message) or plunging into disingenuousness. But in the age of spin, who is dainty enough to care about the connection between an advertisement and the product it is intended to promote?

Have you seen the ubiquitous TV commercial for the hotel chain where, the ad suggests, every employee is prepared to give a guest detailed strategic advice and encouragement for a forthcoming business meeting? Unlike a more traditional advertising claim—that, say, an angel flies out of a can of cleanser to banish grime with her magic wand—this hotel's claim is not inherently or obviously metaphorical. Yet it's clearly not true—a point that probably didn't even occur to the producers of the ad or 99% of its viewers. The deception is not on purpose; few are deceived. But the process of producing a spin for this hotel chain apparently did not include reality as even a minor consideration.

2000 began with all those Super Bowl dotcom commercials aimed at brand awareness, where you did in fact become aware of the brand. You just had no idea what the brand did. ("ProtoLink: the Enterprise Solution for Internet Strategy. Because the future is where decisions will be made.") And throughout the year there were more and more of those ads for prescription drugs that didn't supply the smallest clue to what disease the miracle drug was supposed to cure. ("Sue, have you tried Protozip? It sure worked for me!" "No, Donna, I haven't, but I'm going to call my doctor today and ask for Protozip." Announcer: "Protozip should not be used by pregnant women or anyone who wears button-down collars. Bankers with a net worth of more than $5 million should consult a doctor before using.")

These ads are naked spin. They don't distort reality; they simply dispense with it. That's why 2000 was the year of spin. It couldn't go further in 2001. Could it?

[Condensed from: Michael Kinsley, "The Great Spin Machine," *Time*, Vo. 156, No. 26, December 25, 2000, pp. 100–1.]

The Summary Paragraph

A summary paragraph is a condensed version of a longer article or piece of writing. In a summary paragraph, you briefly restate, in your own words, the article's thesis, main points, and a few key details. A summary paragraph uses an objective style of writing. It does not contain your personal (subjective) opinions, evaluation, or original ideas.

Writing an effective summary paragraph begins with critical reading and thinking skills. You must have full understanding of the article and the author's ideas before you begin writing a summary paragraph. After carefully reading the article or the essay, identify the controlling idea of the entire article or essay. This controlling idea is called the **thesis statement.** You can discover the author's thesis statement by using the following strategies:

1. Read any introductory statements that appear before the beginning of the article. Such introductory material often states the author's purpose and controlling idea. In the article "The Great Spin Machine," the introductory material provides you with a clue to the thesis. The information in italics is the clue.

   Spin is sometimes seen as a euphemism for lying, but as Michael Kinsley shows in the following article, *spin is an indifference to the truth. Politicians, lawyers, journalists, and marketing experts all use spin to promote themselves, their clients, or their products.*

2. Think about the title selected for the article or the essay. Often the title suggests the controlling idea. The title "The Great Spin Machine," suggests that the *spin machine* is a heavy-duty machine that in some way is massive, incredible, or for some reason, highly recognized, respected, or honored.
3. Read the first paragraph of the article or the essay. The thesis statement usually appears within the first paragraph; however, the thesis statement can be implied, or more than one sentence can be used to state the thesis. After you read the introductory paragraph, ask yourself the following questions:
   a. Is there a sentence that states a controlling idea that is similar to the clues provided in the introductory material?
   b. Is there an overall idea expressed that could be developed throughout the article?
   c. Is there a controlling idea that reflects the thought presented in the title of the article?

   In the first paragraph of "The Great Spin Machine," the following sentence is the thesis statement with the controlling idea of the article. This thesis statement controls the content of the remaining paragraphs in the article.

"But 2000 turned out to be a milestone year for the Great American Spin Machine."

4. Read the entire article or essay slowly and carefully. Take time to understand the author's points. When you encounter unfamiliar words, use a dictionary to learn the meaning of the words. You can know for sure you have correctly identified the author's thesis statement only after you have read the entire piece of writing; this is especially true for more complex articles or essays. After you have read the entire piece of writing, you will have a clearer picture of the content and the ideas that the author wished to express. You can then return to the introductory paragraph in the essay to see if the sentence you initially identified as the thesis statement provides a controlling idea for the entire piece of writing. If you understand the information in the article or essay but do not see a controlling idea clearly stated in the introductory paragraph, the thesis is most likely implied.

Reading for Meaning

A summary paragraph condenses the information from a larger piece of writing. In order to condense the information accurately, you must understand the author's ideas and point of view without distorting, altering, or expanding his or her ideas. Critical reading is the key to an accurate summary. Complete each of the following eight critical reading steps when you read a longer piece of writing, such as an article or an essay.

1. **Read the title of the article.** Take a moment to think about its meaning and predict the content of the article based on the title.
2. **Read any introductory materials that may precede the article.** Highlight or underline key words or phrases that may be clues about the thesis or controlling idea of the article.
3. **Survey the article.** Read the first paragraph carefully, but then switch to a quick skimming of the article to get a general idea about the subject. Look at the headings, the subheadings, graphic materials, pictures, and the overall length of the article. Stop the quick skimming when you reach the concluding paragraph. Read the concluding paragraph carefully.
4. **Begin careful reading and comprehension.** Read the first paragraph. Stop reading. Think about each sentence and whether it could be the controlling idea (the thesis statement) for the entire article or essay.
5. **Read one paragraph at a time.** At the end of each paragraph, stop reading. Look through the paragraph for a sentence that states the main idea, the controlling idea of the entire paragraph. **Highlight the main idea completely.** Then look for the most important supporting details. **Highlight only key words or phrases** that serve to trigger your memory and provide supporting

details to explain the main idea. If you have difficulty understanding the paragraph, try one or more of the following techniques:

a. *Read the paragraph out loud.* Often you will more readily understand the meaning when you hear the words spoken.

b. *Visualize or picture the content of the paragraph in your mind.* Try to make a "movie in your mind" of the information in the paragraph.

c. *Use a dictionary to learn the meaning of unfamiliar words.* Write down the definitions in the margins of your copy of the article or on separate paper.

d. *Substitute familiar words for unfamiliar words.* Read the sentences again using the familiar words in place of the unfamiliar ones.

e. *Look for the type of discourse used in the paragraph.* Does the paragraph contain narration, process, comparison, contrast, cause-effect, or exemplification?

6. **Continue to read one paragraph at a time.** In addition to highlighting or underlining, make brief notes in the margins of your copy of the article or the essay. These notes will be useful when it is time to write the summary paragraph.
7. **Read the concluding paragraph carefully.** Think about how it relates to the introductory paragraph or paragraphs, the title, and the introductory material that preceded the article, if there was any.
8. **Identify and restate the article's thesis.** Use the information you gathered throughout Steps 1–7 to help you express the thesis statement in your own words.

10.1 What do you think?

Working with a partner or on your own, use the eight reading steps on pages 382–383 to read the following article. Read the title and the introductory materials. Survey the entire article before you begin careful reading. Then, read one paragraph at a time. Highlight the main idea completely. Highlight key words or phrases that are supporting details. Add brief notes in the margins. (See the examples of highlighting and marginal notes.) Continue the process for all the paragraphs. When you reach the concluding paragraph, think about its relationship to other parts of the article. At the bottom of the article, restate the author's thesis.

Step 1: Read the title. The title implies that some place other than Vietnam was hell. Could it be his own country?

Step 2: Read the introductory material. Identify a sentence that could possibly be the thesis statement.

From Vietnam to Hell (Shirley Dicks)

The Vietnam War left in its wake many men who were unable to return to the life they had known, and many of these veterans suffered from post-traumatic stress disorder (PTSD). Some became abusive, alcoholic, and unable to find satisfying work. Many of their marriages ended in divorce.

Author
men suffering from PTSD
John's story

Step 3: Survey or skim the article.

Shirley Dicks, whose former husband was a Vietnam veteran, interviewed several men diagnosed with PTSD. These veterans speak of suffering from depression, emotional paralysis, headaches, isolation, and nightmares about Vietnam. Here is a story of John, who reveals his anger and suffering as he speaks about his experience. He feels his story must be told.

From Vietnam to Hell

Step 4: Read one paragraph at time. Highlight. Make notes in the margin.

don't trust people
been through hell since Vietnam War
life ruined
no one cared
outraged
went to war at 19
upset with him at home
time bomb—jail
can't handle authority

My name is John and I'd prefer not to use my last name. I don't trust many people anymore, but the story of Vietnam needs to be told. I've been through hell since the Vietnam War. My life was ruined and no one cared. I'm outraged at the whole thing. I went to war at the age of nineteen to fight for this country, and when I came home, they were upset with me. I feel like a time bomb, that I could go to jail at any time because I might do something stupid. I can't handle authority or someone telling me what to do. Right now I'm out in the woods by myself.

When I first went to Vietnam, I was scared like all the others. We were young and knew we were going to war to be killed, wounded, or whatever and it was scary. When we landed in the country, we didn't know what to do. The people who had been there awhile didn't want anything to do with us because we didn't know anything, and they felt their lives would be jeopardized. The jungle itself was beautiful, green, blue vegetation, and the water in the mountain streams was crystal clear. I was a rifleman during the Tet Offensive in nineteen sixty-eight. I stayed basically in the jungle, so my contact was mostly with the NVA* soldiers.

The NVA were trained soldiers, and we would fight face to face. They usually outnumbered us. The United States would tell the people back home how many we had killed. In reality they were hitting us hard, and that's where the Agent Orange came in. They decided that they would kill the foliage so we could see the NVA. They sprayed chemicals over the jungles, and it killed the foliage, but it also sprayed on the men and later caused cancer.

We never got much sleep in the jungles. Even the days we didn't see the NVA, at least three men would be shot in the head by snipers. You never knew if it would be you that day or if you were one of the lucky ones. I was eating lunch one day with my buddy, and we were talking about his girl back in the States. A round hit him in the head, and I had his brains in my lunch and all over me. He never felt a thing, but I did: I've never gotten over it and I don't think I ever will.

*NVA: North Vietnamese Army.

They would tell us that we had to stay up at night, that this was the night the NVA would come in and we needed to be ready. Can you imagine thinking that all night long? We were all so tired, but we didn't sleep. Nothing happened that night. I became so unfeeling at nineteen years old that, after a fight, I would pack up the wounded and send them off. I would pick up the dead and throw them in bags, and then we'd eat lunch. We'd sit down and eat lunch. We had to be hard; we were Marines and you couldn't let anyone see that it bothered you. You had to be a man and take it. I opened up my lima beans and ate them. Do you know why we ate the lima beans after a fight? We hated them but after seeing the death and destruction, you didn't taste them. That's why we ate them at that time.

I had been in the country about six weeks when we had to go out on patrol one night. I had dysentery and asked the sergeant if I could miss that one patrol. I was sick and didn't think I could make it, or be of help to anyone else. He said in no uncertain terms that I was going if I was dying. So I went down the trail with them. I was so sick, and it was uncomfortable. I wasn't trying to get out of going into the bush, I was just plain sick. My temperature was going up as the day wore on. The medic said that I should go back, that I was too sick to go on, but the sergeant said I would go on or die. They were not going to send a chopper in to take me out. I drank all of my water because I was so hot and feverish. Then I traded my fruit cocktail for a couple of swigs of water from the guy in front of me. I didn't have any more valuables on me, so I didn't get any more water. These guys didn't want to have anything to do with me because I was new in the country. They thought I couldn't take it, getting sick and all. We didn't make contact all day with the enemy. We reached our destination and got some water to drink. It was Thanksgiving Day, and they were cooking turkey and instant potatoes. I wanted to eat so badly, but I was so sick that I couldn't. The sergeant came over and asked me if I was going to eat. I told him that I was too sick, so he just left me there and went down to eat. Finally I was put on a chopper and sent to the hospital. I woke up and the nurses were cleaning me. I smelled so bad and had sores all over my body. Two weeks later, I was back in the bush again.

One day on patrol three of our men disappeared. We didn't know what had happened to them until the second day. We came upon their bodies on the trail. The NVA had defaced them, cut off their penises and stuck them in their mouths. We were uptight now. We were scared because they might do this to us if they got a chance.

I remember it was Christmas, and I felt tears in my eyes. I said to myself that I was in some serious trouble. My nerves were getting bad, guys were dying like flies all around me, and it was kill or be killed. We were fighting in their backyards, and we stood out like sore thumbs, ready to be ambushed. They would use snakes to get us, put them about face height so we'd walk into them. They called them the five step snake. You couldn't go five steps after being bitten before you died. They had all kinds of booby traps. Sometimes they used poison gas, but the greatest fear we had was to be a POW.

When I came back to the United States, I couldn't believe the people would be mad at us. We thought we were heroes for laying our lives down for our country. We were warriors and had fought our war. They called me "baby killer" and "rapist," and I couldn't understand it. I hadn't done any of that over there, but the people here didn't understand the war. All they could do was place the blame.

I couldn't hold on to a job because of the PTSD. At first I thought it was normal for me to have hallucinations and dreams about Vietnam. I thought the flashbacks and the tiredness were normal, too, but they weren't. It was a symptom of post-traumatic stress disorder. I would take sleeping pills to get some sleep at night. The pills kept me drugged, but the VA wanted me to take them. I needed outside help since the VA wasn't doing anything but giving me sleeping pills. I went to a psychiatrist who treated me for the PTSD. I tried to get money from the government because of the PTSD, but the government refused. I think the veterans have a real problem and should be helped for their safety as well as for the safety of other people. We went to war to fight for our country. They send us out here with no money and some of us are unable to work because of the mental and physical stresses. If you can't work and support your family and it's because you fought for the government, then they should help us. They should have deprogrammed us as soon as we reached the U.S. I think it would have helped a lot of us if they had had some sort of programs for us.

For years after Vietnam, I lived out in the woods. I would wash in the stream, eat cold food, and go to the bathroom in the woods. Finally I got a little heater and would heat some of the canned food that I ate. I was getting modern then.

I've been diagnosed as having severe PTSD. I went to the veterans' centers and they helped. I couldn't hold a job for very long, and I couldn't sleep. I began to smoke a little marijuana; then I needed something to wake me up. It was a merry-go-round. I keep on having nightmares and flashbacks about Vietnam. I get into fights all the time because I can't stand somebody telling me what to do. I find myself on the edge of life all the time. Vietnam did that to me.

I used to sleep with a gun all the time until one night I was having a flashback and found myself shooting at some trees. I decided not to take a chance on that happening again. My wife could have come walking down the path and been killed.

I don't believe we belonged in Vietnam. They told us in training we were going over there because they didn't want the Vietnamese over here fighting on our backdoor and raping our women. They said it was necessary to go over and fight the war. I didn't see any necessity in it. We went over there with the good intentions of cleaning up these bad guys and coming home as heroes. That was a joke. The other wars were necessary, but not this one. My child isn't going to war for this country.

I can remember the happiest day in Vietnam. We were on the jet on our way back home, so high that the Vietnamese couldn't fire at us and that was a very happy feeling. We knew that now the only way we were going to die was if the jet were to crash. We were almost home with all our arms and legs. We weren't going home in a basket; we were going home in one piece. Little did we know, most of us were eaten up with Agent Orange, PTSD, and traumas. We thought we were all set; we were going back. We got home and found out differently.

I've driven eighteen wheelers all over the country but can't seem to last very long at any one place. Vietnam haunts me today; I hear the groans of the dying. Everyone yells out to God when they know they're dying, and I used to wonder if I would do the same.

A man can't kill another man and be the same as he was when he was a child. You can cover it up and pretend, and try to forget it, but it never goes away. It poisons you, robs you, and changes you from what you once were. What I once was I can never be again because I fought for my country. A child went to war, and a crazy man came home. I don't know of any other way to put it.

[Source: Sattler, Shabatay, *Psychology in Context*, Houghton Mifflin, 2000, pp. 263–266.]

I think the thesis of this article is: ______________________________

____

Writing Informal and Formal Summaries

After you carefully read and comprehend an article or essay, you are ready to begin the process of using the main ideas, the key details you highlighted, and the marginal notes you wrote to write a summary paragraph. Keep these important points in mind when you write your summary paragraph. You are going to do the following:

1. Condense what the author has said about the subject. Your summary should be considerably shorter than the original work.
2. Limit the statements in your summary to the author's ideas. A summary paragraph is not the forum for opinions, comments, or your own ideas.
3. Use your own words to summarize what the author said. You may use some of the key words and factual information, but rephrase them. Do not copy them directly from the original writing. Your summary should not include word-for-word full sentences that were a part of the original writing.
4. Summarize the key ideas in an order that seems logical. You do not need to summarize the details in the exact order that they appear in the article.

Writing Informal Summaries

Compare your highlighting and marginal notes with the content of the following summary for the article "From Vietnam to Hell." Notice how some, but not all, of the details that you may have written in the margins are included in this summary. The summary format that follows is an *informal summary*. Read the comments about this summary that point out important elements of summary paragraph writing.

INFORMAL SUMMARY: "FROM VIETNAM TO HELL"

Thesis statement

This information appeared later in the article but the writer placed it here in the summary to provide important background setting.

In "From Vietnam to Hell," Shirley Dicks tells about an interview with a Vietnam veteran, John, who wants his story about Vietnam to be known and not forgotten. When John came back from Vietnam, he expected to be treated as a hero. Instead, he was ostracized and called a baby killer and a rapist. He felt that many Americans did not understand the suffering the soldiers endured to serve their country. John was extremely distraught by the fact that the government did not deprogram the soldiers, nor did the government provide

The writer reveals John's disorder and the symptoms of the disorder.

The writer selected a few of John's experiences to demonstrate the horrors he had to face. Not all the examples in the article appear in the summary.

The writer mentions other veterans' problems.

The concluding sentence summarizes John's attitude and feelings. The writer uses several of John's key words in the conclusion.

adequate financial or medical support. John experienced symptoms of PTSD (post-traumatic stress disorder): hallucinations, flashbacks, tiredness, and haunting dreams about Vietnam. John tells about the horrors that he experienced as a young, scared nineteen-year-old. A sniper blew out a friend's brains; the brains splattered on his lunch. He found missing soldiers who had been defaced. Death was so common that he became desensitized; he would fight, kill, bag the dead bodies, and then sit down to eat lunch. He had to stay up all night to be ready for an attack; he had to trudge through the jungle on night patrol even when he had dysentery and was barely able to walk. The suffering continued for many veterans long after the war ended. In addition to PTSD, many Vietnam veterans who had been exposed to Agent Orange, a chemical used to kill the foliage, now had cancer. For John, his rage and his dangerous, destructive behavior forced him to retreat from society and to live alone in the woods. John knows that the war changed him forever. The killings, the atrocities, and the haunting memories will forever be a part of this man who once was a child who went to war.

Writing Formal Summaries

The guidelines below apply to the structure of a formal summary paragraph, the type of summary paragraph you will write most frequently in college courses. If your instructor prefers an informal structure, or a formal structure that varies from the following, use those instructions and guidelines for writing your summary paragraphs.

As with an informal summary, when you write a *formal summary,* you condense and summarize the author's ideas by using an objective style of writing. However, in a formal summary, the topic sentence and the sentences in the body of the paragraph that introduce each main idea are more highly structured than in an informal summary paragraph. As you will notice by reading the marginal notes for the following summary, the author's name appears more frequently throughout the paragraph. In this formal structure, a present-tense action verb follows the author's name; however, you may use past-tense verbs in sentences that refer to action that has been completed.

The topic sentence includes the name of the article, the author's full name, and the thesis statement.

As shown in bold print, each new main idea is introduced with the author's last name and a present-tense verb:

Kinsley states . . .
Kinsley reveals . . .
Kinsley reports . . .
Kinsley continues . . .
Kinsley concludes . . .

Sentences in the body of the paragraph that explain the main ideas use past tense for actions that have already taken place.

Only a few supporting details are used to explain the main ideas.

The concluding sentence restates or reinforces the thesis statement of the article.

FORMAL SUMMARY: "THE GREAT SPIN MACHINE"

In "The Great Spin Machine," Michael Kinsley claims that the year 2000 was a significant year for *spin*, the indifference to truth and the distortion of reality to suit a person's purpose. Kinsley states that despite claims by politicians that sincerity was of the upmost importance, politicians used *spin* quite liberally during the election campaign and the postelection recount crisis. Instead of intellectual honesty, in which politicians say only what they know to be true and say it with consistency, politicians used *spin* during the election campaign of 2000 to elude the real problems and create an argument for the desired outcome or conclusion. The five weeks of confusion that surrounded the Florida recount demonstrated how quickly the spin machine can shift points of view and analyze situations with new slants, with little concern about previous statements or positions. **Kinsley reveals** that politicians are not the only ones who use spin. He says that lawyers are "in a way, the fathers of spin." Lawyers often mislead lay people and turn courtrooms into battlefields with their high-powered statements and their spins designed to represent their clients regardless of the truth about their clients. **Kinsley** also **reports** that journalists have "bought into the spin culture." For example, he recounts how journalists flocked to hear spinners for specific presidential candidates recite their speeches, written before the presidential debates occurred, telling how their candidates won the debate. **Kinsley continues** to give examples of the widespread acceptance of spin in our society. He discusses ways in which the private sector, mainly marketing, uses spin to design a product around a sales message, a message that often dispenses altogether with logic or reality. **Kinsley concludes** that spin was rampant in 2000 in many sectors of our society. With so many examples of spin in the year 2000, **he questions** whether or not spin in 2001 could possibly go any farther than it has this year.

Developing the Topic Sentence

Use the following guidelines to write an effective topic sentence that includes the following elements.

1. Give the **title of the article** in the topic sentence. Place the title inside quotation marks. Capitalize the first word and all the key words of the title. Do not capitalize the small words, such as *a, an,*

the, and, or, and *of* that are not the first word of the title. Follow the title with a comma and then the closing quotation marks.

In **"From Vietnam to Hell,"** . . .

2. Give the **author's full name** in the topic sentence.

   In "From Vietnam to Hell," **Shirley Dicks** . . .

3. Use a **present-tense verb** to introduce the thesis statement.

   In "From Vietnam to Hell," Shirley Dicks **tells** . . .

4. State the **thesis,** the controlling idea of the entire piece of writing, in the topic sentence. As mentioned previously, you can use introductory material, the title, and the first paragraph to help identify the thesis of the article. After careful reading and comprehension of the article, identify or use your own words to state the thesis.

Notice how the following topic sentences for a formal summary paragraph include four elements of a topic sentence.

In "From Vietnam to Hell," (title) Shirley Dicks (author's full name) tells (present-tense verb) about an interview with a Vietnam veteran, John, who wants his story about Vietnam to be known and not forgotten. (thesis)

In "The Great Spin Machine," (title) Michael Kinsley (author's full name) claims (present-tense verb) that the year 2000 was a significant year for *spin*, (thesis) the indifference to truth and the distortion of reality to suit a person's purpose. (definition)

Developing the Body of the Paragraph

Use the following guidelines to develop the body of your paragraph and the thesis stated in your topic sentence.

1. Summarize the main ideas of the entire article or essay in the body of your summary paragraph. A summary paragraph should be shorter than the original writing.

2. Introduce each new main idea by using the author's last name (or a subject pronoun) and then a present-tense action verb. Strive to achieve word variety by using different present-tense action verbs to introduce each new main idea. The following verbs may be useful when you write summary paragraphs.

Present-Tense Action Verbs							
advises	argues	ascertains	asserts	claims	clarifies	comments	compares
confesses	debates	declares	demonstrates	describes	discusses	disputes	emphasizes
examines	explains	gives	holds	illustrates	informs	interprets	justifies
lists	maintains	mentions	notes	presents	proclaims	provides	recounts
remarks	reports	restates	reveals	reviews	says	shows	states
suggests	teaches	tells	thinks				

3. Include only a few key details. Combine or condense the details to avoid excessive wordiness.
4. Achieve coherence by organizing the details in a logical sequence that will be easy for your reader to follow. You do not need to summarize the details in the exact order they appear in the paragraph.
5. Use your own words to summarize. If you have the tendency to copy too many of the sentences or phrases from the article, put the article away. Write the summary without referring to your notes. Then, check the accuracy of the information and check to see if you need to add any additional main ideas or key points to the paragraph.
6. Use quotation marks around any words or phrases that are direct quotations when you feel the exact wording strengthens your summary paragraph.

Developing the Concluding Sentence

Use the following guidelines to bring your paragraph to an end.

1. Restate or summarize the thesis that is stated in the topic sentence.
2. Be sure that the concluding sentence reflects the author's point of view. Do not include extra information or your personal opinion in the concluding sentence.

10.2 What do you think?

Working with a partner or on your own, use the eight steps for reading for meaning (pages 382–383) to read and comprehend the following excerpt from a longer article written by Susan Jacoby. Answer the questions that follow the paragraph. Write your answers on separate paper.

In this excerpt, Susan Jacoby explores the love-hate relationship Americans have with money and wealth. The results of several national surveys shatter the myth that all Americans want to be wealthy. Several reasons explain why many Americans do not want to be wealthy; however, as contradictory as it sounds, many of these same Americans long for the benefits of having money and financial security. Thus, we see the love-hate relationship Americans have with the almighty dollar.

Money: America's Love-Hate Relationship with the Almighty Dollar (Susan Jacoby)

Who doesn't want to be a millionaire? More people than you might think. In an exclusive AARP-Modern Maturity survey, "Money and the American Family," 27 percent of men and a startling 40 percent of women said *no* when asked if they would like to become wealthy. More than half defined being wealthy as requiring $500,000 or less in total assets (including savings, investments, and real estate); in fact, only 8 percent said it would take $1 million to make them feel wealthy.

Why do so many have an aversion to getting rich at a time when the most popular show on TV is *Who Wants to Be a Millionaire?* and the new Internet economy is creating instant millionaires by the nanosecond? Four out of five of those surveyed said they feared that wealth would turn them into greedy people who consider themselves superior, and three-fourths said that wealth promotes insensitivity. Even those who said they would like to be wealthy shared the negative view of how the rich behave.

Does this really mean that a huge number of people would turn down a million-dollar windfall and that they hate the rich? "No and no," says Andrew Hacker, professor of political science at Queens College in New York city and the author of *Money: Who Has How Much and Why*. What it does indicate, Hacker argues, is that most Americans aren't all that interested in doing what it takes to amass great wealth. "There are certain types, the driven young men you read about on Wall Street, who want to make lots of money as a way of keeping score," he says. "But most of us just want enough to feel comfortable and secure. Would you take the million if it fell from the sky? Sure. Do you want to work seven days a week and think about money 24 hours a day? Probably not."

As for the negative stereotypes of the rich, Hacker believes they are almost entirely the result of publicity about celebrities. "I'll bet if you asked those polled to list ten rich people, they'd be hard put to come up with very many names after they thought of people such as Donald Trump, Michael Jordan, and Bill Gates." In fact, in the interviews that were conducted after the survey was completed, the only other name that emerged was Oprah Winfrey.

Three-fourths of Generation-Xers (age 18–35) said they would like to become wealthy, but the desire for wealth steadily dropped with age, hitting its lowest point among those 65 and over. Arlie Russell Hochschild, professor of sociology at the

University of California at Berkeley and co-director of the Center for Working Families, suggests that some Gen-Xers may believe that money is all they can rely on. "There's a sense of impermanence about both marriage and career for many young adults today," she notes. "The older you are, the more likely you were to have grown up believing in lasting marriage and also in lasting career choice. Money is what's left when you feel you can't count on those other things." Gen-Xers also appear to depend less on religion, with just two-thirds—compared with more than three-fourths in older age groups—believing that strong religious faith is absolutely essential for them to consider their lives a success.

Men at every age and income level were more interested than women in getting rich. Even among the financially ambitious 35-and-under generation, more men (82%) than women (68%) said they would like to become wealthy. When men and women entered the realm of financial "what-ifs," the survey revealed more differences of opinion. Asked the *main* thing they would do with a $1 million windfall, 41 percent of women said they would either use it to help friends and family or donate it to charity. Only 32 percent of men chose that response.

Many women spoke of the pleasure that they would derive from being able to provide financial support to an aging parent. "What I would do first is take my mom somewhere really nice," said a 39-year-old African-American government administrator in Chicago. "I would reward her for raising all nine of us by herself. She would be rewarded—and so would I."

Men also were twice as likely as women to say that they would save or invest a windfall." "That scares me a little," says Linda Barbanel, a New York psychotherapist and the author of *Sex, Money, and Power.* "I do think women's attitudes are changing, but maybe not fast enough for our own good—especially when you think about what happens to so many women in midlife if they get divorced."

On the question of what money *can* and *cannot* buy, a large majority of Americans said that money could buy "freedom to live as you choose" (which may include the freedom to leave an unhappy marriage), "excitement in life," and "less stress." In a number of follow-up interviews, many people commented that having extra money would immediately alleviate one source of profound stress—the need to work overtime.

Can money buy peace of mind? Fifty-two percent of Americans said no. "It all depends on what 'peace' means to you," observed a businesswoman in California who is nearing 60 and would like to retire at 62 and go back to college. "For my husband, peace of mind means working as long as he can and collecting the biggest possible pension. For me, it means knowing I've worked long enough so that I can afford to go after an old dream."

[Excerpt from: Susan Jacoby, "Money: America's Love-Hate Relationship with the Almighty Dollar," *Modern Maturity*, July–August 2000, pp. 36–41.]

1. Before you read the article, what were your thoughts about the title of this article? What did you predict would be discussed?
2. What is the thesis or the controlling idea of "Money: America's Love-Hate Relationship with the Almighty Dollar"?
3. Compare your highlighting to the highlighting done by another student. Did you both identify and highlight the same sentence in each paragraph as the topic sentence? Did you both highlight the same key words or phrases? Explain.
4. Compare the key words you wrote in the margin to the key words another student wrote in the margins. Are they similar or quite different? Explain.

10.3 What do you think?

Working with a partner or on your own, read the following summary of "Money: America's Love-Hate Relationship with the Almighty Dollar." After you read the summary, carefully compare its main points to the main points you highlighted and wrote in the margins of the excerpt. Then answer the questions that follow the summary. Write your answers on separate paper.

Summary: "Money: America's Love-Hate Relationship with the Almighty Dollar"

Susan Jacoby looked at American's attitudes toward money. She found that 27 percent of men and 40 percent of women in the survey had no desire to become wealthy. Many people did not want to become wealthy because they thought they might become greedy, feel superior to others, and develop an insensitivity to other people. Jacoby tells how one professor of political science believes that people would not reject a million-dollar windfall. He believes people do not want to be wealthy because they do not want to do the work that it takes to become rich. Seventy-five percent of the people between the ages of eighteen and thirty-five, known as the Generation-Xers, did want to become wealthy. One sociology professor believed that this group wants to be wealthy because money, not marriage or careers, can be relied upon or counted on to remain in their lives. Jacoby found, however, that men and women would use money differently. Women frequently would like to use their wealth to help family, friends, and charities. In addition to differences in how money would be spent, men and women have different attitudes about what money can buy. Even though many people did not wish to be wealthy, they had opinions about ways they would spend their wealth if they had it.

1. Is the topic sentence of this formal summary paragraph effective and complete? Does it have all the key elements? Explain.
2. Write a new topic sentence that includes the key elements of a topic sentence for a formal summary paragraph.
3. How many paragraphs are in the excerpt? How many main ideas are in the excerpt?
4. Does the writer include all the main ideas in the summary paragraph? If not, which main ideas are missing in the summary?
5. Does the writer introduce the main ideas effectively? Does the writer use the recommended standard structure for a formal summary paragraph? Explain.
6. The writer of this summary shows confusion with verb tenses. Each main idea should be introduced with the author's last name and a present-tense action verb. Actions that are expressed in the remaining sentences in the body of the paragraph should use past-tense verbs to express actions that already occurred. Change the verbs in the paragraph to show correct usage of verb tenses.
7. Write an alternative concluding sentence.

The Writing Process for Summary Paragraphs

Step 1: Generate ideas.

In a summary paragraph, you do not need to generate any original ideas. You will be working only with the author's words, point of view, and content.

Step 2: Get a focus.

Begin the initial steps to identify the author's thesis or controlling idea. Is the thesis statement explicit? What meaning does the title convey? Read any introductory information. Read the first paragraph. Identify or formulate a possible thesis sentence for your summary paragraph.

Step 3: Gather and organize information.

Begin by reading the article or essay carefully. Examine the information as a whole to determine the author's controlling idea, the thesis statement. Highlight the main ideas and a few key details and make a brief list in the margins of the key words you may want to use in your summary paragraph.

Write a **topic sentence** for your summary paragraph. Use the standard format for a formal summary paragraph. The topic sentence should show the title of the article inside quotation marks, the author's full name, and the thesis statement.

Step 4: Write the rough draft.

Write your topic sentence. Continue your summary paragraph by summarizing each of the author's main points or main ideas. Introduce each main idea by using the author's last name and a present-tense verb. (See page 392 for a helpful list of action verbs.) Include a few supporting details to clarify or strengthen your summary. Be very selective and include only the most important supporting details. End the summary paragraph with a concluding sentence that restates or reinforces the thesis.

Step 5: Revise, revise, revise.

Examine your rough draft for ways to strengthen your summary paragraph. Revise your rough draft at least one time. Use the following checklist to guide your revision work.

1. Does the topic sentence include the name of the article, the author's full name, and a statement of the author's thesis?
2. Do you introduce each main idea with the author's last name (or a subject pronoun for the author) and a present-tense action verb?
3. Does your summary paragraph include each of the article's main ideas? Do you summarize the ideas in your own words?
4. Do you include only a few important supporting details in the paragraph?
5. Is there coherence? Do the ideas flow together smoothly? Do you use transition words effectively to link ideas together?
6. Does the paragraph have unity? Does every sentence relate to the thesis statement and function to summarize the author's ideas?
7. Does the concluding sentence restate or summarize the thesis statement?

Step 6: Proofread and edit.

Check for grammatical or mechanical errors. Check for accurate spelling and punctuation. Edit to eliminate any errors and avoid wordiness. Your writing should be error-free.

Step 7: Prepare the final version of your summary paragraph.

WRITING ASSIGNMENT

Write a formal summary of an article or an essay. Condense the information in the article. Demonstrate that you understand the thesis statement and the most important ideas by including them in your summary paragraph.

Step 1: Generate ideas.
Four articles appear on pages 401–407. Follow your instructor's directions. You may be asked to write a summary paragraph for one specific article, or you may be instructed to choose one of the four articles to summarize, or you may be asked to locate your own article to summarize.

Step 2: Get a focus.
Unless your teacher assigns a different approach, use the Summary Paragraph Planning Sheet on page 399. Complete each of the steps.

Step 3: Gather and organize information.
Use the eight steps for reading for meaning (pages 382–383). Read the article carefully. Highlight and make notes in the margin. Use your highlighting and marginal notes to write an effective topic sentence that has the essential elements of a topic sentence for a formal summary.

Step 4: Write a rough draft. Complete Step 4 on the Planning Sheet.

Step 5: Revise, revise, revise.
Refer to the checklist on page 397. Ask a partner to read your revised paragraph and answer the Partner Feedback questions on the Planning Sheet.

Step 6: Proofread and edit.

Step 7: Prepare the final version of your summary paragraph.
You may be asked to turn in your highlighting and marginal notes, your rough draft, and your revision work when you turn in your final summary paragraph.

SUMMARY PARAGRAPH PLANNING SHEET

Name ______________________________

Step 1: For a summary paragraph, you do not need to generate any original ideas.

Step 2: Based on the title, introductory information, and the first paragraph, state the author's thesis or main controlling idea.

____

____

Step 3: Using the eight steps to read for meaning, read the article carefully, one paragraph at a time. Underline the main idea in each paragraph. Underline a few significant key details. List the main ideas and details in the margin.

Write a topic sentence for your formal summary paragraph:

____

____

Step 4: When did you complete your rough draft? ______________________________

Step 5: Revise your paragraph at least one time. Use the checklist on page 397. Give your revised paragraph to a partner. Ask your partner to complete the Partner Feedback Form.

PARTNER FEEDBACK FORM

1. Does the topic sentence contain all the key elements for a topic sentence for a formal summary? Explain. ______________________________

____

____

2. How many main ideas are in the article? __________ How many main ideas does your partner include in the summary? __________ Does your partner's summary include all of the important ideas that are in the article? Explain. ______________________________

____

____

____

(Continue on page 400)

PARTNER FEEDBACK FORM

3. Does the writer introduce each main idea by using the author's last name and a present-tense action verb? Explain. ____________________

4. Does the paragraph have an adequate number of supporting details? Explain. ____________________

5. Does the paragraph have coherence? Explain. ____________________

6. Does the writer summarize the article by using mostly his or her own words? Are there sentences that could be more effective by rewording? Explain. ____________________

7. Is the concluding sentence effective? Explain. ____________________

8. Is the summary paragraph an appropriate length? Explain. ____________________

Partner's name ____________________

Step 6: Proofread and edit your summary paragraph so it is free of errors

Step 7: Prepare the final version of your summary paragraph.

Article 1: Misuse of Native American Symbols

Many schools across the United States use Native American names and mascots. The messages conveyed about Native Americans through these symbols and mascots are being questioned and challenged. Mixed opinions exist as to whether the practices are disrespectful to the Native American culture and aspirations. The author, Gurleen Grewal, an associate professor in women's studies in Tampa, hopes to take action to set things right.

MISUSE OF NATIVE AMERICAN SYMBOLS

Our silences often tell more about us than our most informed lectures. The silence of most faculty in our universities and colleges about the continued use of Native American images and sacred items as mascots for college and professional sports teams is telling indeed.

A diverse coalition of Native American groups is demanding the elimination of Native images as mascots, but the typical reaction of too many faculty is to make light of the issue.

Symbols are extremely powerful and convey complex messages. The use of Native American symbols—such as Chief Illiniwek at the University of Illinois or team names such as the Florida State University Seminoles or the Atlanta Braves, the Cleveland Indians, the Washington Redskins, and many others—conveys a message that is far from amusing.

Oddly, those in favor of preserving these mascots and team names often argue that they seek to "honor" Native peoples.

In reality, the practice is an exercise in power that disregards the sanctity of Native cultures and aspirations. These symbols are neither "compliments" to the Native American people nor acknowledgements of their "heritage." They are part of an old tradition—racism.

One does not need to recall the murders of 18 Lakota men in South Dakota over the last year—none of which has been solved—to recognize that the life of a Native American person holds little value in our society.

The systematic decimation of Native peoples during the U.S. colonial period—a population reduced from over 13 million in 1500 to fewer than 250,000 by the turn of the 20th century—was justified through racist depictions of Native peoples as "savages,"—exactly the image portrayed by the popular ballgame gesture, the "Tomahawk Chop."

This colonial relationship is perpetuated by the use of Native American images as mascots.

Raising our voices—on our campuses, in our classrooms, and elsewhere—against the use of Native American symbols as sports' mascots is only the beginning.

What must follow is the clear recognition of the historical and contemporary oppression of Native peoples, as well as the recognition of how the dominant society benefits from that colonial relationship. From that recognition must come the willingness to take action to set things right.

[Source: Gurleen Grewal, "Misuse of Native American Symbols," *National Education Association*, January 2000, p. 12.]

Article 2: Technological Wonderland

In the following excerpt from a longer article titled "Solitude," Ester Buchholz, Ph.D., explores the impact that computer technology has on the way people deal with problems related to being alone. Does this computer technology strip us of the benefits of solitude? If so, what price will we pay for ignoring the basic human need for true solitude? Buchholz questions whether we truly understand our own attraction to computer technology.

TECHNOLOGICAL WONDERLAND

In the classic silent film *Modern Times,* Charlie Chaplin's "modern" man runs around in circles tightening screws and bolting bolts in mad precision. Today, Chaplin's postmodern equivalent punches the keyboard, moves from chat room to e-mail to game screen, and sails into virtual reality with an earnestness that can cause equal delirium. Computer life is, I believe, an attempt to solve the problem of alonetime and social needs. In a culture that no longer provides wilderness or stretches of solitary time, the computer is the one machine that seemingly offers it all: stimulation, knowledge, news, alonetime, relationships, and even sex. One might say it has universal appeal. However, if we are not aware of why computer technology is attracting us, we cannot use it to our best advantage. The question is, are we routinely using the computer and television to find alonetime without really realizing our unfulfilled alone need? Or are we becoming incapable of living in the moment except in technological time-outs like the computer?

A friend of mine wishes he could be lost in the woods with a cellular phone: that way, there could be utter silence with the opportunity to connect if he so desired. Yet the explorer of the Internet is never completely freed from the world.

Tuned in to electronic information, he is inundated with knowledge. More and more, people are getting annoyed by the accessibility of modern hookups and the prevalence of telephones (on airplanes and in hotel rooms) because it makes them feel like they must work. At no other time in history have people's minds and bodies been so accessible. Today, being online seems the Western way to meet our needs for solitude and together time, but at what cost? Keeping silent about the pleasures of aloneness leaves us blind to the real allure of computer marvels. When an experience is altering our consciousness and we do not discriminate either how or why, then the experience is regulating us.

[Source: Ester Buchholz, Ph.D., "Solitude," *Psychology Today*, January/February 1998, pp. 54, 80.]

Article 3: Yes, America Is Mine . . . and Yours

The author, Jeremiah Holmes, uses historical information to develop the idea that a long history of African American citizenship makes America his and yours. At the time this article was published, Jeremiah Holmes was a thirteen-year-old who attended Marshwood Junior High School in South Berwick, Maine.

YES, AMERICA IS MINE . . . AND YOURS

My Aunt Sis told me that the great W.E.B. Du Bois once asked, "Would America have been America without her Negro people?" I would not have used the word "Negro," but my dad said that in Mr. Du Bois's day African Americans were referred to as "Negroes" and even "colored." So, I guess I understand.

Would America be America without me, without my brothers and sisters, without my mother and father or grandpop and grandmom or all the people I know? No way, I don't think so.

From the beginning, America was mine. True, our people did not ask to come here, but once they were here, their suffering and struggle for freedom made this country as much mine as any of my white friends whose ancestors came from Ireland, Germany, France, England or Italy.

My ancestors—beginning with Crispus Attucks, the leader of the Boston Massacre—paid a very high price for our share of America. Crispus Attucks gave his life so that all of us in this country could live free. He was the first martyr of the American Revolution, which, to me, makes him the founding father of Black America.

Crispus Attucks had to be awesome. He was born into slavery circa 1723. At age 27, he escaped and went to sea. And on the cold night of March 5, 1770, when a British soldier fired the shot that triggered the Revolutionary War into a crowd of patriots lead by Crispus Attucks on the Boston Commons, it was Attucks, a former slave, who would forever more be known as the first person to die for his country, the United States of America.

Thousands of Black freedmen and slaves served in the military during the Revolutionary War right alongside the white revolutionaries. Together they created an independent nation dedicated to democracy. Of course, the African American patriots never received proper recognition for their bravery. We were not taught about them in school. I learned most of my African American history at home from my mom and dad.

However, it is never too late to honor heroes. The Black Patriots Foundation has been established to build a memorial on the Mall in Washington D.C. in tribute to the brave African Americans who shed their blood for America's independence. Last year (1998), through an act of Congress, the U.S. Mint struck 500,000 silver dollars denoting the memorial. Philip Diehl, the Mint's director said, "The Black Revolutionary War Patriots Silver Dollar will recall and commemorate history by focusing on Crispus Attucks's sacrifice as a symbol of commitment of all Black American patriots."

"It was not for their own land they fought, not even for a land which had adopted them," Harriet Beecher Stowe, author of *Uncle Tom's Cabin,* said in 1855, "but for a land which had enslaved them, and whose laws, even in freedom, more often oppressed than protected. Bravery under such circumstances has a peculiar beauty and merit." And I say that Crispus Attucks and the thousands of African Americans who served the revolutionary cause, began the long history of African American citizenship that 229 years later, makes America mine . . . and yours.

[Jeremiah Holmes, "Yes, America is Mine . . . and Yours," *Crisis*, January/February, 1999, p. 17.]

Article 4: Why We're Destroying the Earth

Awareness of our depleting natural resources is at an all-time high and, yet, so is their destruction. A new field of research hopes to explain why we damage the environment even though we think we are protecting it—and how we can stop. Robert Gifford, Ph.D., is a professor of psychology at the University of Victoria in Canada.

WHY WE'RE DESTROYING THE EARTH

In November, nearly 80,000 people flocked to Seattle, Washington, to protest the disregard of the World Trade Organization (WTO) for environmental concerns. Impassioned demonstrators from San Diego to France inundated the streets of downtown Seattle for days, railing against the toll that free trade often exacts on endangered wildlife.

Unfortunately, the protestors' admirable pilgrimage to save the environment actually hurt it more than they knew. Consider how many well-intentioned individuals who normally would have stayed home flew across the country, sapping tons of energy and releasing vast amounts of carbon dioxide into the air. According to the U.K's Royal Commission on Environmental Pollution, aircraft emissions of carbon dioxide could triple over the next 50 years, highly exacerbating global warming. This is just one of the ways we destroy the environment even as we're trying to protect it—a tragic irony that is one of the major themes of environmental psychology.

Many people, based perhaps on well-publicized disasters like the 1989 Exxon Valdez oil spill, believe that environmental problems are most often caused—and best solved—by government or big business. Most environmental damage, however, begins not with government or large companies, but with the cumulative actions of individuals. If there is a solution to this global crisis, it is to understand—and remedy—the decision-making of individual consumers of energy before nature pays the price.

For about 30 years, environmental psychologists have struggled to understand the way we treat our surroundings, which ultimately harms our own well-being, since environmental assault can wreak havoc on our health, even leading to illnesses such as cancer. Over 100 studies conducted in the last two decades have examined the ways individuals influence the environment—from deciding to have another child to turning on the air conditioner—and why they make such decisions. We know that some people do refrain from overusing nonrenewable resources, from forests and fish to less tangible resources such as clean air and physical space. Environmental psychologists are now examining the mindset of such individuals, hoping eventually to encourage others to consider our resources in the same way.

More and more people are environmentally aware these days—curbside recycling, insulated homes and Woodsy

Owl's slogan "Give a hoot, don't pollute" are now ingrained in our cultural consciousness. You might think that awareness would lead to environmentally friendly behavior, but it does not: Well-educated, middle-class North Americans, the people most likely to have high environmental awareness, use far more energy than Third World residents—and other North Americans too.

Why the discrepancy between words and deeds? So far, scientists have identified at least 30 different personal, social or structural influences that affect whether a given person uses natural resources wisely or takes more than their share. There are four overriding ways that people, mostly unconsciously, hurt the environment every day:

• *Energy use.* Perhaps our biggest priority is to curb our heavy use of fossil fuel energy sources, like oil. Burning these fuels produces greenhouse gases and ground-level pollutants, leading to global warming, a planetary danger no longer questioned by experts. A 1998 study in the journal *Bioscience* showed that 40% of deaths worldwide are caused by pollution and other environmental factors. Furthermore, energy use is growing: Dutch researcher Linda Steg, Ph.D., reports that in the Netherlands, a region typical of developed nations, consumers now use 25% more energy than they did just 14 years ago.

• *Convenience.* Taking a plane is several times less fuel-efficient even than driving, but we often choose to fly to save time. In a typical recent year, U.S. commercial airliners carried 60 million passengers 158 billion miles, using 21 billion gallons of jet fuel in the process. Similarly, cars afford us speed and comfort compared to cycling or walking. But a Dutch study found that about 20% of car trips are for journeys of less than one mile. Is this truly necessary?

• *Overpopulation.* In a classic 1968 article, biologist Garrett Hardin, Ph.D., theorized that environmental destruction stemmed from the fact that there are just too many mouths to feed, even with great agricultural improvements. The Population Reference Bureau reports that the 20th century began with 1.6 billion people on the planet and likely ended with 6 billion. This is the end result of every parent's personal decision to have a child, whether they realize it or not.

• *Ignorance.* Robyn Dawes, Ph.D., a professor at Carnegie Mellon University, blames "limited processing": People simply don't place their daily behaviors in an environmental context; their decisions are literally thoughtless. Some progress has been made since Dawes' initial research (witness the growth of recycling), but how many people consider the environment when they flip a light switch or use an electric toothbrush?

Many people take whatever they can, believing that natural resources are inexhaustible. A review of 59 studies by Donald Hine, Ph.D., and myself revealed that individuals use resources more wisely when the group sharing the resource is small in number, communicates well and is informed that goods are limited. Unfortunately, groups that share real-world resources are usually large, often communicate poorly and don't realize the resource crisis they face. In a 1994 study that simulated ocean fishing in groups of up to 200 in size, I found that participants would cut back their fishing when they learned that the fish stocks were depleting. But the cutbacks they made were too little to save the fish population over the long run. People were destroying a resource just as they believed they were helping it, not unlike those who flew to protest the WTO or who travel to far-off national parks to revel in nature.

To reverse this ill-fated trend, you can construct your life to make conservation easy. For example, the next time you move, place environmental considerations near the top of your list by relocating as close as possible to work or school. Then you won't drive as much, and won't have to ride a bike or walk too far, either. Residing in a slightly smaller home would consume less energy for heating or cooling without forcing you to sacrifice much comfort. Do you need to fly as much as you do? Perhaps there are undiscovered vacation spots close to home. And instead of flying to your next business meeting simply because your company will pay for it, try carpooling or taking a train, or telecommuting via phone, fax or the Internet.

Adopting these measures would significantly reduce pollution and global warming and its ill-effects on our well-being. Celebrate this April 22, Earth Day, by making a few of these changes. The world depends on it.

[Robert Gifford, Ph.D., "Why We're Destroying the Earth," *Psychology Today,* March/April 2000, pp. 68–9.]

CHAPTER 10 • Summary Paragraphs • Proofreading and Editing Exercise

Return to Writing Warm-Up 10. Reread the essay, "The Great Spin Machine." Now that you understand the structure of a summary paragraph and have read one summary paragraph for this article, revise your Warm-Up as needed so it reflects the skills you learned in this chapter for writing a formal summary. Revise, proofread, edit, and prepare the final version of your Writing Warm-Up 10.

Internet Enrichment

Log on to the web site for this textbook for additional exercises and links for the following topics:

Summary Paragraphs
Reading for Meaning
Action Verbs
Excerpts to Summarize

Go to: http://college.hmco.com. Click on "Students." Type *Paragraph Essentials* in the "Jump to Textbook Sites" box. Click "go," and then bookmark the site. Click on Chapter 10.

CHAPTER 11

Paragraph Answers for Test Questions

In Chapter 11 you will learn about the following:

1. Answering definition and short-answer questions
2. Understanding direction words
3. Using key words
4. Preparing for tests
5. Using prewriting techniques
6. Writing a paragraph answer
7. Practicing writing test answers
8. Learning from your tests

Answering Definition and Short-Answer Questions

In college, you will encounter three general kinds of test questions of varying difficulty: recognition (objective) questions, recall questions, and essay questions. The following chart shows the types of questions associated with each general category and the skills required to answer the questions.

TYPES OF TEST QUESTIONS			
KIND OF QUESTION	LEVEL OF DIFFICULTY	EXAMPLES	REQUIREMENTS
1. Recognition (objective)	Easiest	True-False Multiple Choice Matching	Read and recognize whether information is correct; apply a skill and then recognize the correct answer.
2. Recall	More demanding	Fill-in-the-blanks Listing Definition Short answer	Retrieve the information from your memory. For definitions and short answers, pull information from your memory, analyze it, and organize it in a meaningful, logical way.
3. Essay	Most difficult	Essay with multiple	Retrieve the information from memory, analyze it, organize it, paragraphs and use effective writing skills.

[Source: Wong, *Essential Study Skills*, Houghton Mifflin 2000, p. 227.]

This chapter focuses on writing answers for definition and short-answer test questions. (Chapter 12 focuses on writing answers for essay questions.) The paragraph-writing skills that you have learned throughout this textbook can be applied to writing effective, thorough answers for short-answer questions.

WWW Understanding Direction Words

To provide answers that directly answer test questions, focus immediately on the **direction word** in the test question so you can identify the type of answer your instructor expects. Some direction words require a descriptive paragraph; others require a process, comparison or contrast, exemplification, classification, definition, cause-effect, or summary answer. After you identify the direction word, create a prewriting plan to guide you through the writing of the paragraph. Take time to learn the meaning of the following direction words.

DIRECTION WORDS		
DIRECTION WORD	TYPE OF PARAGRAPH	WHAT YOU NEED TO DO
Analyze	Classification	Identify the parts and discuss each part individually.
Compare	Comparison	Show likenesses and differences between two subjects.
Contrast	Contrast	Show the differences between two subjects.
Define	Definition	Provide an expanded definition of a term.
Describe	Descriptive	Give a detailed description of the required elements.
Discuss	Any paragraph style	Discuss or tell about the topic. Read the rest of the question for clues as to the paragraph style that is expected (For example, *discuss how* = process; *discuss the reasons for* = cause-effect.)
Explain/Explain why	Cause-Effect	Give reasons or show the cause-effect relationship between two or more actions or events.
Explain how/how	Process	Explain the steps or stages for something to occur.
Evaluate/Critique	Exemplification, Classification, Cause-Effect	Offer your opinion or judgment on a topic and support it with factual details, reasons, and explanations.
Illustrate	Exemplification	Give examples and supporting details to illustrate or show a concept, its application, or its significance.
Trace/Outline	Process	Discuss a sequence of events in chronological order.
Summarize	Summary	Identify and discuss the main points and key details.
What are/were	Any paragraph style	Read the rest of the question for clues as to the paragraph style expected. (For example, *What are the types of* = classification; *what are the reasons for* = cause-effect.)

As you use the direction word as a clue to the type of paragraph answer to develop, remember that each form of discourse may include elements or characteristics from other types of paragraphs as well. For example, a cause-effect paragraph may also have elements of description and process. A comparison paragraph may have elements of exemplification. In actuality, few paragraphs are purely one form of discourse. The basic structure of a paragraph usually follows one of the specific types of paragraphs, but the elements within the paragraph may also be common to other paragraph types.

Using Key Words

In addition to identifying the direction words, identify the key words and phrases in the question itself. These key words and phrases are signal words that can help you develop an appropriate controlling idea. Read the test question carefully. Highlight or circle the key words and phrases in the question. For a stronger, effective topic sentence, use these key words and phrases in the topic sentence.

direction word ↘ ↙ key word ↓ key phrase

Question: Discuss the characteristics of a figurehead leadership role, which is one of the functions of management.

Topic Sentence: A figurehead leadership role in management has four characteristics.

Type of Paragraph: Classification

11.1 What do you think?

Read the following test questions. Focus on the direction word as a clue to the type of answer that the instructor expects. Circle the direction word. On the line below the question, write the type of paragraph you would write to answer each question. Highlight or circle key words and key phrases in the question that you will want to include in your topic sentence.

Example: Discuss the primary differences between individual branding and family branding.

Paragraph requires: contrast

1. Explain why so many Europeans emigrated to North America in the late nineteenth and early twentieth centuries. What were the motivating factors?

   Paragraph requires: ______________________________

2. Why did Mahatma Gandhi designate the spinning wheel as his symbol?

   Paragraph requires: ______________________________

3. Illustrate ways the Chen Pu addressed the problem of feeding China adequately.

   Paragraph requires: ______________________________

4. How did Napoleon's rule differ from the previous rule of the Directory?

   Paragraph requires: ______________________________

5. Summarize the main characteristics of any four of the eight kinds of leadership roles.

   Paragraph requires: ______________________________

6. Leaders often encounter the need to transform organizations from low performance to acceptable performance, or from acceptable

performance to high performance. How does a transformational leader overhaul the organizational culture or subculture?

Paragraph requires: ______________________

7. What is *charisma* and how is it developed?

   Paragraph requires: ______________________

8. What effect did the early Europeans have on the indigenous people of North and South America?

   Paragraph requires: ______________________

11.2 What do you think?

Bring questions from recent tests to class. Discuss with the class the direction word, key words and key phrases, and the type of paragraph that the instructor expects in the answer. You can also share with the class how you organized and composed your answer.

Preparing for Tests

Knowing how to write strong test answers is only one aspect of being successful in college. Unless you are given an open-book test, you must prepare for tests by learning the information thoroughly. Use a variety of study strategies to prepare for tests, and allow ample time to review textbook and classroom notes. Many causes of test anxiety and poor performance on tests are the result of being underprepared. To avoid being underprepared, use the following study strategies prior to facing tests.

1. Use time management to schedule ample time to complete your textbook reading assignments. Staying current with your reading assignments enables you to participate more actively in class discussions and understand lectures.
2. Take notes as you read. Look for main ideas and important supporting details. Highlight, make marginal notes, and write separate notes on paper. Take time to think about relationships between ideas and how the concepts can be applied in life. Use the eight steps of reading for meaning. (See Chapter 10, pages 382–383.)
3. Spend time studying your notes. Review them frequently. Recite information out loud and in your own words. When you are not able to explain information in your own words, return to your notes or your textbook for further review.
4. Quiz yourself. Try to predict test questions. Write your own test questions and practice answering them without looking at the textbooks or your notes.

5. Find a "study buddy," someone with whom you can study and discuss the course content. Practice writing test questions for each other and quizzing each other orally.
6. Participate in study groups and/or work with tutors. Frequently, discussing information with others, listening to the ideas they believe are the most important, and contributing your own ideas reinforce the learning process.

KINDS of SUMMARY NOTES to PREPARE for TESTS

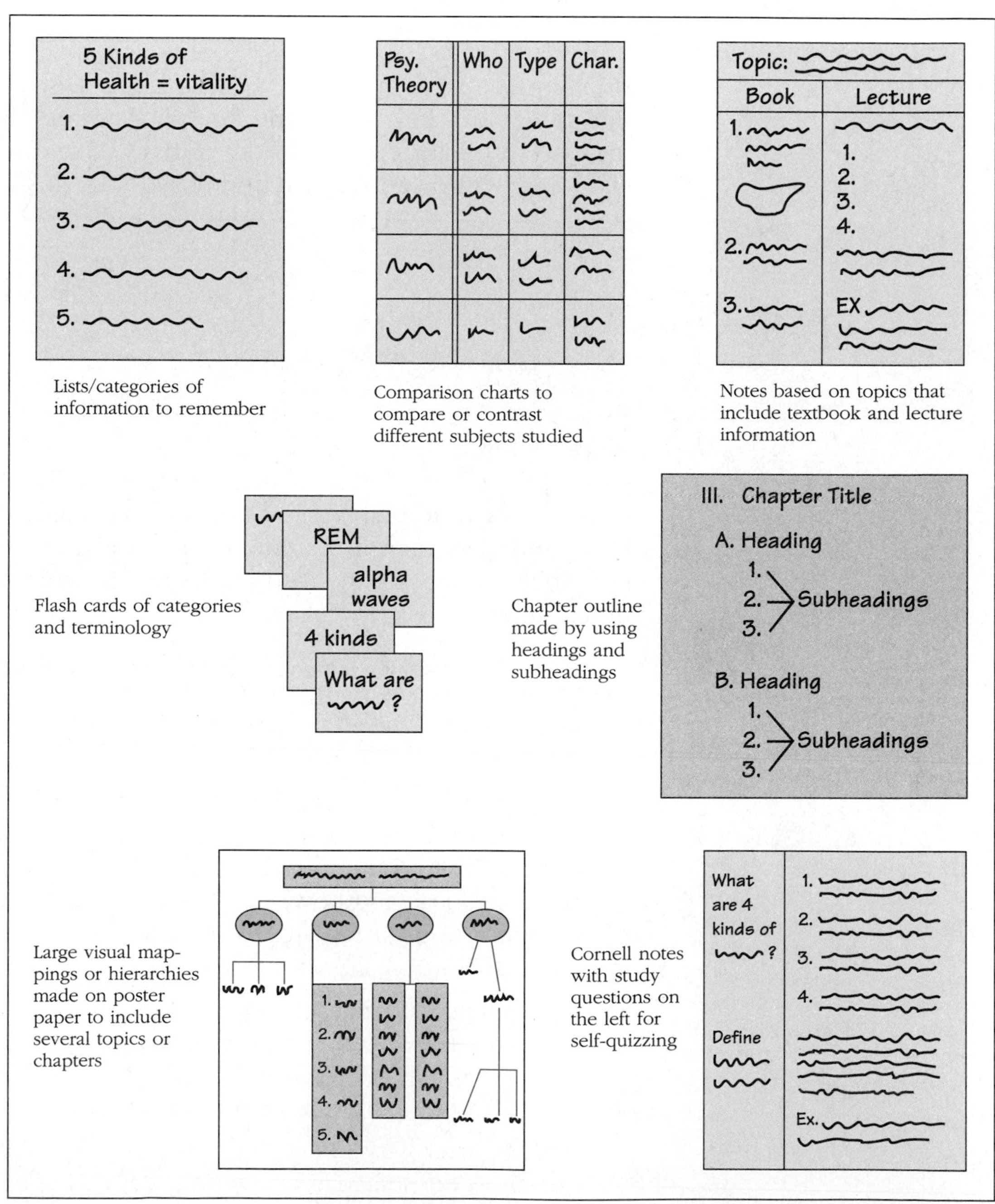

[Source: Wong, *Essential Study Skills*, Houghton Mifflin 2000, p. 226.]

7. Make a five-day study plan prior to a test. Each day, plan which chapters and sets of notes you will review to prepare for the test. Plan carefully so that you have time to review each chapter systematically.
8. Make a separate set of summary notes that contains only the information that you feel you need to review further. See several options for summary notes on page 414.
9. Find out as much as possible about the test. Ask your instructor which topics and chapters will be covered. Ask if you can write on the test (highlight, underline, or make notes) and if you can bring blank paper to use to plan your answers. Ask what kinds of questions will be on the test. Talk to other students who have taken the class in the past. Ask them for study suggestions and information about the kinds of tests that are typical for the class.
10. Get a good night's sleep the night before a test. Staying up late to cram often backfires and affects your mental alertness.

Using Prewriting Techniques

In previous chapters, you learned several prewriting techniques. You can use these same techniques to organize information for paragraph answers on tests.

1. **Brainstorm** a list of concepts and details for any type of paragraph.
2. Make a **list** of individual steps for a process paragraph.
3. Make a **cluster** or a **hierarchy** of key details for any type of paragraph.
4. Make a basic **outline** of the main ideas and details.
5. Make a **grid** for a comparison or a contrast paragraph.
6. Make a **diagram** to show a cause-effect relationship.

During a test, time is usually limited, so you will not have a lot of time to develop your writing plan or your prewriting materials. However, spending a few minutes planning your answer before you begin writing is time well spent. With a plan as a guide, you will be able to develop your paragraph much more quickly, and your ideas will flow together more coherently. If by chance you run out of time, you can turn in your prewriting plan so the instructor can see that you know the information and know what you would have included in your answer.

Writing Your Paragraph Answer

Use the following techniques to develop a paragraph answer for a test question:

1. In the topic sentence, be direct. Get right to the point to show that you know the answer to the question and know how to focus your paragraph.
2. Include key words from the question in your opening sentence. Doing so helps you to stay focused and to develop the controlling idea. Using key words from the question also serves as a signal to the instructor that you know which concepts need to be discussed.
3. Use the techniques presented throughout this book for writing effective topics sentences. Include the key elements associated with a topic sentence for the various kinds of paragraphs.
4. Use the techniques presented throughout this textbook to develop the body of the paragraph. Include pertinent details to develop and support your topic sentence. Do not assume "that the instructor knows that I know that so I don't need to put that in the paragraph." Your instructor should not have to read between the lines to determine whether you know the answer.
5. Be very specific with your details. Include facts, such as dates, names, and statistics. If you have memorized exact quotations, you can include them in your answer.
6. Review your paragraph. Check to see that you have unity, coherence, and adequate development. Usually you will not have time to rewrite your answer, so if you remember additional details you want to use, neatly insert them in the paragraph to expand the body of the paragraph.
7. Use **assisted response** when your paragraph lacks adequate development. Look through other test questions for details that you could add to your paragraph. Sometimes the wording of a different question or an individual word in another question triggers an association to details that could strengthen your paragraph. In other words, use your test to assist you in finding pertinent details.
8. Include course-specific terminology to show that you understand the terminology and can use it effectively in your response.
9. Close with a concluding sentence that echoes the topic sentence. A concluding sentence shows that you have said all that you wanted to say about the subject. It finishes your answer and summarizes the main point you intended to develop in the paragraph.

Practice Writing Test Answers

Carefully read the following textbook excerpts. Then, using the content they provide, practice writing paragraph answers. Though you seldom will have access to your textbook during a test, for these practice exercises, you may refer to the excerpts as you develop your answer. As you read each selection, highlight and mark marginal notes. Choose *one* of the questions that follow the excerpt. Decide which type of paragraph you will need to write for the answer.

Follow these steps to write your one-paragraph answer:

1. Make a brief prewriting plan.
2. Write an effective topic sentence.
3. Develop the body of the paragraph. Be careful not to copy anything word for word from the text excerpt. Your test answers must be in your own words.
4. Write a concluding sentence.

Unless instructed otherwise, use the Paragraph Answers For Test Questions Planning Sheet on page 425 for the paragraph answer you write. The Planning Sheet may be duplicated if your instructor assigns more than one paragraph to write.

Excerpt 1

Read the excerpt carefully. Write a one-paragraph answer for *one* of the questions that follow the excerpt. This excerpt from a global history book looks at the attitude of early Europeans in the Americas and the effects they had on the indigenous people of North and South America.

EUROPEANS IN THE AMERICAS

As Columbus's letter of 1493 indicates, Europeans almost instantly discovered that the world across the Atlantic contained exploitable sources of wealth (such as silver, gold, timber, and furs) and was capable of supporting large-scale agricultural production of such crops as sugar and tobacco, for which there was an eager European market. All these things seemed theirs for the taking, not only in the thinly populated regions of North America and eastern and southern South America, but even in the densely populated regions of Mexico, Peru, and the Caribbean.

The consequences of this attitude were catastrophic for America's indigenous peoples. By 1650 Spaniards and Portuguese ruled and exploited Mexico, the Caribbean, Central and South America, and southern portions of North America; the English, French, Dutch, and other Europeans had begun to settle the northern portions of North America's Atlantic coast and the St. Lawrence River Basin. In the wake of these European incursions, Native American political structures disintegrated, uncounted millions of Amerindians died, and traditional patterns of life and belief managed only a tenuous (but tenacious) survival.

While this sad story is true enough, it would be incorrect to say that the majority of the European colonists and the governments who supported them attempted to exterminate the Native Americans. Certainly most European colonists sought to exploit the Amerindians, and even the Amerindians' protectors sought to convert them to European religious beliefs, thereby offering the natives a form of cultural suicide. Moreover, there is no denying the fact that the European newcomers contained within their ranks a number of ruthless thugs who did not hesitate to brutalize and kill, sometimes on a large scale. Still, there is no credible evidence of any widespread attempts at *genocide,* or the systematic, state-sponsored annihilation of an entire people. Such a notion was inconsistent with the world view and aims of the European colonizers who, as we saw in Columbus's letter of 1493, sought souls to save and slaves for servitude.

Europeans might have lacked the intention of killing off millions of Native Americans, but they managed unintentionally to do so, as a consequence of the viruses, bacteria, and other parasites that they carried across the Atlantic in their bodies. What is more, when West African slaves were brought to the Caribbean to replace the native populations that were rapidly dying off, additional fatal diseases came into the Americas. Smallpox, measles, diphtheria, chicken pox, whooping cough, influenza, malaria, yellow fever—all of these and more became killers when introduced into populations that lacked genetic resistance, due to their thousands of years of isolation from the Afro-Eurasian world.

The Tainos, who greeted Columbus in 1492, numbered about one million in 1492; by 1530 they numbered a few thousand. In 1519, the year of Cortés's arrival, the population of Mexico was about twenty-one and one-half million people; in 1532 it had fallen to about sixteen million; at midcentury, following the epidemic of 1545–1548, it was possibly as low as two and one-half million. That is a ninety percent decrease in the short space of thirty years! No part of the Americas was untouched; even areas not visited personally by Europeans felt the devastating effects of killer epidemics. The Mississippian Mound Culture of North America seems to have disappeared as an identifiable entity in the mid-sixteenth century as a result of European diseases that traveled along native trade routes to its population centers well before Europeans ever saw the magnificent mound complexes that this culture left behind as silent witnesses of its former greatness.

[Source: Andrea, Overfield, *The Human Record*. Houghton Mifflin 1998, pp. 446–7.]

Question 1: What negative effects did the early European explorers and settlers have on the lifestyle and beliefs of the native people of the Americas?

Question 2: Why did the indigenous populations of North and South America decrease after the arrival of the Europeans?

Excerpt 2

Read the excerpt carefully. Write a one-paragraph answer for *one* of the questions that follow the excerpt. This excerpt from a book on leadership skills examines the cultural differences and values that effective leaders understand and use in relating to diverse populations in the work force.

CULTURAL FACTORS INFLUENCING LEADERSHIP PRACTICE

A **multicultural leader** is a leader with the skills and attitudes to relate effectively to and motivate people across race, gender, age, social attitudes, and lifestyles. To influence, motivate, and inspire culturally diverse people, the leader must be aware of overt and subtle cultural differences. Such culturally based differences are generalizations, but they function as starting points in the leader's attempt to lead a person from another culture. For example, many Asians are self-conscious about being praised in front of the group because they feel that individual attention clashes with their desire to maintain group harmony. A manager might refrain from praising an Asian group member before the group until he or she understands that group member's preferences. The manager is likely to find that many Asians welcome praise in front of peers, especially when working outside their homeland.

One way to understand how national cultures differ is to examine their values. Here we examine seven different values and how selected nationalities relate to them. Geert Hofstede identified the first five value dimensions in research spanning eighteen years, involving over 160,000 people from over sixty countries. The qualitative research of Arvind V. Phatak identified the other two values.

1. *Individualism/collectivism*. At one end of the continuum is **individualism,** a mental set in which people see themselves first as individuals and believe their own interests and values take priority. **Collectivism,** at the other end

of the continuum, is a feeling that the group and society should receive top priority. Members of a society that value individualism are more concerned with their careers than with the good of the firm. Members of a society who value collectivism, on the other hand, are typically more concerned with the organization than with themselves. Individualistic cultures include the United States, Canada, and Great Britain; collectivistic cultures include Japan, Hong Kong, Mexico, and Greece.

2. *Power distance.* The extent to which employees accept the idea that members of an organization have different levels of power is referred to as **power distance.** In a high-power-distance culture, the boss makes many decisions simply because he or she is boss, and group members readily comply. In a low-power-distance culture, employees do not readily recognize a power hierarchy. They accept directions only when they think the boss is right or when they feel threatened. High-power-distance cultures include France, Spain, Japan, and Mexico. Low-power-distance cultures include the United States, Israel, Germany, and Ireland.

3. *Uncertainty avoidance.* People who accept the unknown, and tolerate risk and unconventional behavior, are said to have low **uncertainty avoidance.** In other words, these people are not afraid to face the unknown. A society ranked high in uncertainty avoidance contains a majority of people who want predictable and certain futures. Low-uncertainty-avoidance cultures include the United States, Canada, and Australia. At the other end of the continuum, workers in Israel, Japan, Italy, and Argentina value certainty and predictability more highly.

4. *Masculinity/femininity.* The terms *masculinity* and *femininity* are now considered sexist in relation to work. Nevertheless, Hofstede used the terms to refer to the useful distinction between materialism and concern for personal welfare. In this context, **masculinity** refers to an emphasis on assertiveness and the acquisition of money and material objects, and a deemphasis on caring for others. At the other end of the continuum is **femininity,** which refers to an emphasis on personal relationships, concern for others, and a high quality of life. "Masculine" countries include Japan and Italy, whereas "feminine" cultures include Sweden and Denmark.

5. *Long-term orientation/short-term orientation.* Workers from a culture with a **long-term orientation** maintain a long-range perspective, and thus are thrifty and do not

demand quick returns on their investments. A **short-term orientation** is characterized by a demand for immediate results, and a propensity not to save. Pacific Rim countries are noted for their long-term orientation. In contrast, the cultures of the United States and Canada are characterized by a more short-term orientation.

6. *Formality/informality.* A country that values **formality** attaches considerable importance to tradition, ceremony, social rules, and rank. In contrast, **informality** refers to a casual attitude toward tradition, ceremony, social rules, and rank. Workers in Latin American countries highly value formality, such as lavish public receptions and processions. American and Canadian workers are much more informal.

7. *Urgent time orientation/casual time orientation.* Long- and short-term orientations focus mostly on planning and investment. Another time-related value dimension is how much importance a person attaches to time. People with an **urgent time orientation** perceive time as a scarce resource and tend to be impatient. People with a **casual time orientation** view time as an unlimited and unending resource and tend to be patient. Americans are noted for their urgent time orientation. They frequently impose deadlines and are eager to "get down to business." Asians and Middle Easterners, in contrast, are patient negotiators. In fact, businesspersons in the Middle East are known to allow a business meeting to run over while another visitor waits outside the office.

How might a manager use information about cultural differences in values to become a more effective leader? A starting point would be to recognize that a person's national values might influence his or her behavior. Assume that a leader wants to influence a person with a low-power-distance orientation to strive for peak performance. The "low-power" person will not spring into action just because the boss makes the suggestion. Instead, the leader needs to patiently explain the personal payoffs of achieving peak performance. Another example is a leader who wants to improve quality and therefore hires people who value collectivism. A backup tactic would be to counsel people who value individualism on the merits of collective action, and thereby achieve high quality.

[Source: DuBrin, *Leadership*, Houghton Mifflin 1998, pp. 365–6.]

Question 1: Hofstede and Phatak identified seven cultural values and studied how different nationalities relate to these values. Define the value of *urgent time orientation/casual time orientation*. Include examples of nationalities that tend to relate to *urgent time* and ones that relate to *casual time*.

Question 2: According to Hofstede and Phatak, Americans relate to the following cultural values: individualistic, low-power distance, low-uncertainty avoidance, short-term orientation, informal, and urgent-time orientation. Do you agree that Americans relate to these values? Explain.

Excerpt 3

Read the excerpt carefully. Write a one-paragraph answer for one of the questions that follow the excerpt. This excerpt from a communication textbook addresses the issue of sexual harassment, an issue that affects men and women at work and on college campuses. This excerpt reminds us that communication is a powerful medium that can produce negative and positive consequences and misinterpretation.

SEXUAL HARASSMENT

"Human communication performs a central yet complex role in sexual harassment. Communication is the primary medium through which sexual harassment is expressed; it is the means by which those who are harassed respond to harassment, and it is also the primary means by which policies for eliminating sexual harassment can be implemented. **Sexual harassment** may be described as "generalized sexist remarks or behavior; inappropriate and offensive, but essentially sanction-free, sexual advances; solicitation of sexual activity or other sex-linked behavior by promise of rewards; coercion of sexual activity by threat of punishment; and assaults." It also includes "unwanted and unwelcome sexual actions in work and educational contexts."

The effect of sexual harassment, as a communicative event, was summarized by writer Toni Morrison in her 1993 acceptance speech for the Nobel Prize for literature when she stated, "Oppressive language does more than violence . . . it is violence."

Sexual harassment is a serious and pervasive problem in modern organizational life, with both the targets and those accused (falsely or not) suffering personal anguish and dehumanization. A survey of female employees found that 43 percent had experienced sexual harassment.

Sexual harassment takes place not only in the workplace but on college campuses. Students at one university report that as many as 89 percent of women experienced sexual harassment at least once, and that many experienced it more than once.

"Sexual harassment is experienced primarily by women." This does not mean that men are not also victims. However, in our society, where men may perceive a come-on as positive, women perceive the same advances as negative. Men, therefore, instead of feeling like victims, may perceive harassment as an ego booster, a cause for bragging.

Men's perceptions of what their behavior means are vastly different from women's. The harasser may see himself as intending to exercise his power over women, protect his professional turf, enhance his macho self-image, and demonstrate his friendliness and helpfulness. The harassed may want to stop the harassment; deter future incidents; preserve her reputation; avoid retaliation; maintain rapport; and preserve self-respect, physical safety, and psychological well-being.

Sexual harassment has not changed over the years. "What has changed is that people now are more willing to label these behaviors as being sexual harassment, people are more willing to talk about it, and people are more angry about it.

[Source: Berko, Wolvin, Wolvin, *Communicating*, Houghton Mifflin 1998, pp. 148–9.]

Question 1: What constitutes sexual harassment? Define the term and expand the definition with examples.

Question 2: Perceptions about words and behaviors differ between men and women. This difference can lead to charges of sexual harassment. How do men's perceptions about their behavior differ from women's perceptions of male behavior?

Excerpt 4

Read the excerpt carefully. Write a one-paragraph answer for one of the questions that follow the excerpt. This excerpt from a global history textbook discusses concerns about environmental threats and actions that have been taken to reduce further destruction of the environment.

RESPONDING TO ENVIRONMENTAL THREATS

Despite the gravity of environmental threats, there were many successful efforts to preserve and protect the environment. The Clean Air Act, the Clean Water Act, and the Endangered Species Act were passed in the United States in the 1970s as part of an environmental effort that included the nations of the European Community and Japan. Environmental awareness spread by means of the media and grassroots political movements, and most nations in the developed world enforced strict antipollution laws and sponsored massive recycling efforts. Many also encouraged resource conservation by rewarding energy-efficient factories and the manufacturers of fuel-efficient cars and by promoting the use of alternative energy sources such as solar and wind power.

These efforts produced significant results. In western Europe and the United States, air quality improved dramatically. In the United States, smog levels were down nearly a third from 1970 to 2000 even though the number of automobiles increased more than 80 percent. Emissions of lead and sulfur dioxide were down as well. The Great Lakes, Long Island Sound, and Chesapeake Bay were all much cleaner at the end of the century than they had been in 1970. The rivers of North America and Europe also improved. Still, more than thirty thousand deaths each year in the United States are attributed to exposure to pesticides and other chemicals.

New technologies made much of this improvement possible. Pollution controls on automobiles, planes, and factory smokestacks reduced harmful emissions. Similar progress was made in the chemical industry. Scientists identified the chemicals that threaten the ozone layer, and the phase-out of their use in new appliances and cars began.

Clearly the desire to preserve the natural environment was growing around the world. In the developed nations, continued political organization and enhanced awareness of environmental issues seemed likely to lead to step-by-step improvements in environmental policy. In the developing world and most of the former Soviet bloc, however, population pressures and weak governments were major obstacles to effective environmental policies. In China, for example, respiratory disease caused by pollution was the leading cause of death. Thus it was likely that the industrialized nations would have to fund global improvements, and the cost was likely to be high. Achieving this global redistribution of wealth and political power will be the most difficult task facing the environmental movement in the coming years.

[Source: Bulliet, Crossley, Headrick, Hirsch, Johnson, Northrup, *The Earth and Its People*, Houghton Mifflin 2001, p. 878.]

Question 1: What global changes have occurred in the environmental movement since the early 1970s?

Question 2: Why have developing nations made less progress with preservation of the natural environment than the developed nations? What factors slow down their progress?

PARAGRAPH ANSWERS FOR TEST QUESTIONS PLANNING SHEET

Name ______________________________

1. Title of the excerpt: ______________________________
2. Which question are you answering? Question # ______________________________
3. What is the **direction word** in the question? ______________________________
4. What kind of paragraph will answer the question? ______________________________
5. Show your prewriting plan in the space below.

6. Ask a partner to read your paragraph and to complete the Partner Feedback Form.

PARTNER FEEDBACK FORM

1. Does your partner use an appropriate type of paragraph to answer the question? Explain.

2. Is the topic sentence effective? Does the topic sentence have the key elements for an effective topic sentence for this type of paragraph? Explain.

3. Does the writer include adequate details in the body of the paragraph to explain, develop, or support the topic sentence? Explain.

4. Does your partner use his or her own words throughout the paragraph? Explain.

5. Does the paragraph have coherence? Do the ideas flow together smoothly? Explain.

6. Does your partner need to add any important details to strengthen his or her answer? Explain.

7. Does the paragraph have an effective concluding sentence? Explain.

Partner's name ______________________________

Grammar Checklist to be Completed by your Instructor:

_______# fragments, comma splice errors, or run-on sentence errors

_______# spelling errors

_______# comma and semicolon errors

_______# subject-verb agreement errors

_______# errors in verb forms

Other:

_______ good sentence variety

_______ appropriate paragraph structure

_______ accurate details

_______ minimal/no punctuation errors

_______ adequate details, unity, and coherence

Learning from Your Tests

Immediately after your instructor returns your test to you, take time to analyze the test and identify ways you can strengthen your test-taking skills. The following questions and strategies can help you learn from your tests:

1. Did you read the direction words carefully and write a paragraph that directly answered the question? If not, review the list of direction words on page 411 and the types of paragraphs they tend to require.
2. Were you underprepared for one or more of the questions? Did your paragraph lack sufficient or accurate details? Return to your notes and your textbook. Identify significant information that you should have included in your answer. Cross out inaccurate information and substitute the correct information so you have the accurate information in your memory.
3. Did you use effective paragraph structure? Did you have a strong, to-the-point topic sentence? Did you use appropriate techniques to develop the body of the paragraph? Did you include a concluding sentence that reflects or echoes the topic sentence?
4. Did you have mechanical or sentence-level errors? Study any comments your instructor made on your paper.
5. Rewrite your answer for additional practice. The same information, in one form or another, may appear on a final exam.
6. Adjust your study strategies. Take a careful look at the study strategies you used to prepare for the test. Identify which strategies were effective and which strategies need to be modified for future tests. Review the list of study strategies on pages 413–415. Identify those that you need to use more consistently for improved results.
7. Discuss your test with your instructor if you have any questions or concerns. Ask him or her for additional suggestions for writing stronger test answers.

Writing thorough paragraph answers on tests is a skill that improves with practice and time. As you gain more experiences writing paragraphs in a nonpressure setting, you learn to formulate your ideas, structure your paragraphs, and write paragraph answers more quickly. This comfort and familiarity with writing effective paragraphs carries over to test-taking situations. You may find that you actually prefer tests that require paragraph-level answers over those with true-false, multiple-choice, or matching questions. A paragraph question allows you a better opportunity to express your ideas and show all that you have learned.

Internet Enrichment

Log on to the web site for this textbook for additional exercises and links for the following topics:

Direction Words
Preparing for Tests

Go to: http://college.hmco.com. Click on "Students." Type *Paragraph Essentials* in the "Jump to Textbook Sites" box. Click "go," and then bookmark the site. Click on Chapter 11.

CHAPTER 12

Essays

The first paragraph introduces the topic, key words from the question or assignment, and your thesis statement.	Introductory paragraph with a thesis statement
Each paragraph in the body has a main idea and supporting details. Paragraphs within the essay do not need concluding sentences.	Paragraph 1 with a main idea + supporting details
Each paragraph explains, supports, or develops a portion of the thesis statement.	Paragraph 2 with a main idea + supporting details
Each paragraph has unity, coherence, and adequate development.	Paragraph 3 with a main idea + supporting details
The concluding paragraph reinforces the thesis statement.	Concluding paragraph

In Chapter 12 you will learn about the following:

1. The differences between paragraphs and essays
2. The structure of an essay
3. Understanding your essay assignment
4. The writing process for essays
5. Learning from model essays
6. Writing essay answers on tests

From Paragraphs to Essays

An essay is a form of writing that consists of a series of well-developed paragraphs that together explain, develop, or support one controlling idea. Though essays vary in length, a standard essay consists of five paragraphs: an introductory paragraph, three paragraphs for the body, and a concluding paragraph. The main controlling idea of the entire essay is called a **thesis statement.** The thesis statement usually appears in the first paragraph, the **introductory paragraph.** The **body** of the essay consists of a series of paragraphs; each paragraph has its own main idea and supporting details. A **concluding paragraph** may summarize the main ideas, reinforce the thesis statement, or draw conclusions that are based on the content of the essay.

Throughout the discussion of paragraphs in previous chapters, you learned that you need to narrow a topic to a manageable size for a paragraph. Topics that are too large for a paragraph are better suited for an essay. An essay offers you the opportunity to develop larger topics effectively through a structured series of paragraphs. In the following diagrams, notice both the similarities and the differences between the structures of paragraphs and essays.

Paragraph Structure

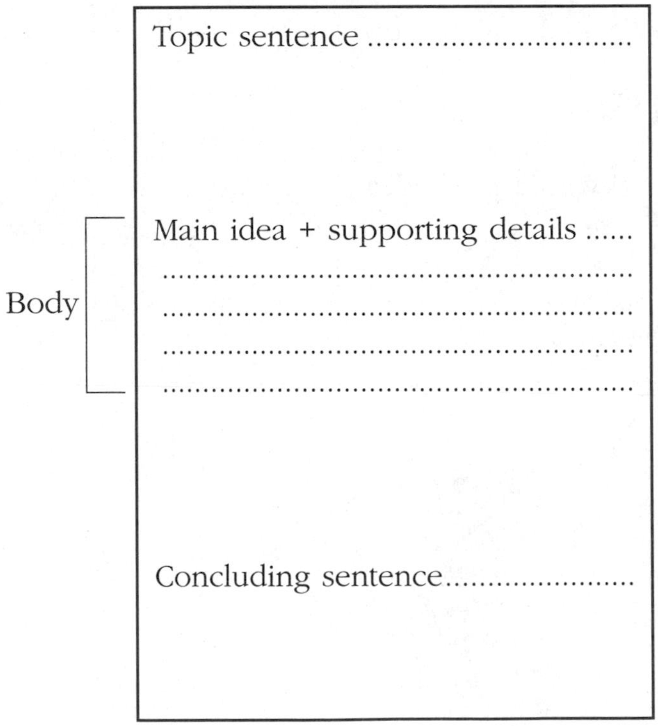

Topic sentence ....

Body: Main idea + supporting details ......
....
....
....
....

Concluding sentence......................

Essay Structure

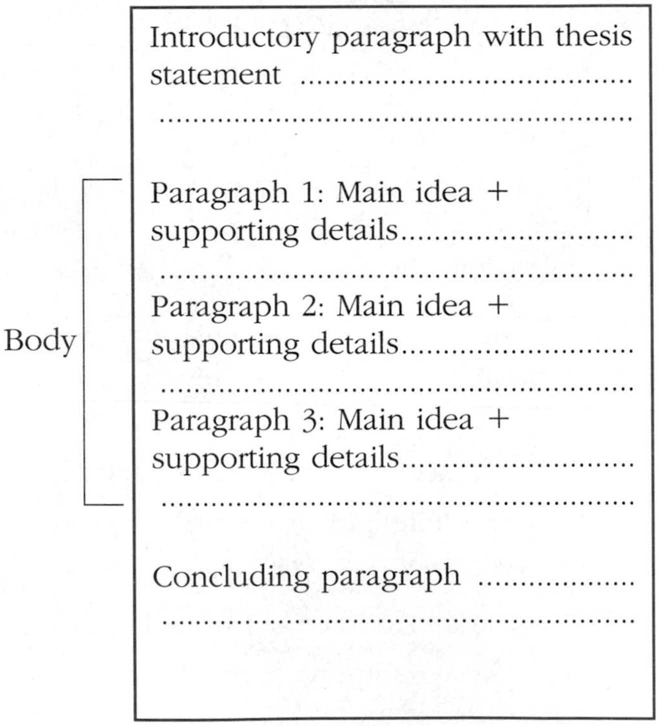

Introductory paragraph with thesis statement ....
....

Body:
Paragraph 1: Main idea + supporting details..........................
....
Paragraph 2: Main idea + supporting details..........................
....
Paragraph 3: Main idea + supporting details..........................
....

Concluding paragraph ....
....

Many paragraphs have the potential to be expanded into essays. For example, a classification paragraph may have three subtopics or three categories of information. When there are sufficient details for each of the categories, you can expand the paragraph into an essay. The following classification paragraph introduces the reader to the defense in football. Then, to provide the reader with more extensive details, the writer expands the paragraph into an essay.

The Defense

Topic sentence

Body

Concluding Sentence

In American football, the defense is comprised of three basic groups of players. The first group of defensive players is called the *defensive linemen*. These players line up on the line of scrimmage, an invisible line that touches the end of the ball when the referee places the ball on the field at the beginning of a play. Defensive linemen consist of defensive tackles and defensive ends. Though the number of defensive linemen varies according to the play plan, it is common to have four linemen. The second group of defensive players is called the *linebackers*. These players line up behind the defensive linemen. A common defensive game plan or formation uses three linebackers. The middle linebacker has an outside linebacker to his left and to his right. The third group of defensive players is called the *secondary*. The secondary lines up farther back in the field and behind the linebackers. The secondary frequently consists of four players. Two of the players in the secondary are cornerbacks. The other two are called safeties. The defense in football, which always consists of eleven players, uses combinations of these three groups of players each time it defends its side of the field from the team with the ball.

Essay: The Defense

Introductory Paragraph

Thesis Statement

American football, one of America's passions, is a complex game that requires athleticism and intelligence. Each player has a role to play and must learn an array of formations in order to be in the right place at the right time. Each team consists of two subteams: the offense and the defense. The roll of the defense is to defend its territory from invasion and to prevent the other team from entering its territory and scoring points. A common football saying is that "you don't win a game by offense alone." The defense, which consists of eleven players, plays a crucial role in every game. To better understand the value of the defense and truly appreciate the defense, understanding the defensive positions and the responsibilities of each position is essential.

Body: First Paragraph

Topic Sentence (main idea)

Position

The first group of defensive players is called the *defensive linemen*. These players line up on the line of scrimmage, an invisible line that touches the end of the ball when the ball is placed on the field at the beginning of a play. They line up opposite the offensive linemen. These players squat down or bend over at the line of scrimmage and have one hand or their fingertips in the dirt. Though the number of

Kinds of linemen

Main role

defensive linemen varies according to the play, four linemen is common: two *tackles* and two *defensive ends.* The two tackles are in the middle of the line and face the center of the opposing team. The main job of the tackles is to push the center of the other team back as soon as the play begins and to cover a gap to prevent a player with the ball from running through the gap to move the ball forward. The two defensive ends line up on each end of the line of scrimmage. They face the tackles on the other team. The main job of the defensive ends is to get to the quarterback to disrupt the play and sometimes *sack* the quarterback, which means to tackle him while he has the ball behind the line of scrimmage.

Body: Second Paragraph

Topic sentence (main idea)

Position

Kinds of linebackers and their main roles

The second group of defensive players is called the *linebackers.* The linebackers line up behind the four defensive linemen. They begin each play in a more upright or standing position. A common defensive game plan or formation uses three linebackers: a strong outside linebacker, a middle linebacker, and a weak outside linebacker. The *strong outside linebacker,* nicknamed "Sam," lines up across from an offensive player (a tight end) who may run down the field for a pass. The strong outside linebacker's role is to disrupt the running path and the player so he cannot catch a pass and run down field. Sometimes he also tries to get through the offensive line to reach the quarterback before the quarterback has a chance to throw or pass the ball. The *middle linebacker,* nicknamed "Mike," has an outside linebacker to his left and to his right. The middle linebacker often tells the other defensive players which defensive play to use. His other main role is to tackle any ball carrier who comes his way. The *weak outside linebacker,* nicknamed "Will," has multiple roles. Sometimes he defends his side of the field, sometimes he goes after and tries to tackle the quarterback, and sometimes he goes further back in the field to be ready to tackle a player who catches a pass.

Body: Third Paragraph

Topic Sentence (main idea)

Kinds of secondary players

Main roles

The third group of defensive players is called the *secondary.* The secondary is also called the *defensive backs;* they are in the back of the field behind the linebackers. The secondary frequently consists of four players: two cornerbacks, one strong safety, and one free safety. The *free safety* is the farthest back in the field and the closest to the goal line where the other team scores. The secondary's job is to defend the backfield from pass plays and to prevent any ball carrier from getting into the end zone to score. The secondary's main job is to tackle the ball carrier to end the play. These players are the last line of the defense. If a ball carrier makes it past the secondary, there is no defense left; the ball carrier will "hit his head on the goal post," which means he will score for his team.

Concluding Paragraph

The defense in football, which always consists of eleven players, uses combinations of these three groups of players each time it defends its side of the field from the team with the ball. The defensive linemen, the linebackers, and the secondary each have crucial roles to play. They share one common objective: keep the other team from advancing the ball down the field and scoring.

[Adapted from: Wong, *Mom's Pocket Guide to Watching Football,* TV Books 2000, pp. 80–96.]

The Structure of an Essay

An essay has three distinct parts: an introduction, a body, and a conclusion. The standard five-paragraph essay has one introductory paragraph, three paragraphs for the body, and one concluding paragraph.

	Introductory paragraph
Body	Paragraph 1
Body	Paragraph 2
Body	Paragraph 3
	Concluding paragraph

Essays are not restricted to the standard five-paragraph essay format. An essay may be considerably longer than the standard five-paragraph essay. For a complex topic with many different main ideas, you will need more than three paragraphs to develop each main idea. (Examples of longer paragraphs appear at the end of this chapter.) The length of an essay is determined not by a formula, but by the amount of information and the number of main ideas the writer needs to include in the essay to develop the thesis statement.

Writing the Introductory Paragraph

Use the following guidelines to write an effective introductory paragraph that reveals your thesis statement with the controlling idea for your essay.

1. Capture your reader's interest by using an anecdote, quotation, interesting background information, a statement of the significance of your topic, or a question.
2. Introduce the topic (the subject) and the controlling idea, which is called the thesis statement. The thesis statement states the central purpose of the essay and lets your reader know your position, your point of view, or the direction you intend to use to develop your controlling idea.

3. Place the thesis statement in the introductory paragraph. The thesis statement is often the last sentence in the introductory paragraph, but you can place it within the paragraph as well.
4. Provide your reader with signals words or clues as to how you structured the essay. For example, number words often signal the structure of the essay and make it possible for your reader to predict the structure and the content of the essay. In the following example, the last sentence, the thesis statement, provides you with a "roadmap" for the remainder of the essay. You can easily predict the three categories of information that will follow in the body of the paragraph.

    Giving a speech is challenging for most people. Giving an effective speech for a diverse audience is even more challenging. When the audience is diverse, such as an audience with members of different genders, cultural or ethnic identities, ages, sexual orientations, religions, and occupations, the speaker must find ways to relate to all the members of his or her diverse audience. An effective speaker must learn to avoid stereotyping and using language that is offensive to one or more of the members of the audience. To communicate effectively to a diverse audience, an effective speaker must avoid the three most common problems that impede communication with a diverse audience: sexism, ethnocentrism, and racism.

    [Adapted from: Osborn, Osborn, *Public Speaking*, Houghton Mifflin 1997, pp. 118–121.]

5. Get right to the point in the introductory paragraph. Avoid weak or meaningless sentences such as the following:

    There are things you should know before I write this essay.

    I wanted to write about endangered animals, but I decided to write instead about preservation of our national forests.

    I am going to write about something that really concerns me.

    I am not quite sure how to write an essay, but here it goes.

    Here are my ideas about school vouchers.

Developing the Body of the Essay

Use the following guidelines to develop the body of your essay and the controlling idea that is stated in your thesis statement.

1. Plan to include a series of paragraphs, each of which explains, develops, or supports your thesis statement in the introductory paragraph.

2. Write a strong, effective topic sentence for each paragraph. The topic sentence is usually, but not always, placed at the beginning of each new paragraph. Placing the topic sentence at the beginning of the paragraph keeps your reader focused on the main point you intend to develop in the paragraph.

3. Achieve *coherence* in the essay, within the paragraphs, and from one paragraph to the next. Ideas within a paragraph and from one paragraph to another should flow smoothly and logically. The following techniques can help you achieve coherence:

   a. Construct a well-developed organizational plan before you begin writing. In this plan, show a logical sequence for the paragraphs within the body of your essay.

   b. Use key words from the introductory paragraph and the thesis statement in the beginning of each paragraph in the body of the essay. Repetition of key words strengthens your essay by consistently relating the paragraphs to your controlling idea.

   c. Use transition sentences at the end of one or more of your paragraphs. A transition sentence serves as a lead into the next paragraph.

4. Achieve *unity* throughout your essay by including main ideas and details that explain, develop, support, or reinforce the controlling idea of your thesis statement. You should exclude information that is not directly related to the controlling idea. Do not wander off course or lose the focus of your overall purpose for the essay.

5. Achieve *adequate development* within the individual paragraphs and within the essay. The writing skills you have learned for different kinds of paragraphs apply to the paragraphs within the essay. Each paragraph must have a main idea that you develop through supporting details. The same is true for the thesis statement. You must develop each part or aspect of the thesis statement through a well-planned series of paragraphs.

   For example, the following thesis statement from page 434 lays the foundation for an essay that will discuss sexism, ethnocentrism, and racism.

   > To communicate effectively to a diverse audience, an effective speaker must avoid the three most common problems that impede communication with a diverse audience: sexism, ethnocentrism, and racism.

   If the writer develops only two of the three ideas into paragraphs, the essay will be incomplete and underdeveloped. Likewise, if the body of the essay includes a paragraph for each of the three concepts, but the paragraphs lack content or sufficient details, the essay will lack adequate development and be underdeveloped.

Underdeveloped	Underdeveloped	Adequately Developed
Introductory Paragraph with Thesis	Introductory Paragraph with Thesis	Introductory Paragraph with Thesis
Paragraph 1: sexism (includes adequate details)	Paragraph 1: sexism (with too few details)	Paragraph 1: sexism (with adequate details)
Paragraph 2: ethnocentrism (includes adequate details)	Paragraph 2: ethnocentrism (with too few details)	Paragraph 2: ethnocentrism (with adequate details)
Concluding Paragraph	Paragraph 3: racism (with too few details)	Paragraph 3: racism (with adequate details)
	Concluding Paragraph	Concluding Paragraph

6. Use a variety of paragraph styles when it seems appropriate. For example, one paragraph may develop the main idea through exemplification. Another paragraph may develop the main idea through narration, definition, comparison, or contrast. An essay does not need to use the same type of paragraph for every paragraph in the body. Use the type of paragraph style that is most suited to develop the main idea of each paragraph.

Developing the Concluding Paragraph

Use the following guidelines to bring your essay to an end.

1. Use the concluding paragraph to bring your essay to a satisfactory close for your reader. You may be able to create this closure in one or two sentences, but a three- to six-sentence concluding paragraph is more typical for an essay.
2. Use one of the following options to develop your concluding paragraph:
   a. If you posed a question in the introductory paragraph, state the answer to the question in this closing paragraph.
   b. Conclude the essay by reinforcing the thesis statement and the main ideas that you presented in the essay. Restate or summarize these main elements of the essay in different words.
   c. Leave your reader with a powerful final thought by ending with a thought-provoking statement, a new anecdote, a quotation, or a definition that relates to or reinforces the thesis statement.

Understanding Your Essay Assignment

The same seven steps that you have used to write paragraphs are used to write essays. Because essays are longer and contain more details, you will need more time to complete each of the steps. Before you begin the steps of the writing process for essays, you must first attend to three aspects of the assignment:

1. What is the essay assignment? Be very certain that you understand the assignment, the scope of information your instructor expects you to cover, the general guidelines for the assignment, and the maximum length that will be accepted.
2. What is the direction word in the essay assignment? (See the list of direction words in Chapter 11, page 411.) Highlight key words in the question. You will want to include these key words in your introductory paragraph and throughout your essay.
3. When is the essay due? Because each step requires significantly more time to complete for an essay than for a paragraph, create a time management plan. Use a calendar to plan each step of the writing process. Your goal should be to complete the final version of the essay the day before it is due. On your calendar, indicate a target date for each step of the process. The more often you write essays, the more accurately you can estimate the amount of time you need for each step. It is in your best interest to begin the assignment immediately.

Step	**Complete by . . .**
Step 1: Generate ideas.	____________
Step 2: Get a focus.	____________
Step 3: Gather and organize information.	
Do prewriting. Do an outline.	
Write a thesis statement.	____________
Step 4: Write the rough draft.	____________
Step 5: Revise, revise, revise.	____________
Step 6: Proofread and edit.	____________
Step 7: Complete the final version.	____________

The Writing Process for Essays

Step 1: Generate ideas.

Sometimes essay assignments are very specific and do not offer a choice of topics. When your instructor gives a specific assignment, move to Step 2. When your instructor gives a specific assignment for an essay, but you must select a topic, you will need to generate ideas to consider for your essay. The same techniques that you used to generate ideas for paragraphs work effectively to generate ideas for essays.

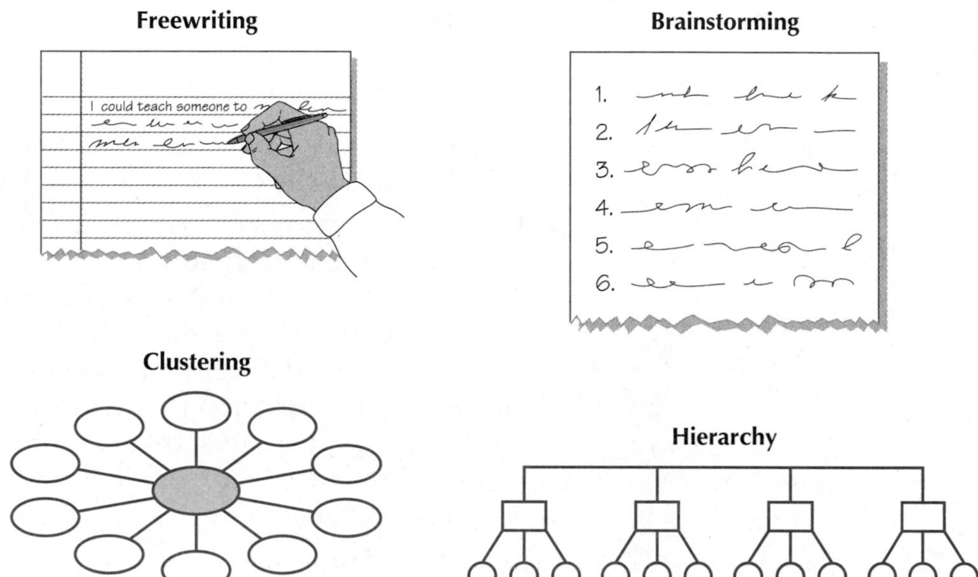

The following techniques also work effectively to generate ideas for essays.

1. **Card catalogs.** An interesting way to explore possible ideas is to use electronic media in your college's library or at home. A card catalog system (online or file cards) can help you discover possible topics for your essay. Assume your essay needs to be on *eating disorders*. When you look up *eating disorders* in a catalog system, you will find many subcategories that you could consider as topics for an essay.
2. **The Internet.** Another electronic source of information is the Internet. Use several different search engines to explore possible topics for your essay. At each web site that you visit, explore other connecting links as well. Compile a list of possible topics from the various web sites. Record or bookmark sites that you may want to return to later for information to use in your essay.
3. **Your textbook.** Most essay assignments in college relate in some way to the content of the course. Your textbook can provide you with possible topics to use. Turn to the index at the end of the book. Look up the key words in the essay assignment. Refer to all

the pages listed for those key words to locate essay topics that interest you.

Step 2: Get a focus.

Once you select a topic, the next step is to give it a focus. This often involves narrowing the topic to a specific time frame or a specific aspect of the subject. A topic that is too broad is too unmanageable, even for an essay. Broad topics are also difficult to develop within the length requirements of the assignment. For example, volumes of books have been written about developing strong writing skills. Narrowing the topic to a specific aspect of writing, such as using the three essential elements of all paragraphs, is better focused and manageable.

Step 3: Gather and organize information.

Step 3 involves three separate processes: gathering information to use in your essay, organizing the information in a logical way, and formulating a thesis statement that will control the content of the essay. These three steps require time and a time management plan with a realistic time frame for each task. Because this step can lead you in new directions and down time-consuming paths, you may want to estimate the time needed to gather and organize information and then double it. If you overestimate the amount of time a task will require, you will be ahead of your schedule and able to move on to Step 4.

Gathering Information

Unless your essay is a personal narrative, you will often need to research your topic to find significant details to include in your essay. The majority of essays in college are expository, which means the purpose is to expose or present concepts and factual details to support your thesis statement. If you do not have a wealth of knowledge and an abundance of factual information, you will need to use the resources that are available to you to locate information for your essay.

Use the following guidelines to gather information:

1. Take notes on information that you may want to use in your essay.
2. Always record the bibliographic information of each resource. If you photocopy the information, you can write the bibliographic information on the copy. If you take notes but do not photocopy, you can write the information in your notes or code your notes with a number. On a separate piece of paper, make a numerical list of the resources you use.
3. If you are copying information word-for-word from the book or the resources, place the information inside quotation marks so you will know later that those are not your words. If you read information and then summarize it in your own words, do not use the quotation marks.

4. Many students find that large index cards work most effectively to record research notes. Limit each index card to one main idea or one aspect of your topic. This way, when it is time to organize the information, you can sort and group the index cards according to the ideas presented in the cards. Be sure to write a bibliographic reference note or code on the card so you later know the source.
5. Include the following bibliographic information in your notes:
   - name of the author
   - name of the book
   - name of the publisher
   - copyright date
   - page numbers

   Different formats can be used for bibliographies. Use the formats provided by your instructor, or use the following formats as guides.

   Authors
   Bulliet, Crossley, Headrick, Hirsch, Johnson, Northrup,
   Title of the Book — Publisher — Copyright — Page Number
   The Earth and Its People, Houghton Mifflin, 2001, p. 814.)
   Author's Name — Name Source of Article
   Mihaly Csikszentmihalyi, Ph. D, "Finding Flow,"
   Publication — Date — Page Numbers
   Psychology Today, July/August 1997, pp. 46–8.

6. Make good use of the resources that are available to you. As you gather information for your essay, you may encounter other interesting aspects or subtopics that you had not previously considered. If you wish to revise your focus, or even change your topic during the stage of gathering information, you may do so. The following resources can provide you with details for your essay:
   a. Your textbook. Use the index in the back of the book to locate pages throughout the book that contain related information.
   b. The library. Access reference books, shelved books, magazines, databases, card catalog, and audio-visual materials. Do not hesitate to ask a reference librarian to assist you in locating information.
   c. The Internet. Use several different search engines to seek out relevant information. Pay close attention to the source, as some information on the Internet is inaccurate, biased, or incomplete.
   d. Interviews. Talk with experts or authorities in the field for firsthand knowledge about the topic of your essay.

Organizing Information

From the process of gathering information, you should have a variety of notes and information that may be essential for your essay. Your task now is to sort through the information and organize it in a meaningful way. You can use the following guidelines to help you organize the information.

1. Read through the information you have gathered. Look for commonalities or similar categories. If you are working with notes on index cards, sort the cards by placing cards with similar concepts together. If you are working with photocopied notes or notes on paper, you can cut the notes apart and then sort or regroup similar concepts together. Be sure that each piece has the bibliographic code or reference on it when you separate it from its original format.
2. Use any of the techniques that you have already learned to organize your information. Select the format that seems most appropriate and useful for the topic. Seeing the information presented in a visual form is helpful and effective. Each main section of your organizational plan becomes the roadmap for a paragraph.

Cluster

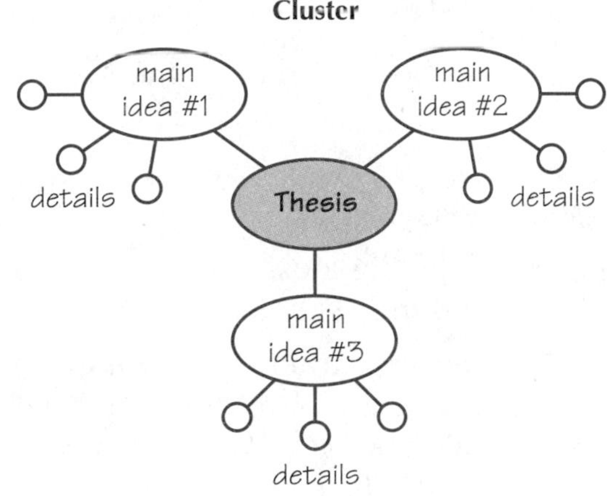

Hierarchy

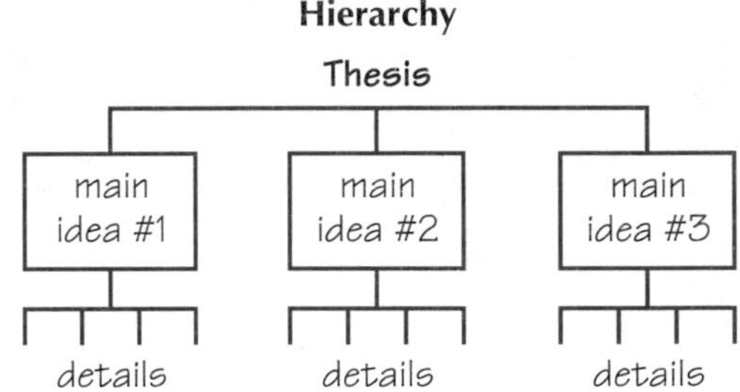

Grid

Subtopics	Subject A	Subject B	Subject C

Outline

Title
I. Introductory Paragraph
   A. General background
   B Thesis statement
II. Main Idea #1
   A.
   B. details
   C.
III. Main Idea #2
   A.
   B. details
   C.
IV. Main Idea #3
   A.
   B. details
   C.
V. Concluding Paragraph

Some instructors will require you to turn in a formal outline for your essay. If this is the case, you can begin to plan your essay by creating a cluster, a hierarchy, or a grid to use as your first prewriting organizer. You can easily convert the information in any one of these organizers into an outline before you begin writing the rough draft. Some students prefer to write their formal outline *after* they have written the rough draft. While this may seem to be in a reverse order, writing a formal outline after writing a rough draft helps you to identify the strengths and the weaknesses of your rough draft, including coherence and adequate development. This information can help you with your revision work.

Writing a Thesis Statement

The thesis statement is the controlling idea of the entire essay, so you need to give careful thought to the development of the thesis statement. As with topic sentences, plan on writing and refining several possible thesis statements until a strong, effective thesis statement emerges. Use these questions and guidelines to develop your thesis statement.

1. What is the purpose or the big idea you want to express in this essay? Try to put your idea on paper as a thesis statement. Then, try to write two or three other possible thesis statements. Select the one that seems most effective and reflects the idea you want to express.
2. Is the big idea something that interests you, will interest your reader, and has some significance?
3. Does your purpose and the big idea meet the criteria established by the direction word and the essay assignment?
4. Do you have adequate material to use to develop the thesis statement? Everything in your essay must support the topic sentence of the paragraph it is in, and it must support the thesis statement either directly or indirectly. Do you have enough material so your essay will have adequate development? You need to have a variety of information in order to have several different topic sentences. If you feel you do not have enough information, continue searching and gathering more information.
5. Does the thesis statement serve as a roadmap for you to write the essay and for your reader to follow your thoughts? If not, refine the thesis statement.

12.1 What do you think?

Assume that your assignment is to write an essay about the paragraph-writing skills you have learned in this course. Your assignment is to discuss the three essential elements of all paragraphs: unity, coherence, and adequate development. Complete each of the following prewriting tasks.

1. Complete the following cluster to show the three main ideas that you need to develop in this writing assignment.

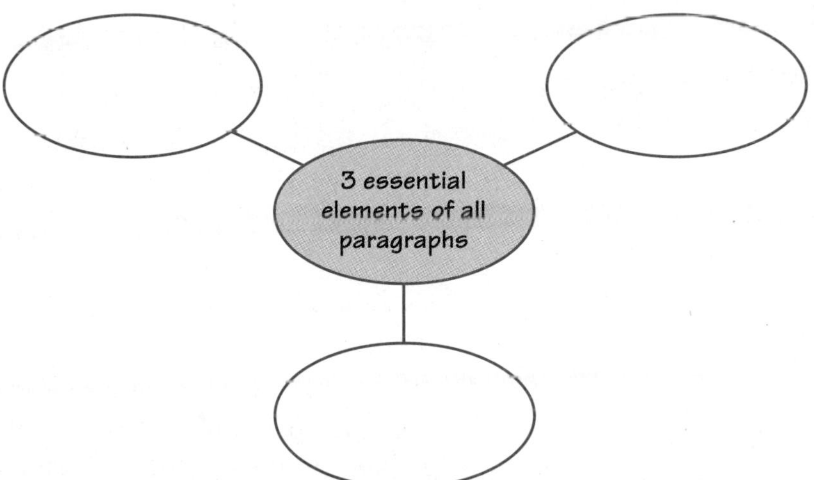

2. This assignment can be developed in a five-paragraph essay. Label each paragraph by telling in general terms what you plan to include in each paragraph.

Assignment: Discuss the three essential elements of all paragraphs: unity, coherence, and adequate development.

Your Essay Diagram

3. Write several possible thesis statements for your essay. Star the thesis statement that you prefer.

____

____

____

____

Step 4: Write the rough draft.

Use your prewriting materials, which include your notes, an organizational plan, and a thesis statement, to write a rough draft. Use the following sequence to write your draft.

1. Write the introductory paragraph, which includes your thesis statement.
2. Use your notes and your organizational plan to write a series of paragraphs. Develop only one main idea in each paragraph.
3. As your write, if you feel some information is out if place, move the information to a more appropriate location. In other words, modify your organizational plan as needed during the draft-writing step.
4. Remember that your goal for writing a rough draft is to get your ideas on paper so you can analyze them more thoroughly and make revisions in the next step. Do not expect a polished essay at this point in the writing process.
5. Double-space your work when your write the rough draft. Space between the lines makes adding words, phrases, or sentences easier. It also gives you room to add comments or questions to yourself. If you know how to use a computer and have access to one, writing a draft on a computer facilitates the revision work. Cutting and pasting to move ideas and adding or deleting ideas is much easier to do on a computer than by hand.

Step 5: Revise, revise, revise.

This step of the writing process often requires a considerable amount of time, for there are many elements of an essay to consider. Instead of trying to make revision a one-step process, plan to revise several times. Each time you revise, analyze the essay for different elements and continue to look for ways to strengthen your essay. Ask writing tutors, other students, or your instructor to provide feedback for you on your essay. As you revise, use these questions to analyze your essay.

1. Are you using an effective structure for your essay? Do you have a strong introductory paragraph that captures your reader's interest and serves as a roadmap for you and your reader? Do you have a sufficient number of paragraphs to develop the body of the paragraph and the thesis statement? Is the concluding paragraph effective?
2. Does each paragraph serve a clear purpose? Does the essay reflect your audience? Does each paragraph have a well-developed topic sentence? Does each topic sentence support the thesis statement? Is the topic sentence placed effectively in the paragraph? Does the topic sentence control the contents of the paragraph?

3. Do you use an effective form of discourse or paragraph style for each paragraph? Does the paragraph style incorporate the elements for that style of paragraph that you learned in previous chapters?
4. Does every paragraph have unity, coherence, and adequate development? Do you avoid wandering off course? Are all the details relevant to the topic? Do you have a sufficient number of quality details to explain, support, or develop the thesis statement? Do the ideas in the paragraphs flow smoothly? Do the paragraphs flow together smoothly? Are transitions needed?
5. On the sentence level, can you strengthen some of the sentences by using more effective word choices? Do you use a variety of sentence structures? Can you combine some ideas more effectively? Do you use transition words where they are needed to connect words, phrases, and sentences effectively?

With such a lengthy list of essay and paragraph elements to consider, you may feel that the revision process never ends. In some ways this is true. There will always be other ways to express the ideas and organize the information. Your goal is to reach a point at which you are pleased with your essay and feel the essay expresses your thoughts clearly, powerfully, and effectively. When you achieve this feeling, it is an appropriate time to end the revision process. Even though you know other changes could be made, accept the notion that your work is representative of your knowledge and your effort, and that it is woven with quality. Move to the next step.

Step 6: Proofread and edit.

Proofreading and editing occurs on the sentence level. Apply the skills you have learned to check each sentence for punctuation, spelling, subject-verb agreement, pronoun-antecedent agreement, correct usage of verb tenses, parallelism, and complete sentences. Correct any errors and move on to Step 7.

Step 7: Prepare the final version of your essay.

Use your instructor's guidelines for preparing the final version of your essay. You may be asked to include a title page, a bibliography, prewriting materials, and an outline. Before turning your paper in, review the assignment. Check that you have complied with all the requirements, have met all the criteria, and have prepared the final version in the format requested. If you have followed the seven steps for essay writing, have completed each of the steps to the best of your ability, and have allowed ample time for the entire writing process, your effort will be reflected in your final version.

Learning from Model Essays

The following exercises provide you with opportunities to read, examine, and discuss model essays. Work with a partner or on your own to complete the following tasks:

1. Read each essay carefully.
2. Underline the thesis statement and the main idea of each paragraph.
3. Highlight or underline key points, and make brief notes in the margins.
4. Answer the questions that follow the essay. Write your answers on separate paper.

12.2 What do you think?

Moving from one's native country to the United States takes courage and a willingness to face language and cultural barriers. Hiromi Hasegawa made the decision to come to America from Japan. In her essay, she reveals the many frustrations and uncomfortable situations she has encountered in her life in America. Language barriers, American customs, and common behaviors of some American people create numerous pressures, but she is determined to make life in America work for her.

My Life in America

P1 Talking with people in Japan was never a problem, but I feel uncomfortable talking with people in America. I used to talk with my friends in Japanese about many things occurring in our daily lives, such as our jobs, our families, and our feelings. I had no hesitations when I talked with them because I was able to communicate in my native language. I did not need to translate my words in my head; they just came out of my mouth naturally. I never thought I would struggle this much with my nonproficiency in English. Actually, I have many things to say to people, but I don't feel I have the proper English words in my head to use. When people speak to me in ten or more words, I reply to them using only a few words. I have to translate in my head; I feel frustrated because I am too slow to respond. Living in America has brought new kinds of stress and pressure to my life.

P2 In Japan, I worked at an apparel company as a sales chief for ten years. Meeting people from all different backgrounds was an inspiring experience. We had a buyers' meeting and a collection show in Tokyo four times a year. All of the buyers gathered to determine which merchandise they would purchase for their shops. I was a part of the trend, telling people what the latest fashions would be for the next season. I was a part of a resource tour in New York, Boston, and Los Angeles. This career gave me many chances to learn how to manage customers and the shop, and how to work with my colleagues cooperatively.

P3 I was pleased and satisfied with my job, but then my company's situation changed. It started cutting employees to save labor costs. We were put on a commission system. We had to work more after we lost some of our colleagues. We often worked overtime, but our union did not allow us to work overtime every day. Our union was very weak and did not have power to protect our rights against the company. I was exhausted and stressed every day. I was growing tired of the relentless career competition. That was when I decided to change my career and come to the United States to study. I came here last June with two suitcases, not realizing how much I would be stressed out in my dream country, America.

P4 One of the stresses when I first arrived was that I needed somebody's help all the time except when I was sleeping. Things that would have been easy if I had been born in the United States, such as how to get to the post office, how to use a checkbook, and how to open a bank account, were not easy. They created some uncomfortable feelings. I had to ask someone to help me out every day, all the time. The problem at the post office, the bank, and other places was the English language. I still struggle emotionally to communicate with people. It is often hard to tell people exactly what I need. For example, there was the time I called the Social Security office to ask for my Social Security number. The lady who received my phone call asked me my name and my date of birth. After I told her, she said my number wasn't ready yet even though I had applied a week earlier. I told her my number should have been ready by then; she hung up. I called again and received my number from another person.

P5 I also encountered problems when I decided I needed a car and insurance. Driving in America at first was a nightmare. In Japan, people drive on the left side, but in most other countries such as America, people drive on the right, which is very hard to get used to. I was frightened to practice driving the American way. I really hated it. People here make a right turn when they have a red light, but we cannot make a left turn when we have a red light in Japan.

I was afraid to make a right turn at a red light at a busy intersection here. Nevertheless, I needed a car so I had to study for and pass the written and the driving tests. I then had to decide which auto insurance to buy, but I had no idea which kind was the best for me. I asked some people but could not get a proper answer. So, I opened the phone book and made several phone calls to insurance companies and asked about their auto insurance. Basically, I felt they didn't want to sell their insurance to someone who doesn't speak English and doesn't have much driving experience here. I was always stressed out and felt pressure whenever I had to take care of these kinds of things. It was overwhelming.

P6 Some people are very nice and try to understand me, but some just think I am stupid because of my English. I can listen and understand, and I can talk, but English makes me a disabled person. I still have moments when I hesitate to speak English to somebody. I am bothered by this hesitation, and now I am obsessed about becoming a perfect speaker. If I am not, I think I must be too incompetent to live and study here. English is such a monster.

P7 It has been ten months since I started living here, but the pressures still have not gone away. They always surround me like a dim fog in a deep forest. I have so many examples of my frustrations. One day I didn't know what to say when my former landlady rebuked me, saying that my English, which was not correct to explain my feelings at the time, was ugly. Honestly, my mind became blank, and I felt humiliated by her harshness. Not having the words to express my emotions or feelings makes me feel insecure. I do open my dictionary to look for words that show exactly how I feel, but often I cannot tell if the word is the right word or not. Some days when I wake up in the morning, I have to push myself hard to keep a positive mood.

P8 Strange to say, I have never thought I wanted to go back to Japan, but sometimes I wonder why I am still here with all these stresses and pressures. I feel that perhaps I am not clever enough to do this. These feelings get me down, and it takes a while to get my feelings back up so I can carry on. It's nobody's fault; I will just keep trying until the pressure and stress go away. I will not give up. I know time will pass, and life will get better.

Hiromi Hasegawa
Bellevue Community College
Bellevue, Washington

1. In Paragraph 1, where is the thesis statement located? Does the thesis statement help you predict the direction the essay will be developed? Explain.
2. What is the purpose of Paragraphs 2 and 3? Why are these paragraphs important for the development of the essay?
3. Copy the following cluster, in larger size, on your paper. Fill in the missing details so the cluster reflects the thesis, the main ideas of each paragraph, and the conclusion in "My Life in America."

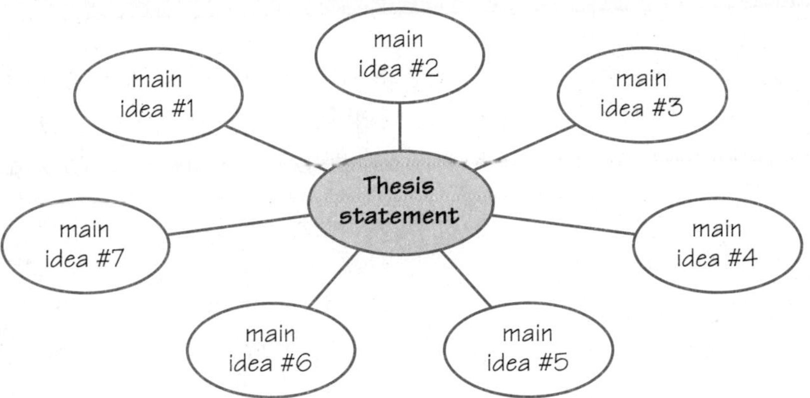

12.3 What do you think?

The following essay uses a variety of strategies to define the term *Spanglish,* a free-form blend of Spanish and English. The authors discuss the increased usage, popularity, and functionality of Spanglish.

Spanglish

P1 In Manhattan a first-grader greets her visiting grandparents, happily exclaiming, "Come here, *siéntate!*" Her bemused grandfather, who does not speak Spanish, nevertheless knows she is asking him to sit down. A Miami personnel officer understands what a job applicant means when he says, "*Quiero un* part time." Nor do drivers miss a beat reading a billboard alongside a Los Angeles street advertising CERVEZA—SIX-PACK! This free-form blend of Spanish and English, known as Spanglish, is common linguistic currency wherever concentrations of Hispanic Americans are found in the United States.

P2 In Los Angeles, where 55 percent of the city's 3 million inhabitants speak Spanish, Spanglish is as much a part of daily life as sunglasses. Unlike the broken-English efforts of earlier immigrants from Europe, Asia, and other regions, Spanglish has become a widely accepted conversational mode used casually—even playfully—by Spanish-speaking immigrants and native-born Americans alike.

P3 Consisting of one part Hispanicized English, one part Americanized Spanish, and more than a little fractured syntax, Spanglish is a bit like a Robin Williams comedy routine: a crackling line of cross-cultural patter straight from the melting pot. Often it enters Anglo homes and families through the children, who pick it up at school or at play with their young Hispanic contemporaries. In other cases, it comes from watching TV; many an Anglo child watching *Sesame Street* has learned *uno dos tres* almost as quickly as one two three.

P4 Spanglish takes a variety of forms, from the Southern California Anglos who bid farewell with the utterly silly "*hasta la* bye-bye" to the Cuban-American drivers in Miami who *parquean* their *carros.* Some Spanglish sentences are mostly Spanish, with a quick detour for an English word or two. A Latino friend may cut short a conversation by glancing at his watch and excusing himself with the explanation that he must "*ir al* supermarket."

P5 Many of the English words transplanted in this way are simply handier than their Spanish counterparts. No matter how distasteful the subject, for example, it is still easier to say "income tax" than *impuesto sobre la renta.* At the same time, many Spanish-speaking immigrants have adopted such terms as *VCR, microwave,* and *dishwasher* for what they view as largely American phenomena. Still other English words convey a cultural context that is not implicit in the Spanish. A friend who invites you to *lonche* most likely has in mind the brisk American custom of "doing lunch" rather than the languorous afternoon break traditionally implied by *almuerzo.*

P6 Mainstream Americans exposed to similar hybrids of German, Chinese, or Hindi might be mystified. But even Anglos who speak little or no Spanish are somewhat familiar with Spanglish. Living among them, for one thing, are 19 million Hispanics. In addition, more American high school and university students sign up for Spanish than for any other foreign language.

P7 Only in the past ten years, though, has Spanglish begun to turn into a national slang. Its popularity has grown with the explosive increases in U.S. immigration from Latin American countries. English has increasingly collided with Spanish in retail stores, in offices and classrooms, in pop music, and on street corners. Anglos whose ancestors picked up such Spanish words as *rancho, bronco, tornado,* and *incommunicado,* for instance, now freely use such Spanish words as *gracias, bueno, amigo,* and *por favor.*

P8 Spanglish is a sort of code for Latinos: the speakers know Spanish, but their hybrid language reflects the American culture in which they live. Many lean to shorter, clipped phrases in place of the longer, more graceful expressions their parents used. Says Leonel de la Cuesta, an assistant professor of modern languages at Florida International University in Miami: "In the United States, time is money, and that is showing up in Spanglish as an economy of language." Conversational examples: *taipiar* (type) and *winshi-wiper* (windshield wiper) replace *escribir a máquina* and *limpiaparabrisas.*

P9 Major advertisers, eager to tap the estimated $134 billion in spending power wielded by Spanish-speaking Americans, have ventured into Spanglish to promote their products. In some cases, attempts to sprinkle Spanish through commercials have produced embarrassing gaffes. A Braniff airlines ad that sought to tell Spanish-speaking audiences they could settle back *en* (in) luxuriant *cuero* (leather) seats, for example, inadvertently said they could fly without clothes (*encuero*). A fractured translation of the Miller Lite slogan told readers the beer was "Filling, and less delicious." Similar blunders are often made by Anglos trying to impress Spanish-speaking pals. But if Latinos are amused by mangled Spanglish, they also recognize these goofs as a sort of friendly acceptance. As they might put it, *no problema.*

[Source: "Bazerman, *Side by Side—A Multicultural Reader*, "Spanglish," by Janice Castro, Dan Cook, and Cristina Garcia, Houghton Mifflin 1996, pp. 159–61.]

1. What is the thesis statement for this essay? Copy it on your paper.
2. In Paragraph 2, what two kinds of discourse does the author use? (The word "unlike" signals one type of discourse.)
3. How does Spanglish enter Anglo homes? (Paragraph 3)
4. Why is Spanglish convenient to use?
5. Why has the popularity of Spanglish grown in the past ten years?
6. What type of paragraph structure does the author use in Paragraph 9? Explain your answer.
7. Write an appropriate concluding paragraph for this essay.

12.4 What do you think?

The following five-paragraph essay is longer than usual because the writer inserts a personal narrative to support the thesis statement. This essay, which includes a personal narrative from Rosa Parks, reveals why many people consider Rosa Parks to be a symbol of courage and determination to make democracy work in the United States. Rosa Louise McCauley was born and raised by her mother in Alabama. When Rosa was 19 years old, she married Raymond Parks, who was a barber and a courageous civil rights activist. The incident discussed in the following essay led to nationwide familiarity with the name Rosa Parks.

Rosa Parks

P1 On a cold evening in December 1955, a simple act of protest gave way to a new era of the civil rights movement. It was on that day that Rosa Parks, weary from her job as a seamstress, was ordered to give up her bus seat to a white passenger. Her refusal to move to the back of the bus demonstrated not only her courage but her defiance of society's injustices. Her subsequent arrest sparked a 381-day bus boycott and earned her recognition as the "mother of the civil rights movement."

P2 Rosa Parks was undaunted by the fact that affiliation with any social work was dangerous for her during this time in history. In 1943 Rosa Parks joined the NAACP and became secretary of the Montgomery chapter, where she met Edgar Daniel Nixon, president of the state branch. From the onset of her social activism, Parks worked hard to motivate the young people of Mississippi. That has remained important and constant in the 87-year old's life to this day.

P3 Parks reflected in her autobiography, *Quiet Strength:* "Four decades later I am still uncomfortable with the credit given to me for starting the bus boycott. Many people do not know the whole truth . . . I was just one of many who fought for freedom." As an excerpt from her personal narrative shows, many fought for freedom, but her actions triggered the Montgomery boycott and ignited the civil rights movement.

> "On Thursday, December 1, 1955 at 5:30 p.m., I, Mrs. Rosa Lee McCauley Parks, 42, left my job as a tailor's assistant in the Montgomery Fair Department Store and walked to the Court Square bus stop. I boarded the bus and sat in the "colored" section behind the seats reserved for whites. I sat on the aisle next to a black man. Two black women sat in the seat across the aisle. The bus

filled up quickly at the next two stops. By the third stop, the white section was filled, and a white man remained standing at the front. This meant that all four of the passengers in my row would have to move in order for this white man to sit down. According to custom, a black person could not sit in the same row as a white person. The driver, James F. Blake, said that he expected passengers to comply with company policy. He called out, "All right, you folks, I want those two seats!" No one moved. "Y'all better make it light on yourselves and let me have those seats!" he said.

The two women across the aisle from me got up and moved. The man next to me got up, too. I shifted to let him out, then moved to the window seat. I didn't say anything to Blake. But he said, "Look woman, I told you I wanted that seat. Are you going to stand up?" "No," I said. "I'm tired of being treated like a second-class citizen." "If you don't stand up, I'm going to arrest you," Blake warned me. "You can do that," I told him. Blake then parked the bus in front of the Empire Theater and telephoned his supervisor. "Did you warn her, Jim?" his boss asked. "I warned her," Blake said. "Well then, Jim, you do it; you got to exercise your powers and put her off, yuh hear?" Blake called the police, who arrived in a few minutes.

Officers Day and Nixon boarded the bus and Blake pointed to me, telling the officers, "I needed that seat. The other ones stood up." The officers approached me and asked if the driver had asked me to stand. "Yes," I said. "Why didn't you stand up?" they asked. I said," I didn't think I should have to. I paid my fare like everybody else." "Well," said one of the officers, "the law is the law, and you are under arrest." I stood up and the officers took me to the patrol car. They went back to talk to the driver who wanted to press charges against me under Montgomery's bus segregation ordinance. The officers drove me to police headquarters, then to the city jail. I asked to drink from a water fountain but was told that it was for whites only. So I called my husband after the officers completed the paperwork for my arrest. My bond was $100. Dr. E.D. Nixon and Clifford and Virginia Durr signed my bond and took me home. On December 5, the day the boycott started, the court found me guilty and fined me $10 plus $4 in court costs. The Movement begins!"

[Source: Rose Parks, *Crisis*, January/February, 1999, p. 73.]

P4 In 1980, at the twenty-fifth anniversary celebration of the bus boycott, Parks received the Martin Luther King, Jr., Nonviolent Peace Prize; she was the first woman recipient of the award. In 1984, she received the Eleanor Roosevelt Woman of Courage Award at a ceremony in New York. Three years later, she received the E. Joseph Prize of the Jewish Institute of Religion for being the "mother of the modern freedom movement." The award, accompanied by $10,000, helped fund the Rosa and Raymond Parks Institute for Self-Development. The institute offers guidance to young people pursuing their education to prepare for successful careers and positions of leadership. On June 15, 1999, Parks received the greatest honor awarded by Congress, the Congressional Gold Medal.

P5 Rosa Parks undoubtedly stands out as a symbol of courage and the continuing fight to make democracy work in the United States.

[Adapted from: *Crisis*, "March/April 2000.]

Crisis, January/February 1999, p. 74. *Crisis* is a magazine founded by NAACP in 1910. The founding editor was W.E.B. DuBois.

1. The author inserted a personal narrative from Rosa Parks in this essay. How does the inclusion of this narrative strengthen the essay? Explain.
2. Explain the relationship of each of the following paragraphs to the controlling idea that Rosa Parks was the "mother of the civil rights movement."
   a. Paragraph 2
   b. Paragraph 3
   c. Paragraph 4
3. Write your own concluding paragraph for this essay.

Writing Assignment

Write an essay that discusses the three elements of all paragraphs: unity, coherence, and development. Use the skills you have learned in this chapter to write a five-paragraph essay. Refer to 12.1 What do you think? on page 442.

WWW Writing Essay Answers on Tests

In addition to writing assignments that require essays, many tests in college consist of essay questions. Writing strong answers on essay tests involves essentially the same steps as writing an essay for a class assignment. The main difference, of course, is that you need to recall information from memory, organize it quickly, formulate a thesis statement, and write the essay in a limited amount of time. Suggestions in this section will provide you with guidelines and techniques for writing effective answers for essay questions.

Preparing for Essay Tests

Preparation for essay tests involves gathering information about the "big picture," which includes concepts, trends, and relationships that have been covered in the course. Test preparation strategies vary depending on the following testing situations:

1. The instructor does not announce the topics for an in-class essay test.
2. The instructor announces the topics for an in-class essay test.
3. The essay test is an open-book test.
4. The essay test is a take-home test.

Preparing for Essay Tests When Topics Are Unannounced

The most challenging type of essay test is one in which the instructor does not announce the topics for the essay questions in advance. If you have used ongoing study techniques for class notes and reading assignments throughout the term, you will be quite familiar with the course materials and need only to organize information to study for the test. This type of test is most difficult for students who have not learned the content thoroughly throughout the term, for now they will need to learn the material and find time to organize their thoughts. The following strategies will help you prepare for essay tests when the instructor does not announce topics in advance.

1. Use the course description and the course syllabus to identify major themes that the instructor discussed throughout the course. After reading the course description and the syllabus, predict possible test questions based on the themes, topics, and relationships stated in the materials.
2. Review all the visual study tools, such as hierarchies, grids, or clusters, that you have created throughout the term. Review all your class notes. Formulate possible test questions that could come from these materials. Make a list of possible questions, and then create prewriting organizational plans, such as outlines, clusters, hierarchies, or grids, to organize main ideas and details you could use in an essay answer.
3. Create summary sheets for major themes. Use the table of contents, chapter outlines, and chapter summaries in your textbook to identify major recurring themes. Your summary sheets once again can be in the form of outlines, clusters, hierarchies, or grids. Your main goal at this point is to practice grouping and organizing information that might be used to answer an essay question.

4. Predict test questions and practice writing answers. What topics received the most time and emphasis in lectures or discussions? What themes or "big pictures" did you identify in 1–3 above? How could you convert these into questions? Consider working with a study partner so you can write practice test questions for each other. If you practice writing a variety of essay answers before the day of the test, essay questions will feel more comfortable, more familiar, and less stressful.

Preparing for Essay Tests When Topics Are Announced in Advance

Some instructors will give you the topics for the essay questions in advance; others will give you a set of questions from which one or more will appear on the test. This advance notice offers you the opportunity to prepare thoroughly, organize answers, and practice writing the essays. When the instructor gives essay questions in advance, the expectation is that your answers will be better organized, developed, and supported with relevant supporting details than might have been possible if the questions were not announced in advance. You are expected to have the answer formulated though you most likely will not be allowed to bring notes or outlines with you the day of the test. Your answer needs to be recorded in your mind. The following strategies will help you organize for essay tests in which the instructor provided you with the questions in advance.

1. Gather information for each answer.
   a. Use the index in the back of your textbook to locate pages in the textbook that have information relevant to the topic of the essay.
   b. Review all your class notes from lectures and discussions. Seek out information relevant to the essay questions.
   c. Review all your homework assignments to locate additional information related to the essay topics.
2. Organize the information you gathered. Make a special set of summary notes that highlight the major themes, main ideas, trends, and significant relationships between ideas. After reading the question carefully and identifying the type of answer the instructor expects from you, create a prewriting organizational plan that includes the information in your summary notes. Once again, your prewriting organizational plan can be a cluster, hierarchy, outline, or grid. You can memorize each of these four organizational plans quite efficiently; they can then become your guide for writing the essay answer in class.
3. Practice writing answers to the essay questions. Use your organizational plan to guide you. You may want to write practice answers several times to reinforce the important ideas and details you want to include in your answer during the test.

Preparing for Open-Book Essay Tests

You may be excited and relieved to learn that an essay test will be an open-book test. However, the previous strategies for preparing for tests by anticipating test questions, preparing summary sheets, and practicing writing essay answers should still be used. In addition, you can use the following strategies so you do not waste valuable test time searching for needed information.

1. Become familiar with the index in your book so you can look up topics quickly.
2. Use a special highlighter to highlight important information, such as dates, names, events, statistics, terminology, or quotations that may be useful to include in your answers.
3. Use tabs to mark significant pages such as summaries, charts, tables, lists, steps, or visual materials.

Organizing and Developing Answers for Take-Home Essay Tests

Expectations for polished essays are higher when the instructor gives the essay questions as a take-home test. The major problems many students face with take-home tests is that they do not allow enough time to develop their essay answers. Use your essay-, paragraph-, and sentence-writing skills to produce an effective, polished essay for take-home tests.

Additional Test-Taking Strategies for Essays

In addition to the strategies used to write any essay, you can use the following strategies to make the process of writing test essays easier.

1. If you have several choices of questions to answer, look at the choices carefully. The majority of students tend to choose the questions that are the shortest and look the easiest. However, these questions are usually more general and sometimes more difficult to answer. Often the questions that look the most difficult or contain more information are actually more specific and easier to answer. Consider your choices carefully.
2. If you are required to do more than one essay, begin with the one that is the most familiar and easiest for you. Your confidence will be boosted, and your mind will shift into the essay-writing mode.
3. Strive to write as neatly as possible. Illegible handwriting will hurt your grade. If you need to delete some information, delete it by crossing it out with one neat line. You may also want to use a correction pen with white liquid that covers the information you want to delete.
4. Consider writing on every other line unless your instructor asks you not to do this. The space between the lines gives you room to revise or add information if time permits.

5. If you do not budget your time effectively, turn in your prewriting organizational plan so your instructor can see what you would have included in your essay. You may earn a few points for your effort.
6. If you have more than one essay to complete on a test, be sure to write something for each question. When you ignore questions, you will obviously earn no points at all.
7. Weigh the value of different questions. If one question is worth more points, allow more time to plan and write the answer to that question.
8. If your keyboarding skills are good and you have a laptop computer, ask if you can write your essay on the computer and save it on a disk that you can give to the instructor. Work always appears neater, easier to read, and void of spelling errors when it is done on a computer.

[Adapted from: Wong, *Essential Study Skills*, Houghton Mifflin, 2000, pp. 289–292, 294–300.]

Enjoy the Process of Writing Essays

With practice, essay writing becomes easier, ideas flow more smoothly, and your personal style becomes more defined. You may find that you prefer writing essays to other forms of writing, and you prefer essay tests over objective tests, such as multiple choice. Essay writing provides you with a channel to be creative, to explore interesting ways to express your ideas, and to communicate meaningful information effectively and powerfully to your readers.

Internet Enrichment

Log on to the web site for this textbook for additional exercises and links for the following topics:

The Structure of an Essay
Writing a Thesis Statement
Writing Essay Answers on Tests

Go to: http://college.hmco.com. Click on "Students." Type *Paragraph Essentials* in the "Jump to Textbook Sites" box. Click "go," and then bookmark the site. Click on Chapter 12.

APPENDIX A

Student Answer Keys

How to Use These Answer Keys

After you complete an exercise, check your work with the following answer keys. Each answer is worth one point unless the directions specify using a different method for scoring. Write your number of errors on the score line on the exercise page in the chapter. In the margin of your textbook next to the exercise, write questions about the grammar and usage points that you would like to discuss in class or with your instructor.

Chapter 1

Exercise 1.1 (page 31) Possible: 11

The following words should be circled:

1. papers, mail
2. Homeowners, expenses
3. development, park, mall
4. workers, sun
5. house, roof

Exercise 1.2 (page 32) Possible: 14

The following words should be circled:

1. We, them, our
2. Many, me
3. Someone, your, us
4. Who, their, my
5. No one, who, him

Exercise 1.3 (page 33) Possible: 14

The following words should be circled:

1. marching, sporting, school
2. band, red, gold

3. band, tall
4. Loud, energetic, immediate
5. special, creative, loud

Exercise 1.4 (page 35) Possible: 6

The following words should be circled:

1. darkened
2. moved
3. were running
4. fell, damaged
5. are

Exercise 1.5 (page 36) Possible: 10

The following words should be circled:

1. barely
2. quickly, today
3. obviously, not
4. too, directly
5. definitely, not, again

Exercise 1.6 (page 38) Possible: 13

The following prepositional phrases should be marked with parentheses:

1. (from cradle) (to ashes) (in a lifetime)
2. (about growing up) (with different values and beliefs)
3. (for hours) (without ever tiring)
4. (During one vacation) (at our cabin) (in the woods) (till dawn)
5. (by the fire) (under the stars)

Exercise 1.7 (page 39) Possible: 5

1. and
2. or
3. but
4. so
5. for

Chapter 2

Exercise 2.1 (page 74) Possible: 10

The following words should be underlined:

1. whales
2. addresses
3. hurricanes
4. winner
5. Hepatitis
6. headaches
7. reader
8. I
9. government
10. Neither

Exercise 2.2 (page 75) Possible: 30

The following subjects and prepositional phrases should be marked. Give one point for each subject and each prepositional phrase. Do not deduct points for marking other words incorrectly.

1. rage (at youth sports events) (at an alarming rate)
2. forms (of the flu virus) (in the United States)
3. muscles (around the scalp) (in the back) (of the neck) (throughout the shoulder area) (in stressful situations)
4. Each (of the following paragraphs) (with coherence)
5. kinds (of federal taxes) (of federal tax revenue)
6. show (on inspirational personal stories)
7. (On a separate piece) (of paper) you
8. (In two hours) we
9. Lack (of eye contact) (with the speaker)
10. report (of our new product)

Exercise 2.3 (page 76) Possible: 35

The following subjects and prepositional phrases should be marked. Give one point for each subject and each prepositional phrase. Do not deduct points for marking other words incorrectly.

1. areas schools hospitals
2. Examples facts definitions reasons (in the body) (of a paragraph)
3. Tempers (at intersections) (on freeways)
4. geologists (from the U.S. Geological Survey Team)
5. date (under the line) (with the city, state, and ZIP code information)
6. quantity quality (of supporting details)
7. They (under the same roof)
8. families families (in many countries)
9. Fidgeting doodling daydreaming (of interest) (in the speaker or the topic)
10. shoes backpack supply (of food) (for the hiking event)

Exercise 2.4 (page 79) Possible: 40

Sentences should be marked as follows. Give one point for each prepositional phrase, each infinitive, each complete verb, and each subject. Do not deduct points for marking other words incorrectly.

1. A foot (of rain) flooded the coastal towns.
2. A person (with an internal locus) (of control) feels (in charge) (of his or her life).

3. We rode (with them) (for the next three hundred miles).
4. People respond (to praise) (in many different ways).
5. The public safety officials wanted [to evacuate] the entire area.
6. The plant supervisor requested a meeting (with the union) [to discuss] several problems.
7. Neither (of the contestants) knew the correct answer.
8. Lack (of eye contact) (during an interview) signals a lack (of confidence and shyness).
9. Preschool children need vaccinations [to prevent] childhood diseases.
10. (During the test), I remembered [to develop] each answer (with sufficient details).

Exercise 2.5 (page 80) Possible: 40

Sentences should be marked as follows. Give one point for each prepositional phrase, each infinitive, each verb, and each subject. Do not deduct points for marking other words incorrectly.

1. The young children grew restless (during the long concert).
2. Anyone is eligible [to apply] (for the scholarship).
3. Three forms (of hepatitis) are common (in the United States).
4. The comet appears once every one hundred years.
5. Detergent, floor wax, mops, and air freshener are (on sale) (at Mickey's Market).
6. The fresh bread (from the bakery) (across the street) smells wonderful.
7. Homemade vegetable soup tastes good (on a cold winter day).
8. Scientists were eager [to study] the effects (of genetically altered food).
9. Many ridiculous and outdated laws remain (on the books) (in some states).
10. Lately, you seem [to be] unhappy and (under a lot) (of stress).

Exercise 2.6 (page 83) Possible: 36

Sentences should be marked as follows. Give one point for each prepositional phrase, each infinitive, each verb or verb phrase, and each subject. Do not deduct for marking other words incorrectly.

1. The topic sentence should capture the reader's attention.
2. Sentences (in the body) (of the paragraph) should not stray (from the main idea).

3. The sisters were hoping [to win] (at Wimbledon).
4. Some species (of whales) have been (on the brink) (of extinction) (for many years).
5. Technology has created new concerns (about copyright infringements).
6. The movie industry will never sanction duplication (of movies) (over the Internet).
7. International companies must understand the cultural practices (of other countries).
8. The prosecution has listed the evidence (in chronological order).
9. The tourists (from Switzerland) had planned [to visit] Washington, D.C.
10. His temporary manager had treated him badly.

Exercise 2.7 (page 84) Possible: 42

Sentences should be marked as follows. Give one point for each prepositional phrase, each infinitive, each verb or verb phrase, and each subject. Do not deduct points for marking other words incorrectly.

1. Baleen hangs (inside whales' mouths) and sifts food (from the water).
2. Roller coasters (at theme parks, carnivals, and fairs) draw large crowds and provide fun (for thrill-seekers.)
3. The writer does not wander (from the topic) or include unrelated information.
4. Sunburn ointments can reduce the burning sensation (on your skin) and prevent blisters.
5. Sarina was pruning the roses and the bushes and fertilizing all the plants.
6. An underdeveloped paragraph lacks sufficient details and fails [to explain] the main idea.
7. An effective speaker acknowledges and respects differing points (of view).
8. The music industry will find ways [to stop] the abuse and force compliance (of copyright laws).
9. Biotech farming can increase food production and improve the quality (of crops).
10. (At work), I set goals well and manage my time efficiently.

Exercise 2.8 (page 87) Possible: 10

1. S
2. F
3. F
4. S
5. F
6. S
7. S
8. F
9. F
10. S

Exercise 2.9 (page 88)

Your instructor may score this exercise.

The topic sentence and the concluding sentence should not be changed. The answers will vary within the body of the paragraph. Check that you have combined sentences by using compound verbs. One possible answer is shown below. Changes are shown in bold print.

> The Chinese still favor their *bu xie,* cloth slip-on shoes. The shoes are soft and cool **and** do not pinch their feet. The shoes are inexpensive **and** cost an equivalent of one dollar. Some Chinese wear Italian-style leather shoes **or** Nike sneakers and their knockoffs. However, the traditional Chinese cloth shoes are still frequently worn with business suits **and** used by construction workers instead of steel-toed construction boots. Though shoes with support and more durability seem to make more sense, many Chinese continue to favor their traditional *bu xie.*

Proofreading Exercises

Proofreading exercises will be discussed in class or graded by your instructor.

Chapter 3

Exercise 3.1 (page 121) Possible: 12

1. chose
2. rang
3. hung
4. spun, shook
5. struck
6. shut, swore
7. paid
8. stole
9. slit
10. ground

Exercise 3.2 (page 121) Possible: 30

1. rode
2. bought
3. bit
4. bent
5. spread
6. swept
7. wept
8. set
9. fought
10. laid
11. rose
12. crept
13. broadcast
14. kept
15. sped
16. stung
17. swung
18. lent
19. drew
20. felt
21. clung
22. bore
23. lay
24. slung
25. shook
26. knew
27. shot
28. took
29. drank
30. bled

Exercise 3.3 (page 126) Possible: 10

Give one point per sentence. The answers shown below are the most common answers. You may have arranged the words differently to create a different answer than the one that is shown. Ask your instructor if an alternative sentence is correct. Check that a comma is used before the coordinating conjunction.

1. I could not move, **nor** could I cry out for help.
   I could not move, **and** I could not cry out for help.
2. I crouched down behind the bushes, **and** I started to pray.
3. The bear picked up my scent, **but** (or **yet**) he did not head in my direction.
4. He brushed against the tree to scratch his back, **but** (or **yet**) I was still too frightened to move.
5. He worked his way toward the river, **for** he was hungry and wanted to catch some fish.
6. The bear was out of sight, **but** (or **yet**) he might still return.
7. I could sit quietly for a few more minutes, **or** I could move slowly to my car.
8. I decided to ease my way toward my car, **for** the car would be safer than staying out in the open air.
9. I unlocked the car door, **and** I got in.
10. From the car, I could see the bear down by the river, **but** (or **yet**) I had no desire to get a closer look.

Exercise 3.4 (page 127) Possible: 14

Arrows show where commas need to be added. Xs show where commas need to be deleted. C indicates the sentence is correct.

1. A young woman straddled her surfboard and scanned the ocean, [X] for a sign of the perfect wave.
2. Two weeks of women's surfing competition started [↓] and fifty women came to compete.
3. The women wore body suits, [X] and board shorts [↓] but their attire was fashionable.
4. C
5. The popularity of surfing among women has steadily increased [↓] yet many people still see surfing as a man's sport.
6. C
7. Promoters of the sport, [X] and sponsors of surfing competitions tend to support the male surfers [↑] but such favoritism may change in the near future.
8. Female surfers will not accept a lower status, [X] for long [↓] nor will they accept the status quo quietly.

9. Marketing experts, clothes designers ↓ and surfing schools are paying more attention now to female surfers ↑ for the women have money to spend on the sport.

10. C

Exercise 3.5 (page 130) Possible: 10

1. C
2. C
3. C
4. S
5. S
6. C
7. C
8. S
9. C
10. C

Exercise 3.6 (page 131) Possible: 50 points

Each sentence is worth five points. Deduct 1 point in a sentence for every error. If you have more than five errors in a sentence, your score for that sentence is 0. Sentences should be marked as shown below. Pay close attention to the punctuation.

1. (In early American history), women did not publicly demand suffrage; that changed (in 1848).
2. Women publicly demanded their rights (in 1848); in fact, they organized a Women's Rights Convention and adopted twelve resolutions (for equal rights).
3. The press ignored the women's demands; (in addition), opponents pelted women's rights advocates (with rotten fruit) and chastised them.
4. (By 1900), women suffragists became more vocal and more aggressive (with their demands), yet the men (in power) still ignored and ridiculed their demands.
5. Consequently, women started [to march] (in the streets) and [to voice] stronger demands (for their equal rights); twenty years later, they won the right [to vote].
6. Women were happy [to win] the right [to vote], but there were other inequities [to confront].
7. Many women wanted access (to education, the military, politics, and employment opportunities), but many men and even some women tried [to stop] the feminist movement and [to maintain] the status quo.
8. (In the 1960s), a powerful activist surfaced [to add] momentum (to the women's struggle) (for equality); Gloria Steinem was her name.

9. The feminist movement (in the 1960s) fought many forms (of gender discrimination); (as a result), women today earn higher wages and have greater access (to education, employment opportunities, military positions, and women's sports programs).
10. The women's rights movement (throughout the last century) fought and won many rights (for women); however, the fight (for gender equality) continues (in the courts), (in the media), and (at the ballot box).

Exercise 3.7 (page 135) Possible: 10

Give on point per sentence. Answers may vary. One possibility is shown. If your answer differs, ask your instructor if it is correct.

1. Not all women enjoy working outside of the home**; in fact,** some prefer to remain at home with their children.
2. C
3. Children learn to work in small groups, to share their toys, and get along with each other; they also learn to handle their emotions in new ways.
4. For some children, separation from their parents is difficult**;** they cry and throw temper tantrums in the initial separation process.
5. C
6. C
7. Many children look to their fathers for one kind of advice**; however,** they turn to their mothers for other kinds of advice.
8. Communication between parents and children is more open than in previous generations**;** unfortunately, communication during the teenage years continues to be difficult.
9. Generation gaps have always existed**;** our parents would acknowledge this fact.
10. Healthy children feel safe, loved, and protected**;** parents contribute greatly to the physical, social, and emotional health of their children.

Exercise 3.8 (page 137) Possible: 10

Answers will vary. If your answer is different than the following, ask your instructor if your answer is correct.

1. The House of Representatives voted to increase the minimum wage by one dollar an hour**;** the increase will be phased in by the year 2002.
2. C
3. The average pay for corporate chief executives has risen nearly 770 percent since 1980**;** however, the average worker has seen only a 68 percent pay increase since 1980.

4. C
5. About 4 million workers in America are paid the minimum wage, but all four million are not full-time workers.
6. The concept of minimum wage began in October 1938; the minimum wage then was 25 cents.
7. Workers do not receive minimum wage increases every year; in fact, a trend of annual raises in minimum wages occurred only during 1974 to 1976 and 1978 to 1981.
8. C
9. The latest minimum wage increase is the largest in American history; the increase typically varies from ten cents to forty cents.
10. C

Proofreading Exercises

Proofreading exercises will be discussed in class or graded by your instructor.

Chapter 4

Exercise 4.1 (page 165) Possible: 20

Give one point for the dependent clause and one point for circling the subordinate conjunction. The dependent clause should be boxed. The subordinate conjunction should be circled.

1. Although the power was off,
2. because a construction crew accidentally cut the power line.
3. as soon as the power company repairs the line.
4. While the power was off,
5. Before the power was turned on,
6. After the power company repaired the line,
7. Even though some homes use solar energy,
8. Whenever power lines go down,
9. If you are in your home during a power outage,
10. When you are without electricity,

Exercise 4.2 (page 165) Possible: 10

The missing punctuation should appear between the following words. C indicates the sentence is correct.

1. new planets; the planets
2. now known; of course
3. Earth, but
4. Jupiter; it
5. Earth, it
6. C
7. C
8. C
9. new planets, but
10. future, for

Exercise 4.3 (page 167) Possible: 30

Give one point for each dependent clause marked correctly, one point for the correct subject in the dependent clause, and one point for the correct complete verb in each dependent clause. The following dependent clauses should be boxed. The subjects and verbs in the dependent clauses should be marked as follows:

1. that is wrinkled
2. that I am truly in the South Pacific
3. which was brown with mud
4. which I could see through his glasses
5. that came out of the piano
6. that you requested for the meeting tomorrow morning
7. so that users can personalize the watering cycles
8. who use the Water Wizard
9. that no one with normal eyesight can read
10. that a person with average intelligence can understand

Exercise 4.4 (page 171) Possible: 10

Be sure the dependent clause is placed next to the noun it refers to or renames. If your sentence is different, ask your instructor if it is correct.

1. The house has one bay window, which overlooks the canyon.
2. This logo, which Sean designed, will appear on our letterhead.
3. Clint Eastwood stars in *Space Cowboys,* which is a movie about four retired pilots.
4. My neighbors, who do not own a dog, complain about my dog at least once a week.
5. The Lion's Club's car raffle, which is for a new Chrysler PT Cruiser, takes place in September.
6. Jake, who is a native of Colorado, is a rodeo rider.
7. My cousin wrote this book, which is about a Native American bounty hunter.
8. My grandmother raised five children and also two grandchildren, who lived with her for five years.
9. Patrick Summers, whose son served in the Persian Gulf, is a retired Navy officer.
10. A memo, which went out via E-mail, had several errors.

Exercise 4.5 (page 172) Possible: 10

C indicates the sentence is correct. The missing punctuation should appear as follows in the other sentences:

1. C
2. C
3. C
4. transcripts, which arrived yesterday, have

5. brother, who considers himself an honest person,
6. can, which I have had for years, is
7. attendance policy, several
8. C
9. C
10. on the table, his

Exercise 4.6 (page 173) Possible: 10

Your answers will vary, but the following can be used as examples. If you are uncertain about the correct punctuation or method to correct the fragment, ask your instructor.

1. After the fishermen reached the dock, they weighed their catch for the day.
2. When the flood level rises, some people evacuate their homes.
3. My grandfather, whom I regard as an intelligent person, has a vivid imagination.
4. Several people hinted that I should resign.
5. As soon as the final report is ready, I will be ready for the meeting.
6. Marsha was advised to see a counselor because she had a lot of anger.
7. My student teaching assignment, which turned out to be a wonderful experience, lasted four months.
8. Martin, who needs attention from other people, always clowns around.
9. If you know the difference between right and wrong, why do you do these things?
10. Before you file your taxes, you need to organize your receipts.

Proofreading Exercises

Proofreading exercises will be discussed in class or graded by your instructor.

Chapter 5

Exercise 5.1 (page 206) Possible: 8

The following words should be crossed out. The correct verbs should be written above the errors.

	takes	join	
1.	~~took~~	~~joined~~	
	offers	blow	enable
2.	~~will offer~~	~~blew~~	~~enabled~~
	fills	bumps	are
3.	~~filled~~	~~bumped~~	~~were~~

Exercise 5.2 (page 210) Possible: 35

Give one point for each subject and one point for each complete verb in each clause. The subjects and verbs should be marked as follows:

1. The marketing director is distributing the marketing plans for three new products.
2. My daughters are playing on two different soccer teams and enjoying this new sport.
3. The highway crews are sanding and salting the icy overpasses.
4. Whether you are planning to drive or carpool, you will find hazardous conditions today.
5. The computers are running on backup batteries until the electricity comes on.
6. The computer lab assistants were documenting the problems when the department head announced the decision to buy new hardware and software.
7. Paying college tuition gets harder and harder; many students are working part-time jobs to pay their bills.
8. I will be paying two times more rent, but I will have two additional roommates.
9. Ramos was studying for his physics test, so he could not attend the concert.
10. Earning solid grades in his major is his primary goal; he is reaching his goal so far this term.

Exercise 5.3 (page 214) Possible: 10

1. forgotten	3. come	5. given	7. hidden	9. rung
2. flown	4. broken	6. gone	8. spoken	10. stolen

Exercise 5.4 (page 215) Possible: 10

1. considered	3. found	5. arriving	7. offered	9. spoken
2. working	4. having	6. taken	8. hoping	10. written

Exercise 5.5 (page 216) Possible: 10

1. **had suffered** a heart attack
2. **have had** financial problems
3. **had lived** in California
4. **have existed** for several months
5. **had cancelled** every morning flight

6. **had encountered** a porcupine
7. **had given** the directions
8. **has recorded** two new albums
9. **had worked** ten-hour shifts
10. **had argued** with Janet

Exercise 5.6 (page 218) Possible: 10

Give one point per sentence. Answers may vary. If your answers differ from the following, ask your instructor if your sentences are correct.

1. Drivers on the freeway ~~swerving~~ swerved to miss the garbage can in the middle of the road.
2. I got this computer mouse pad free because the store ~~giving~~ was giving it away with every twenty-dollar purchase.
3. The man ~~choosing~~ chose to end his contract with the company, for he could no longer support the company's goals.
4. ~~Wanting~~ The company wants to expand the operation and move into three new states before the end of the year.
5. Determined to get to the bottom of the problem that was bothering him, Jason met with a counselor.
6. Family values were the topic of the debate; however, candidates ~~wandering~~ wandered off the topic and ~~talking~~ talked about economic and medical topics.
7. Every student in our study group ~~contributing~~ contributes study aids and study notes for specific chapters of the textbook, but I still like to make my own for every chapter.
8. Many financial planners ~~getting~~ get vital information about investments from the Internet.
9. Preston ~~hoping~~ had hoped to prevent bankruptcy, so he scheduled an appointment with a loan officer to discuss his financial situation.
10. She was charging up the stairs and shoving people aside.

Proofreading Exercises

Proofreading exercises will be discussed in class or graded by your instructor.

Chapter 6

Exercise 6.1 (page 249) Possible: 11

The following appositives should be circled:

1. a 1995 Harley Davidson
2. a woman of Hawaiian heritage
3. Anna Marie, Rosie O'Donnell
4. a famous tourist spot in San Francisco
5. a primitive hominid
6. a thousand-word essay
7. an experienced therapist
8. a portrait of a strong Native American woman
9. a freelance photographer
10. a system of physical and mental exercise

Exercise 6.2 (page 250) Possible: 10

Give two points per sentence: one for creating the appositives and one for using correct punctuation. Answers may vary. If your answers vary from the following, ask your instructor if your sentences are correct.

1. Many large corporate headquarters are located in Minneapolis, the home of the Vikings, the Timberwolves, and the Twins.
2. Denver, the capital of Colorado, is the hub for United Airlines, one of America's largest airlines.
3. The company, a chain of retail stores, conducts drug screening on all its employees.
4. My car, an old, beat-up Plymouth, stalled in the middle of a busy intersection.
5. An antique clock, a relic from the Civil War years, caught my eye.

Exercise 6.3 (page 252) Possible: 10

The following participial phrases should be circled:

1. tired of studying for her nursing exam
2. Trying to understand my feelings
3. Believing in traditional Japanese superstitions
4. Trying to keep me away from bad luck
5. Elected to the highest office in the nation
6. Running from the warehouse
7. Emphasizing formal rules, patterns, and structures
8. depicting different aspects of human nature
9. Known as the "warm event"
10. spreading colder water across the Pacific

Exercise 6.4 (page 253) Possible: 10

The following appositives and participial phrases should be circled:

1. a former monk
2. believing in gender stereotypes
3. *Men Are from Mars, Women Are from Venus*
4. the contemporary psychologist
5. Dr. John Gottman
6. A prolific writer
7. a professor of psychology at the University of Washington
8. wanting to strengthen their relationships
9. a cultural historian and relationship expert
10. Equalizing the balance between men and women

Exercise 6.5 (page 254) Possible: 10

Answers will vary. Ask another classmate or your instructor to check your sentences. The following sentences are only examples of possible sentences:

1. *Wanting to work part-time,* the woman hired a new babysitter for after-school childcare.
2. *Concerned about the consequences,* the soldiers followed all the instructions.
3. Mario, *needing a little help with his science paper,* scheduled an appointment with a tutor.
4. The clothes *hanging on the line in the backyard* were stolen during the night.
5. *Enraged by the insinuation,* Rachel did not respond.
6. *Seeing strange lights behind the warehouse,* the night patrol reported the unusual situation.
7. *Bothered by the clerk's rude behavior,* the customers asked to talk with the manager.
8. *Showing disregard for the rules,* the band was banned from future football games.
9. *Concerned for everyone's safety,* the teachers instructed everyone to leave the building.
10. *Huffing and puffing,* the reporter arrived for the interview early.

Exercise 6.6 (page 255) Possible: 10

Answers will vary. The following sentences may be used as examples. Ask another classmate or your instructor to check your sentences. C indicates the sentence is correct.

1. Wishing to stay anonymous, a donor left a cash donation in a sealed envelope.
2. C
3. Because it had been damaged extensively by the water, Eduardo's magazine ended up in the garbage.
4. Surprised by the announcement of the merger, stockbrokers sold stocks rapidly.

5. After the loud explosion, chaos erupted in the streets.
6. C
7. C
8. C
9. C
10. Because people were worried about heavy holiday traffic, the parking lot of the arena was half empty before the event ended.

Exercise 6.7 (page 257) Possible: 10

Answers will vary. The following sentences may be used as examples. Ask another classmate or your instructor to check your sentences.

1. Listening to the pitter-patter of the rain on the roof, I felt relaxed and safe.
2. Starving after the long hike, the children ran to the refrigerator for something to eat.
3. Destroyed by the flames, the house and all our belongings were nothing more than ash.
4. Hanging from the telephone wire, the kite was not safe to touch.
5. Beaten and defeated, the boxer left the ring without talking to reporters.
6. Sneezing, coughing, and wheezing, the sick man decided to go to the clinic.
7. Wanting to attend school next term, I met with an adviser to plan my classes.
8. Concerned about the consequences, Ali hired a lawyer to look into the situation.
9. Dancing and singing on stage for the first time, Maya was apprehensive.
10. Living in the utmost poverty, the village people appreciated even small amounts of food and supplies.

Proofreading Exercises

Proofreading exercises will be discussed in class or graded by your instructor.

Chapter 7

Exercise 7.1 (page 293) Possible: 46

Give one point for each subject, one point for correctly marking S or P for each subject, and one point for each prepositional phrase. The prepositional phrases and subjects should be marked as follows:

P P

1. Many elected officials do not keep the promises that they make (during election campaigns).

2. (During his entire term), he [S] wrote one column; needless to say, everyone [S] was very surprised.

3. Nothing [S] that I [S] do is quite right (in the opinion) (of my father).

4. Controllers [P] often want to feel that they [P] are powerful and superior.

5. Men [P] and women [P] share many common interests.

6. Some [P] (of the writers) use excessive stereotyping, which [S] reduces their credibility.

7. Migrating geese [P] fly (over the lake) and land (near the cabin) (on a daily basis).

8. The committee [S] meets twice a month to discuss employee performance.

9. The summons [S] to appear (in court) (at the end) (of the month) arrived yesterday.

10. Athletics [S] (at our school) encourages excellent performance (on the court or fields) as well as (in the classrooms).

Exercise 7.2 (page 296) Possible: 31

The subjects and verbs should be marked as follows:

1. Links (include)
2. hub (utilizes), visitors (receive)
3. cornucopia (awaits)
4. wallpaper (is)
5. Managers (tend), that (functions)
6. manager who (uses) (is), that (meets) (does)
7. linemen (consist)
8. linebacker (has)
9. dish (represents)
10. name (has), that (means)

Exercise 7.3 (page 297) Possible: 10

The crossed-out verbs are incorrect. The correct verb is shown next to the crossed-out verb. C indicates the sentence is correct.

1. ~~pay~~ pays
2. C
3. ~~is~~ are
4. ~~attend~~ attends
5. C
6. C
7. ~~varies~~ vary ~~is~~ are
8. ~~get~~ gets
9. ~~provide~~ provides
10. ~~decreases~~ decrease

Exercise 7.4 (page 299) Possible: 10

1. explains
2. considers
3. have
4. are
5. bother
6. make
7. recommend
8. have
9. expects
10. has

Exercise 7.5 (page 302) Possible: 15

1. he or she
2. their
3. its
4. their
5. their, their
6. it
7. their, its
8. their, its *or* their
9. his or her
10. its, them, their

Exercise 7.6 (page 304) Possible: 10

1. his or her
2. his or her
3. their
4. their
5. their
6. them
7. their
8. he or she
9. his or her
10. their

Exercise 7.7 (page 305) Possible: 10

1. conj
2. A
3. A
4. IP
5. conj
6. conj
7. A
8. conj
9. A
10. IP

Proofreading Exercises

Proofreading exercises will be discussed in class or graded by your instructor.

Chapter 8

Exercise 8.1 (page 336) Possible: 10

Give one point per complete answer. Answers will vary depending on the dictionary that you use. Your answers should cite the name of the dictionary. Quotation marks should be placed around the exact dictionary definition, as shown in the following example.

1. irony: According to *The American Heritage Dictionary,* irony is "the use of words to express something different from and often opposite to their literal meaning."

Exercise 8.2 (page 337) Possible: 10

1. begged
2. fastidious
3. mob
4. exuberant
5. flabbergasted
6. disadvantaged
7. immense
8. admire
9. vehicle
10. embellishes

Exercise 8.3 (page 339) Possible: 21

Answers will vary. If your answers differ from the ones below, ask your instructor if your answers are correct. You may be asked to share your answers in class.

1. ticked off = annoyed
   as dumb as a doorknob = foolish
2. crashed = relaxed
   snooze = nap
3. a bunch of = many
   get a handle on = address
   get the best of her = overwhelm her
4. kind of cute = attractive
   duds = clothes
5. the bomb = excellent
   cruise by = go to
6. uptight = upset
   chill = spend time with
7. cool = intriguing
   mess up = create problems in
8. stumped by = unable to answer
   a nerd = an expert
9. really bushed = extremely tired
   worked my tail off = worked so hard
10. awfully stupid = naive
    baloney = nonsense

Exercise 8.4 (page 341) Possible: 20

Answers will vary. Give one point for replacing each cliche with a word or expression that is formal language. Give one point for correctly punctuating each of your sentences. You may be asked to share your answers in class, or your instructor may grade your work.

Exercise 8.5 (page 342) Possible: 10

Possible answers are given for each euphemism. If your answers vary, ask your instructor if your answers are correct.

1. janitor
2. killed
3. liar
4. hair dye
5. lazy person
6. divorce
7. stolen
8. unaffordable, too expensive
9. expensive
10. failed, flunked

Proofreading Exercises

Proofreading exercises will be discussed in class or graded by your instructor.

Chapter 9

Exercise 9.1 (page 369) Possible: 10

The following words, which show parallelism, should be underlined:

1. skiing, inline skating, swimming
2. direct, honest
3. from the critics, from the public
4. The reduction of violence, the improvement of test scores
5. see the ancient ruins, visit the museums, shop at the local markets
6. the toddlers, the kindergarteners
7. rude, insensitive, disrespectful
8. managed the front office, ordered supplies, coordinated the work orders
9. rain, snow
10. traveled from all over the world, participated in their specific events, left Olympic Village with fond memories

Exercise 9.2 (page 369) Possible: 10

The C before sentences indicates the sentences have no errors. Corrections for sentences with faulty parallelism are shown above the crossed-out errors. Answers may vary. If your answers vary from the following, ask your instructor if your sentences are correct.

1. My professor told us that his role is to *guide* us through the curriculum, *instill* a sense of enthusiasm for the content, and
   evaluate
   ~~the evaluation of~~ our work.
2. C

3. Before I begin my paragraph, I need to *generate* ideas and narrow ~~narrowing~~ the topic ~~is important~~.
4. C
5. C
6. Preschool *children* and adolescents ~~even older children in adolescent years~~ need a stable life.
7. C
8. The wind *tossed* garbage cans in the air, *blew* over fences, and knocked out the electricity ~~the electricity was knocked out~~.
9. C
10. I do not understand *why you want to move* out of the state or why you plan ~~planning~~ *to change* your major.

Exercise 9.3 (page 371) Possible: 14

The words that are crossed out can be eliminated to avoid wordiness.

1. When the wind suddenly, ~~unexpectedly, quickly~~ shifted, the hot air balloon drifted off course.
2. ~~Ever~~ Since I became a vegan ~~and decided not to eat meat or dairy products~~, my cholesterol level has improved.
3. Fast, ~~rapid~~ global warming will have ~~dire~~, serious consequences for our planet.
4. I was injured ~~and hurt~~ during a routine inspection of the wiring in the attic ~~upstairs~~.
5. Poor urban planning resulted in the lack of essential, ~~necessary~~ infrastructures.
6. ~~To the best of my knowledge~~ I think the woman should be charged with fraud.
7. Lying ~~in the form of being dishonest~~ to your best friend causes many problems.
8. At the age of thirty ~~years old~~, I was getting bald ~~because I was losing hair~~.
9. My doctor told me that I have a genetic condition ~~that I inherited~~.
10. The decrease of chlorophyll in the fall causes the vivid, ~~bright~~ colors in the ~~autumn~~ leaves.

Proofreading Exercises

Proofreading exercises will be discussed in class or graded by your instructor.

APPENDIX B

Helpful Charts

PAST PARTICIPLES OF IRREGULAR VERBS					
Infinitive (base form)	Past (simple past)	Past Participle (Use with has, have, had)	Infinitive (base form)	Past (simple past)	Past Participle (Use with has, have, had)
abide	abode, abided	abode	cost	cost	cost
arise	arose	arisen	creep	crept	crept
awake	awoke	awaked, awoken	cut	cut	cut
bear	bore	born, borne	deal	dealt	dealt
beat	beat	beat, beaten	dig	dug	dug
become	became	become	dive	dove, dived	dived
begin	began	begun	do	did	done
bend	bent	bent	draw	drew	drawn
bid	bid, bade	bid, bidden	dream	dreamed, dreamt	dreamed, dreamt
bind	bound	bound			
bite	bit	bit, bitten	drink	drank	drunk
bleed	bled	bled	drive	drove	driven
blow	blew	blown	eat	ate	eaten
break	broke	broken	fall	fell	fallen
bring	brought	brought	feed	fed	fed
broadcast	broadcast	broadcast	feel	felt	felt
build	built	built	fight	fought	fought
burst	burst	burst	find	found	found
buy	bought	bought	flee	fled	fled
cast	cast	cast	fling	flung	flung
catch	caught	caught	fly	flew	flown
choose	chose	chosen	forbid	forbade, forbad	forbidden, forbid
cling	clung	clung			
come	came	come	forget	forgot	forgotten

Infinitive (base form)	Past (simple past)	Past Participle (Use with has, have, had)	Infinitive (base form)	Past (simple past)	Past Participle (Use with has, have, had)
forsake	forsook	forsaken	seek	sought	sought
freeze	froze	frozen	sell	sold	sold
get	got	got, gotten	send	sent	sent
give	gave	given	set	set	set
go	went	gone	sew	sewed	sewed, sewn
grind	ground	ground	shake	shook	shaken
grow	grew	grown	shine	shone	shone
hang	hung (object)	hung	shoot	shot	shot
have	had	had	show	showed	shown
hear	heard	heard	shrink	shrank,	shrunk,
hide	hid	hidden		shrunk	shrunken
hold	held	held	sing	sang	sung
hurt	hurt	hurt	sink	sank	sunk
keep	kept	kept	shut	shut	shut
knit	knit, knitted	knit, knitted	sit	sat	sat
know	knew	known	slay	slew	slain
lay	laid	laid	sleep	slept	slept
lead	led	led	slide	slid	slid
leave	left	left	sling	slung	slung
lend	lent	lent	slink	slunk	slunk
lie	lay	lain	slit	slit	slit
light	lit	lit, lighted	sneak	sneaked,	sneaked,
lose	lost	lost		snuck	snuck
make	made	made	speak	spoke	spoken
mean	meant	meant	speed	sped	sped
meet	met	met	spend	spent	spent
pay	paid	paid	spread	spread	spread
prove	proved	proved, proven	spin	spun	spun
put	put	put	spring	sprang	sprung
quit	quit	quit	stand	stood	stood
read	read	read	steal	stole	stolen
rid	rid, ridded	rid, ridded	stick	stuck	stuck
ride	rode	ridden	sting	stung	stung
ring	rang	rung	stink	stank, stunk	stunk
rise	rose	risen	stride	strode	stridden
run	ran	run	strike	struck	struck
say	said	said	string	strung	strung
see	saw	seen	strive	strove	striven

Infinitive (base form)	Past (simple past)	Past Participle (Use with has, have, had)	Infinitive (base form)	Past (simple past)	Past Participle (Use with has, have, had)
swear	swore	sworn	throw	threw	thrown
sweep	swept	swept	thrust	thrust	thrust
swim	swam	swum	understand	understood	understood
swing	swung	swung	wake	woke, waked	waked, woken
take	took	taken	wear	wore	worn
teach	taught	taught	weave	wove	woven
tear	tore	torn	weep	wept	wept
tell	told	told	win	won	won
think	thought	thought	wring	wrung	wrung
thrive	thrived, throve	thrived thriven	write	wrote	written

COORDINATING CONJUNCTIONS	
Coordinating Conjunction	Functions
And	• shows clauses of equal value • adds information • means "in addition to" or "along with"
But	• shows an opposite idea, a contrast, or a difference • means "except" or "however"
For	• shows how the first clause occurs because of the action of the second clause • shows a reason or cause • means "because"
Nor	• joins two negative ideas • means "not"
Or	• shows a choice between two equal options or possibilities
So	• shows that the first clause causes the action in the second clause to occur • means "therefore"
Yet	• shows that one action occurs in spite of the other action • means "however," "nevertheless," or "but still"

Subordinate Conjunctions			
after	even though	provided that	until
although	if	since	when
as	in order that	so	whenever
as if	in that	so long as	where
as long as	less than	so that	whereas
as soon as	more than	than	wherever
as though	no matter how	though	whether
because	now that	till	while
before	once	unless	

Conjunctive Adverbs				
Relationship	; conjunctive adverb,			
addition, continuation of the same thought,	accordingly furthermore	again likewise	also in addition	besides moreover
comparison, similarity	also in comparison	in the same way likewise	 similarly	
contrast, opposition	however instead on the other hand still	in contrast nevertheless unfortunately	in comparison on the contrary otherwise	
time	afterward first later second	at the same time furthermore meanwhile subsequently	finally in the meantime next then	
illustration, example	for example	for instance	in fact	
concession	admittedly	however	nevertheless	
result, effect	as a result hence thus	accordingly then	consequently therefore	
summation, conclusion	finally in short overall	hence in summary therefore	in general in conclusion	
emphasis	certainly	in fact	indeed	

Relative Pronouns				
who	whom	whose	which	that

TEXT CREDITS

Page 51: Linda Wong, *Essential Study Skills,* Third Edition. Copyright (c) 2000 by Houghton Mifflin Company. Reprinted with permission.

Pages 130-131: Exercise based on Amy Goldstein's article, "Breadwinner Wives Tip Marriage Scales." Copyright (c) 2000 The Washington Post. Reprinted with permission.

Pages 137-138: "House OKs Minimum Wage." Reprinted with permission of The Associated Press.

Pages 165-166: Kathy Sawyer, "Ten More Planets Discovered: Extrasolar System Relatively Nearby." Copyright (c) 2000 The Washington Post. Reprinted with permission.

Pages 180-181: "Iowa Caucuses Q & A." Reprinted with permission of The Associated Press.

Page 206: Reprinted by permission of the author, Jay Heinrichs, from "Rise and Shine." *VIA Magazine,* September/October 2000.

Pages 224-225: David Osborne, "Districts Should Try Charter Schools." Reprinted by permission of International Creative Management, Inc. Copyright (c) 1999 by Davis Osborne.

Pages 232-233: Libby Quaid, "Feds Distribute Sacagawea Coins." Reprinted with permission of The Associated Press.

Page 239: Hara Estroff Marano, "Contracts of Two Johns," "Gottman and Gray: The Two Johns." Reprinted with permission from *Psychology Today Magazine,* Copyright (c) 1997 Sussex Publishers, Inc.

Pages 259-260: Janet Filips, "Diabetes Fair: Time is of Essence." This article appeared in its correct form in *The Register-Guard,* January 28, 2000, pg. 6A, 6B. Adapted and reprinted with permission.

Page 266: Karen S. Peterson, "In Charge, Out of Control." Copyright (c) 2000, USA TODAY. Reprinted with permission.

Page 272: Reprinted with permission of the author from Buffy Sainte-Marie, "Native American Culture," *Yahoo! Internet Life,* July 1999.

Pages 276-277: Andrew J. DuBrin, *Leadership,* Third Edition. Copyright (c) 2001 by Houghton Mifflin Company. Reprinted with permission.

Pages 309-310: Amy Goldstein, "Breadwinner Wives Tip Marriage Scales." Copyright (c) 2000 The Washington Post. Reprinted with permission.

Pages 312-313: Patricia Wen, "To Be Happy, Look on the Bright Side," *The Register-Guard,* March 15, 2000, pg.1. Republished by permission of *The Boston Globe* via Copyright Clearance Center, Inc. (c) 2000 The Boston Globe. All rights reserved worldwide.

Page 323: "Greenhouse Effect," Microsoft (r) Encarta (r) Online Encyclopedia 2000 http://encarta.msn.com (c) 1997-2000 Microsoft Corporation. All rights reserved.

Page 336: Definition of "comfortable". Copyright (c) 2000 by Houghton Mifflin Company. Reproduced by permission of *The American Heritage Dictionary of the English Language,* Fourth Edition.

Page 341: Definition of "euphemism". Copyright (c) 2000 by Houghton Mifflin Company. Reproduced by permission of *The American Heritage Dictionary of the English Language,* Fourth Edition.

Pages 378-380: Michael Kinsley, "The Great Spin Machine." Copyright (c) 2000 Time, Inc. Reprinted by permission.

Pages 383-387: From *From Vietnam to Hell: Interviews with Victims of Post-Traumatic Stress Disorder.* Copyright (c) Shirley Dicks by permission of McFarland & Company, Inc., Box 611, Jefferson, NC 28640.

Pages 393-395: "Money: America's Love-Hate Relationship with the Almighty Dollar," by Susan Jacoby. Copyright (c) 2000 by Susan Jacoby. Originally appeared in *Modern Maturity.* Reprinted by permission of Georges Borchardt, Inc.

Pages 401-402: Gurleen Grewal, "Misuse of Native American Symbols," *National Education Association Higher Education Advocate,* January 2000, pg. 12. Reprinted with permission.

Pages 402-403: Ester Buchholz, "Solitude." Reprinted with permission of Simon & Schuster and the author, from The Call of Solitude by Ester Buchholz. Copyright (c) 1997 by Ester Buchholz.

Pages 403-404: Jeremiah Holmes, "Yes, America is Mine...And Yours." Reprinted by permission of the author. This article originally appeared in *The Crisis,* January/February 1999.

Pages 405-407: Robert Gifford, "Why We're Destroying the Earth." Reprinted with permission from *Psychology Today Magazine,* Copyright (c) 2000 Sussex Publishers, Inc.

Page 410: Illustration, "Types of Test Questions." Linda Wong, *Essential Study Skills,* Third Edition. Copyright (c) 2000 by Houghton Mifflin Company. Reprinted with permission.

Page 414: Illustration, "Kinds of Summary Notes to Prepare for Tests." Linda Wong, *Essential Study Skills,* Third Edition. Copyright (c) 2000 by Houghton Mifflin Company. Reprinted with permission.

Pages 417-419: Alfred J. Andrea and James Overfield, *The Human Record*, Third Edition. Copyright (c) 1998 by Houghton Mifflin Company. Reprinted with permission.

Pages 419-421: Andrew J. DuBrin, *Leadership,* Third Edition. Copyright (c) 2001 by Houghton Mifflin Company. Reprinted with permission.

Pages 422-423: Roy M. Berko, Andrew D. Wolvin, and Daryln R. Wolvin, *Communicating,* Seventh Edition. Copyright (c) 1998 Houghton Mifflin Company. Reprinted with permission.

Pages 423-424: Richard Bulliet et al., *The Earth and Its Peoples,* Seond Edition. Copyright (c) 2001 by Houghton Mifflin Company. Reprinted with permission.

Pages 431-433: Reprinted by permission of the author from Linda Wong, *Mom's Pocket Guide to Watching Football.* Copyright (c) 2000, pp. 80-96.

Page 434: "What constitutes effective Listening." Michael Osborn and Suzanne Osborn, *Public Speaking*, Fourth Edition. Copyright (c) 1997 by Houghton Mifflin Company. Reprinted with permission.

Pages 449-451: Janice Castro et al., "Spanglish Spoken Here." Copyright (c) 1988 Time, Inc. Reprinted with permission.

Pages 452-454: Reprinted with permission from "The Narrative of Rosa Parks," as appeared in *The Crisis,* January/February 1999. The publisher wishes to thank The Crisis Publishing Co., Inc., the publisher of the magazine of the National Association for the Advancement of Colored People, for the use of this work.

Pages 457-458: Linda Wong, *Essential Study Skills,* Third Edition. Copyright (c) 2000 by Houghton Mifflin Company. Reprinted with permission.

INDEX

Action verbs
explanation of, 34
list of, 392
in narratives, 100
review of, 77–78
Adequate development
in cause-effect paragraphs, 350, 353
in classification paragraphs, 276
in comparison-contrast paragraphs, 230, 240
in descriptive paragraphs, 149
elements of, 17, 59–62
in essays, 435–436
in exemplification paragraphs, 269
in narrative paragraphs, 100
in process paragraphs, 185
for test question answers, 416
Adjectives, 323
Adverbs
conjunctive, 38–39, 53–55, 128–129
explanation of, 35
between helping verb and main verb, 81–82
list of common, 36
Analogy, 227
and, 125–126, 298
Antecedents
agreement between pronouns and, 300–304
explanation of, 31, 166, 300
Appositives
explanation of, 247–248
use of, 248–249, 257
Assignments, 4
Assisted response, 416
Audiences, 11–12
Author citations, 24–25

because, 125
Bibliographies, 440
Block method
example of, 233–234
explanation of, 231–232
Body of paragraphs
cause-effect, 352–354
for classification paragraphs, 275–276
clustering to generate ideas for, 8
for comparison-contrast paragraphs, 228–232
for definition paragraphs, 317–319
for descriptive paragraphs, 148–149
for exemplification paragraphs, 269–271
function of, 43, 45
guidelines for developing, 48, 59
for narrative paragraphs, 99–100
for narratives, 99–100
for process paragraphs, 185–186
rough draft of, 23
for summary paragraphs, 391–392
for test question answers, 416
verb tense in, 205
Brainstorming
clustering as form of, 7–8
for comparison-contrast paragraphs, 235
for definition paragraphs, 325
for descriptive paragraphs, 153–154
for essay idea generation, 438
for exemplification and classification paragraphs, 281–282
explanation of, 6
for narrative paragraphs, 105
Business letter format
elements of, 65
example of, 68, 69

Card catalogs, 438
Cause-effect paragraphs
body of, 352–354
concluding sentence in, 355–356
elements of, 64
explanation of, 13–14, 348–349
gathering and organizing information for, 358–359
generating ideas for, 357
getting focus for, 358
partner feed back form for, 364
planning sheet for, 363
proofreading and editing, 360
revision of, 359–360
rough draft for, 359
topic sentence in, 350–351
Central impression
creation of, 144
methods to strengthen, 148
selecting, 155
Chronological order
in cause-effect paragraphs, 352
in descriptive paragraphs, 149
explanation of, 56
Circular definitions, 315
Classification
elements of, 64
explanation of, 13–14
Classification paragraphs
body of, 275–276
concluding sentence in, 280
elements of, 64
explanation of, 13–14, 264–267
final version of, 287
gathering and organizing information in, 283–284
generating ideas for, 281–282
getting focus for, 282–283
partner feedback form for, 290
planning sheet for, 289
proofreading and editing, 287
revision for, 285
rough drafts for, 285
topic sentence in, 267–268
Clichés, 340–341
Clustering
for cause-effect paragraphs, 357–358
for descriptive paragraphs, 155–156
for essay writing, 438, 441, 443
to generate ideas, 7–8

for narrative paragraphs, 106–107
to organize information and details, 21–22
Coherence
in cause-effect paragraphs, 350, 352
in classification paragraphs, 276
in comparison-contrast paragraphs, 229, 240
in definition paragraphs, 317
in descriptive paragraphs, 148
in essays, 435
in exemplification paragraphs, 270
methods to achieve, 53–56
in narrative paragraphs, 99
in narratives, 99
in process paragraphs, 185–186
Collective nouns, 291
Colloquial language, 338–341
Commas
after conjunctive adverbs, 128
after transition words, 185
to correct run-on sentences, 134
with relative pronoun clauses, 169–170
use of, 136
Comma splice errors
explanation of, 135–136
identifying, 136
methods for correcting, 136–137
Common nouns, 30
Comparison
elements of, 63
explanation of, 13–14
Comparison-contrast paragraphs
body of, 228–232
concluding sentence in, 234
elements of, 63
explanation of, 13–14, 224
final version of, 243
gathering and organizing information in, 237–238
getting focus in, 236–237
idea generation for, 235
partner feedback form for, 246
planning sheet for, 245
proofreading and editing, 243
revision of, 240
rough drafts in, 240
topic sentence in, 225–227
Complex sentences
explanation of, 164
transition words in, 54–55
Compound sentences
explanation of, 122–123
transition words in, 54–55
use of conjunctive adverbs to form, 128–130
use of coordinating conjunctions to form, 123–126
use of semicolons to form, 127–128
Compound subjects
illustrations of, 75–76
joined by *and,* 298
joined by *either/or* or *neither/nor,* 299
joined by *or,* 298
Compound verbs, 83–84
Computer use, 24
Concluding sentences
in cause-effect paragraphs, 355–356
for classification paragraphs, 280
for comparison-contrast paragraphs, 234
in definition paragraphs, 322
for descriptive paragraphs, 152
evaluating effectiveness of, 49
for exemplification paragraphs, 280
function of, 43–45
guidelines for developing, 49
for narrative paragraphs, 103
rough draft of, 23
in summary paragraphs, 392
for test question answers, 416
Conjunctions
correlative, 365
explanation of, 38, 123
subordinate, 38–39, 54–55, 164
types of, 38–39
use of, 53
Conjunctive adverbs
explanation of, 38
list of, 129
semicolons followed by, 128–129
use of, 39, 53–55
Connotation, 335
Contractions, 340
Contrast
elements of, 63
explanation of, 13–14
Contrast paragraphs, 224. *See also* Comparison-contrast paragraphs
Controlling ideas
in exemplification and classification paragraphs, 264, 267
for topic sentences, 18, 45
Controlling sentences. *See* Topic sentences
Coordinating conjunctions
explanation of, 38, 365
list of, 365
use of, 39, 54–55, 123–125
Correlative conjunctions
examples of, 367–368
explanation of, 365, 367
list of, 367
Cover letters
function of, 65
illustration of, 68–69
steps for writing, 65–68, 70

Dangling participles, 255
Deductive order, 149
Definition paragraphs
body of, 317–319
concluding sentence in, 322
elements of, 64
explanation of, 13–14, 312–313
final version of, 331
gathering and organizing information for, 326–328
generating ideas for, 325
getting focus for, 326
partner feedback form for, 334
planning sheet for, 333
proofreading and editing, 331
revision of, 328–329
rough draft for, 328
topic sentence in, 314–317, 322
Definitions
circular, 315
formal, 315
signal words for, 314
Demonstrative pronouns, 32, 73
Denominator, 267
Denotation, 335
Dependent clauses
explanation of, 163
fragments created by, 172–173
in parallel structures, 366–367
relative pronoun clauses as, 166
Description
explanation of, 13
objective, 144–145
subjective, 144–146
Descriptive paragraphs
body of, 148–149
body of paragraph in, 148–149
concluding sentence in, 152
elements of, 63
explanation of, 13–14, 144
final version for, 159
gathering and organizing information for, 155–157
generating ideas for, 153–154
getting focus for, 155

partner feedback form for, 162
planning sheet for, 161
proofreading and editing, 159
revision of, 158–159
rough draft for, 157
topic sentence in, 146, 157
verb tense in, 204–206
Descriptive words, 99
Diagrams, 350
Diction
clichés and, 340
connotation and, 336
denotation and, 335
euphemisms and, 341–342
explanation of, 335
levels of, 338–339
Directional process paragraphs, 181, 189
Direction words, 410–411
Drafts. *See* Rough drafts
Due dates, 4, 23

-ed, 78, 81–82, 119–120, 202–203
Editing
cause-effect paragraphs, 360
checklist for, 115, 159, 196, 243
of classification and exemplification paragraphs, 287
definition paragraphs, 331
of essays, 445
explanation of, 27, 114
either/or, 299
Emotion, 100
Emphatic order
in cause-effect paragraphs, 352–353
in descriptive paragraphs, 149
explanation of, 56
Essay questions, 410
Essays
body of, 434–436
concluding paragraph for, 436
enjoy writing, 458
expanding paragraphs into, 430–433
explanation of, 430
final version of, 445
gathering and organizing information for, 439–442
generating ideas for, 438–439
getting focus for, 439
introductory paragraphs for, 433–434
learning from model, 446
proofreading and editing, 445
revision of, 444–445
rough draft for, 444
test-taking strategies for, 457–458
understanding assignments for, 437
Essay tests
guidelines for, 454–455
preparing for, 445–447
Essential clauses, 169–170
Euphemisms, 341, 342
Examples
elements of, 64
explanation of, 13, 14
extended, 269
organizational patterns for, 271
Exemplification paragraphs
body of, 269–271
concluding sentence in, 280
explanation of, 264–266
final version of, 287
gathering and organizing information in, 283–284
generating ideas for, 281–282
getting focus for, 282–283
partner feedback form for, 290
planning sheet for, 289
proofreading and editing, 287
revision for, 285
rough drafts for, 285
topic sentence in, 267–268
Expository paragraphs, 13, 224, 264. *See also* Cause-effect paragraphs; Classification paragraphs; Definition paragraphs; Exemplification paragraphs
Extended examples, 269

Faulty parallelism, 368
Feedback
form for partner, 118, 162, 200
during revision process, 109
Final version
of classification and exemplification paragraphs, 287
of comparison-contrast paragraphs, 243
of definition paragraphs, 331
of descriptive paragraphs, 159
of essays, 445
of narrative paragraphs, 115
preparation of, 28
of process paragraphs, 197
First person
cause-effect paragraphs in, 349
narratives in, 94–95
Focus
for cause-effect paragraphs, 358
for comparison-contrast paragraphs, 236–237
for definition paragraphs, 326
for descriptive paragraphs, 155
for essays, 439
for exemplification and classification paragraphs, 282–283
identifying a purpose to establish, 13–15
knowing your audience to establish, 11–13
for narrative paragraphs, 105–106
narrowing topic to gain, 10–11, 105
for process paragraphs, 190
Footnotes, 25
for, 125–126
Formal definitions, 315
Formal language, 338–340
Formal summary paragraphs, 389–390
Fragments
caused by participial phrases, 256, 257
examples of, 85–86
explanation of, 85
methods to correct, 86, 87, 172–173
relative pronoun clauses as, 166, 170
tips for avoiding, 85, 216–218
Freewriting
for essay idea generation, 438
example of, 9
explanation of, 9, 189
to generate ideas, 9
Fused sentences, 133. *See also* Comma splice errors; Run-on sentences
Future perfect tense, 212
Future progressive tense, 207–208
Future tense, 202

Gerunds, 209
Grids
for essay writing, 441
explanation of, 237–238

Heading, 28
Helping verbs
explanation of, 81–82
list of, 81, 203
in progressive verb phrases, 209
types of, 203
use of, 207
Hierarchies
in classification and exemplification paragraphs, 283
for essay writing, 438, 441
explanation of, 265

Idea generation
brainstorming used for, 6
for cause-effect paragraphs, 357
clustering used for, 7–8
for comparison-contrast paragraphs, 235
for definition paragraphs, 325
for descriptive paragraphs, 153–154
for essays, 438–439
for exemplification and classification paragraphs, 281–282
freewriting used for, 9
importance of, 3–4
for narrative paragraphs, 104–105
for process paragraphs, 189
selecting a topic and, 5–6
understanding the assignment and, 4
Imperative sentences, 185
Implied subjects, 185
Indefinite pronouns
explanation of, 32, 73
use of, 292–293, 303
Independent clauses
examples of, 87
explanation of, 85–86, 122, 163
in parallel structures, 366–367
punctuation between, 133
relative pronoun clauses and, 169–170
run-on sentences and, 133–134
Index cards, 440
notetaking using, 17
Inductive order, 149
Infinitives, 78
Informal definitions, 315
Informal language, 338–339
Informal summary paragraphs, 388–389
Information gathering and organizing
for cause-effect paragraphs, 358–359
clustering as element of, 21–22
for comparison-contrast paragraphs, 237–238
for definition paragraphs, 326–328
for descriptive paragraphs, 155–157
determining correct amount of, 17–18
developing topic sentences as, 18–19
for essays, 439–442
for exemplification and classification paragraphs, 283–284
explanation of, 15–16
listing as element of, 21
for narrative paragraphs, 106–107
outlining as element of, 20
taking notes for, 16–17
using resources for, 16
Informational process paragraphs, 180
-ing
as gerund ending, 209
as present participle ending, 217
as verbal ending, 209
as verb ending, 81, 82, 203, 211
Interjections, 39
Internet, 438
Interrogative pronouns, 32
Irregular verbs
explanation of, 78
in perfect tenses, 213
simple past tense of, 120–121

Key words, 4

Letters, cover, 65–70
Linking verbs
adjectives following, 33
explanation of, 34
list of, 80
review of, 79–80
Listing, 21
-ly, 35, 81

Main idea sentences. *See* Topic sentences
Main verbs, 81–82
Mapping. *See* Clustering
Media searching, 282
Mood, 100

Narrative paragraphs
body of, 99–100
concluding sentence in, 103
elements of, 63
explanation of, 13–14, 94
gathering and organizing information for, 106–108
generating ideas for, 104–105
getting focus for, 105–106
paragraphs rough draft for, 108
partner feedback form for, 118
planning sheet for, 117
preparing final versions of, 115
proofreading and editing, 114–115
revisions of, 108–109
topic sentence in, 97–98
verb tense in, 204
Narratives
explanation of, 13, 94
first-person, 94
third-person, 95–96
neither/nor, 299
Nonessential clauses, 169–170
nor, 125
not, 125
Note taking
for information gathering, 16–17, 439–440
while reading, 413
Noun phrases, 366
Nouns
collective, 291–292
common, 30
explanation of, 30–31
review of, 71–72
Number, 207

Objective description, 144–145
Object pronouns
explanation of, 72–73, 301
use of, 74
Open-book essay tests, 457
or, 298
Organization. *See also* Information gathering and organizing
deductive, 149
inductive, 149
of supporting details, 56, 327
Outlines
for definition paragraphs, 327
for essay writing, 441–442
explanation of, 238
guidelines for, 20

Paragraphs
adequate development in, 17, 59–62 (*See also* adequate development)
coherence in, 53–58 (*See also* Coherence)
explanation of, 44
overdevelopment of, 59–61
skills for effective, 44
structure of, 19, 23, 44–52 (*See also* Body of paragraphs; Concluding sentences; Topic sentences)
types of, 13, 62–64, 411
unity in, 52 (*See also* Unity)
Parallelism
among verbs in clauses or sentences, 209
clauses and, 366–367

explanation of, 365
faulty, 368
phrases and, 366
use of, 56
words and, 365–366
Participial phrases
errors with, 255, 257
explanation of, 250–251
fragments caused by, 256
use of, 251–252, 257
Participles
incorrect use of, 216–218
past, 203, 212–213
present, 203, 209–210
Partner feedback forms
for cause-effect paragraphs, 364
for classification and exemplification paragraphs, 290
for comparison-contrast paragraphs, 246
for definition paragraphs, 334
for descriptive paragraphs, 162
for narrative paragraphs, 118
for process paragraphs, 200
for summary paragraphs, 399–400
for test question answers, 426
Parts of speech
review of, 30–39
summary of, 39–40
Past participles
explanation of, 203, 212
fragments with, 217–218
use of, 212–213
Past perfect tense
explanation of, 212
use of, 82, 213–214
Past progressive tense, 207–208
Past tense
shifts between present and, 204–206
simple, 202
Past-tense verbs, 78, 119
Patterns of discourse, 13
Pencil use, 24
Pen use, 24
Perfect tenses
avoiding errors in, 213–214
helping verbs to form, 203
Perfect tense verbs
explanation of, 210–211
progressive forms of, 211–212
Personal pronouns, 32, 73
Persuasive discourse, 13
Plural nouns, 30, 291
Plural subjects, 294–296
Plural verbs, 294–296
Point-by-point method
example of, 232–233
for subtopic organization, 230–231
Possessive case, 72
Possessive pronouns, 32, 301
Predicate adjectives, 33
Prepositional phrases
examples using, 72
explanation of, 36–37, 71
list of common, 37
use of pronouns in, 74
Prepositions
explanation of, 36–38
list of common, 37
use of, 38
Present participles
explanation of, 203
fragments with, 217–218
use of, 209–210
Present perfect tense, 211, 213
Present progressive tense, 207–208
Present tense
shifts between past and, 204–206
simple, 201–202
Present-tense verbs
action, 392
explanation of, 77–78
Prewriting plans
clustering as element of, 21–22
guidelines for developing, 19
listing as element of, 21
outlining as element of, 20
to study for tests, 415
Prewriting techniques
brainstorming as, 6
clustering as, 7–8
freewriting as, 9
Process paragraphs
body of, 185–186
directional, 181
elements of, 63
explanation of, 13–14, 180
final version of, 197
generating ideas for, 189–190
getting focus for, 190
informational, 180
information gathering and organizing for, 190–192
partner feedback form for, 200
planning sheet for, 199
proofreading and editing, 196
revision of, 194
rough draft for, 192
topic sentence in, 183–184
Progressive forms
of perfect tense verbs, 210–212
of simple tense verbs, 207–208
Progressive verb phrases, 207–208
Progressive verbs, 203
Pronoun cases, 72
Pronouns
agreement between antecedents and, 300–304
demonstrative, 32, 73
explanation of, 31
indefinite, 32, 73, 292–293, 303
object, 72–74, 301
possessive, 32, 301
reflexive, 32
review of, 72–74
subject, 72–73, 300
third-person, 291
types of, 32
Proofreading
cause-effect paragraphs, 360
checklist for, 115, 159, 243
of classification and exemplification paragraphs, 287
definition paragraphs, 331
of essays, 445
explanation of, 27, 114
sentences for complete subject and verbs, 172
Proper nouns, 30
Purpose
identifying your, 13–14
paragraphs for specific, 13–15

Questions. *See* Test questions
Quotations, 319

Reading, for meaning, 382–383
Recall questions, 410. *See also* Test questions
Recognition questions, 410. *See also* Test questions
Reflexive pronouns, 32
Regular verbs, 78, 120
Relative pronoun clauses
essential and nonessential, 169–170
examples of, 167
explanation of, 166
as fragment, 170
placement of, 170
subjects and verbs in, 167
use of, 170–171, 173
Relative pronouns
dependent clauses beginning with, 173
explanation of, 32, 73, 166
Resource use, 16
Revision
of cause-effect paragraphs, 359–360

of classification and exemplification paragraphs, 285
of comparison-contrast paragraphs, 240
of definition paragraphs, 328–329
of descriptive paragraphs, 158
of essays, 444–445
guidelines for, 25–26, 158
of narrative paragraphs, 108–109
of process paragraphs, 194

Rough drafts
for cause-effect paragraphs, 359
citing sources in, 24–25
for classification and exemplification paragraphs, 285
for comparison-contrast paragraphs, 240
of cover letters, 65
for definition paragraphs, 328
for descriptive paragraphs, 157
for essays, 444
goals of, 23
importance of, 22–23
for narrative paragraphs, 108
paying attention to due dates in, 23–24
for process paragraphs, 192
using basic paragraph structure in, 23
using pencils, pens, or computers for, 24

Run-on sentences, 133–134

Secondary details, 230

Semicolons
to correct run-on sentences, 134
explanation of, 127–128
followed by conjunctive adverbs, 128–129

Sensory details, 148

Sentences. *See also* Concluding sentences; Topic sentences
complex, 54–55, 164
guidelines for developing topic, 18–19
imperative, 185
run-on, 133–134
simple, 85

-s/-es, 77, 81, 201

Signal words
for cause-effect, 351
for definitions, 314
in test questions, 411–412

Simple future tense, 202

Simple past tense
explanation of, 119–120, 202
of irregular verbs, 120–121, 202
of regular verbs, 120, 202
shifting between present and, 204–206

Simple present tense
explanation of, 201–202
shifting between past and, 204–206

Simple sentences, 5

Singular nouns, 30, 123

Singular subjects, 294–296

Singular verbs, 294–296

Source citations, 24–25

Spatial order, 56, 149

Stated subjects, 185

Study groups, 414

Subjective description
examples of, 145–146
explanation of, 144

Subject pronouns, 72–73, 300

Subjects
compound, 75–76
implied, 185
nouns as sentence, 71
in relative pronoun clauses, 167
stated, 185
third person and singular and plural, 294–296
of topic sentences, 18, 226–227

Subject-verb agreement
avoiding errors in, 209, 294–295, 298
types of errors in, 291, 294

Subordinate conjunctions
dependent clauses beginning with, 173
explanation of, 38, 164
list of, 164, 175
use of, 39, 54, 55

Subtopics
block methods for, 231–232
in classification paragraphs, 265
examples of, 228–229
organizational methods for, 229
point-by-point method for, 230–231
secondary details for, 230
transition words to connect, 229

Summary notes, 414–415

Summary paragraphs
body of, 391–392
concluding sentence in, 392
elements of, 64
explanation of, 13–14, 381
formal, 389–390
informal, 388–389
partner feedback sheet for, 399–400
planning sheet for, 399
reading for meaning and, 382–383
strategies for writing, 381–382
topic sentence in, 390–391
writing process for, 396–398

Superscript, 25

Supporting details
function of, 44, 48
number and relevance of, 59
organization of, 56

Synonyms, 318, 336

Take-home essay tests, 457

Technical writing, 144

Test questions
identifying direction words in, 410–411
identifying key words in, 411–412
partner feedback form for answers to, 426
planning sheet for answers to, 425
practice writing answers to, 417–424
types of, 410

Tests
guidelines to prepare for, 413–415
learning from past, 427
preparing for essay, 445–457
using prewriting techniques to prepare for, 415
writing essay answers on, 454–455
writing paragraph answers to, 416

Textbooks, 438–439

that, 166, 170–171

Thesis statement
development of, 391
for essays, 430, 433–434, 442
explanation of, 381

Third person
cause-effect paragraphs in, 349
informational process paragraphs in, 180
narratives in, 95–96
singular and plural subjects in, 291–293
singular and plural verbs in, 294–296

Third-person narratives, 95–96

Time management, 413

Timetables, 23–24

to be, 203, 207, 295

to do, 203, 295

to have
forms of, 203
perfect tenses and, 211–213
use of, 295
Topics
brainstorming to generate, 6
clustering to generate, 7–8
for essays, 430
freewriting to generate, 9
guidelines for selecting, 5–6
method for narrowing, 10–11, 105
specific or open-ended, 4
Topic sentences
in cause-effect paragraphs, 350–351
in classification paragraphs, 267–268, 284
in comparison-contrast paragraphs, 225–227
for definition paragraphs, 314–317, 322
for descriptive paragraphs, 146, 157
elements of, 18
for exemplification paragraphs, 267–268, 284
function of, 43–45
guidelines for developing, 18–19, 45–46, 59
for narrative paragraphs, 97–98, 107
for process paragraphs, 183–184
rough draft of, 23
in summary paragraphs, 390–391
for test question answers, 416
Transition words
in cause-effect paragraphs, 353
in classification paragraphs, 276
in comparison-contrast paragraphs, 229
in descriptive paragraphs, 149
in exemplification paragraphs, 270
explanation of, 128–129
function of, 53, 130
lists of, 54–55
in narrative paragraphs, 99
in process paragraphs, 185

Unity
in cause-effect paragraphs, 350, 352
in comparison-contrast paragraphs, 229, 240
in definition paragraphs, 317
in descriptive paragraphs, 148
in essays, 435
in exemplification paragraphs, 269–270
methods to achieve, 52
in narrative paragraphs, 99
in process paragraphs, 186

Verbals, 209
Verb phrases
as compound verbs, 84
examples of, 204
explanation of, 34, 81, 203
helping verbs in, 207
in parallel structures, 366
progressive, 207
review of, 81–82
Verbs
action, 34, 77–78, 100, 392
compound, 83–84
explanation of, 34, 77
helping, 81–82, 203, 207, 209
irregular, 78, 120–121, 202, 213
linking, 33, 34, 79–80
main, 81
past-tense, 78
present-tense, 77
progressive, 203, 210–212
in relative pronoun clauses, 167
third person and singular and plural, 294–296
Verb tenses
avoiding errors in, 208–210
explanation of, 34, 119
number and, 207
shifting, 204–206
simple future, 202
simple past, 119–121, 202
simple present, 201–202
Visual images, 99, 100

when, 314
where, 314
which, 166, 171
who, 166, 169, 171
whom, 166, 169, 171
whose, 166, 169, 171
Wordiness
explanation of, 370
sentence combining to eliminate, 371–373
Words
to convey emotion, 100
to convey mood, 100
descriptive, 99
direction, 410–411
parallelism and, 365–366
signal, 314, 351, 411–412
Writing
as communication, 5–6
methods used for strong, 2
Writing file system, 16–17
Writing process. *See also specific types of paragraphs*
elements of, 2–3
gathering and organizing information as step in, 15–22
generating ideas as step in, 3–10
getting focused as step in, 10–15
preparing a final version as step in, 28
proofreading and editing as step in, 27
revising as step in, 25–26
rough draft as step in, 22–25
summary of, 29